# Computer Communications and Networks

**Series editors**

Jacek Rak, Department of Computer Communications, Faculty of Electronics, Telecommunications and Informatics, Gdansk University of Technology, Gdansk, Poland

A. J. Sammes, Cyber Security Centre, Faculty of Technology, De Montfort University, Leicester, UK

The **Computer Communications and Networks** series is a range of textbooks, monographs and handbooks. It sets out to provide students, researchers, and non-specialists alike with a sure grounding in current knowledge, together with comprehensible access to the latest developments in computer communications and networking.

Emphasis is placed on clear and explanatory styles that support a tutorial approach, so that even the most complex of topics is presented in a lucid and intelligible manner.

More information about this series at http://www.springer.com/series/4198

Krishna Raj P. M. · Ankith Mohan
K. G. Srinivasa

# Practical Social Network Analysis with Python

Springer

Krishna Raj P. M.
Department of ISE
Ramaiah Institute of Technology
Bangalore, Karnataka, India

K. G. Srinivasa
Department of Information Technology
C.B.P. Government Engineering College
Jaffarpur, Delhi, India

Ankith Mohan
Department of ISE
Ramaiah Institute of Technology
Bangalore, Karnataka, India

Additional material to this book can be downloaded from http://extras.springer.com.

ISSN 1617-7975 ISSN 2197-8433 (electronic)
Computer Communications and Networks
ISBN 978-3-030-07241-4 ISBN 978-3-319-96746-2 (eBook)
https://doi.org/10.1007/978-3-319-96746-2



This Springer imprint is published by the registered company Springer Nature Switzerland AG
The registered company address is: Gewerbestrasse 11, 6330 Cham, Switzerland

# Preface

Although there are innumerable complex systems and therefore such a large number of networks, the focus of this book is *social networks*. A social network contains individuals as nodes and links representing the relationship between these individuals. The study of social networks is of particular interest because it focuses on this abstract view of human relationships which gives insight into various kinds of social relationships ranging all the way from bargaining power to psychological health.

We describe in detail graph theory, statistical properties and graph algorithms. Through this, we hope to describe the various patterns and statistical properties of networks, introduce design principles and models for looking at these properties, provide an understanding as to why networks are organized the way they are and apply our understanding to predict behaviour of networks.

The world around us provides a plethora of instances of *complex systems*. Transportation networks, social media applications, protein–protein interactions, auction houses, spreading of diseases and so on are all examples of complex systems we all encounter in our daily lives. All of these systems are extremely complicated to comprehend because they contain several seemingly disparate components which may be directly or indirectly related to one another. These components exhibit behaviour which is increasingly difficult to reason about and too risky to tinker with. Even a slight seemingly innocuous change in one of the components can have a domino effect which could have unexpected consequences.

Figure 1 depicts the Internet on a global scale. This figure can help paint a sort of picture as to how complicated a system really is, and how one must proceed in order to understand such a complex system.

Each of these complex systems (especially the Internet) has its own unique idiosyncrasies but all of them share a particular commonality in the fact that they can be described by an intricate wiring diagram, a *network*, which defines the interactions between the components. We can never fully understand the system unless we gain a full understanding of its network.

**Fig. 1** Illustration of the global Internet. Online at https://www.weforum.org/projects/internet-for-all

## Network

A network is a collection of objects where some pairs of these objects are connected by links. These objects are also sometimes referred to as nodes. By representing a complex system through its network, we are able to better visualize the system and observe the interconnections among the various nodes. From close examination of networks, we can gather information about which nodes are closely linked to one another, which are sparsely linked, whether there is a concentration of links in a particular part of the network, do some nodes have a very high number of links when compared to others and so on.

Figure 2 illustrates network corresponding to the ARPANET in December 1970 (what the Internet was called then). It consisted of 13 sites where the nodes represent computing hosts and links represent direct communication lines between these hosts.

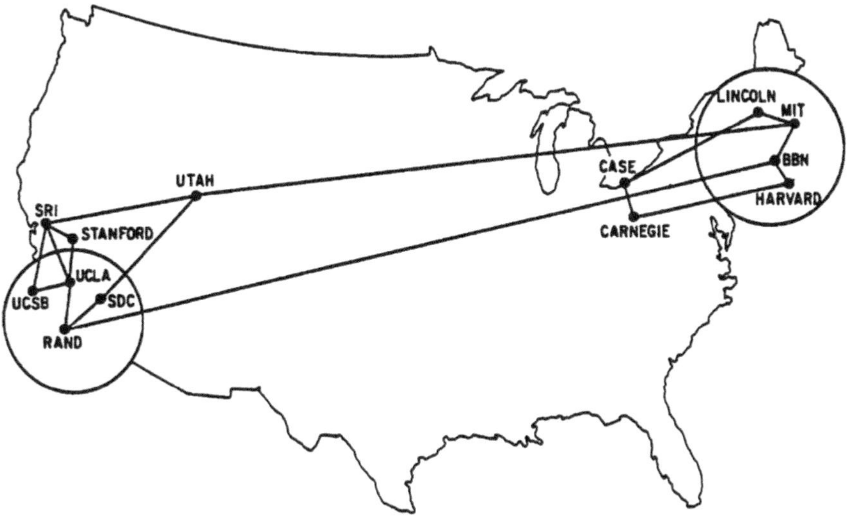


**Fig. 2** ARPANET in December 1970. Computing hosts are represented as nodes and links denote the communication lines. Online at https://imgur.com/gallery/Xk9MP

## Graph

Several properties can be retrieved from these networks but there are some others which require a more mathematical approach. In the purview of mathematics, networks in its current state fail to be amenable. To allow for this amenability, a network is represented as a *graph*. In this view, a graph can be described as a mathematical representation of networks which acts as a framework for reasoning about numerous concepts. More formally, a graph can be defined as $G(V, E)$ where $V$ denotes the set of all vertices of $G$ and $E$ denotes the set of edges of $G$. Each edge $e = (u, v) \in E$ where $u, v \in V$ describes an edge from $u$ to $v$. If an edge exists between $u$ and $v$ then they are considered as *neighbours*. The number of vertices in $G$ is denoted as $|V|$ and the number of edges is denoted by $|E|$. These notations will be used throughout the book.

Figure 3 represents the graph corresponding to the network in Fig. 2 where the vertices of the graph correspond to the computing hosts and the edges correspond to the linking communication lines.

## Organization of the Book

We reason about each graph and therefore its networks in the following manner. First, we study the data therein and use it to find organizational principles that help measure and quantify networks. Second, using graph theory and statistical models,

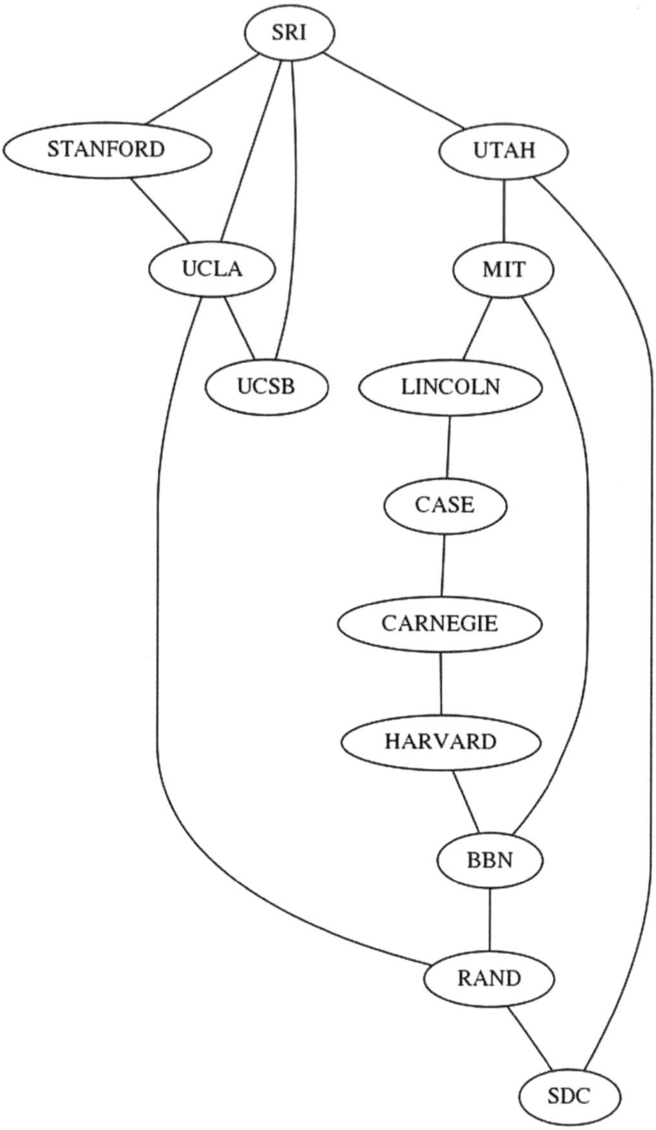


**Fig. 3** Graph corresponding to Fig. 2 consisting of 13 vertices and 17 edges

we attempt to understand behaviours and distinguish surprising from expected phenomena. Finally, we apply graph algorithms to analyse the graphs representing the networks.

Although there are innumerable complex systems and therefore such a large number of networks, the focus of this book is *social networks*. A social network contains individuals as nodes and links representing the relationship between these individuals. The study of social networks is of particular interest because it focuses on this abstract view of human relationships which gives insight into various kinds of social relationships ranging all the way from bargaining power to psychological health.

Completeness of a network is important in this study of online social networks because unlike other offline and certain online networks, the members of online social networks are not controlled random samples and instead are biased samples.

In this book, we follow the possible convention: a complex system has components interconnected by interactions, a network consists of nodes with links representing connections and a graph contains vertices with connecting edges. Wherever possible, we will try to stick to this convention but these terms may be used interchangeably.

We describe in detail graph theory, statistical properties and graph algorithms. Through this, we hope to accomplish the following goals: Describe the various patterns and statistical properties of networks, introduce design principles and models for looking at these properties, provide an understanding as to why networks are organized the way they are, and apply our understanding to predict behaviour of networks.

## Network Datasets

In this age of information technology, we are blessed with an ever increasing availability of large and detailed network datasets. These datasets generally fall into one or more of the following groups.

- *Collaboration graphs*: Collaboration graphs show the collaborators as vertices and an edge between vertices indicating a collaboration between the corresponding collaborators. Co-authorship among scientists, co-appearances in movies among performers and Wikipedia collaboration networks are all instances of collaboration graphs.
- *Who-talks-to-whom graphs*: These graphs have conversers as vertices and an edge between a pair of them if they have shared a conversation. Phone call logs, e-mail logs, SMS logs and social media message logs are examples of who-talks-to-whom graphs. However, these graphs have a certain amount of regulation with it because it involves private information that can be accessed. Certain privacy concerns must be resolved before these graphs can be subject to any form of analysis.
  A variant of these graphs are a "Who-transacts-with-whom graphs" where the nodes represent individuals and edges denote a transaction between individuals. These graphs are of particular interest to economists.
- *Information Linkage graphs*: The Web is an example of these graphs where the webpages denote the vertices and a hyperlink between webpages are represented by edges. Such graphs which contain a large amount of information in both the

vertices and the edges, whose manipulation is a task *per se* connotes information linkage graphs.

- *Technological graphs*: In these graphs, physical devices such as routers or substations represent the vertices and an edge represents a communication line connecting these physical devices. Water grid, power grid, etc. are examples of technological graphs.
  There is a specific kind of technological graphs called the *autonomous systems (AS)* graph where the vertices are autonomous systems and the edges denote the data transfer between these systems. AS graphs are special in that they have a two-level view. The first level is the direct connection among components but there is a second level which defines the protocol regulating the exchange of information between communicating components. A graph of communication between network devices controlled by different ISPs, transfer between bank accounts, transfer of students between departments, etc. are all instances of these AS graphs.
- *Natural-world graphs*: Graphs pertaining to biology and other natural sciences fall under this category. Food webs, brain, protein–protein interactions, disease spread, etc. are natural-world graphs.

Bangalore, India Krishna Raj P. M.
Bangalore, India Ankith Mohan
Jaffarpur, India K. G. Srinivasa

# Contents

# List of Figures

# List of Tables

# Chapter 1
# Basics of Graph Theory

A graph can shed light on several properties of a complex system, but this is incumbent on the effectiveness of the network. If the network does not fully represent all the features described in the system, then the graph will also fail to describe all the properties lying therein. Therefore, the choice of a proper network representation of the complex system is of first importance.

A network must be chosen in such a way that it weighs every component of a system individually on its own merit. In some cases, there is a unique, unambiguous representation. While in others, the representation is not unique.

## 1.1 Choice of Representation

*Undirected graphs* and *directed graphs* are the most common choices for representation of networks.

### *1.1.1 Undirected Graphs*

A graph $G(V, E)$ is said to be an undirected graph if every edge is bidirectional, i.e, every edge is symmetrical and reciprocal. Therefore, an edge $e$ between $u$ and $v$ in $G$ can be represented as $e = (u, v)$ or $e = (v, u)$. Figure 1.1 depicts an undirected graph with 4 vertices connected by 5 edges.

Collaborations and friendships on social media applications are some of the instances in the real-world that can be represented as undirected graphs.



K. Raj P. M. et al., *Practical Social Network Analysis with Python*,
Computer Communications and Networks,
https://doi.org/10.1007/978-3-319-96746-2_1

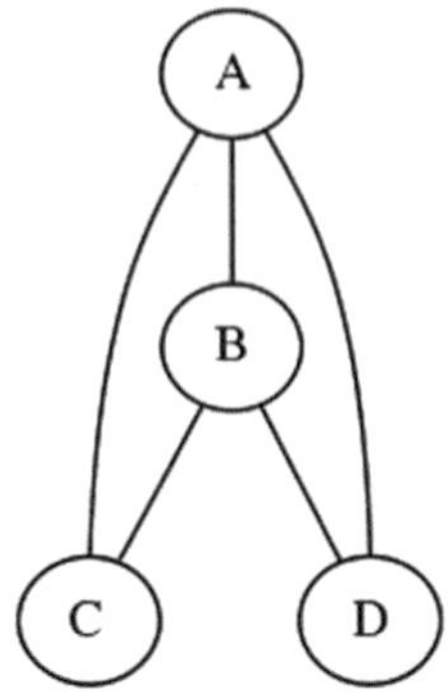


**Fig. 1.1** An undirected graph comprising of 4 vertices $A$, $B$, $C$ and $D$, and 5 edges, $(A,B)$, $(A,C)$, $(A,D)$, $(B,C)$, $(B,D)$

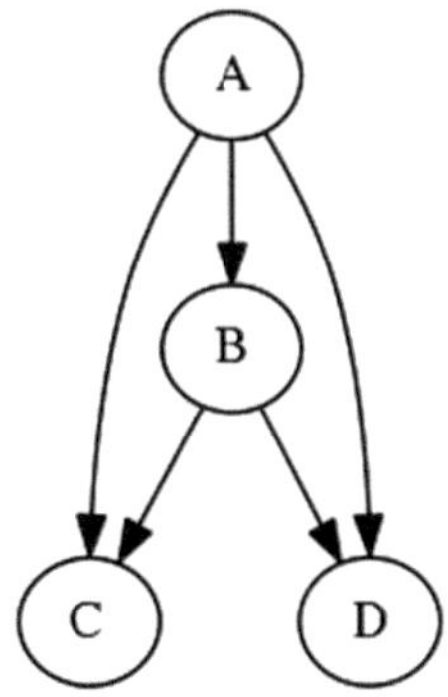


**Fig. 1.2** A directed graph comprising of 4 vertices $A$, $B$, $C$ and $D$, and 5 edges, $(A,B)$, $(A,C)$, $(A,D)$, $(B,C)$, $(B,D)$

### *1.1.2 Directed Graphs*

A graph $G(V, E)$ is said to be a directed graph if every edge is directional, i.e, every edge is asymmetrical and non-reciprocal. An edge $e$ from $u$ to $v$ in $G$ must be represented as $e = (u, v)$. Figure 1.2 represents a directed graph with 4 vertices interconnected by 5 edges.

Voting and followings on social media applications are examples of real-world that can be described by directed graphs.

## 1.2 Degree of a Vertex

The degree of a vertex $i$, denoted as $k_i$, is defined as the number of edges that are adjacent to this vertex $i$.

The definition of the degree of a node in a directed graph is slightly more nuanced. The *in-degree* of a vertex $i$, denoted as $k_i^{in}$, is defined as the number of edges directed towards this vertex $i$. The *out-degree* of a vertex $i$, denoted as $k_i^{out}$, is defined as the number of edges directed away from this vertex $i$. The degree of vertex $i$ in

**Table 1.1** Table shows the vertices of the graph in Fig. 1.1 and their corresponding degrees

| Vertex | Degree |
|---|---|
| *A* | 3 |
| *B* | 3 |
| *C* | 2 |
| *D* | 2 |
| Total | 10 |

**Table 1.2** Table shows the vertices of the graph in Fig. 1.2 and their corresponding in-degrees, out-degrees and degrees

| Vertex | In-degree | Out-degree | Degree |
|---|---|---|---|
| *A* | 0 | 3 | 3 |
| *B* | 1 | 2 | 3 |
| *C* | 2 | 0 | 2 |
| *D* | 2 | 0 | 2 |
| Total | 5 | 5 | 10 |

a directed graph is therefore defined as the sum of the in-degree of this vertex $i$ and its out-degree. This is represented as $k_i = k_i^{in} + k_i^{out}$.

Tables 1.1 and 1.2 tabulate the degrees of all the vertices in Figs. 1.1 and 1.2 respectively.

A vertex with zero in-degree is called a *source vertex*, a vertex with zero out-degree is called a *sink vertex*, and a vertex with in-degree and out-degree both equal to zero is called an *isolated vertex*.

## 1.3 Degree Distribution

The degree distribution of a graph $G(V, E)$, denoted by $P(k)$, is defined as the probability that a random chosen vertex has degree $k$. If $|V|_k$ denotes the number of vertices with degree $k$,

$$P(k) = \frac{|V|_k}{|V|} \tag{1.1}$$

The degree distribution is plotted either as a histogram of $k$ vs $P(k)$ (Fig. 1.3) or as a scree plot of $k$ vs $|V|_k$ (Fig. 1.4).

## 1.4 Average Degree of a Graph

The average degree of a graph $G(V, E)$, denoted by $\bar{k}$, is defined as the average of the degrees of all the vertices in $G$. More formally, the average degree is given by Eq. 1.2.

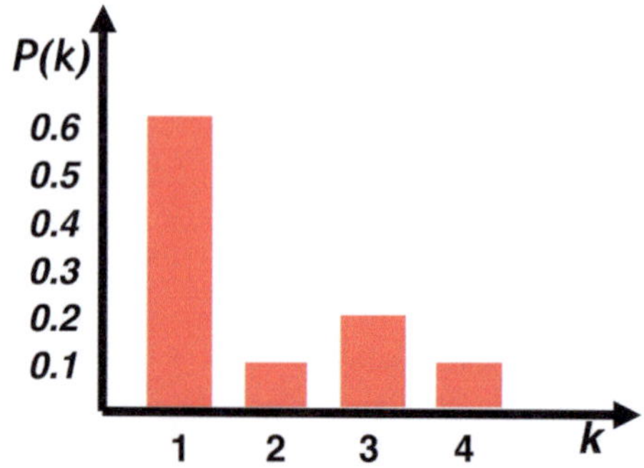


**Fig. 1.3** Histogram of $k$ versus $P(k)$

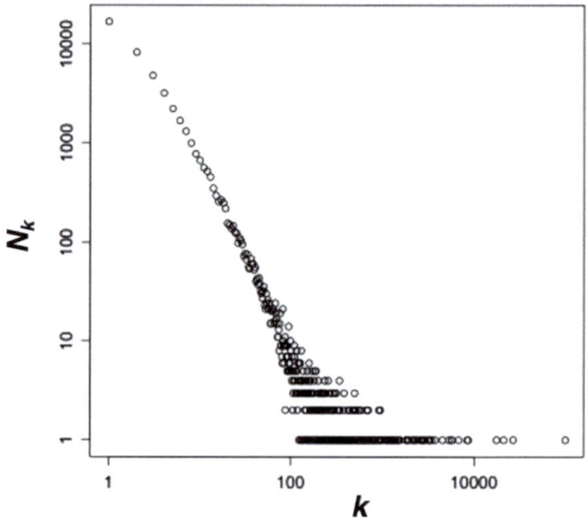


**Fig. 1.4** Scree plot of $k$ versus $|V|_k$

$$\overline{k} = \frac{1}{|V|} \sum_{i=1}^{|V|} k_i \tag{1.2}$$

The average degree of a graph satisfies the properties given in Eqs. 1.3 and 1.4.

$$\overline{k} = \frac{2|E|}{|V|} \tag{1.3}$$

$$\overline{k^{in}} = \overline{k^{out}} \tag{1.4}$$

The average degree of the graph in Fig. 1.1 as well as the graph in Fig. 1.2 is $\frac{10}{4} = 2.5$. Since there are 4 vertices and 5 edges in both of these graphs, Eq. 1.3 is satisfied. The average in-degree of the graph in Fig. 1.2 is $\frac{5}{4} = 1.25$, and its average out-degree is $\frac{5}{4} = 1.25$. This satisfies Eq. 1.4.

**Fig. 1.5** A complete undirected graph having 20 vertices and 190 edges

## 1.5 Complete Graph

The maximum number of edges that a graph with $|V|$ number of vertices, as denoted by $E_{max}$, is given by Eq. 1.5.

$$E_{max} = \begin{cases} \binom{|V|}{2} = \frac{|V|(|V|-1)}{2} \text{ for undirected graphs} \\ 2\binom{|V|}{2} = |V|(|V|-1) \text{ for directed graphs} \end{cases} \tag{1.5}$$

A graph with $|E| = E_{max}$ number of edges is called a complete graph. The average degree of a complete graph is $|V| - 1$.

Figures 1.5 and 1.6 illustrate complete undirected and directed graphs each having 20 vertices and therefore 190 and 380 edges respectively.

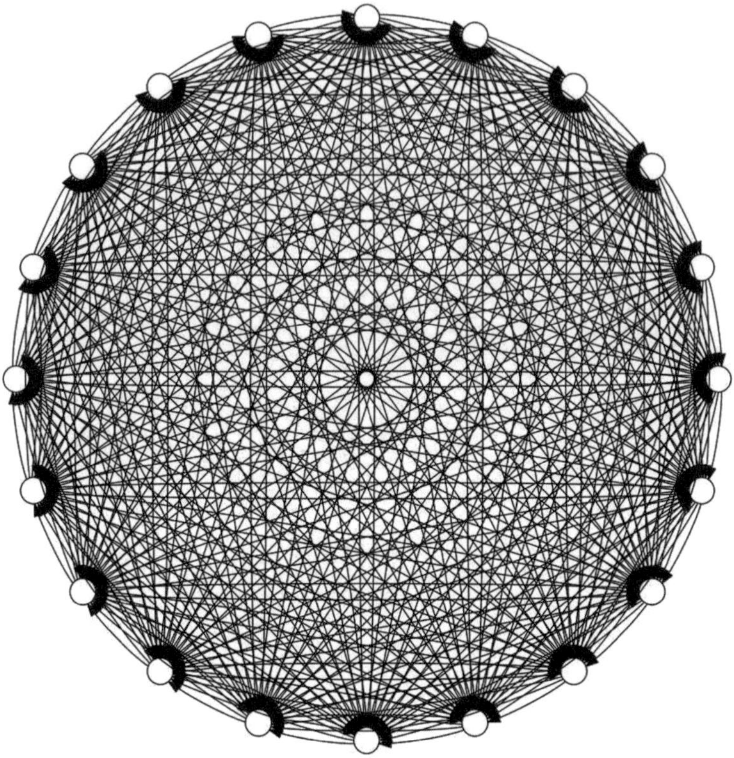

**Fig. 1.6** A complete directed graph having 20 vertices and 380 edges

## 1.6 Regular Graph

A regular graph is defined as a graph where each vertex has the same degree, i.e, $k_1 = k_2 = \cdots = k_{|V|}$. A regular directed graph must also satisfy the stronger condition that the in-degree and out-degree of each vertex be equal to each other, i.e, $k_1^{in} = k_1^{out}$, $k_2^{in} = k_2^{out}, \ldots, k_{|V|}^{in} = k_{|V|}^{out}$. A regular graph with vertices of degree $k$ is called a $k$-regular graph or regular graph of degree $k$. Figure 1.7 shows a 5-regular graph having 10 vertices.

## 1.7 Bipartite Graph

A bipartite graph is a graph whose vertices can be divided into two independent sets $L$ and $R$ such that an edge connects a vertex in $L$ to one in $R$. The corresponding graph that does not have these independent set partitions is called a *folded graph*.

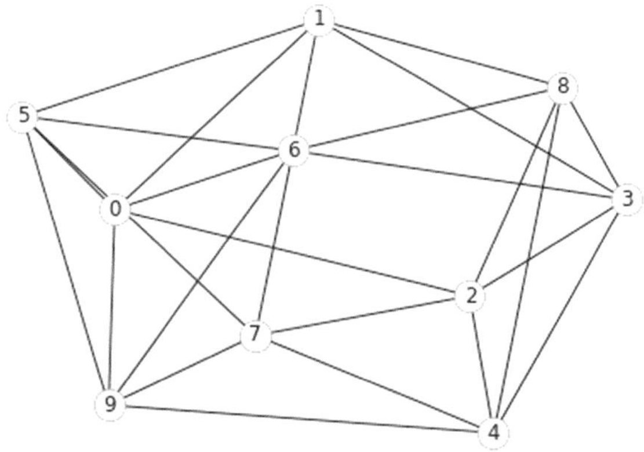


**Fig. 1.7** A 5-regular random graph on 10 vertices

Figure 1.8 depicts the undirected bipartite graph with its corresponding folded graph and Fig. 1.9 illustrates the directed bipartite graph and its corresponding folded graph.

## 1.8 Graph Representation

So far, we have only looked at the visualisation of a graph which is very tedious to work with in the case of graph algorithms. Instead, we look at several other representations of graphs.

### *1.8.1 Adjacency Matrix*

The adjacency matrix of a graph, denoted by $A$, is defined as a matrix where 1 indicates the presence of an edge and 0 indicates the absence of one. More formally, an adjacency matrix is defined as in Eq. 1.6.

$$A_{ij} = \begin{cases} 1 \text{ is an edge exists between the vertex } i \text{ and the vertex } j \\ 0 \text{ otherwise} \end{cases} \tag{1.6}$$

The adjacency matrix for the graph in Fig. 1.1 is as shown in the matrix below.

$$\begin{bmatrix} 0 & 1 & 1 & 1 \\ 1 & 0 & 1 & 1 \\ 1 & 1 & 0 & 0 \\ 1 & 1 & 0 & 0 \end{bmatrix}$$

**Fig. 1.8** A folded undirected graph with its corresponding bipartite undirected graph

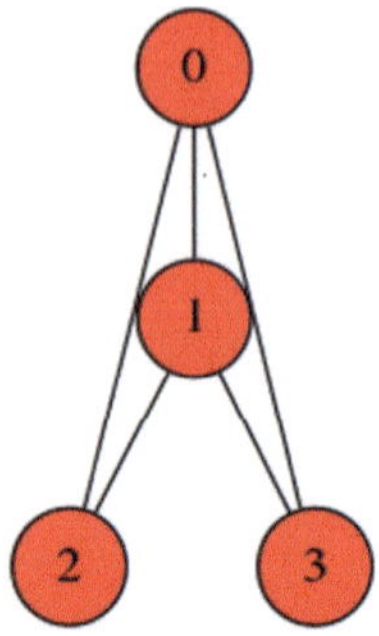


(a) An undirected graph with 4 vertices, 0, 1, 2 and 3 with 5 edges, (0,1), (0,2), (0,3), (1,2), (1,3)

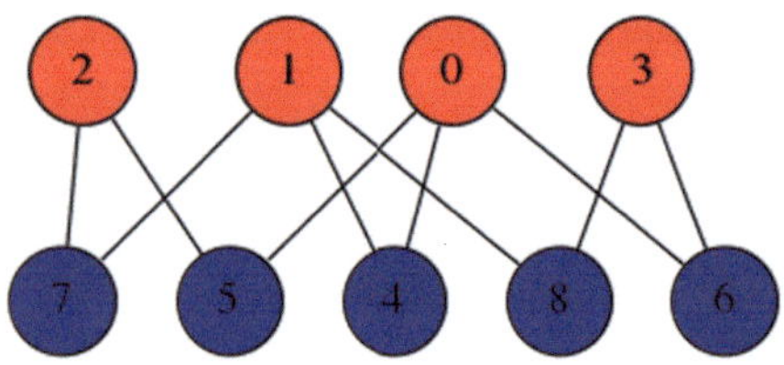


(b) The bipartite graph corresponding to Figure 2.8a where the vertices 0, 1, 2 and 3 in red, denote the set $L$ and the vertices 4, 5, 6, 7 and 8 in blue denote the set $R$

Similarly, the adjacency matrix for the graph in Fig. 1.2 is described in the following matrix.

$$\begin{bmatrix} 0 & 1 & 1 & 1 \\ 0 & 0 & 1 & 1 \\ 0 & 0 & 0 & 0 \\ 0 & 0 & 0 & 0 \end{bmatrix}$$

We can summarize the following properties from adjacency matrices.

$$A_{ii} = 0 \tag{1.7}$$

$$A_{ii} \neq 0 \tag{1.8}$$

$$A_{ij} = A_{ji} \tag{1.9}$$

$$A_{ij} \neq A_{ji} \tag{1.10}$$

**Fig. 1.9** A folded directed graph with its corresponding bipartite directed graph

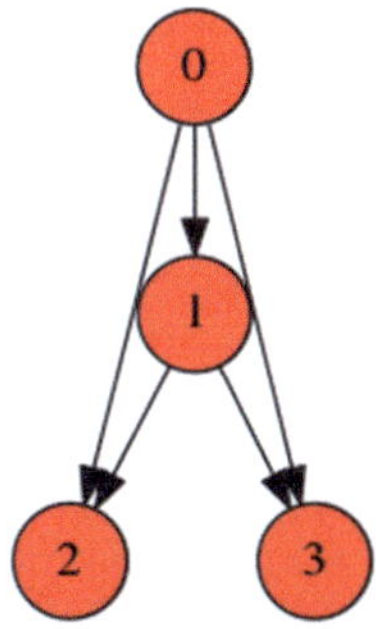


(a) A directed graph with 4 vertices, 0, 1, 2 and 3 with 5 edges, (0,1), (0,2), (0,3), (1,2), (1,3)

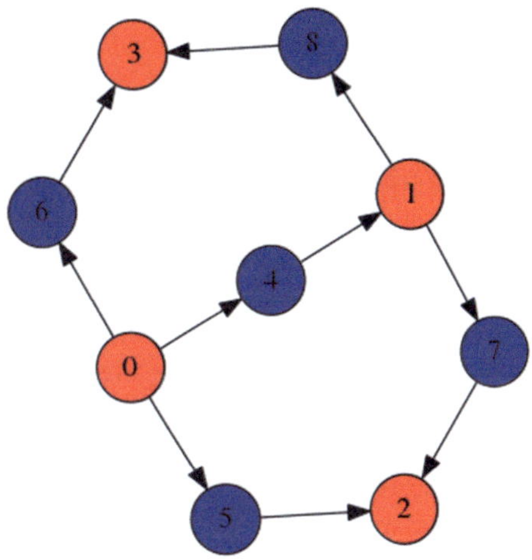


(b) The bipartite graph corresponding to Figure 2.9a where the vertices 0, 1, 2 and 3 in red, denote the set $L$ and the vertices 4, 5, 6, 7 and 8 in blue denote the set $R$

$$|E| = \frac{1}{2}\sum_{i,j=1}^{|V|} A_{ij} \tag{1.11}$$

$$|E| = \sum_{i,j=1}^{|V|} A_{ij} \tag{1.12}$$

Undirected graphs satisfy Eqs. 1.7, 1.9 and 1.11 while directed graphs satisfy Eqs. 1.7, 1.10 and 1.12.

### 1.8.2 Edge List

The edge list of a graph $G(V, E)$ is its representation as a list of edges where each edge $e \in E$ is represented as a tuple $e = (u, v)$ where $u$ denotes the source vertex and $v$ denotes the destination vertex of $e$.

The edge list for both the graph in Fig. 1.1 and for the graph in Fig. 1.2 is given by $\{(A,B), (B,C), (B,D), (A,C), (A,D)\}$.

### 1.8.3 Adjacency List

The adjacency list of a graph $G(V, E)$ is defined as $\{u\colon [v_1, v_2, \ldots], \exists\, e_1 = (u, v_1) \in E, e_2 = (u, v_2) \in E, \ldots;\ \forall u, v_1, v_2, \ldots \in V\}$

The adjacency list for the graph in Fig. 1.1 and that for the graph in Fig. 1.2 is as shown in Tables 1.3 and 1.4 respectively.

When the graphs are small, there is not a notable difference between any of these representations. However, when the graph is large and sparse (as in the case of most real world networks), the adjacency matrix will be a large matrix filled mostly with zeros. This accounts for a lot of unnecessary space and account for a lot of time that could have been avoided during computations. Although edge lists are concise, they are not the best data structure for most graph algorithms. When dealing with such graphs, adjacency lists are comparatively more effective. Adjacency lists can be easily implemented in most programming languages as a hash table with keys for the source vertices and a vector of destination vertices as values. Working with this implementation can save a lot of computation time. SNAP uses this hash table and vector representation for storing graphs [1].

**Table 1.3** Adjacency list for the graph in Fig. 1.1

| |
|---|
| $A : [B, C, D]$ |
| $B : [A, C, D]$ |
| $C : [A, B]$ |
| $D : [A, B]$ |

**Table 1.4** Adjacency list for the graph in Fig. 1.2

| |
|---|
| $A : [\phi]$ |
| $B : [A]$ |
| $C : [A, B]$ |
| $D : [A, B]$ |

## 1.9 Edge Attributes

Some networks may sometimes have to store information on the edges to properly represent the corresponding complex system. This information could be any of the following:

- *Weight*: The frequency of communication between the connected vertices, the strength of this connection, etc.
- *Type*: The type of the relationship between the connected vertices. Eg: Family, friends, colleagues.
- *Ranking*: Best friend, second best friend, third best friend, so on.
- *Sign*: Friend vs foe, trust vs distrust, etc.
- Properties dependent on the structure of the rest of the graph. Such as the number of common neighbours, centrality measure, etc.

Based on edge attributes, the number of edges between vertices and the source and destination of an edge, graphs can be further classified.

### *1.9.1 Unweighted Graph*

Unweighted graphs are graphs where the edges do not have any associated weights. Figures 1.1 and 1.2 are instances of an undirected unweighted graph and a directed unweighted graph respectively.

Friendships and hyperlinks are real-world instances of unweighted graphs.

### *1.9.2 Weighted Graph*

Weighted graphs are graphs where the edges are associated with a certain weight. Figures 1.10 and 1.11 depict an undirected weighted graph and a directed weighted graph respectively.

The adjacency matrix for the graph in Fig. 1.10 is given below

$$\begin{bmatrix} 0 & 1 & 2.5 & 13.75 \\ 1 & 0 & 0.3 & 100 \\ 2.5 & 0.3 & 0 & 0 \\ 13.75 & 100 & 0 & 0 \end{bmatrix}$$

The adjacency matrix for the graph in Fig. 1.11 is as depicted below

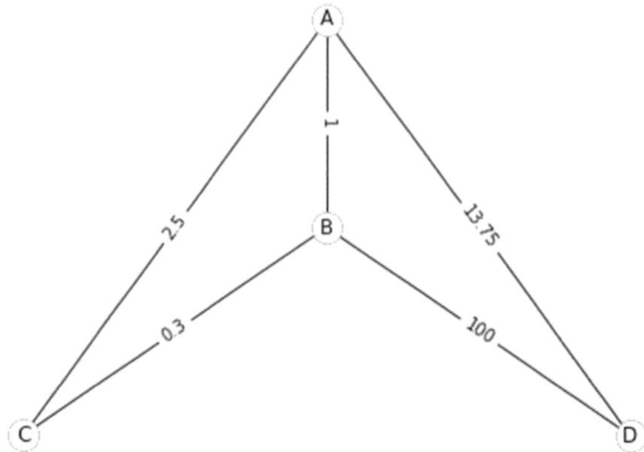


**Fig. 1.10** An undirected weighted graph with 4 vertices and 5 weighted edges

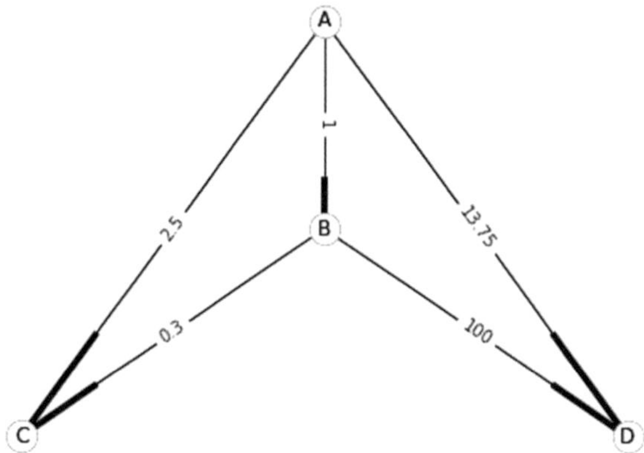


**Fig. 1.11** A directed weighted graph with 4 vertices and 5 weighted edges

$$\begin{bmatrix} 0 & 1 & 2.5 & 13.75 \\ 0 & 0 & 0.3 & 100 \\ 0 & 0 & 0 & 0 \\ 0 & 0 & 0 & 0 \end{bmatrix}$$

Undirected weighted graphs satisfy properties in Eqs. 1.7, 1.9 and 1.13.

$$|E| = \frac{1}{2} \sum_{i,j=1}^{|V|} nonzero(A_{ij}) \tag{1.13}$$

Directed weighted graphs on the other hand satisfy properties in Eqs. 1.7, 1.10 and 1.14.

$$|E| = \sum_{i,j=1}^{|V|} nonzero(A_{ij}) \tag{1.14}$$

Collaborations and transportation networks are some examples of weighted graphs.

### 1.9.3 Self-looped Graph

Self-loops are defined as edges whose source and destination vertices are the same. More formally, an edge $e \in E$ is called a self-looped edge if $e = (u, u)$ where $u \in V$. A graph that contains one or more self-loops is called a self-looped graph. Figures 1.12 and 1.13 illustrate an undirected self-looped graph and a directed self-looped graph respectively.

The adjacency matrix for the graph in Fig. 1.12 is as shown below

$$\begin{bmatrix} 1 & 1 & 1 & 1 \\ 1 & 1 & 1 & 1 \\ 1 & 1 & 1 & 0 \\ 1 & 1 & 0 & 1 \end{bmatrix}$$

The adjacency matrix for the graph in Fig. 1.13 is illustrated as follows

$$\begin{bmatrix} 1 & 1 & 1 & 1 \\ 0 & 1 & 1 & 1 \\ 0 & 0 & 1 & 0 \\ 0 & 0 & 0 & 1 \end{bmatrix}$$

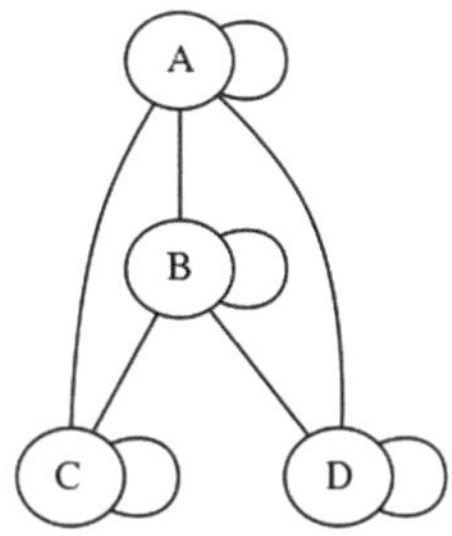


**Fig. 1.12** An undirected self-looped graph with 4 vertices and 9 edges

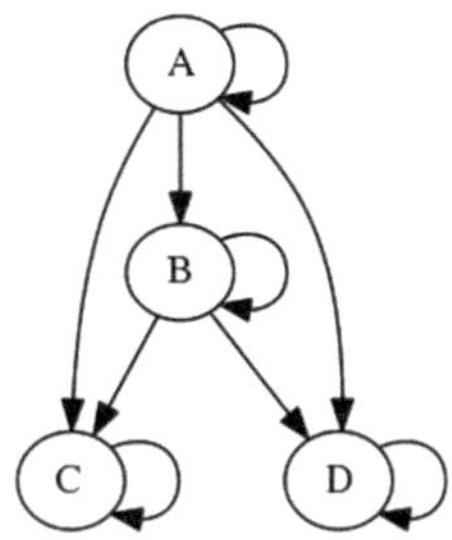


**Fig. 1.13** A directed self-looped graph with 4 vertices and 9 edges

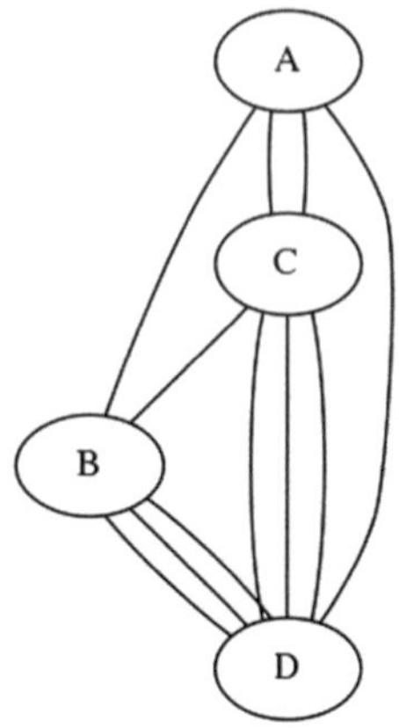


**Fig. 1.14** An undirected multigraph with 4 vertices and 9 edges

Undirected self-looped graphs satisfy properties in Eqs. 1.8, 1.9 and 1.15.

$$|E| = \frac{1}{2} \sum_{i,j=1;i \neq j}^{|V|} A_{ij} + \sum_{i=1}^{|V|} A_{ii} \tag{1.15}$$

Directed weighted graphs on the other hand satisfy properties in Eqs. 1.8, 1.10 and 1.16.

$$|E| = \sum_{i,j=1;i \neq j}^{|V|} A_{ij} + \sum_{i=1}^{|V|} A_{ii} \tag{1.16}$$

Proteins and hyperlinks are some commonly encountered examples of self-looped graphs.

### 1.9.4 Multigraphs

A multigraph is a graph where multiple edges may share the same source and destination vertices. Figures 1.14 and 1.15 are instances of undirected and directed multigraphs respectively.

The adjacency matrix for the graph in Fig. 1.14 is as shown below

$$\begin{bmatrix} 0 & 1 & 2 & 1 \\ 1 & 0 & 1 & 3 \\ 2 & 1 & 0 & 3 \\ 1 & 3 & 3 & 0 \end{bmatrix}$$

The adjacency matrix for the graph in Fig. 1.15 is illustrated as follows

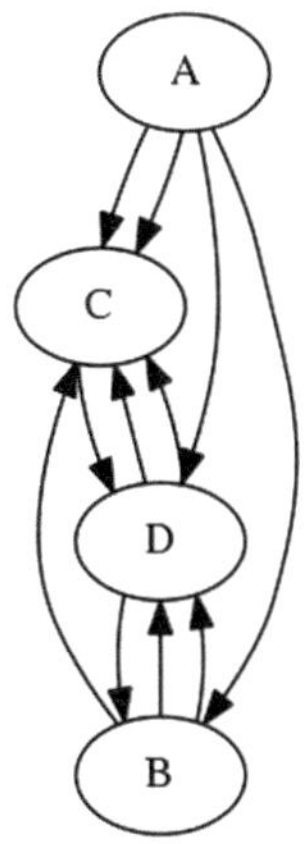


**Fig. 1.15** A directed multigraph with 4 vertices and 9 edges

$$\begin{bmatrix} 0 & 1 & 2 & 1 \\ 0 & 0 & 1 & 2 \\ 0 & 0 & 0 & 1 \\ 0 & 1 & 2 & 0 \end{bmatrix}$$

Undirected multigraphs satisfy properties in Eqs. 1.7, 1.9 and 1.13. Directed multigraphs on the other hand satisfy properties in Eqs. 1.7, 1.10 and 1.14.

Communication and collaboration networks are some common instances of multigraphs.

## 1.10 Path

A path from a vertex $u$ to a vertex $v$ is defined either as a sequence of vertices in which each vertex is linked to the next, $\{u,u_1,u_2,\ldots,u_k,v\}$ or as a sequence of edges $\{(u,u_1), (u_1,u_2), \ldots, (u_k,v)\}$. A path can pass through the same edge multiple times. A path that does not contain any repetition in either the edges or the nodes is called a *simple path*. Following a sequence of such edges gives us a *walk* through the graph from a vertex $u$ to a vertex $v$. A path from $u$ to $v$ does not necessarily imply a path from $v$ to $u$.

The path $\{A,B,C\}$ is a simple path in both Figs. 1.1 and 1.2. $\{A,B,C,B,D\}$ is a path in Fig. 1.1 while there are no non-simple paths in Fig. 1.2.

## 1.11 Cycle

A cycle is defined as a path with atleast three edges, in which the first and the last vertices are the same, but otherwise all other vertices are distinct. The path $\{A,B,C,A\}$ and $\{A,B,D,A\}$ are cycles in Fig. 1.1.

Cycles exist in graph sometimes by design. The reason behind this is redundancy. If any edge were to fail there would still exist a path between any pair of vertices.

## 1.12 Path Length

The length of a path is the number of edges in the sequence that comprises this path. The length of the path $\{A,B,C\}$ in both Figs. 1.1 and 1.2 is 2 because it contains the edges $(A,B)$ and $(B,C)$.

## 1.13 Distance

The distance between a pair of vertices $u$ and $v$ is defined as the number of edges along the shortest path connecting $u$ and $v$. If two nodes are not connected, the distance is usually defined as infinity. Distance is symmetric in undirected graphs and asymmetric in directed graphs.

The *distance matrix*, $h$ of a graph is the matrix in which each element $h_{ij}$ denotes the distance from vertex $i$ to vertex $j$. More formally, distance matrix is defined as given in Eq. 1.17.

$$h_{ij} = \begin{cases} \text{the number of edges from vertex } i \text{ to vertex } j \text{ if a path exists from } i \text{ to } j \\ \infty \text{ otherwise} \end{cases} \tag{1.17}$$

The distance matrix for the undirected graph in Fig. 1.1 is

$$\begin{bmatrix} 0 & 1 & 1 & 1 \\ 1 & 0 & 1 & 1 \\ 1 & 1 & 0 & 2 \\ 1 & 1 & 2 & 0 \end{bmatrix}$$

The distance matrix for the directed graph in Fig. 1.2 is

$$\begin{bmatrix} 0 & 1 & 1 & 1 \\ \infty & 0 & 1 & 1 \\ \infty & \infty & 0 & \infty \\ \infty & \infty & \infty & 0 \end{bmatrix}$$

## 1.14 Average Path Length

The average path length of a graph, denoted as $\overline{h}$ is the average of the distances between all pairs of vertices in the graph. Formally, the average path length is given by

$$\overline{h} = \frac{1}{E_{max}} \sum_{i,j} h_{ij} \tag{1.18}$$

All infinite distances are disregarded in the computation of the average path length.

## 1.15 Diameter

The diameter of a graph is the maximum of the distances between all pairs of vertices in this graph. While computing the diameter of a graph, all infinite distances are disregarded.

The diameter of Figs. 1.1 and 1.2 is 2 and 1 respectively.

## 1.16 Connectedness of Graphs

A graph is said to be *connected* if for every pair of vertices, there exists a path between them. A subgraph which is connected is called a *connected component* or simply a *component*. A *disconnected graph* is a graph which breaks apart naturally into a set of components which are connected when considered in isolation without overlap between these components.

When dealing with directed graphs, the definition of connectedness is two-fold. A *strongly connected directed graph* is one where there is a path between every pair of vertices of this graph. While, a *weakly connected directed graph* is considered connected if and only if the graph is considered undirected.

Figure 1.1 is a connected undirected graph because there is a path between all of the vertices. Figure 1.16 is an instance of a disconnected undirected graph because $D$ is an isolated vertex and hence there are no paths connecting $D$ to the rest of the vertices.

Figure 1.2 is a weakly connected directed graph because the following paths do not exist in the directed graph: $A$ to itself, $B$ to $A$, $B$ to itself, $C$ to all other vertices including itself, $D$ to itself and the rest of the vertices. But, there is a path between all pairs of vertices when Fig. 1.2 is considered undirected. Figure 1.17 is a strongly connected directed graph where each vertex in this directed graph has a path to all of the other vertices including itself.

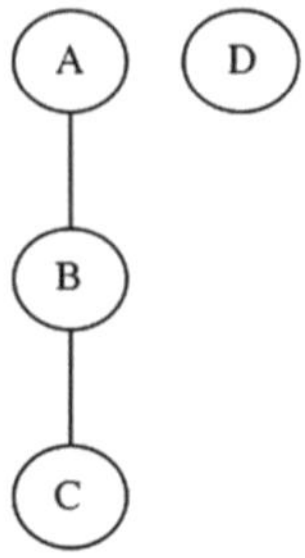


**Fig. 1.16** A disconnected undirected graph with 4 vertices, $A$, $B$, $C$ and $D$, and 2 edges, ($A$,$B$), ($B$,$C$) leaving $D$ as an isolated vertex

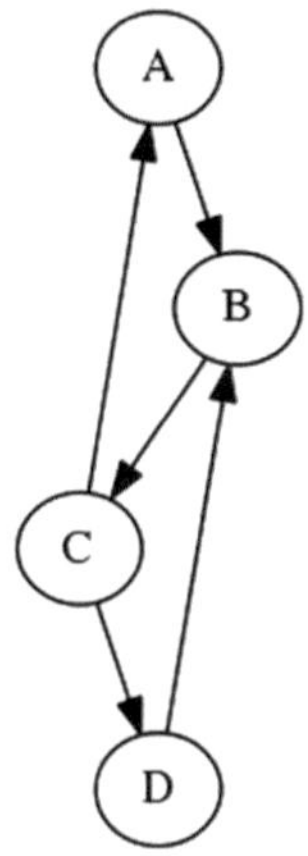


**Fig. 1.17** A strongly connected directed graph with 4 vertices, $A$, $B$, $C$ and $D$, and 5 edges, ($A$,$B$), ($B$,$C$), ($C$,$A$), ($C$,$D$) and ($D$,$B$)

## Giant Component

The largest component of a graph is called its *giant component*. It is a unique, distinguishable component containing a significant fraction of all the vertices and dwarfs all the other components. $A$,$B$,$C$ is the giant component in Fig. 1.16.

## Bridge Edge

A *bridge edge* is an edge whose removal disconnects the graph.Every edge in Fig. 1.17 is a bridge edge. For Fig. 1.1, the combination of edges ($A$,$B$), ($A$,$C$), ($A$,$D$); or ($A$,$C$), ($B$,$C$); or ($A$,$D$), ($B$,$D$) are bridge edges.

## Articulation Vertex

An *articulation vertex* is defined as a vertex which when deleted renders the graph a disconnected one. Every vertex in Fig. 1.17 as well as in Fig. 1.1 is an articulation vertex.

## In and Out of a Vertex

For a graph $G(V, E)$, we define the *In* and *Out* of a vertex $v \in V$ as given in Eqs. 1.19 and 1.20.

$$In(v) = \{w \in V \mid there\ exists\ a\ path\ from\ w\ to\ v\} \tag{1.19}$$
$$Out(v) = \{w \in V \mid there\ exists\ a\ path\ from\ v\ to\ w\} \tag{1.20}$$

In other words if Eq. 1.21 is satisfied by a directed graph, then this graph is said to be a strongly connected directed graph. This means that a weakly connected directed graph must satisfy Eq. 1.22.

$$In(v) = Out(v)\ \forall\ v \in V \tag{1.21}$$
$$In(v) \neq Out(v)\ \forall\ v \in V \tag{1.22}$$

Tables 1.5, 1.6, 1.7 and 1.8 tabulate the $In$ and $Out$ for all the vertices in each of these graphs. From these tables, we observe that Fig. 1.17 is strongly connected and Fig. 1.2 is weakly connected because they satisfy Eqs. 1.21 and 1.22 respectively.

### Directed Acyclic Graph

A *directed acyclic graph* (DAG) is a directed graph that does not have any cycles. Figure 1.2 is an instance of a DAG.

### Strongly Connected Component

A *strongly connected component* (SCC) is a set of vertices $S$ such that it satisfies the following conditions:

- Every pair of vertices in $S$ has a path to one another.
- There is no larger set containing $S$ that satisfies this property.

Figure 1.18 is a weakly connected directed graph having the SCCs, $E$, $A$,$B$,$C$ and $D$.

**Table 1.5** $In$ and $Out$ for all the vertices in Fig. 1.1

| $v \in V$ | $In(v)$ | $Out(v)$ |
|---|---|---|
| $A$ | $A,B,C,D$ | $A,B,C,D$ |
| $B$ | $A,B,C,D$ | $A,B,C,D$ |
| $C$ | $A,B,C,D$ | $A,B,C,D$ |
| $D$ | $A,B,C,D$ | $A,B,C,D$ |

**Table 1.6** $In$ and $Out$ for all the vertices in Fig. 1.2

| $v \in V$ | $In(v)$ | $Out(v)$ |
|---|---|---|
| $A$ | $\phi$ | $B,C,D$ |
| $B$ | $A$ | $C,D$ |
| $C$ | $A,B$ | $\phi$ |
| $D$ | $A,B$ | $\phi$ |

**Table 1.7** $In$ and $Out$ for all the vertices in Fig. 1.16

| $v \in V$ | $In(v)$ | $Out(v)$ |
|---|---|---|
| $A$ | $A,B,C$ | $A,B,C$ |
| $B$ | $A,B,C$ | $A,B,C$ |
| $C$ | $A,B,C$ | $A,B,C$ |
| $D$ | $\phi$ | $\phi$ |

**Table 1.8** $In$ and $Out$ for all the vertices in Fig. 1.17

| $v \in V$ | $In(v)$ | $Out(v)$ |
|---|---|---|
| $A$ | $A,B,C,D$ | $A,B,C,D$ |
| $B$ | $A,B,C,D$ | $A,B,C,D$ |
| $C$ | $A,B,C,D$ | $A,B,C,D$ |
| $D$ | $A,B,C,D$ | $A,B,C,D$ |

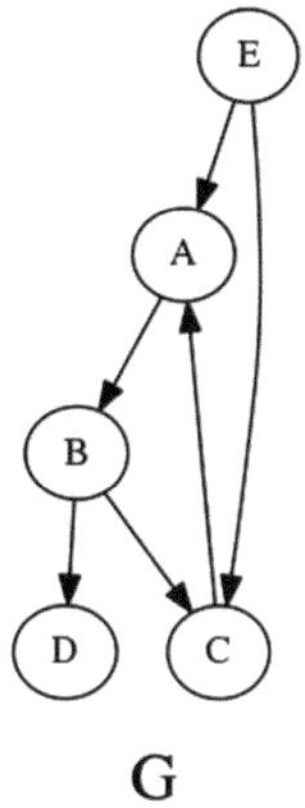


**Fig. 1.18** A weakly connected directed graph $G$ with 5 vertices, $A$, $B$, $C$, $D$ and $E$, with 6 edges, $(A,B)$, $(B,C)$, $(B,D)$, $(C,A)$, $(E,A)$ and $(E,C)$. This graph has the SCCs, $E$, $A,B,C$ and $D$

The SCC containing a vertex $v \in V$ can be computed using Eq. 1.23.

$$In(V) \cap Out(v) \tag{1.23}$$

These definitions of a DAG and SCC gives us Theorem 1.

**Theorem 1** *Every directed graph is a DAG on its SCC.*

1. *SCCs partition vertices of a graph, i.e, each node is in exactly one SCC.*
2. *If we build a graph $G'$ whose vertices are SCCs of $G$ and an edge between vertices of $G'$ exists if there is an edge between corresponding SCCs of $G$, then $G'$ is a DAG.*

For the proof of this theorem, we will use the graphs $G$ in Fig. 1.18 and $G'$ in Fig. 1.19.

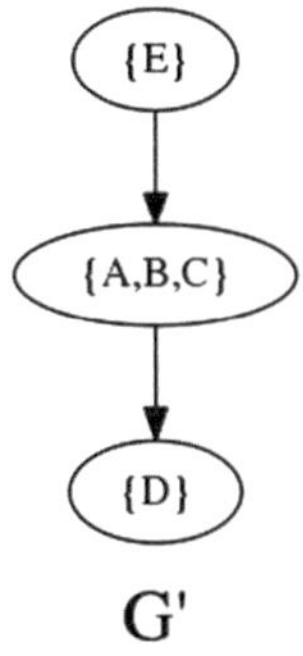


**Fig. 1.19** A weakly connected graph whose vertices are the SCCs of $G$ and whose edges exist in $G'$ because there is an edge between the corresponding SCCs in $G$

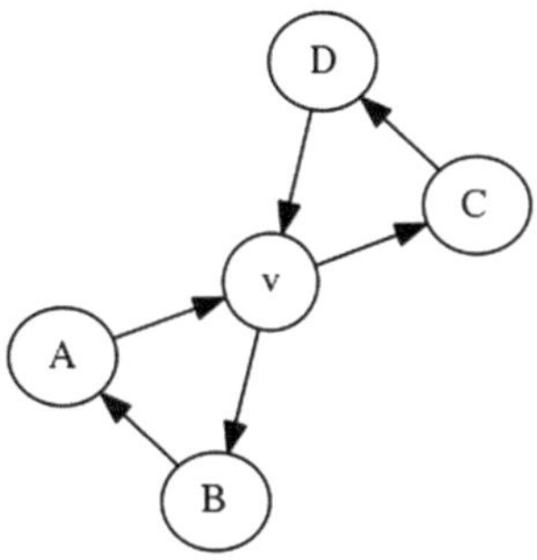


**Fig. 1.20** A strongly connected directed graph where vertex $v$ belongs to two SCCs $A,v,B$ and $C,v,D$

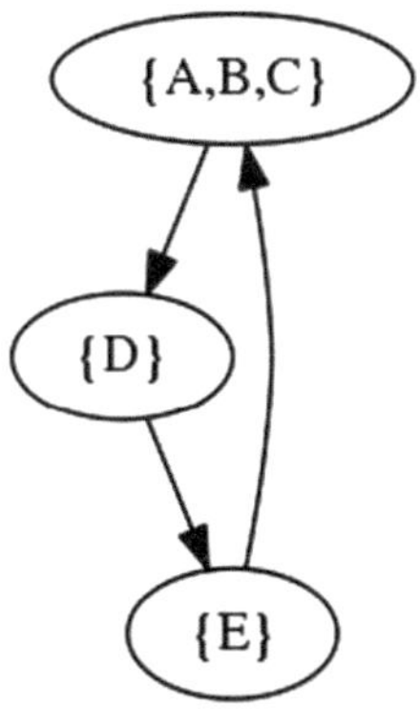


**Fig. 1.21** A graph with the same vertices and edges as shown in Fig. 1.19 with the exception that there exists an edge between $D$ and $E$ to make the graph a strongly connected one

*Proof* 1. Let us assume there exists a vertex $v$ which is a member of two SCCs $S = A,v,B$ and $S' = C,v,D$ as shown in Fig. 1.20. By the definition of a SCC, $S \cup S'$ becomes one large SCC. Therefore, SCCs partition vertices of a graph.

2. Assume that $G'$ is not a DAG, i.e, there exists a directed cycle in $G'$ (as depicted in Fig. 1.21). However, by the definitions of a SCC and a DAG this makes $\{A,B,C,D,E\}$ one large SCC, rendering $G'$ no longer a graph of edges between SCCs. Therefore by contradiction, $G'$ is a DAG on the SCCs of $G$.

## 1.17 Clustering Coefficient

The clustering coefficient of a vertex $i$ in a graph $G(V, E)$, denoted by $C_i$, gives what portion of $i$'s neighbours are connected. Formally, the clustering coefficient is as given in Eq. 1.24

$$C_i = \frac{2e_i}{k_i(k_i - 1)} \epsilon [0, 1] \tag{1.24}$$

where $e_i$ denotes the number of edges between the neighbours of vertex $i$.

The clustering coefficients of the vertices for the graphs in Figs. 1.1 and 1.2 are as tabulated in Table 1.9.

## 1.18 Average Clustering Coefficient

The average clustering coefficient of a graph $G(V, E)$, denoted by $C$, is defined as the average of the clustering coefficients of all the vertices $v \in V$. Formally, the average clustering coefficient is given by

$$C = \frac{1}{|V|} \sum_i |V| C_i \tag{1.25}$$

The average clustering coefficients of the graphs in Figs. 1.1 and 1.2 are both equal to $1.\overline{6}$.

## Problems

Download the *email-Eu-core* directed network from the SNAP dataset repository available at http://snap.stanford.edu/data/email-Eu-core.html.

For this dataset compute the following network parameters:

**1** Number of nodes

**2** Number of edges

**Table 1.9** Clustering coefficient of vertices of Figs. 1.1 and 1.2

| Vertex | Clustering coefficient |
|---|---|
| $A$ | $\frac{2}{3}$ |
| $B$ | $\frac{2}{3}$ |
| $C$ | 3 |
| $D$ | 3 |

**3** In-degree, out-degree and degree of the first five nodes

**4** Number of source nodes

**5** Number of sink nodes

**6** Number of isolated nodes

**7** In-degree distribution

**8** Out-degree distribution

**9** Average degree, average in-degree and average out-degree

**10** Distance between five pairs of random nodes

**11** Shortest path length distribution

**12** Diameter

**13** Is the graph strongly connected? If so, compute the strongly connected component size distribution

**14** Is the graph weakly connected? If so, compute the weakly connected component size distribution

**15** Number of bridge edges

**16** Number of articulation nodes

**17** Number of nodes in $In(v)$ for five random nodes

**18** Number of nodes in $Out(v)$ for five random nodes

**19** Clustering coefficient for five random nodes

**20** Clustering coefficient distribution

**21** Average clustering coefficient

## Reference

1. Leskovec, Jure, and Rok Sosič. 2016. Snap: A general-purpose network analysis and graph-mining library. *ACM Transactions on Intelligent Systems and Technology (TIST)* 8 (1): 1.

# Chapter 2
# Graph Structure of the Web

In this chapter, we will take a close look at the Web when it is represented in the form of a graph and attempt to understand its structure. We will begin by looking at the reasons behind why we must be interested with this problem concerning the Web's structure. There are numerous reasons as to why the structure of the Web is worth studying, but the most prominent ones are as follows: the Web is a large system that evolved naturally over time, understanding such a system's organization and properties could help better comprehend several other real-world systems; the study could yield valuable insight into Web algorithms for crawling, searching and community discovery, which could in turn help improve strategies to accomplish these tasks; we could gain an understanding into the sociological phenomena characterising content creation in its evolution; the study could help predict the evolution of known or new web structures and lead to the development of better algorithms for discovering and organizing them; and we could predict the emergence of new phenomena in the Web.

**Bowtie Structure of the Web**

Reference [1] represented the Web as a directed graph where the webpages are treated as vertices and hyperlinks are the edges and studied the following properties in this graph: diameter, degree distribution, connected components and macroscopic structure. However, the dark-web (part of the Web that is composed of webpages that are not directly accessible (even by Web browsers)) were disregarded. This study consisted of performing *web crawls* on a snapshot of the graph consisting of 203 million URLs connected by 1.5 billion hyperlinks. The web crawl is based on a large set of starting points accumulated over time from various sources, including voluntary submissions. A 465 MHz server with 12 GB of memory was dedicated for this purpose.

Reference [1] took a large snapshot of the Web and using Theorem 1, attempted to understand how its SCCs fitted together as a DAG.



K. Raj P. M. et al., *Practical Social Network Analysis with Python*,
Computer Communications and Networks,
https://doi.org/10.1007/978-3-319-96746-2_2

**Power Law**

The *power law* is a functional relationship between two quantities where a relative change in one quantity results in a proportional relative change in the other quantity, independent of the initial size of those quantities, i.e, one quantity varies as the power of the other. Hence the name power law [3]. Power law distributions as defined on positive integers is the probability of the value $i$ being proportional to $\frac{1}{i^k}$ for a small positive integer $k$.

## 2.1 Algorithms

In this section we will look at several algorithms used by [1] in their experiments.

### 2.1.1 Breadth First Search (BFS) Algorithm

The BFS algorithm (Algorithm 1) takes as input a graph $G(V, E)$ and a source vertex $s$. The algorithm returns the set of vertices that the source vertex has a path to.

**Algorithm 1** BFS algorithm

```
procedure BFS(G(V, E),s)
    Let reachable be an array
    Let Q be a queue
    Q.enqueue(s)
    reachable.add(s)
    while Q is not empty do
        v ← Q.dequeue()
        for each neighbour w of v in V do
            if w is not in reachable then
                Q.enqueue(w)
                reachable.add(w)
            end if
        end for
    end while
    return reachable
end procedure
```

The Web crawl proceeds in roughly a BFS manner, subject to various rules designed to avoid overloading, infinite paths, spam, time-outs, etc. Each build is based on crawl data after further filtering and processing. Due to multiple starting points, it is possible for the resulting graph to have several connected components.

### 2.1.2 *Strongly Connected Components (SCC) Algorithm*

The SCC algorithm (Algorithm 4) takes a graph $G(V, E)$ as input and returns a list of all the SCCs in this graph as output. The SCC of $G$ is computed using Eq. 1.21. The function *unique* returns a list of all the distinct elements in the input list. For instance, *unique*([1,2,1,3,2,2]) will return [1,2,3].

**Algorithm 2** In algorithm

```
procedure IN(G(V, E),s)
    Let In be an array
    for each vertex v in V do
        if s in BFS(G(V, E), v) then
            In.add(v)
        end if
    end for
    return In
end procedure
```

**Algorithm 3** Out algorithm

```
procedure OUT(G(V, E),s)
    Let Out be an array
    Out ← BFS(G(V, E), s)
    return Out
end procedure
```

**Algorithm 4** SCC algorithm

```
procedure SCC(G(V, E))
    Let SCC be an array
    for each vertex v in V do
        SCC.add(In(G(V, E), v) ∩ Out(G(V, E), v))
    end for
    return unique(SCC)
end procedure
```

### *2.1.3 Weakly Connected Components (WCC) Algorithm*

The WCC algorithm (Algorithm 5) computes the list of all WCCs given a graph $G(V, E)$ as input.

---

**Algorithm 5** WCC algorithm

---

**procedure** WCC($G(V, E)$)
  Let $WCC$ be an array
  Let $G'(V', E')$ be $G(V, E)$ as an undirected graph
  **for each** vertex $v$ in $V'$ **do**
    $WCC.add(BFS(G'(V', E'), v)$
  **end for**
  **return** $unique(WCC)$
**end procedure**

---

Three sets of experiments on these web crawls were performed from May 1999 to October 1999.

## 2.2 First Set of Experiments—Degree Distributions

The first set of experiments involved generating in-degree and out-degree distributions on the graph of the Web crawl. The in-degree distribution is observed to follow a power law with exponent of 2.1 as seen in Figs. 2.1 and 2.2. The out-degree distribution is found to also follow a power law with exponent of 2.72 as shown in Figs. 2.3 and 2.4.

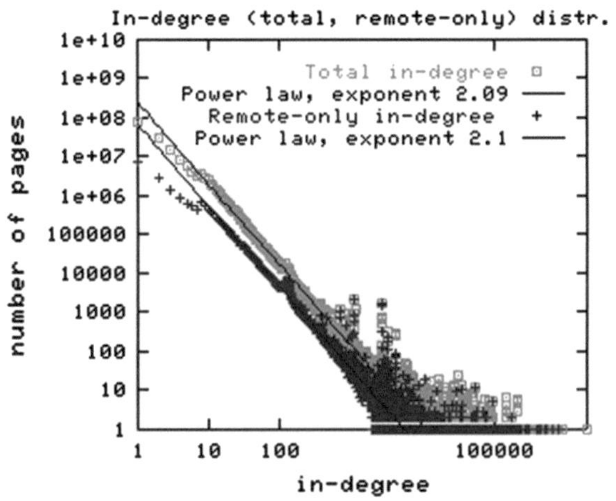


**Fig. 2.1** In-degree distribution when only off-site edges are considered

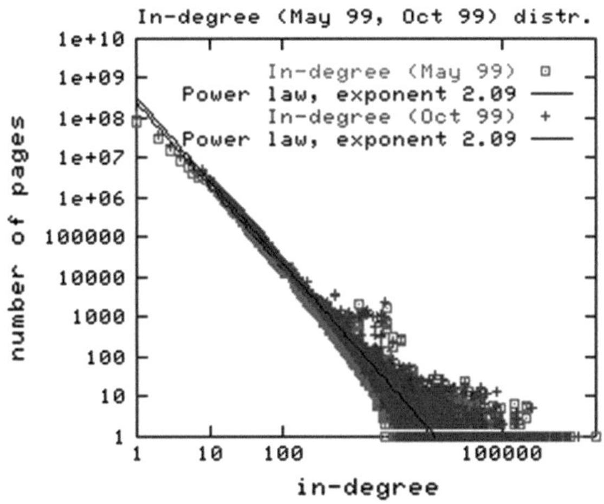


**Fig. 2.2** In-degree distribution over May and October 1999 crawls

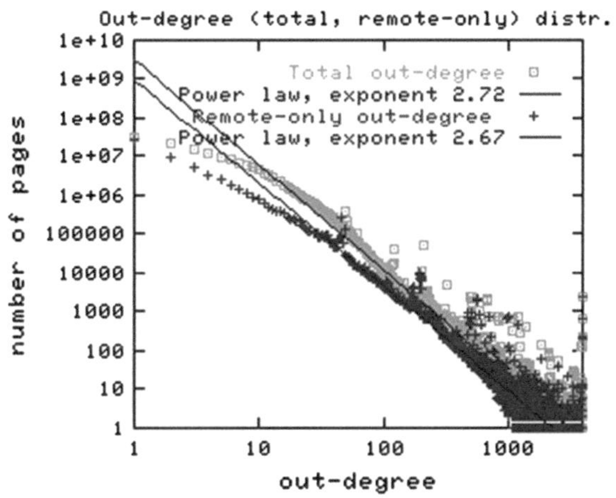


**Fig. 2.3** Out-degree distribution when only off-site edges are considered

## 2.3 Second Set of Experiments—Connected Components

The second set of experiments were concerned with the study of the directed and undirected connected components of the Web. The Web was considered as an undirected graph and the sizes of the undirected component was computed. By running the $WCC$ algorithm on the Web, a giant component comprising of 186 million nodes in which fully 91% of these nodes have a path to one another by following either the forward or the backward edges was identified. The remaining 17 million nodes formed the $DISCONNECTED\ COMPONENTS$. Even the distribution of the sizes of the WCCs exhibits a power law with exponent 2.5 as illustrated in Fig. 2.5.

However, there still exists the question as to whether this widespread connectivity results from a few vertices of large in-degree. The answer is as tabulated in Table 2.1.

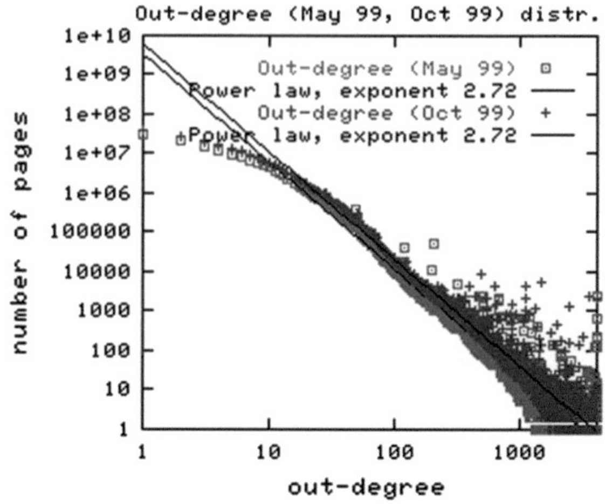


**Fig. 2.4** Out-degree distribution over May and October 1999 crawls

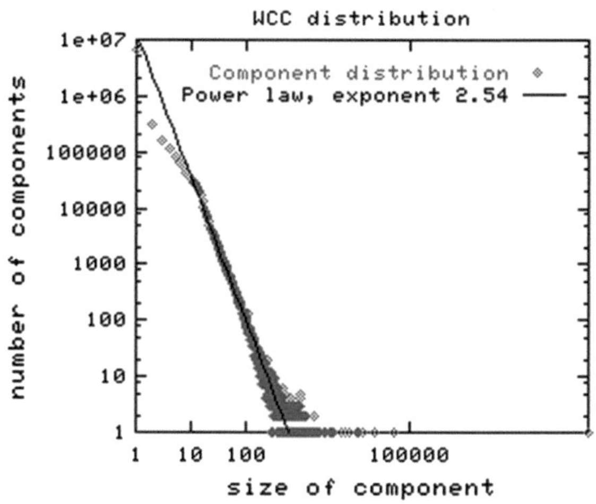


**Fig. 2.5** Distribution of WCCs on the Web

**Table 2.1** Size of the largest surviving weak component when links to pages with in-degree at least k are removed from the graph

| *k* | 1000 | 100 | 10 | 5 | 4 | 3 |
|---|---|---|---|---|---|---|
| Size (millions) | 177 | 167 | 105 | 59 | 41 | 15 |

Table shows the size of the largest surviving weak components when edges to pages with in-degree atleast *k* are removed from the graph.

Table 2.1 gives us the following insights: Connectivity of the Web graph is extremely resilient and does not depend on the existence of vertices of high degree, vertices which are useful tend to include those vertices that have a high PageRank

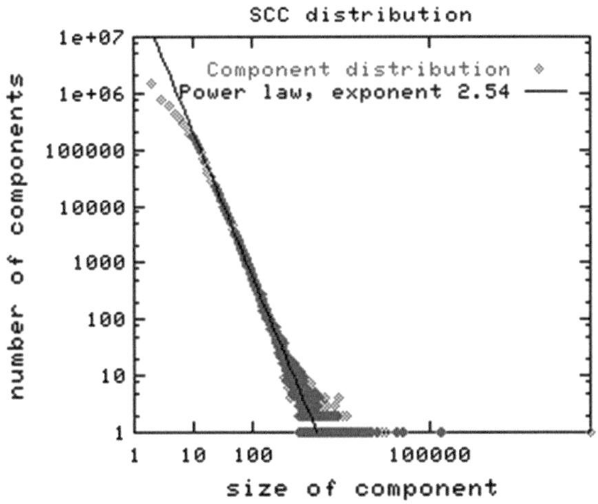


**Fig. 2.6** Distribution of SCCs on the Web

or those which are considered as good hubs or authorities are embedded in a graph that is well connected without them.

To understand what the giant component is composed of, it was subjected to the *SCC* algorithm. The algorithm returned a single large SCC consisting of 56 million vertices which barely amounts to 28% of all the vertices in the crawl. This corresponds to all of the vertices that can reach one another along the directed edges situated at the heart of the Web graph. Diameter of this component is atleast 28. The distribution of sizes of the SCCs also obeys power law with exponent of 2.5 as observed in Fig. 2.6.

## 2.4 Third Set of Experiments—Number of Breadth First Searches

The third set of experiments were related to computing the number of breadth first searches from randomly chosen start vertices in the web crawl to understand what apart from the *SCC* constitutes the giant component.

570 vertices were randomly chosen and the *BFS* algorithm was run twice from each of these selected vertices, once in the forward direction, following the direction of the edges in the Web graph, and the other in the backward direction, following the edges in the reverse direction.

Each of these BFS traversals exhibited a sharp bimodal behaviour: it would either die out after reaching a small set of vertices (90% of the time this set has fewer than 90 vertices, in extreme cases it has a few hundred thousand), or it would explode to cover about 100 million vertices. Further, for a fraction of the starting vertices, both the forward and the backward BFS runs would explode, each covering about 100

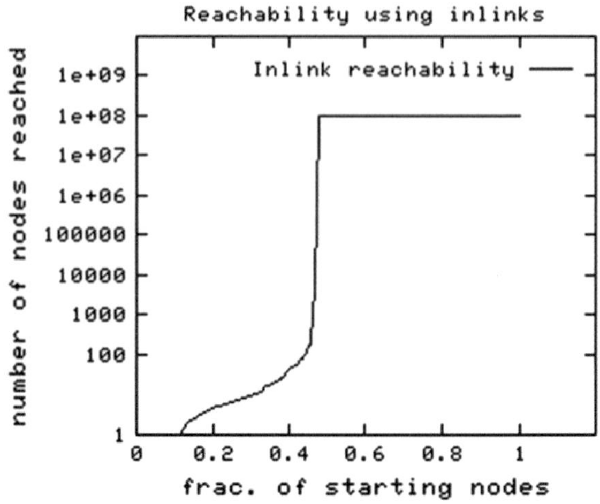


**Fig. 2.7** Cumulative distribution on the number of nodes reached when BFS is started from a random vertex and follows in-links

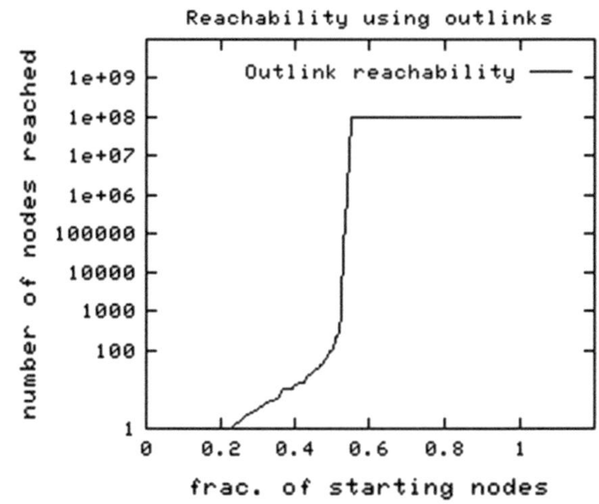


**Fig. 2.8** Cumulative distribution on the number of nodes reached when BFS is started from a random vertex and follows out-links

million vertices ($\approx$ 50%). This behaviour can be observed in Figs. 2.7, 2.8 and 2.9. These explosive nodes are the ones which correspond to the $SCC$.

### Zipf's Law

*Zipf's law* states that the frequency of occurrence of a certain value is inversely proportional to its rank in the frequency table [3]. The in-degree distribution shows a fit more with Zipf distribution than the power law as is evident from Fig. 2.10.

From the previous set of experiments, we got the giant undirected component, the $DISCONNECTED\ COMPONENTS$ and the $SCC$. The 100 million vertices whose forward BFS traversals exploded correspond to either the $SCC$ component or a component called $IN$. Since, $SCC$ corresponds to 56 million vertices, this leaves with

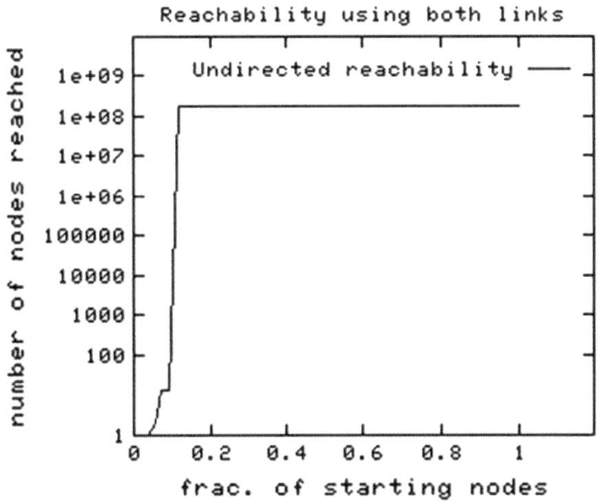


**Fig. 2.9** Cumulative distribution on the number of nodes reached when BFS is started from a random vertex and follows both in-links and out-links

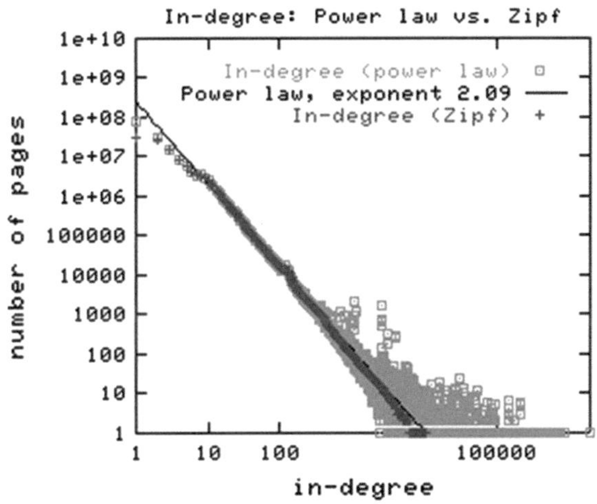


**Fig. 2.10** In-degree distribution plotted as power law and Zipf distribution

44 million vertices ($\approx$ 22%) for $IN$. On similar lines, the 100 million vertices whose backward BFS traversals exploded correspond to either $SCC$ or a component called $OUT$, which will have 44 million vertices ($\approx$ 22%). This leaves us with roughly 44 million vertices ($\approx$ 22%), which are not yet accounted for. These vertices were placed in a component called $TENDRILS$. These components altogether form the famous bowtie structure (Fig. 2.11) of the Web.

The numbers of the vertices in each of these components given above is a rough estimate. The actual numbers are as given in Table 2.2.

The intuition behind these components is that $IN$ corresponds to those webpages that can reach the $SCC$, but cannot be reached back from the $IN$ component. This possibly contains new webpages that have not yet been discovered and linked to. The webpages that are accessible from the $SCC$, but do have a link back to this

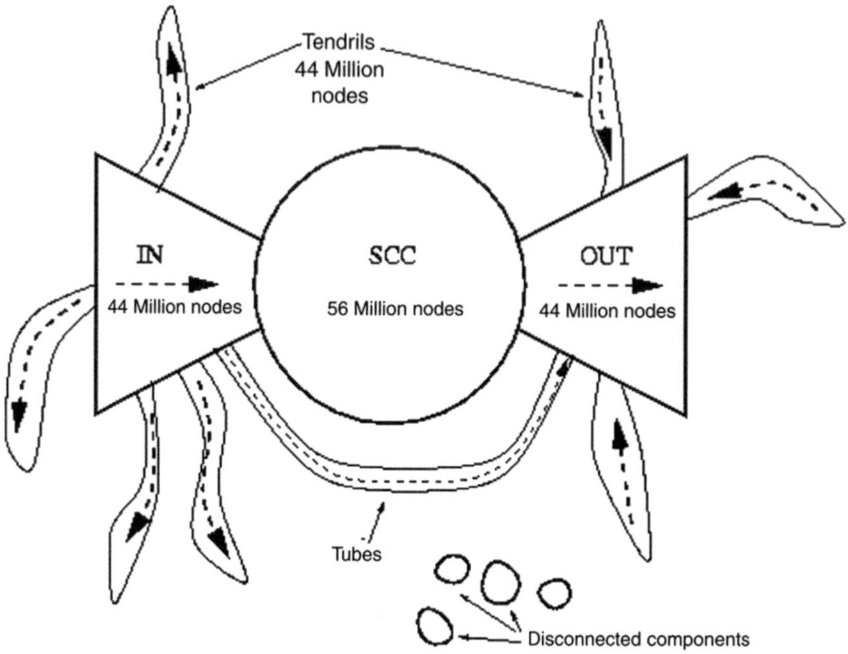


**Fig. 2.11** Bowtie structure of the graph of the Web

**Table 2.2** Sizes of the components forming the bowtie

| Region | Size (number of vertices) |
|---|---|
| SCC | 56,463,993 |
| IN | 43,343,168 |
| OUT | 43,166,185 |
| TENDRILS | 43,797,944 |
| DISC. COMP. | 16,777,756 |
| Total | 203,549,046 |

component correspond to $OUT$. The web sites of private corporations that contain only internal links could be the $OUT$ component. The pages that can neither reach the $SCC$, nor can it be reached by the $SCC$ form the $TENDRILS$.

Of the 570 starting vertices, 172 correspond to the $TENDRILS$ and the $DISCONNECTED\ COMPONENT$. The BFS algorithm cannot differentiate between these. 128 of these vertices correspond to $IN$, 134 correspond to $OUT$ and the remaining 136 correspond to the $SCC$.

### Insights Derived from This Study

The distribution of degrees and the sizes of several various components follow a power law. Therefore, power law phenomenon must be a basic Web property.

It was hypothesized that the Web was more likely to be a single giant SCC. One way to look at this is as follows: Assume that the Web consisted of two equally large SCCs. If there existed even a single link from one of these SCCs to the other, then by the definition of a SCC, these two SCCs would merge into one large SCC. Since the Web easily consists of a million webpages with atleast a billion hyperlinks interconnecting these webpages, the likelihood of a link not crossing over between the SCCs is extremely small. Thus, the Web could plausibly be one large SCC where one could easily go from any page to any other. However, the bowtie Web structure gave us the real organization of the Web.

Although the bowtie structure of the Web explains its conceptual organization, it leaves the following questions unanswered:

- Why are all the pages treated equally? Shouldn't websites of popular search engines or social media sites given more importance than others?
- Which are the most important pages? Is there a certain network property exhibited by these pages that explain its importance?
- What is the internal structure of the giant SCC? Is it a regular graph? Is there a SCC inside this giant SCC? Is there a large central core with several smaller components in its periphery?
- How far apart are the vertices in the SCC? Do all the paths have more or less the same distance? Does the distribution of a path follow a well known probability distribution? If so, is it expected or surprising?

**Study of Properties of Internet**

Reference [2] performed a study exclusively at understanding the power-law exhibition of certain network properties of the Internet between November 1997 and December 1998.

The following four datasets were used:

- *Int-11-97*: This is the inter-domain topology of the Internet in November of 1997 with 3015 nodes, 5156 edges, and 3.42 average outdegree.
- *Int-04-98*: This identifies the inter-domain topology of the Internet in April of 1998 with 3530 nodes, 6432 edges, and 3.65 average outdegree.
- *Int-12-98*: This corresponds to the inter-domain topology of the Internet in December of 1998 with 4389 nodes, 8256 edges, and 3.76 average outdegree.
- *Rout-95*: This lists the routers of the Internet in 1995 with 3888 nodes, 5012 edges, and an average outdegree of 2.57.

The first three datasets signify an evolving network while the last dataset represents the topology of the routers of the Internet in 1995 used in [4].

Here, the out-degree of a node $v$ is denoted by $d_v$, $r_v$ denotes the rank of node $v$ (indexed in order of decreasing out-degree), and $f_d$ denotes the frequency of out-degree $d$.

## 2.5 Rank Exponent $\mathcal{R}$

From the log-log plots of the out-degree $d_v$ as a function of the rank $r_v$ in the sequence of decreasing out-degree (shown in Figs. 2.12, 2.13, 2.14 and 2.15), the paper shows the following results:

- The out-degree, $d_v$, of a node $v$ is proportional to the rank of this node, $r_v$, to the power of a constant, $\mathcal{R}$ (Eq. 2.1).

$$d_v \propto r_v^{\mathcal{R}} \tag{2.1}$$

- If the nodes of the graph are sorted in decreasing order of out-degree, then the *rank exponent*, $\mathcal{R}$ is defined to be the slope of the node versus the rank of the nodes in the log-log scale.
- The out-degree, $d_v$, of a node $v$ is a function of the rank of this node, $r_v$, and the rank exponent, $\mathcal{R}$, as in Eq. 2.2.

$$d_v = \frac{1}{N^{\mathcal{R}}} r_v^R \tag{2.2}$$

- The number of edges, $|E|$, of a graph can be estimated as a function of the number of nodes, $|V|$, and the rank exponent, $\mathcal{R}$, as in Eq. 2.3.

$$|E| = \frac{1}{2(\mathcal{R}+1)} \left(1 - \frac{1}{N^{\mathcal{R}+1}}\right)^{|V|} \tag{2.3}$$

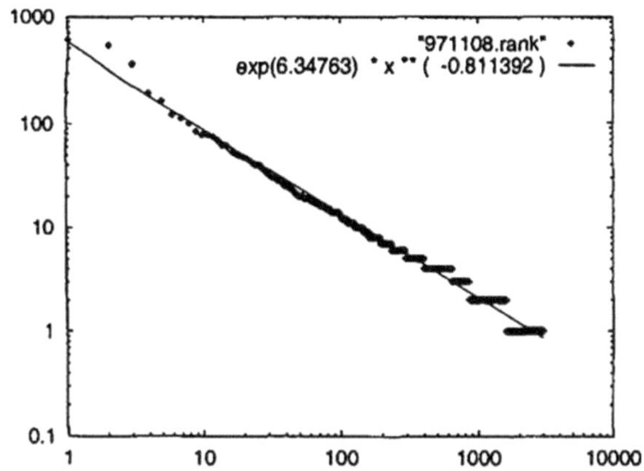


**Fig. 2.12** Log-log plot of the out-degree $d_v$ as a function of the rank $r_v$ in the sequence of decreasing out-degree for *Int-11-97*

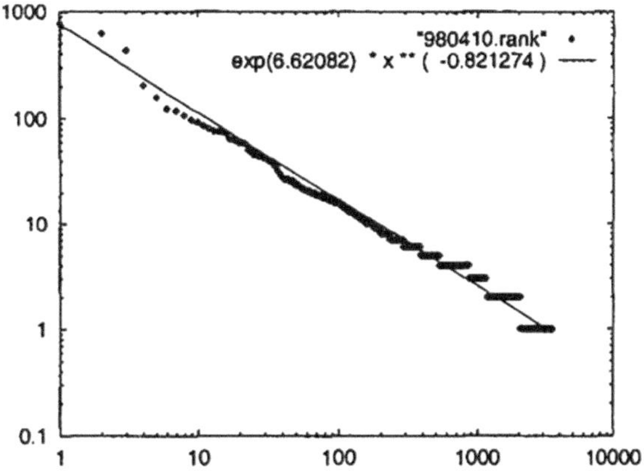


**Fig. 2.13** Log-log plot of the out-degree $d_v$ as a function of the rank $r_v$ in the sequence of decreasing out-degree for *Int-04-98*

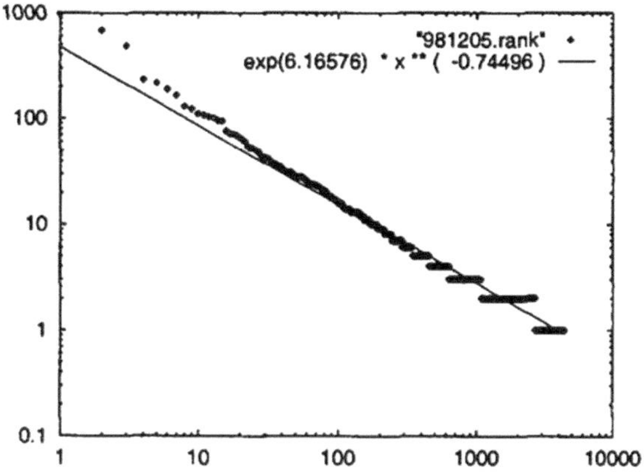


**Fig. 2.14** Log-log plot of the out-degree $d_v$ as a function of the rank $r_v$ in the sequence of decreasing out-degree for *Int-12-98*

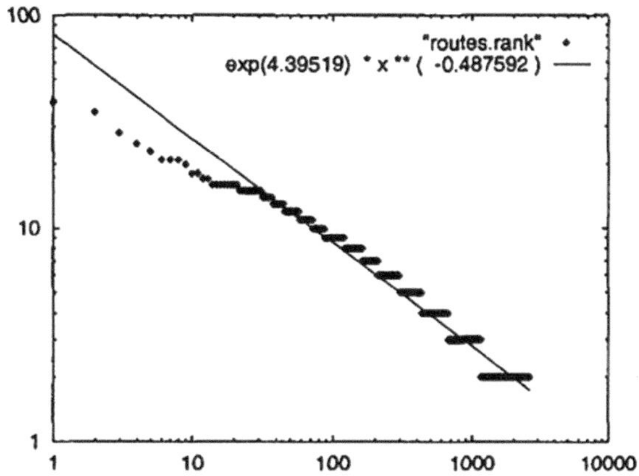


**Fig. 2.15** Log-log plot of the out-degree $d_v$ as a function of the rank $r_v$ in the sequence of decreasing out-degree for *Rout-95*

## 2.6 Out-Degree Exponent $\mathcal{O}$

The log-log plots of the frequency $f_d$ as a function of the out-degree $d$ (illustrated in Figs. 2.16, 2.17, 2.18 and 2.19), gives the following results:

- The frequency, $f_d$, of an out-degree, $d$, is proportional to the out-degree to the power of a constant, $\mathcal{O}$ (Eq. 2.4).

$$f_d \propto d^{\mathcal{O}} \tag{2.4}$$

- The out-degree exponent, $\mathcal{O}$, is defined to be the slope of the plot of the frequency of the out-degrees versus the out-degrees in log-log scale.

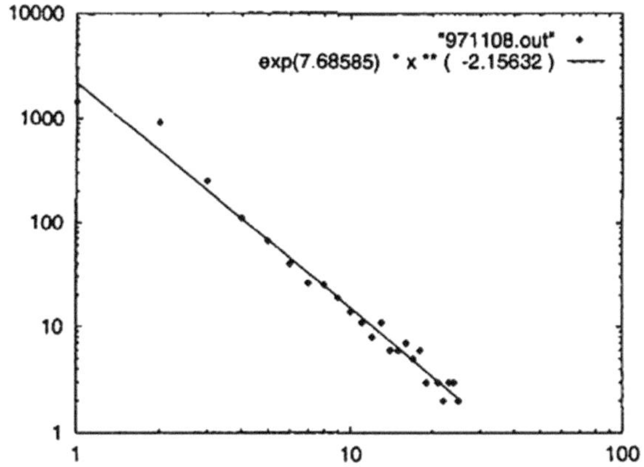


**Fig. 2.16** Log-log plot of frequency $f_d$ versus the out-degree $d$ for *Int-11-97*

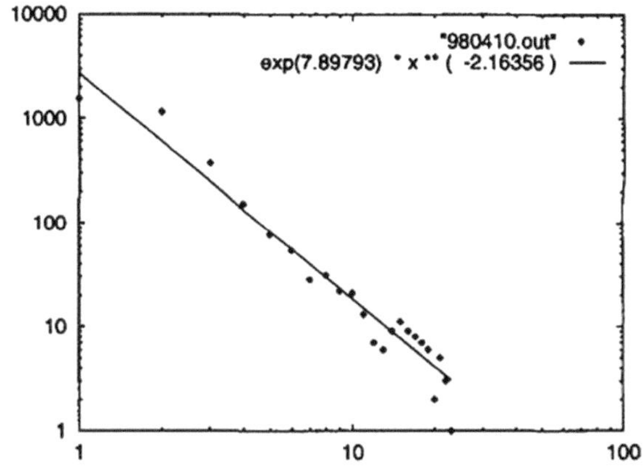


**Fig. 2.17** Log-log plot of frequency $f_d$ versus the out-degree $d$ for *Int-04-98*

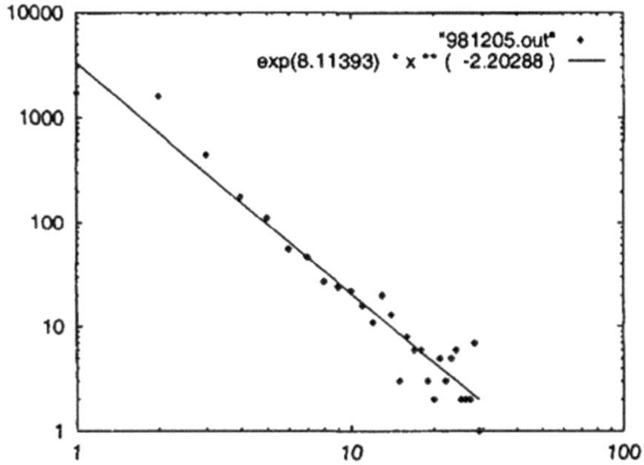


**Fig. 2.18** Log-log plot of frequency $f_d$ versus the out-degree $d$ for *Int-12-98*

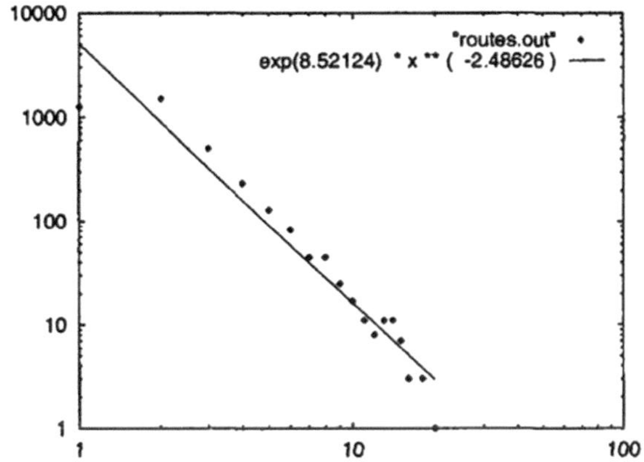


**Fig. 2.19** Log-log plot of frequency $f_d$ versus the out-degree $d$ for *Rout-95*

## 2.7 Hop Plot Exponent $\mathcal{H}$

Here, the total number of pairs of nodes $P(h)$ within $h$ hops, defined as the total number of pairs of nodes within less or equal to $h$ hops, including self-pairs, and counting all other pairs twice, is plotted as the function of the number of hops $h$ in log-log scale (depicted in Figs. 2.20, 2.21, 2.22 and 2.23). This gives the following results:

- The total number of pairs of nodes, $P(h)$, within $h$ hops, is proportional to the number of hops to the power of a constant, $\mathcal{H}$ (Eq. 2.5)

$$P(h) \propto h^{\mathcal{H}}, h << \delta \tag{2.5}$$

where $\delta$ is the diameter of the graph.

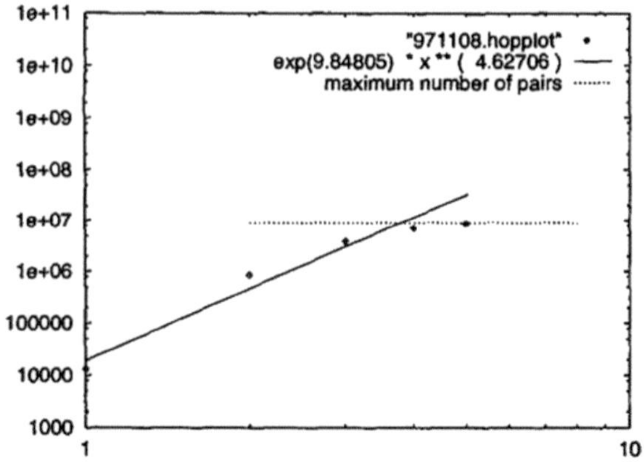


**Fig. 2.20** Log-log plot of the number of pairs of nodes $P(h)$ within $h$ hops versus the number of hops $h$ for *Int-11-97*

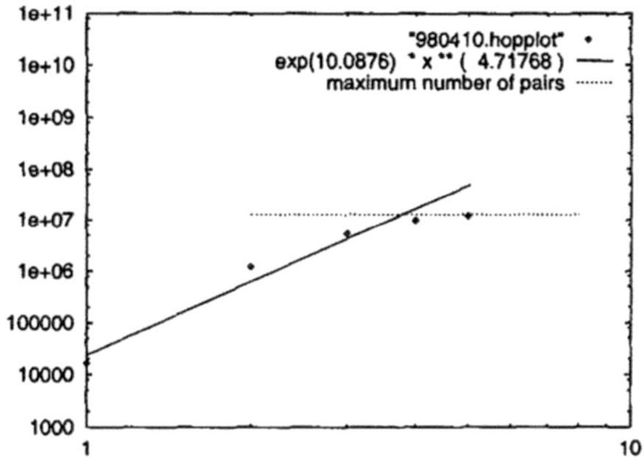


**Fig. 2.21** Log-log plot of the number of pairs of nodes $P(h)$ within $h$ hops versus the number of hops $h$ for *Int-04-98*

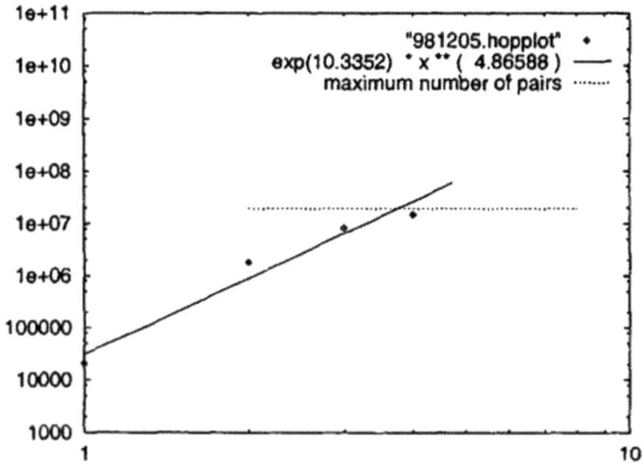


**Fig. 2.22** Log-log plot of the number of pairs of nodes $P(h)$ within $h$ hops versus the number of hops $h$ for *Int-12-98*

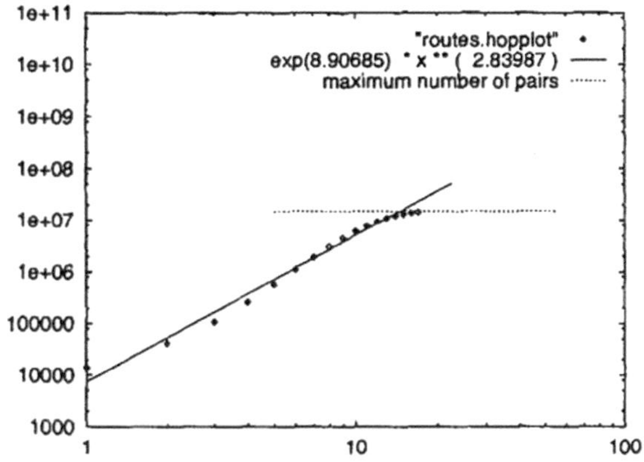


**Fig. 2.23** Log-log plot of the number of pairs of nodes $P(h)$ within $h$ hops versus the number of hops $h$ for *Rout-95*

- If we plot the number of pairs of nodes, $P(h)$, within $h$ hops as a function of the number of hops in log-log scale. For $h << \delta$, the slope of this plot is defined to be the hop-plot exponent $\mathcal{H}$
- The number of pairs within $h$ hops is as given in Eq. 2.6.

$$P(h) = \begin{cases} ch^{\mathcal{H}}, h << \delta \\ |V|^2, h \geq \delta \end{cases} \tag{2.6}$$

  where $c = |V| + 2|E|$ to satisfy internal conditions.
- Given a graph with $|V|$ nodes, $|E|$ edges and $\mathcal{H}$ hop-plot exponent, the *effective diameter*, $\delta_{ef}$ is defined as in Eq. 2.7.

$$\delta_{ef} = \left( \frac{|V|^2}{|V| + 2|E|} \right)^{1/\mathcal{H}} \tag{2.7}$$

- The *average size of the neighbourhood*, $NN(h)$, within $h$ hops as a function of the hop-plot exponent, $\mathcal{H}$, for $h << \delta$, is as given in Eq. 2.8

$$NN(h) = \frac{c}{|V|} h^{\mathcal{H}} - 1 \tag{2.8}$$

  where $c = |V| + 2|E|$ to satisfy internal conditions.
- The *average out-degree estimate* , $NN'(h)$, within $h$ hops with average out-degree $\overline{d}$, is as given in Eq. 2.9

$$NN'(h) = \overline{d}(\overline{d} - 1)^{h-1} \tag{2.9}$$

## 2.8 Eigen Exponent $\mathcal{E}$

The plot of the eigenvalue $\lambda_i$ as a function of $i$ in the log-log scale for the first 20 eigenvalues in the decreasing order (shown in Figs. 2.24, 2.25, 2.26 and 2.27) gives the following results:

- The eigenvalues, $\lambda_i$, of a graph are proportional to the order, $i$, to the power of a constant, $\mathcal{E}$ is as given in Eq. 2.10.

$$\lambda_i \propto i^{\mathcal{E}} \tag{2.10}$$

- The eigen exponent $\mathcal{E}$ is defined as the slope of the plot of the sorted eigenvalues as a function of their order in the log-log scale.

Fig. 2.24 Log-log plot of the eigenvalues in decreasing order for *Int-11-97*

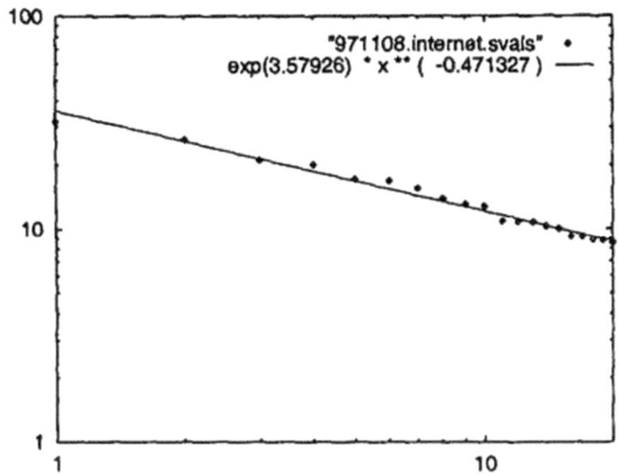


Fig. 2.25 Log-log plot of the eigenvalues in decreasing order for *Int-04-98*

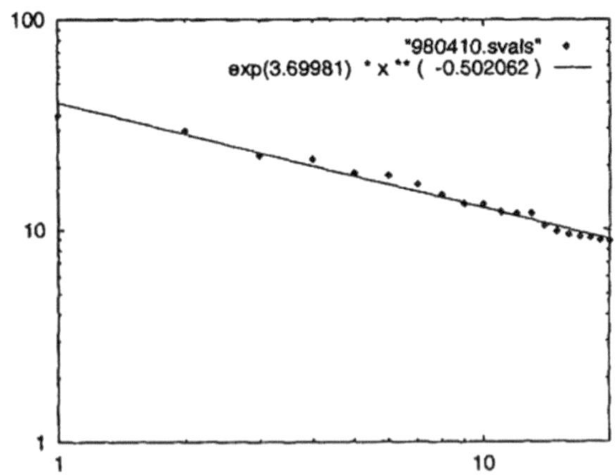

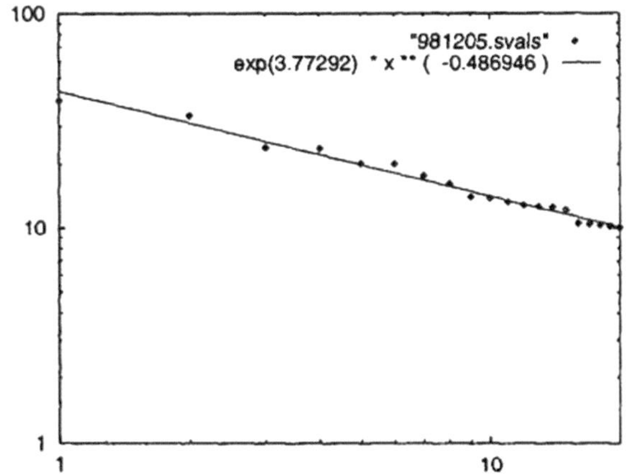


**Fig. 2.26** Log-log plot of the eigenvalues in decreasing order for *Int-12-98*

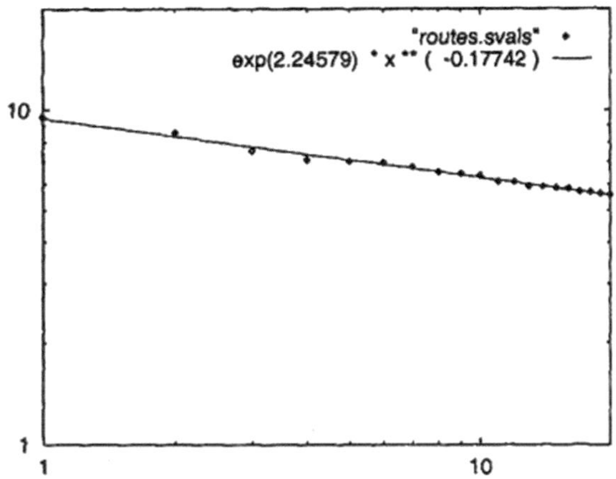


**Fig. 2.27** Log-log plot of the eigenvalues in decreasing order for *Rout-95*

The proofs for many of these results can be found in [2].

## Problems

Download the *Epinions* directed network from the SNAP dataset repository available at http://snap.stanford.edu/data/soc-Epinions1.html.

For this dataset compute the structure of this social network using the same methods as Broder et al. employed.

**22** Compute the in-degree and out-degree distributions and plot the power law for each of these distributions.

**23** Choose 100 nodes at random from the network and do one forward and one backward BFS traversal for each node. Plot the cumulative distributions of the nodes covered in these BFS runs as shown in Fig. 2.7. Create one figure for the forward BFS and one for the backward BFS. How many nodes are in the OUT and IN components? How many nodes are in the TENDRILS component?

(*Hint*: The forward BFS plot gives the number of nodes in SCC+OUT and similarly, the backward BFS plot gives the number of nodes in SCC+IN).

**24** What is the probability that a path exists between two nodes chosen uniformly from the graph? What if the node pairs are only drawn from the WCC of the two networks? Compute the percentage of node pairs that were connected in each of these cases.

## References

1. Broder, Andrei, Ravi Kumar, Farzin Maghoul, Prabhakar Raghavan, Sridhar Rajagopalan, Raymie Stata, Andrew Tomkins, and Janet Wiener. 2000. Graph structure in the web. *Computer Networks* 33 (1–6): 309–320.
2. Faloutsos, Michalis, Petros Faloutsos, and Christos Faloutsos. 1999. On power-law relationships of the internet topology. In *ACM SIGCOMM computer communication review*, vol. 29, 251–262, ACM.
3. Newman, Mark E.J. 2005. Power laws, pareto distributions and zipf's law. *Contemporary Physics* 46 (5): 323–351.
4. Pansiot, Jean-Jacques, and Dominique Grad. 1998. On routes and multicast trees in the internet. *ACM SIGCOMM Computer Communication Review* 28 (1): 41–50.

# Chapter 3
# Random Graph Models

The exercises in Chap. 1 required the computation of several network properties. Are these computed values as expected or surprising? From these values, it is impossible to conclude *per se*. Instead, we require a null model for comparison. One such null model for the study on real-world graphs would be random graphs. There have been numerous approaches to generate random graphs. In this section, we will look at some of the most prominent models used to generate random graphs that are capable of being compared with real-world graphs.

## 3.1 Random Graphs

A random graph, denoted by $G^*(|V|, |E|)$, can be defined as a collection of vertices, with edges connecting pairs of them at random. It is assumed that the presence or absence of an edge between two vertices is assumed to be independent of the presence or absence of any other edge, so that each edge may be considered to be present with probability $p$.

## 3.2 Erdös–Rényi Random Graph Model

*Paul Erdös* and *Alfréd Rényi* were two prominent Hungarian mathematicians who proposed this random graph model which has certain properties which, with surprising accuracy match the properties of real-world networks.

Let $G_{|V|,|E|}$ denote the set of all graphs having $|V|$ vertices, $v_1, v_2, \ldots, v_{|V|}$ and $|E|$ edges. These graphs must not have self-edges or multiple edges. Thus a graph



K. Raj P. M. et al., *Practical Social Network Analysis with Python*,
Computer Communications and Networks,
https://doi.org/10.1007/978-3-319-96746-2_3

belonging to $G_{|V|,|E|}$ is obtained by choosing $|E|$ out of the possible $\binom{|V|}{2}$ edges between the vertices $v_1, v_2, \ldots, v_{|V|}$, and therefore the number of elements of $G_{|V|,|E|}$ is equal to $\binom{\binom{|V|}{2}}{|E|}$. A random graph $\Gamma_{|V|,|E|}$ can be defined as an element of $G_{|V|,|E|}$ chosen as random, so that each of the elements of $G_{|V|,|E|}$ have the same probability to be chosen, namely $\frac{1}{\binom{\binom{|V|}{2}}{|E|}}$.

From a different viewpoint, the formation of a random graph may be considered as a stochastic process defined as follows: At time $t = 1$ we choose one out of the $\binom{|V|}{2}$ possible edges connecting the vertices $v_1, v_2, \ldots, v_{|V|}$, each of these edges having the same probability of being chosen, let this edge be denoted by $e_1$. At time $t = 2$ we choose one of the $\binom{|V|}{2} - 1$ edges different from $e_1$, all of these being equiprobable. Continuing this process at time $t = k+1$ we choose one of the $\binom{|V|}{2} - k$ possible edges different from $e_1, e_2, \ldots, e_k$ already chosen, each of the remaining edges being equiprobable, i.e, having probability $\frac{1}{\binom{|V|}{2}-k}$. This graph consisting of vertices $v_1, v_2, \ldots, v_{|V|}$ and the edges $e_1, e_2, \ldots, e_{|E|}$ is the random graph denoted by $\Gamma_{|V|,|E|}$.

This second point of view gives us the evolution of $\Gamma_{|V|,|E|}$ as $|E|$ increases. This evolution shows very clear-cut features. If $|V|$ is a fixed large positive integer and $|E|$ is increasing from 1 to $\binom{|V|}{2}$, the evolution passes through five clearly distinguishable phases. These phases correspond to ranges of growth of the number $|E|$ of edges, these ranges being defined in terms of the number $|V|$ of vertices. These phases, with increasing $p$, are as follows:

1. $p = 0$: Graph with $|V|$ isolated vertices.
2. *Phase* 1, $p = \frac{1}{|V|-1}$: Giant component appears.
3. *Phase* 2, $p = \frac{C}{|V|-1}$: The average degree is constant but lots of isolated vertices still exist.
4. *Phase* 3, $p = \frac{log|V|}{|V|-1}$: Fewer number of isolated vertices exist.
5. *Phase* 4, $p = \frac{2log|V|}{|V|-1}$: The graph contains no more isolated vertices.
6. *Phase* 5, $p = 1$: A complete graph is obtained.

The proofs for each of these phases can be found in [5].

There are two variants of this graph model,

- $G_{n,p}$ denotes a graph on $n$ vertices where each edge $(u,v)$ appears independent and identically distributed with probability $p$.
- $G_{n,m}$ denotes a graph on $n$ vertices and $m$ uniformly at random picked edges.

$n$, $p$ and $m$ do not uniquely determine the graphs. Since the graph is the result of a random process, we can have several different realizations for the same values of $n$, $p$ and $m$. Figure 3.1 gives instances of undirected graphs generated using this model and Fig. 3.2 are examples of directed graphs also generated using the model. Each of these graphs have $n = 5$ and $m = 5$.

If we consider a random graph $\Gamma_{|V|,|E|}$ having $|V|$ possible vertices and $|E|$ edges, and choose uniformly at random one of the $\binom{\binom{|V|}{2}}{|E|}$ possible graphs which can be

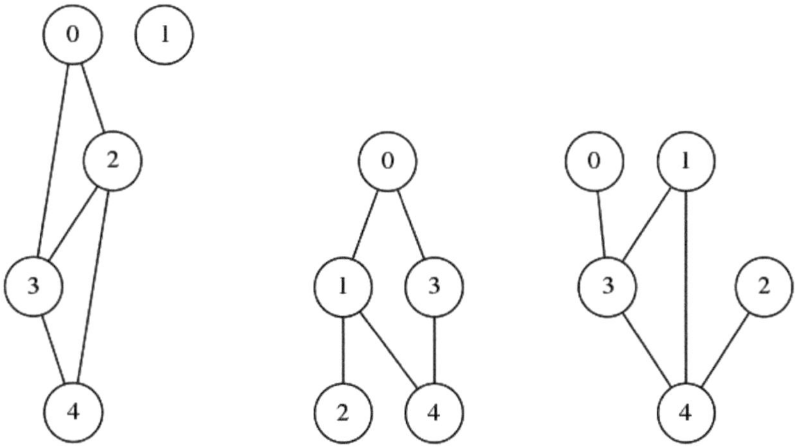

(a) First undirected graph rendering of $G_{5,5}$ (b) Second undirected graph rendering of $G_{5,5}$ (c) Third undirected graph rendering of $G_{5,5}$

**Fig. 3.1** Figure shows three undirected graph variants of $G_{5,5}$

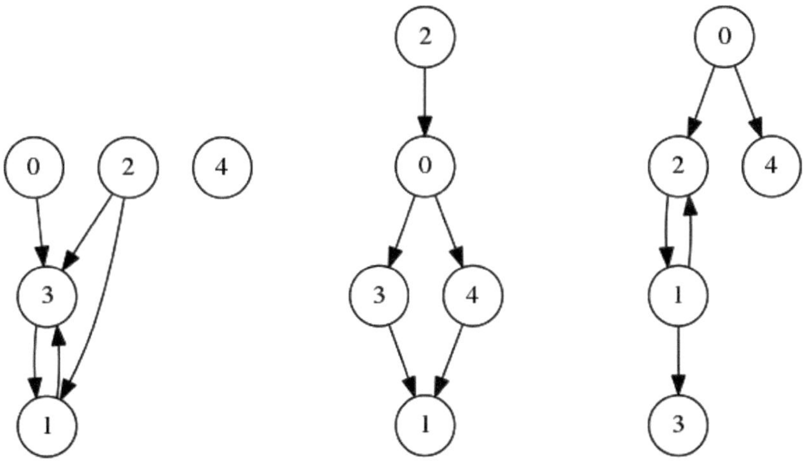

(a) First directed graph rendering of $G_{5,5}$ (b) Second directed graph rendering of $G_{5,5}$ (c) Third directed graph rendering of $G_{5,5}$

**Fig. 3.2** Figure shows three directed graph variants of $G_{5,5}$

formed from the $|V|$ vertices $P_1, P_2, \ldots, P_{|V|}$ by selecting $|E|$ edges from the $\binom{|V|}{2}$ possible edges. The effective number of vertices of $\Gamma_{|V|,|E|}$ may be less than $|V|$ since some vertices $P_i$ may not be connected in $\Gamma_{|V|,|E|}$ with any other vertices. These vertices $P_i$ are the isolated vertices. These isolated vertices are still considered as belonging to $\Gamma_{|V|,|E|}$.

$\Gamma_{|V|,|E|}$ is called *completely connected* if it effectively contains all the vertices $P_1, P_2, \ldots, P_n$.

$\Gamma_{|V|,|E|}$ has the statistical properties stated in the Theorems 2, 3, 4 and 5.

**Theorem 2** *If $P_0(|V|, |E_c|)$ denotes the probability of $\Gamma_{|V|,|E|}$ being completely connected, then we get Eq. 3.1*

$$\lim_{|V|\to\infty} P_0(|V|, |E_c|) = e^{-e^{-2c}} \tag{3.1}$$

*where $|E_c| = [\frac{1}{2}|V|log|V| + c|V|]$. Here, $c \in \mathbb{R}$ and $[x]$ denotes the integral part of $x$.*

**Theorem 3** *If $P_k(|V|, |E_c|)$ $(k = 0, 1, \ldots)$ denotes the probability of the giant component of $\Gamma_{|V|,|E|}$ consisting effectively of $|V| - k$ vertices, then we get Eq. 3.2*

$$\lim_{|V|\to\infty} P_k(|V|, |E_c|) = \frac{(e^{-2c})^k e^{-e^{-2c}}}{k!} \tag{3.2}$$

*i.e, the number of vertices outside the giant component of $\Gamma_{|V|,|E|}$ is distributed in the limit according to Poisson's law with mean $e^{-2c}$.*

**Theorem 4** *If $\prod_k(|V|, |E_c|)$ denotes the probability of $\Gamma_{|V|,|E|}$ consisting of exactly $k+1$ disjoint components ($\prod_0(|V|, |E_c|) = P_0(|V|, |E_c|)$). Then we get Eq. 3.3*

$$\lim_{|V|\to\infty} \prod_k(|V|, |E_c|) = \frac{(e^{-2c})^k e^{-e^{-2c}}}{k!} \tag{3.3}$$

*i.e, the number of components of $\Gamma_{|V|,|E|}$ diminished by one is the limit distributed according to Poisson's law with mean value $e^{-2c}$.*

**Theorem 5** *If the edges of $\Gamma_{|V|,|E|}$ are chosen successively so that after each step, every edge which has not yet been chosen has the same probability to be chosen as the next, and if we continue this process until the graph becomes completely connected, the probability that the number of necessary steps $v$ will be equal to a number $l$ is given by Eq. 3.4*

$$P(v_{|V|}) = \left[\frac{1}{2}|V|log|V|] + l\right] \sim \frac{2}{n} e^{\frac{-2l}{n} - e^{\frac{-2l}{n}}} \tag{3.4}$$

*for $|l| = O(n)$ where $v_{|V|}$ denotes the number of edges of $\Gamma_{|V|,|E|}$ and we get Eq. 3.5*

$$\lim_{|V|\to\infty} P\left(\frac{v_{|V|} - \frac{1}{2}|V|log|V|}{|V|} < x\right) = e^{-e^{-2x}} \tag{3.5}$$

The proofs for these theorems may be found in [4].

## *3.2.1 Properties*

We will look at various graph properties of the $G_{n,p}$ variant of this graph model.

### 3.2.1.1 Edges

Let $P(|E|)$ denote the probability that $G_{n,p}$ generates a graph on $|E|$ edges.

$$P(|E|) = \binom{E_{max}}{|E|} p^{|E|}(1-p)^{E_{max}-|E|} \tag{3.6}$$

From Eq. 3.6, we observe that $P(|E|)$ follows a binomial distribution with mean of $pE_{max}$ and variance of $p(1-p)E_{max}$.

### 3.2.1.2 Degree

Let $X_v$ be the random variable measuring the degree of vertex $v$.

$$X_v = X_{v,v_1} + X_{v,v_2} + \cdots + X_{v,v_{|V|-1}}$$

where $X_{v,u}$ is a $\{0,1\}$-random variable which tells us whether or not the edge $(v,u)$ exists. The expectation of the degree of vertex $v$ is as given in Eq. 3.7.

$$\mathbb{E}[X_v] = \sum_{u=v_1}^{v_{|V|-1}} \mathbb{E}[X_{v,u}] = p(|V|-1) \tag{3.7}$$

### 3.2.1.3 Degree Distribution

The degree distribution of $G_{n,p}$ is given in Eq. 3.8

$$P(k) = \binom{|V|-1}{k} p^k (1-p)^{|V|-1-k} \tag{3.8}$$

Equation 3.8 shows that the degree distribution follows a binomial distribution with mean, $\overline{k} = p(|V| - 1)$ and variance, $\sigma^2 = p(1-p)(|V|-1)$.

$$\frac{\sigma}{\overline{k}} = \left[\frac{1-p}{p}\frac{1}{|V|-1}\right]^{\frac{1}{2}} \rightarrow \frac{1}{|V|-1}\ as\ |V| \rightarrow \infty$$

By the law of large numbers, as the network size increases, the distribution becomes increasingly narrow, i.e, we are increasingly confident that the degree of the vertex is in the vicinity of $k$.

#### 3.2.1.4 Clustering Coefficient

The clustering coefficient of a graph is given by Sect. 3.2.1.4.

$$C_i = \frac{2e_i}{k_i(k_i-1)}$$

where $e_i$ is the number of edges between $i$'s neighbours.

$$e_i = \begin{cases} p\frac{k_i(k_i-1)}{2}\ if\ undirected \\ pk_i(k_i-1)\ if\ directed \end{cases} \tag{3.9}$$

From Eq. 3.9, we get

$$C_i = \begin{cases} \frac{2}{k_i(k_i-1)}p\frac{k_i(k_i-1)}{2}\ if\ undirected \\ \frac{2}{k_i(k_i-1)}pk_i(k_i-1)\ if\ directed \end{cases} = \begin{cases} p\ if\ undirected \\ 2p\ if\ directed \end{cases} \tag{3.10}$$

$C_i \rightarrow 0$ as $|V| \rightarrow \infty$

The clustering coefficient of $G_{n,p}$ is small. As the graph gets bigger with fixed $\overline{k}$, $C$ decreases with $|V|$.

#### 3.2.1.5 Diameter

The path length is $O(log|V|)$ and the diameter is $O(\frac{log|V|}{\alpha})$ where $\alpha$ denotes the expansion of $G_{n,p}$.

A graph $G(V, E)$ has *expansion* $\alpha$ if

$$\begin{aligned} &\forall S \subseteq V:\ number\ of\ edges\ leaving\ S \geq \alpha\ min(|S|, |V \setminus S|) \\ &\implies \alpha = min_{S\subseteq V}\frac{number\ of\ edges\ leaving\ S}{min(|S|, |V \setminus S|)} \end{aligned} \tag{3.11}$$

### 3.2.2 Drawbacks of $G_{n,p}$

The exercise in this chapter will require the computations of the real world graph and the $G_{n,p}$.

These computations will show that the degree distribution of $G_{n,p}$ greatly differs from that of real-world ones. The giant component in most real-world networks does not emerge through phase transition, and the clustering coefficient of $G_{n,p}$ is too low.

### 3.2.3 Advantages of $G_{n,p}$

In spite of these drawbacks, $G_{n,p}$ acts as an extremely useful null model which assists in the computation of quantities that can be compared with real data, and helps us understand to what degree a particular property is the result of some random process.

## 3.3 Bollobás Configuration Model

Béla Bollobás is a British-Hungarian mathematician who proposed this configuration model to generate random graphs. For a graph $G(V, E)$, let $d \in \mathbb{N}$ and $|V| > d$ such that $|V|d$ is even. This model starts with a uniform random $d$-regular graph on $|V|$ vertices, and proceeds by the following steps.

1. Start with $|V|$ vertices and draw $d$ half-edges emanating from each of these vertices, so that the ends of these half-edges are all distinct.
2. Let $W$ be the set of ends of these half-edges. Index these ends by $|V| \times d$, where $(i,1), (i,2), \ldots, (i,d)$ are the ends emanating from vertex $i$. Now choose a random matching $\mathscr{M}$ of the set $W$ of ends (uniformly at random from the set of all matchings of $W$) and use the edges of the random matching to join these pairs of half-edges to produce an edge. This edge could be a self-edge if the matching $\mathscr{M}$ joins two half-edges that emanate from the same vertex, or a multiple edge if the matching has another edge between the same two vertices.
3. Repeat this process of matching half-edges until all pairs of half-edges have been paired. This generates a $d$-regular graph on $|V|$.

Figure 3.3 gives an instance of a random graph generated on $d = 3$ and $|V| = 4$.

Let $G^*(|V|, d)$ denote the random $d$-regular graph produced by this process. However, it is not a uniform random graph. The probability that a particular graph arises depends on the number of loops and on the multiplicities of the edges. The probability that a graph generated using this process is simple is as given in Eq. 3.12.

$$P\{G^*(|V|, d)\ is\ simple\} \rightarrow e^{\frac{-(d^2-1)}{4}}\ as\ |V| \rightarrow \infty \tag{3.12}$$

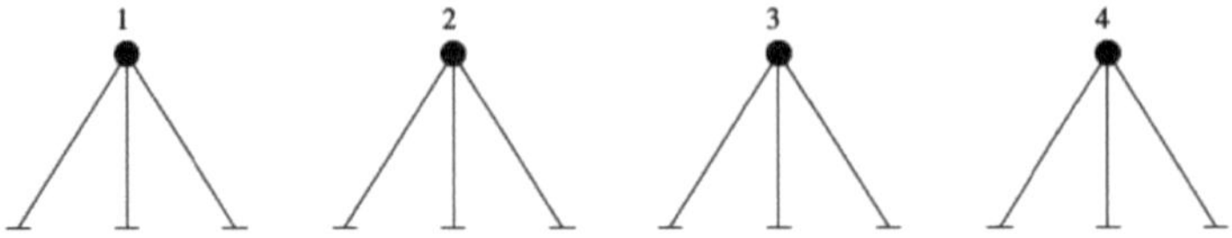


(a) 3 half-edges emanating from each of the 4 vertices

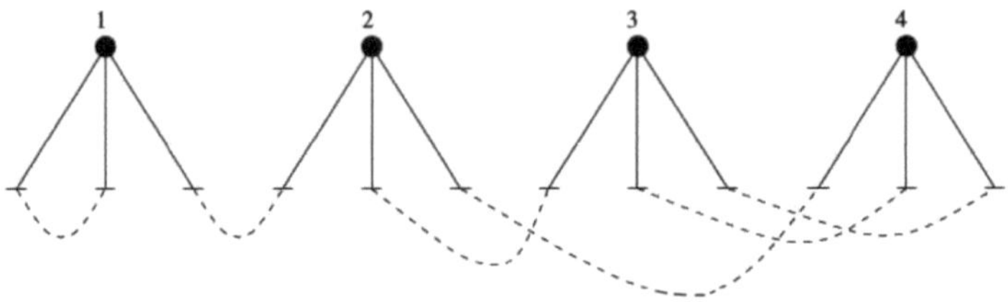


(b) 3 half-edges matched randomly

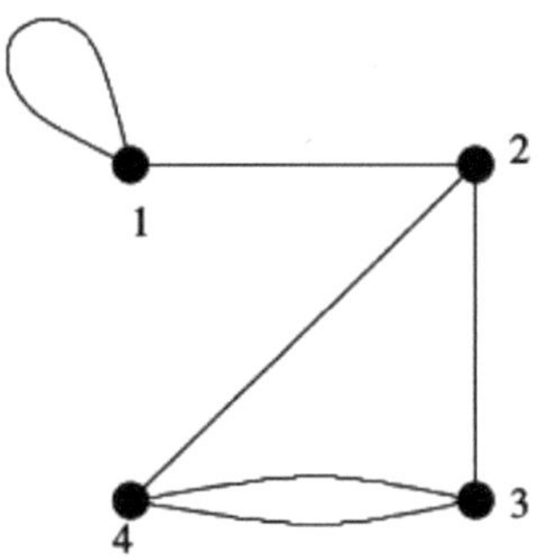


(c) Resultant graph of Fig 4.3b

**Fig. 3.3** A random graph generated using Bollobás configuration model with $d = 3$ and $|V| = 4$

## 3.4 Permutation Model

The permutation model also generates a random graph. It starts with $|V|$ vertices and picks $d$ permutations, $\sigma_1, \sigma_2, \ldots, \sigma_d$, uniformly at random from the symmetric group $S_n$, with replacement. For each $l \in d$ and each $i \in |V|$, join $i$ to $\sigma_i$ (forming a loop if $\sigma_l(i) = i$). This produces a random $(2d)$-regular graph which is commonly denoted as $R^*(|V|, 2d)$.

The graph is simple if and only if the following conditions are satisfied,

1. None of the permutations have any fixed points.
2. None of the permutations have any 2-cycles.
3. No two permutations agree anywhere.

The probability that this graph is simple as given in Eq. 3.13.

$$P\{R^*(|V|, 2d)\ is\ simple\} \rightarrow e^{-d}e^{-2d}e^{-\binom{d}{2}} = e^{\frac{-d^2}{2-d}}\ as\ |V| \rightarrow \infty \qquad (3.13)$$

The proof for Eqs. 3.12, 3.13 and other properties of graphs generated using Bollobás or Permutation models can be found in [1].

## 3.5 Random Graphs with Prescribed Degree Sequences

Reference [2] describes several algorithms used to uniformly generate random graphs with prescribed degree sequences to be used as model of complex networks. Comparing an observed network to an ensemble of such graphs allows us to detect deviations from randomness in network properties.

### *3.5.1 Switching Algorithm*

This algorithm uses a Markov chain to generate a random graph with a given degree sequence. Here, we start from a given random network and carry out a series of Monte Carlo switching steps whereby a pair of edges ($A \rightarrow B$,$C \rightarrow D$) is selected at random and the ends are exchanged to give ($A \rightarrow D$,$C \rightarrow B$). The exchange is only performed if no self-edges or multiple edges occur. Otherwise, it is not performed. The entire process is repeated some number $Q|E|$ times where $Q \in \mathbb{N}$ is chosen large enough so that the Markov chain shows good mixing. As with many Markov chain methods, this method suffers because in general we have no measure of how long to wait for proper mixing. Reference [2] states that empirically $Q = 100$ appears to be adequate.

### *3.5.2 Matching Algorithm*

In this algorithm, each vertex is assigned a set of half-edges according to a desired degree sequence. Then, a pair of half-edges are picked randomly and joined up to create the edges of the graph. If self-edges or multiple edges are created, the entire graph is discarded and the process starts over from scratch.

This process will correctly generate random graphs with desired properties. However, the expected number of edges between two vertices will often exceed one. This makes it unlikely that the procedure will run to completion except in the rarest of cases. To obviate this problem, a modification of the method can be used in which following selection of a pair of half-edges that create a multiple edge, instead of discarding the graph, an alternate half-edge pair is randomly selected. Although the method generates a biased sample of possible graphs, not significantly serving the required purpose.

### 3.5.3 "Go with the Winners" Algorithm

The "go with the winners" algorithm is a non-Markov chain Monte Carlo method for sampling uniformly from a given distribution. Consider a colony of $M$ graphs. Start with the appropriate number of half-edges for each vertex and repeatedly choose at random a pair of half-edges and link them to create an edge. If a multiple edge or self-edge is generated, the graph containing it is removed from the colony and discarded. To compensate for the resulting slow decline in the size of the colony, its size is periodically doubled by cloning each of the surviving graphs; this cloning step is carried out at a predetermined rate chosen to keep the size of the colony roughly constant on average. This process is repeated until all half-edges have been linked, then one of the graphs is chosen at random from the colony and assigned a weight

$$W_i = 2^{-c}\frac{m}{M}$$

where $c$ is the number of cloning steps made and $m$ is the number of surviving graphs. The mean of any quantity $X$ over a set of such graphs is

$$\frac{\sum_i W_i X_i}{\sum_i W_i}$$

where $X_i$ is the value of $X$ in the $i$th graph.

### 3.5.4 Comparison

- Switching algorithm (Sect. 3.5.1):
  - Samples the configurations uniformly, generating each graph an equal number of times within measurement error on calculation.
  - Produces results essentially identical to but faster than "go with the winners" algorithm.
- Matching algorithm (Sect. 3.5.2):
  - Introduces a bias and undersamples the configurations.
  - Faster than the other two methods but samples in a measurable biased way.

- "Go with the winners" algorithm (Sect. 3.5.3):
  - Produces an equal number of graphs which are more statistically correct by sampling ensembles uniformly within permissible error.
  - Far less computationally efficient than the other two methods.

From these points it is evident that any of these methods are adequate for generating suitable random graphs to act as null models. Although the "go with the winners" and the switching algorithms, while slower, are clearly more satisfactory theoretically, the matching algorithm gives better results on real-world problems.

Reference [2] argues in favour of using the switching method, with the "go with the winners" method finding limited use as a check on the accuracy of sampling.

Reference [3] shows how using generating functions, one can calculate exactly many of the statistical properties of random graphs generated from prescribed degree sequences in the limit of the number of vertices. Additionally, the position at which the giant component forms, the size of the giant component, the average and the distribution of the size of the other components, average number of vertices at certain distance from a given vertex, the clustering coefficient and the typical vertex-vertex distances are explained in detail.

## Problems

Download the *Astro Physics* collaboration network from the SNAP dataset repository available at http://snap.stanford.edu/data/ca-AstroPh.html. This co-authorship network contains 18772 nodes and 198110 edges.

Generate the graph for this dataset (we will refer to this graph as the *real world graph*).

**25** *Erdös–Rényi random graph* ($G(n, m)$): Generate a random instance of this model by using the number of nodes and edges as the real world graph.

**26** *Configuration model random graph*: Generate a random instance of this model by using the graph in the dataset.

For each of the *real world graph*, *Erdös–Rényi graph* and *Cofiguration model graph*, compute the following:

**27** Degree distributions

**28** Shortest path length distributions

**29** Clustering coefficient distributions

**30** WCC size distributions

**31** For each of these distributions, state whether or not the random models have the same property as the real world graph.

**32** Are the random graph generators capable of generating graphs that are representative of real world graphs?

## References

1. Ellis, David. 2011. *The expansion of random regular graphs*, Lecture notes. Lent.
2. Milo, Ron, Nadav Kashtan, Shalev Itzkovitz, Mark E.J. Newman, and Uri Alon. 2003. On the uniform generation of random graphs with prescribed degree sequences. arXiv:cond-mat/0312028.
3. Newman, Mark E.J., Steven H. Strogatz, and Duncan J. Watts. 2001. Random graphs with arbitrary degree distributions and their applications. *Physical Review E* 64(2):026118.
4. Paul, Erdös, and Rényi Alfréd . 1959. On random graphs, i. *Publicationes Mathematicae (Debrecen)* 6: 290–297.
5. Paul, Erdös, and Rényi Alfréd. 1960. On the evolution of random graphs. *Publications of the Mathematical Institute of the Hungarian Academy of Sciences* 5: 17–61.

# Chapter 4
# Small World Phenomena

We have all had the experience of encountering someone far from home, who turns out to share a mutual acquaintance with us. Then comes the cliché, "My it's a small world". Similarly, there exists a speculative idea that the distance between vertices in a very large graph is surprisingly small, i.e, the vertices co-exist in a "small world". Hence the term *small world phenomena*.

Is it surprising that such a phenomenon can exist? If each person is connected to 100 people, then at the first step 100 people can be reached, the next step reaches $10^4$ people, $10^6$ at the third step, $10^8$ at the fourth step and $10^{10}$ at the fifth step. Taking into account the fact that there are only 7.6 billion people in the world as of December 2017, the six degrees of separation is not at all surprising. However, many of the 100 people a person is connected to may be connected to one another. Due to the presence of this overlap in connections, the five steps between every inhabitant of the Earth is a longshot.

## 4.1 Small World Experiment

Stanley Milgram, an American social psychologist aimed at answering the following question: "Given two individuals selected randomly from the population, what is the probability that the minimum number of intermediaries required to link them is $0, 1, 2, \ldots, k$?" [16]. This led to his famous "small-world" experiment [15] which contained two studies. The first study, called the "Kansas study" recruited residents from Wichita, Kansas and the next study, called the "Nebraska study" involved volunteers from Omaha, Nebraska. The targets for these studies were located in Massachusetts. The authors particularly selected the volunteers from these two cities because from a psychological perspective, they are very far away from the target's location. The target for the Kansas study was the wife of a divinity student living in Cambridge, MA and that for the Nebraska study was a stockbroker who worked in Boston and lived in Sharon, MA.



K. Raj P. M. et al., *Practical Social Network Analysis with Python*,
Computer Communications and Networks,
https://doi.org/10.1007/978-3-319-96746-2_4

The volunteers were sent a folder containing a document and a set of tracer cards, with the name and some relevant information concerning their target. The following rules were set: (i) The subjects could only send the folder to individuals they knew on a first-name basis. If the subject did not know the target on this basis, they could send it to only one other person who qualified this condition and was more likely to know the target. (ii) The folder contained a roster on which the subject and all subsequent recipients had to write their name. This roster tells the recipients all the people who were part of this chain and thereby prevents endless loop. (iii) Every participant had to fill out in the tracer card the relationship of the person they are sending it to, and send it back to the authors. This helped the authors keep track of the complete and incomplete links.

**Kansas Study**

The Kansas study started with 145 participants which shows a certain pattern: 56 of the chains involved a female sending the folder to another female, 58 of them involved a male sending the folder to a male, 18 of them involved a female sending the folder to a male, and 13 of the chains had a male passing the folder to a female. This shows a three times greater tendency for a same-gender passing. 123 of these participants were observed to send the folder to friends and acquaintances while the other 22 sent the folder to relatives. However, the authors indicate that this preference towards friends could be exclusive to the participants and this does not necessarily generalize to the public.

**Nebraska Study**

The starting population for the Nebraska study was: 296 people were selected, 100 of them were people residing in Boston designated as the "Boston random" group, 100 were blue chip stock holders from Nebraska, and 96 were randomly chosen Nebraska inhabitants called the "Nebraska random" group. Only 64 chains (29%) completed, with 24% by "Nebraska random", 31% by Nebraska stockholder and 35% by "Boston random". There were 453 participants who made up the intermediaries solicited by other participants as people likely to extend the chains towards the target. Similar to the Kansas study, 86% of the participants sent the folders to friends or acquaintances, and the rest to relatives. Men were ten times more likely to send the document to other men than to women, while women were equally likely to send the folder to males as to females. These results were probably affected by the fact that the target was male.

Figure 4.1 shows that the average number of intermediaries on the path of the folders was between 4.4 and 5.7, depending on the sample of people chosen. The average number of intermediaries in these chains was 5.2, with considerable difference between the Boston group (4.4) and the rest of the starting population, whereas the difference between the two other sub-populations were not statistically significant. The random group from Nebraska needed 5.7 intermediaries on average. On average, 6.2 steps to make it to the target. Hence the expression "six degrees of separation". The main conclusion was that the average path length is much smaller than expected, and that geographic location has an impact on the average length whereas

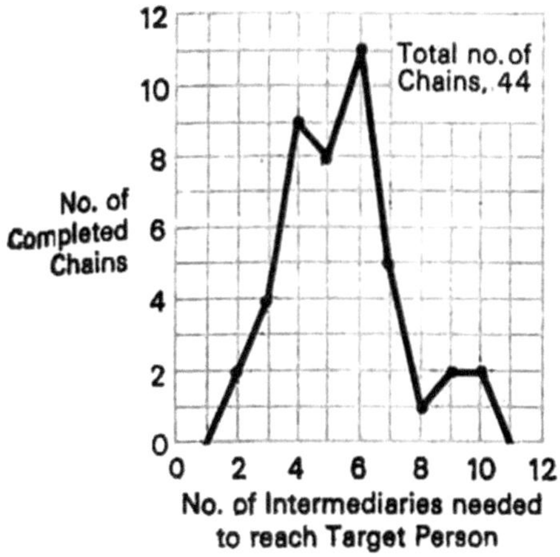


**Fig. 4.1** Frequency distribution of the number of intermediaries required to reach the target

other information, such as profession, did not. It was also observed that some chains moved from Nebraska to the target's neighbourhood but then goes round in circles never making contact to complete the chain. So, social communication is restricted less by physical distance than by social distance. Additionally, a funnelling-like phenomenon was observed because 48% of chains in the last link passed through only 3 of the target's acquaintances. Thereby, showing that not all individuals in a person's circle are equally likely to be selected as the next node in a chain.

Figure 4.2 depicts the distribution of the incomplete chains. The median of this distributions is found to be 2.6. There are two probable reasons for this: (i) Participants are not motivated enough to participate in this study. (ii) Participants do not know to whom they must send the folder in order to advance the chain towards the target.

The authors conclude from this study that although each and every individual is embedded in a small-world structure, not all acquaintances are equally important. Some are more important than others in establishing contacts with broader social realms because while some are relatively isolated, others possess a wide circle of acquaintances.

What is of interest is that Milgram measured the average length of the routing path on the social network, which is an upper bound on the average distance (as the participants were not necessarily sending postcards to an acquaintance on the shortest path to the target). These results prove that although the world is small, the actors in this small world are unable to exploit this smallness.

Although the idea of the six degrees of separation gained quick and wide acceptance, there is empirical evidence which suggests that we actually live in a world deeply divided by social barriers such as race and class.

**Income Stratification**

Reference [3] in a variation of the small world study, probably sent to Milgram for review, not only showed extremely low chain completion rates (below 18%) but also suggested that people are actually separated by social class. This study

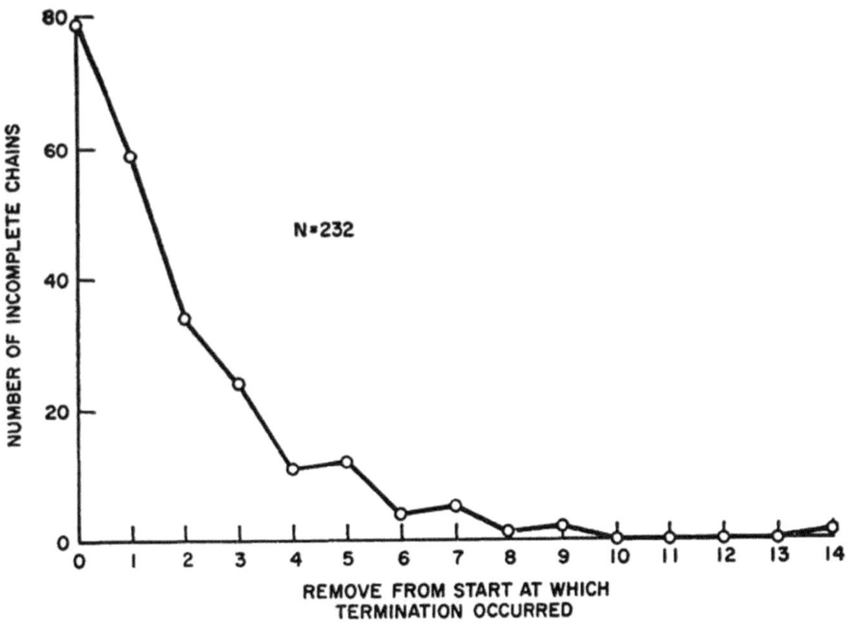


**Fig. 4.2** Frequency distribution of the intermediate chains

consisted of 151 volunteers from Crestline, Ohio, divided into low-income, middle-income and high-income groups. These volunteers were to try to reach a low-income, middle-income and high-income person in Los Angeles, California. While the chain completion rate was too low to permit statistical comparison of subgroups, no low-income sender was able to complete chains to targets other than the low-income target groups. The middle and high income groups did get messages through to some people in every other income group. These patterns suggest a world divided by social class, with low-income people disconnected.

### Acquaintance Networks

Milgram's study of acquaintance networks [11] between racial groups also reveals not only a low rate of chain completion but also the importance of social barriers. Caucasian volunteers in Los Angeles, solicited through mailing lists, were asked to reach both Caucasian and African-American targets in New York. Of the 270 chains started and directed towards African-American targets, only 13% got through compared to 33% of 270 chains directed towards Caucasian targets.

### Social Stratification

Reference [13] investigated a single urbanized area in the Northeast. The research purpose was to examine social stratification, particularly barriers between Caucasians and African-Americans. Of the 596 packets sent to 298 volunteers, 375 packets were forwarded and 112 eventually reached the target—a success rate of 30%. The authors concluded that,

> Communication flows mainly within racial groups. Crossing the racial boundary is less likely to be attempted and less likely to be effective.

### Urban Myth

Reference [10] speculates that the six degrees of separation may be an academic equivalent of an urban myth. In *Psychology Today*, Milgram recalls that the target in Cambridge received the folder on the fourth day since the start of the study, with two intermediaries between the target and a Kansas wheat farmer. However, an undated paper found in Milgram's archives, "Results of Communication Project", reveals that 60 people had been recruited as the starting population from a newspaper advertisement in Wichita. Just 3 of the 60 folders (5%) reached the lady in Cambridge, passing through an average of 8 people (9 degrees of separation). The stark contrast between the anecdote and the paper questions the phenomenon.

### Bias in Selection of Starting Population

Milgram's starting population has several advantages: The starting population had social advantages, they were far from a representative group. The "Nebraska random" group and the stock holders from Nebraska were recruited from a mailing list apt to contain names of high income people, and the "Boston random" group were recruited from a newspaper advertisement. All of these selected would have had an advantage in making social connections to the stockbroker.

The Kansas advertisement was worded in a way to particularly attract sociable people proud of their social skills and confident of their powers to reach someone across class barriers, instead of soliciting a representative group to participate. This could have been done to ensure that the participants by virtue of their inherent social capital could increase the probability of the folder reaching the target with the least amount of intermediaries.

Milgram recruited subjects for Nebraska and Los Angeles studies by buying mailing lists. People with names worth selling (who would commonly occur in mailing lists) are more likely to be high-income people, who are more connected and thus more apt to get the folders through.

Reference [10] questions whether Milgram's low success rates results from people not bothering to send the folder or does it reveal that the theory is incorrect. Or do some people live in a small, small world where they can easily reach people across boundaries while others do not. Further, the paper suggests that the research on the small world problem may be a familiar pattern:

> We live in a world where social capital, the ability to make personal connections, is not widespread and more apt to be a possession of high income, Caucasian people or people with exceptional social intelligence. Certainly some people operate in small worlds such as scientists with worldwide connections or university administrators. But many low-income or minority people do not seem to. What the empirical evidence suggests is that some people are well-connected while others are not. A world not of elegant mathematical patterns where a random connector can zap us together but a more prosaic world, a lot like a bowl of lumpy oatmeal.

**Results and Commentaries**

People who owned stock had shorter paths (5.4) to stockbrokers than random people (6.7). People from Boston area have even closer paths (4.4). Only 31 out of the 64 chains passed through one of three people as their final step, thus not all vertices and edges are equal. The sources and target were non-random. 64 is not a sufficiently large sample to base a conclusion on. 25% of the approached refused to participate. It was commonly thought that people would find the shortest path to the target but the experiment revealed that they instead used additional information to form a strategy.

When Milgram first published his results, he offered two opposing interpretations of what this six degrees of separation actually meant. On the one hand, he observed that such a distance is considerably smaller than what one would naturally intuit. But at the same time, Milgram noted that this result could also be interpreted to mean that people are on average six worlds apart:

> When we speak of five intermediaries, we are talking about an enormous psychological distance between the starting and target points, a distance which seems smaller only because we customarily regard five as a small manageable quantity. We should think of the two points as being not five persons apart, but five circles of acquaintances apart—five structures apart.

Despite all this, the experiment and the resulting phenomena have formed a crucial aspect in our understanding of social networks. The conclusion has been accepted in the broad sense: social networks tend to have very short paths between essentially arbitrary pairs of people. The existence of these short paths has substantial consequences for the potential speed with which information, diseases, and other kinds of contagion can spread through society, as well as for the potential access that the social network provides to opportunities and to people with very different characteristics from one's own.

This gives us the *small world property*, networks of size $n$ have diameter $O(logn)$, meaning that between any two nodes there exists a path of size $O(logn)$.

## 4.2 Columbia Small World Study

All studies concerning large-scale social networks focused either on non-social networks or on crude proxies of social interactions. To buck this trend, Dodds, Muhamad and Watts, sociologists at Columbia University, performed a global, Internet-based social search experiment [4] to investigate the small world phenomenon in 2003. In this experiment, participants registered online and were randomly assigned one of 18 targets of various backgrounds from 13 countries. This was done to remove biases concerning race, gender, nationality, profession, etc. Participants were asked to help relay an email to their allocated target by forwarding it to social acquaintances whom they considered closer than themselves to the target. Of the 98847 individuals who had registered, about 25% had initiated chains. Because subsequent senders were effectively recruited by their own acquaintances, the participation rate after the first step increased to an average of 37%. Including the initial and subsequent senders, data were recorded on 61168 individuals from 166 countries, constituting

24163 distinct message chains. The sender had to provide a description of how he or she had come to know the person, alongwith the type and strength of the resulting relationship.

The study observed the following: When passing messages, the senders typically used friendships in preference to business or family ties. Successful chains in comparison with incomplete chains disproportionately involved professional ties (33.9 versus 13.2%) rather than friendship and familial relationships (59.8 versus 83.4%). Men passed messages more frequently to other men (57%) and women to other women (61%) and this tendency to pass to a same gender contact was strengthened by about 3% if the target was the same gender as the sender and similarly weakened in the opposite case. Senders were also asked why they considered their nominated acquaintance a suitable recipient. Geographical proximity of acquaintance to target and similarity of occupation accounted for atleast half of all choices. Presence of highly connected individuals appear to have limited relevance to any kind of social search involved in this experiment. Participants relatively rarely nominated an acquaintance primarily because he or she had more friends, and individuals in successful chains were far less likely than those in incomplete chains to send messages to hubs (1.6 versus 8.2%). There was no observation of message funneling : at most 5% of messages passed through a single acquaintance of any target, and 95% of all chains were completed through individuals who delivered atmost 3 messages. From these observations, the study concluded that social search is an egalitarian exercise, not one whose success depends on a small minority of exceptional individuals.

Although the average participation rate was 37%, compounding effects of attrition over multiple links resulted in exponential attenuation of chains as a function of their length and therefore leading to an extremely low chain completion rate. Only a mere 384 of 24163 chains reached their targets. There were three reasons for the termination of chains: (i) randomly, because of an individual's apathy or disinclination to participate, (ii) chains get lost or are otherwise unable to reach their target, at longer chain lengths, (iii) individuals nearer the target are more likely to continue the chain, especially at shorter chain lengths. However, the random-failure hypothesis gained traction because with the exception of the first step, the attrition rates remain almost constant for all chain lengths at which there is sufficiently large $N$, and the senders who didn't forward their messages after a buffer time were asked why they hadn't participated. Less than 0.3% of those contacted claimed that they couldn't think of an appropriate recipient, suggesting that lack of interest or incentive, not difficulty, was the main reason for chain termination.

The aggregate of the 384 completed chains across targets (Fig. 4.3) gives us an average length of 4.05 as shown in Fig. 4.4.

However, this number is misleading because it represents an average only over the completed chains, and shorter chains are more likely to be computed. To correct for the 65% dropout per step, the ideal frequency distribution of chain lengths, $n'(L)$, i.e, chain lengths that would be observed in hypothetical limit of zero attrition, may be estimated by accounting for observed attrition as shown in Eq. 4.1.

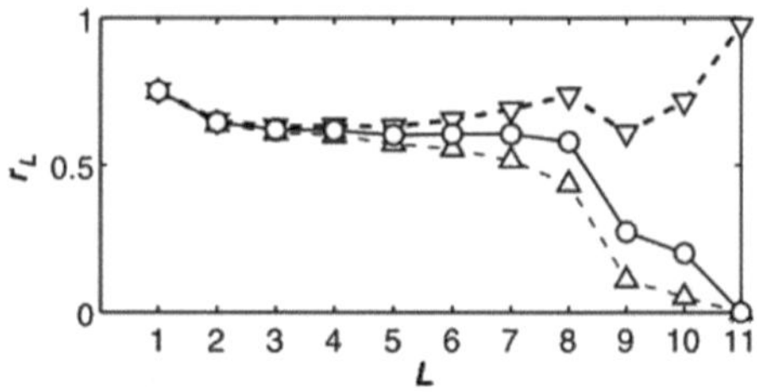


**Fig. 4.3** Average per-step attrition rates (circles) and 95% confidence interval (triangles)

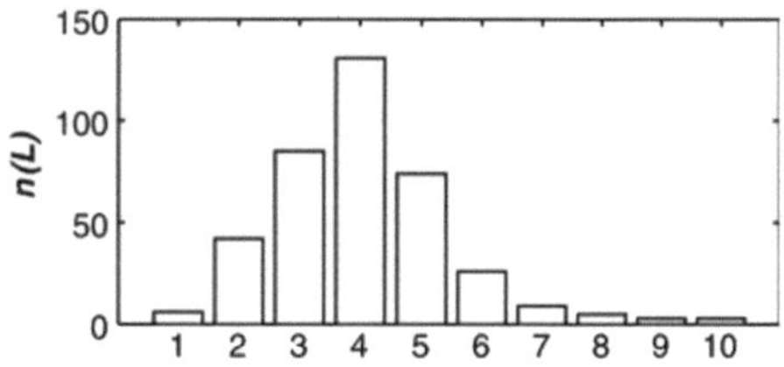


**Fig. 4.4** Histogram representing the number of chains that are completed in $L$ steps

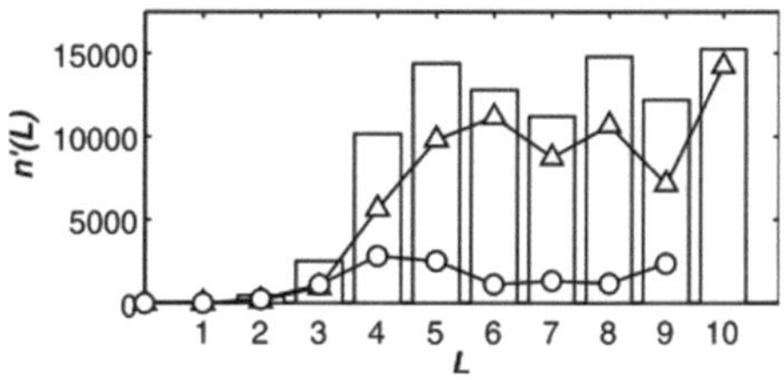


**Fig. 4.5** "Ideal" histogram of chain lengths in Fig. 4.4 by accounting for message attrition in Fig. 4.3

$$n'(L) = \frac{n(L)}{\prod_{i=0}^{L-1}(1 - r_i)} \tag{4.1}$$

where $n(L)$ is the observed number of chains completed in $L$ steps and $r_L$ is the max-likelihood attrition rate from step $L$ to $L + 1$. Figure 4.5 shows the histogram of the corrected number of chains with a poorly specified tail of the distribution, due to the small number of observed chains at large $L$. This gives us the median, $L_* = 7$, the typical ideal chain length for the hypothetical average individual. For chains that started and ended in the same country, $L_* = 5$, or in different countries, $L_* = 7$.

The study finds that successful chains are due to intermediate to weak strength ties. It does not require highly connected hubs to succeed but instead relies on professional relationships. Small variations in chain lengths and participation rates generate large differences in target reachability. Although global social networks are searchable, actual success depends on individual incentives. Since individuals have only limited, local information about global social networks, finding short paths represents a non-trivial search effort.

On the one hand, all the targets may be reachable from random initial seeders in only a few steps, with surprisingly little variation across targets in different countries and professions. On the other hand, small differences in either the participation rates or the underlying chain lengths can have a dramatic impact on the apparent reachability of the different targets. Therefore, the results suggest that if the individuals searching for remote targets do not have sufficient incentives to proceed, the small-world hypothesis will not appear to hold, but that even the slightest increase in incentives can render social searches successful under broad conditions. The authors add that,

> Experimental approach adopted here suggests that empirically observed network structures can only be meaningfully interpreted in light of actions, strategies and even perceptions of the individuals embedded in the network: Network structure alone is not everything.

## 4.3 Small World in Instant Messaging

Reference [5] analyzed a month of anonymized high-level communication activities within the whole of the Microsoft Messenger instant-messaging system. This study was aimed at examining the characteristics and patterns that emerge from the collective dynamics of a large number of people, rather than the actions and characteristics of individuals. The resulting undirected communication graph contained 240 million active user accounts represented as nodes and there is an edge between two users if they engaged in a two-way conversation at any point during the observation period. This graph turned out to have a giant component containing almost all of the nodes, and the distances within this giant component were very small. Indeed, the distances in the Instant Messenger network closely corresponded to the numbers from Milgram's experiment, with an estimated average distance of 6.6, and an estimated median of 7 (as seen in Fig. 4.6). This study containing more than two million times larger than [15], gives "seven degrees of separation". There are longer paths with lengths up to 29. A random sample of 1000 users was chosen and breadth-first search was performed from each of these separately. The reason for this sampling is because the graph was so large that performing breadth-first search from each and every one of these users would have taken an astronomical amount of time.

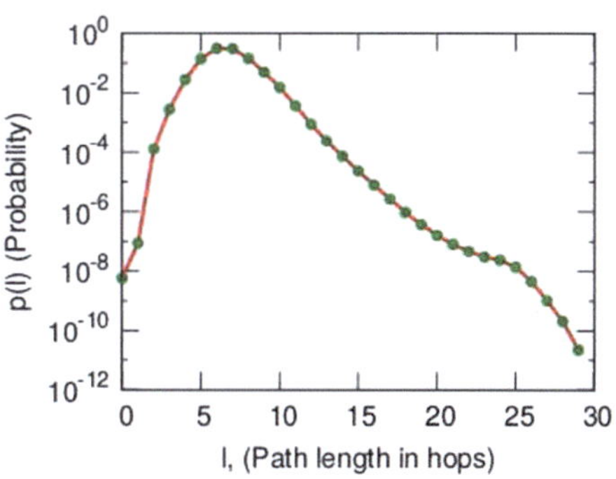


**Fig. 4.6** Distribution of shortest path lengths

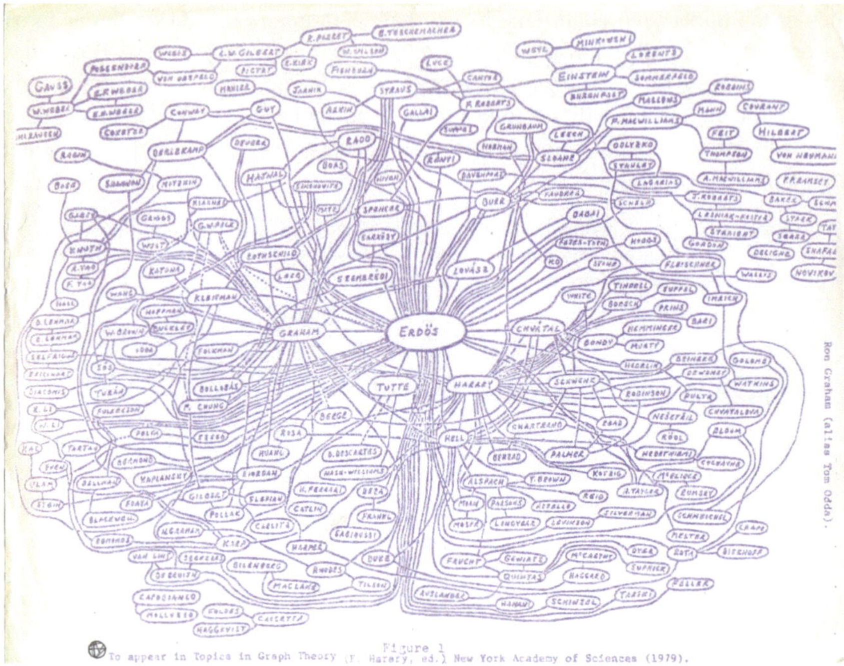


**Fig. 4.7** A hand-drawn picture of a collaboration graph between various researchers. Most prominent is Erdös

## 4.4 Erdös Number

A similar phenomenon is observed in collaborations among researchers. The most popular one is the *Erdös number*. In the collaboration graph of mathematicians as vertices and an edge between mathematicians if they have co-authored a paper, the Erdös number is the distance between a mathematician and Erdös. Figure 4.7 shows a small hand-drawn piece of the collaboration graph, with paths leading to *Paul Erdös*. The highlight is that most mathematicians have an Erdös number of atmost 5 and if scientists of other fields were included, it is atmost 6.

## 4.5 Bacon Number

The compelling belief that the American actor and musician, *Kevin Bacon* was at the center of the Hollywood universe, led three college students to adapt the Erdös number into the *Bacon number*. Here, a collaboration graph has Hollywood performers as nodes and edge between nodes indicates that the performers have appeared in a movie. The Bacon number of a performer gives the number of steps to Kevin Bacon.

The average is 2.9 and there is a challenge to find one that is greater than 5. (there is one with Bacon number 8 that involves a 1928 Soviet pirate movie). Only 12% of all performers cannot be linked to Bacon. There is also a computer game called the "Six Degrees of Kevin Bacon", where players are required to find the shortest path between an arbitrary actor and Kevin Bacon.

## 4.6 Decentralized Search

Given a graph, $s$ has to send a message to $t$, passing it along the edges of this graph, so that the least number of steps is taken. $s$ only knows the location of its neighbours as well as the location of the target $t$, and does not know the neighbours of anyone else except itself. Each vertex has its local information, i.e, a vertex $u$ in a given step has knowledge of:

1. The set of local contacts among among all the vertices
2. The location of the target $t$
3. The locations and long-range contacts of all the vertices who were part of this message chain

Given this information, $u$ must choose one of its contacts $v$ to pass on the message.

## 4.7 Searchable

A graph is said to be searchable or *navigable* if its diameter is $O((log|V|)^{\beta})$, i.e, the expected delivery time of a decentralized algorithm is polylogarithmic. Therefore, a non-searchable or a non-navigable graph is one which has a diameter of $O(|V|^{\alpha})$, i.e, the expected delivery time of a decentralized algorithm is not polylogarithmic.

In other words, a graph is searchable if the vertices are capable of directing messages through other vertices to a specific vertex in only a few hops.

## 4.8 Other Small World Studies

### Small World in an Interviewing Bureau

Reference [7] conducted a small-world study where they analysed 10, 920 shortest path connections and small-world routes between 105 members of an interviewing bureau. They observed that the mean small-world path length (3.23) is 40% longer than the mean of the actual shortest paths (2.30), showing that mistakes are prevalent. A Markov model with a probability of simply guessing an intermediary of 0.52 gives an excellent fit to these observations, thus concluding that people make the wrong small-world choice more than half the time.

**Reverse Small World Study**

Reference [6] attempted to examine and define the network of a typical individual by discovering how many of her acquaintances could be used as first steps in a small-world procedure, and for what reasons. The starting population were provided background information about each of 1267 targets in the small-world experiment and asked to write down their choice, amongst the people they knew, for the first link in a potential chain from them to each of these targets. The subjects provided information on each choice made and the reason that choice had been made. The reason could be in one or more of four categories: something about the location of the target caused the subject to think of her choice; the occupation of the target was responsible for the choice; the ethnicity of the target; or some other reason.

The study drew the following conclusions. First, a mean of 210 choices per subject. However, only 35 choices are necessary to account for half the world. Of the 210, 95 (45%) were chosen most often for location reasons, 99 (47%) were chosen most often for occupation reasons, and only 7% of the choices were mainly based on ethnicity or other reasons. Second, the choices were mostly friends and acquaintances, and not family. For any given target, about 82% of the time, a male is likely to be chosen, unless both subject and target are female, or if the target has a low-status occupation. Over 64% of the time, this trend appears even when female choices are more likely. Lastly, the order of the reasons given were: location, occupation and ethnicity.

The authors conclude that the strong similarity between predictions from these results and the results of [16] suggests that the experiment is an adequate proxy for behavior.

## 4.9 Case Studies

### *4.9.1 HP Labs Email Network*

Reference [1] simulates small-world experiments on *HP Lab* email network, to evaluate how participants in a small world experiment are able to find short paths in a social network using only local information about their immediate contacts.

In the HP Lab network, a social graph is generated where the employees are the vertices and the there is an edge between vertices if there has been atleast 6 emails exchanged between the corresponding employees during the period of the study. Mass emails such as announcements sent to more than 10 individuals at once were removed to minimize likelihood of one-sided communications. With these conditions, Fig. 4.8 shows the graph having 430 vertices with a median of 10 edges and a mean of 12.9. The degree distribution, Fig. 4.9, is highly skewed with an exponential tail. Here, each individual can use knowledge only of their own email contacts, but not their contacts' contacts, to forward the message. In order to avoid loops, the participants append their names to the message as they receive it.

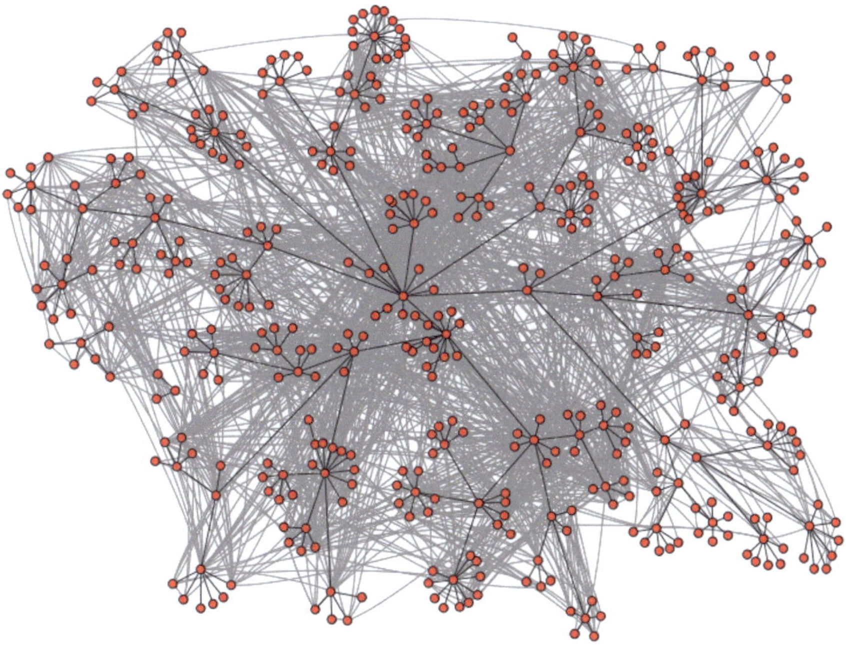

**Fig. 4.8** Email communication between employees of HP Lab

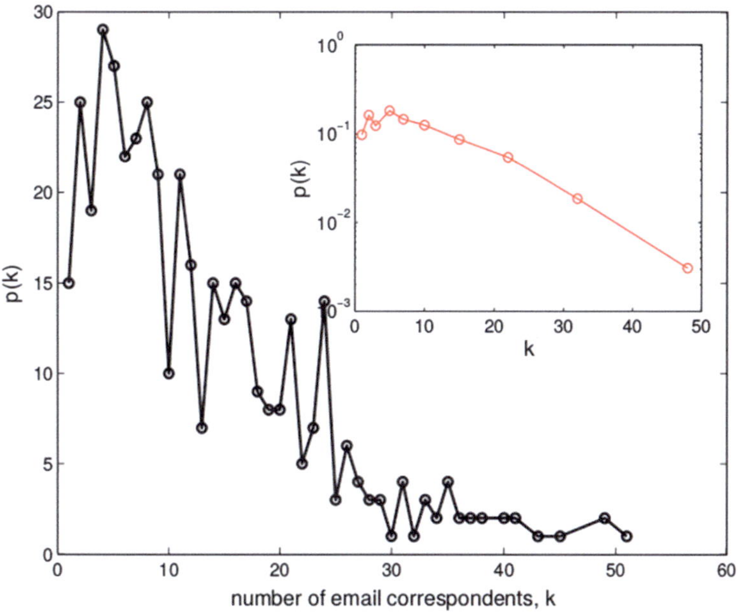


**Fig. 4.9** Degree distribution of HP Lab network

The first strategy involved sending the message to an individual who is more likely to know the target by virtue of the fact that he or she knows a lot of people. Reference [2] has shown that this strategy is effective in networks with power law distribution with exponent close to 2. However, as seen in Fig. 4.9, this network does not have a power law, but rather an exponential tail, more like a Poisson distribution. Reference [2] also shows that this strategy performs poorly in the case of Poisson distribution. The simulation confirms this with a median of 16 and an average of 43 steps required between two randomly chosen vertices.

The second strategy consists of passing messages to the contact closest to the target in the organizational hierarchy. In the simulation, the individuals are given full knowledge of organizational hierarchy but they have no information about contacts of individuals except their own. Here, the search is tracked via the *hierarchical distance* (h-distance) between vertices. The h-distance is computed as follows: individuals have h-distance 1 to their manager and everyone they share a manager with. Then, the distances are recursively assigned, i.e, h-distance of 2 to their first neighbour's neighbour, 3 to their second neighbour's neighbour, and so on. This strategy seems to work pretty well as shown in Figs. 4.10 and 4.11. The median number of steps was only 4, close to the median shortest path of 3. The mean was 5 steps, slightly higher than the median because of the presence of a four hard to find individuals who had only a single link. Excluding these 4 individuals as targets resulted in a mean of 4.5 steps. This result indicates that not only are people typically easy to find, but nearly everybody can be found in a reasonable number of steps.

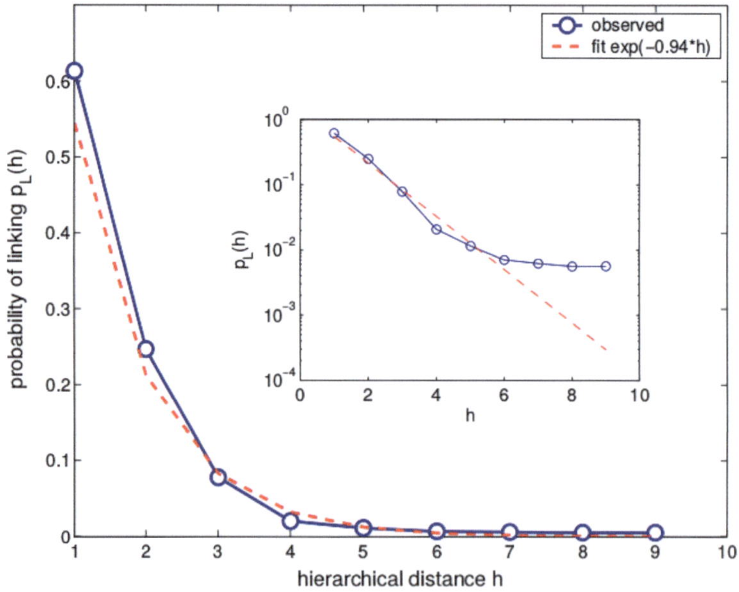


**Fig. 4.10** Probability of linking as a function of the hierarchical distance

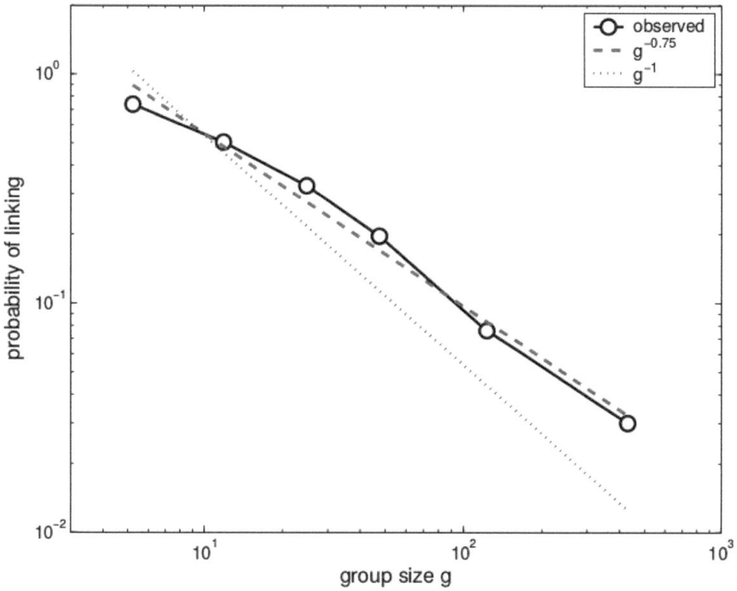


**Fig. 4.11** Probability of linking as a function of the size of the smallest organizational unit individuals belong to

The last strategy was based on the target's physical location. Individuals' locations are given by their building, the floor of the building, and the nearest building post to their cubicle. Figure 4.12 shows the email correspondence mapped onto the physical layout of the buildings. The general tendency of individuals in close physical proximity to correspond holds: over 87% percent of the 4000 emails are between individuals on the same floor. From Fig. 4.13, we observe that geography could be used to find most individuals, but was slower, taking a median number of 6 steps, and a mean of 12.

The study concludes that individuals are able to successfully complete chains in small world experiments using only local information. When individuals belong to groups based on a hierarchy and are more likely to interact with individuals within the same small group, then one can safely adopt a greedy strategy—pass the message onto the individual most like the target, and they will be more likely to know the target or someone closer to them.

### *4.9.2 LiveJournal Network*

Reference [12] performed a study on the *LiveJournal* online community, a social network comprising of 1.3 million bloggers (as of February 2004). A *blog* is an online

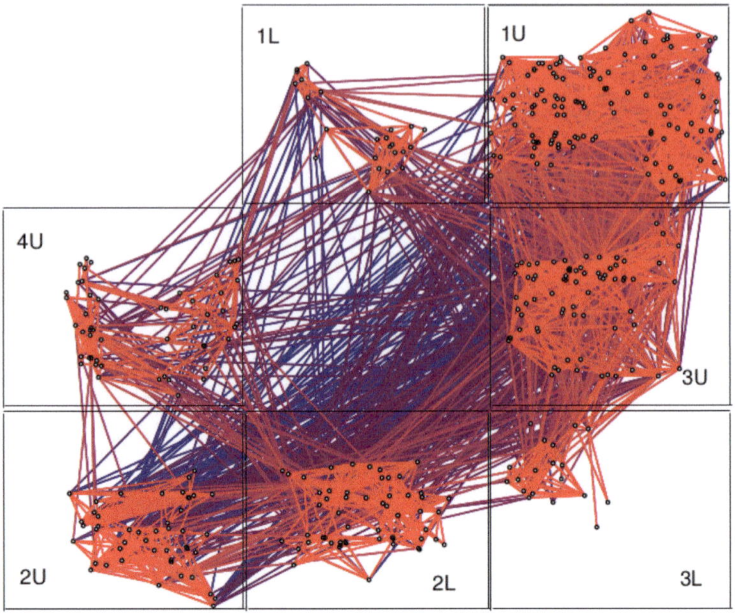


**Fig. 4.12** Email communication mapped onto approximate physical location. Each block represents a floor in a building. Blue lines represent far away contacts while red ones represent nearby ones

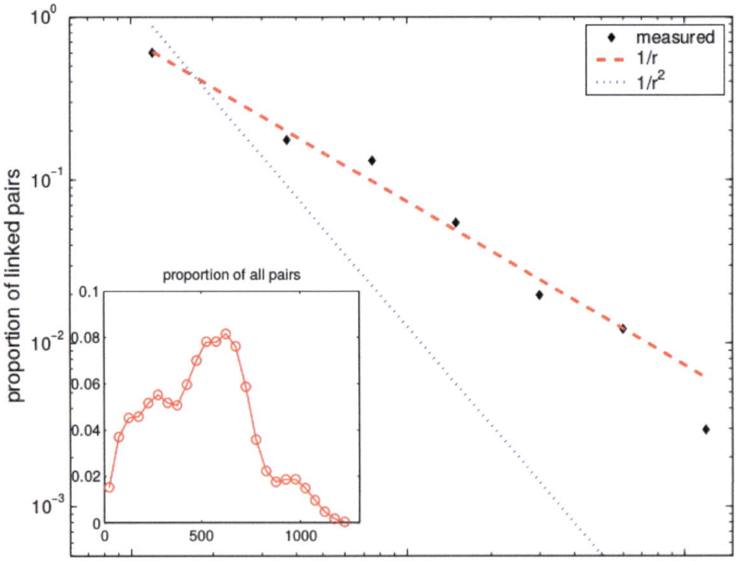


**Fig. 4.13** Probability of two individuals corresponding by email as a function of the distance between their cubicles. The inset shows how many people in total sit at a given distance from one another

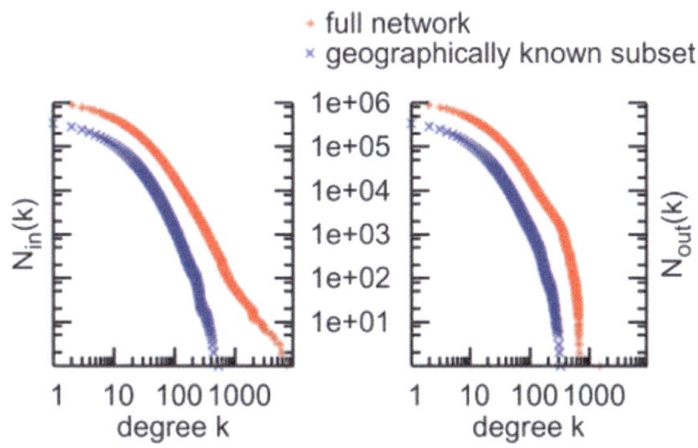


**Fig. 4.14** In-degree and out-degree distributions of the LiveJournal network

diary, often updated daily, typically containing reports on the user's personal life, reactions to world events, and commentary on other blogs. In the LiveJournal system, each blogger also explicitly provides a profile, including geographical location among other information, and a list of other bloggers whom he or she considers to be a friend. Of these 1.3 million bloggers, there were about half a million in the continental United States who listed a hometown and state which could be mapped to a latitude and a longitude. Thus, the discussion of routing was from the perspective of reaching the home town or city of the destination individual.

They defined "$u$ is a friend of $v$" relationship, by the explicit appearance of blogger $u$ in the list of friends in the profile of blogger $v$. Let $d(u, v)$ denote the geographic distance between $u$ and $v$. There are about 4 million friendship links in this directed network, an average of about eight friends per user. It was observed that 77.6% of the graph formed a giant component. Figure 4.14 depicts the in-degree and the out-degree distributions for both the full network and the network of the users who could be geographically mapped. The parabolic shape shows that the distribution is more log-normal than a power law.

They perform a simulated version of the message-forwarding experiment in the LiveJournal, using only geographic information to choose the next message holder in a chain. This was to determine whether individuals using purely geographic information in a simple way can succeed in discovering short paths to a destination city. This approach using a large-scale network of real-world friendships but simulating the forwarding of messages, allowed them to investigate the performance of simple routing schemes without suffering from a reliance on the voluntary participation of the people in the network.

In the simulation, messages are forwarded in the following manner: if a person $s$ currently holds the message and wants to eventually reach a target $t$, then she considers her set of friends and chooses as the next step in the chain the friend in this set who is geographically closest to $t$. If $s$ is closer to the target than all of his or her friends, then $s$ gives up, and the chain terminates. When sources and targets are chosen randomly, we find that the chain successfully reaches the city of the target in

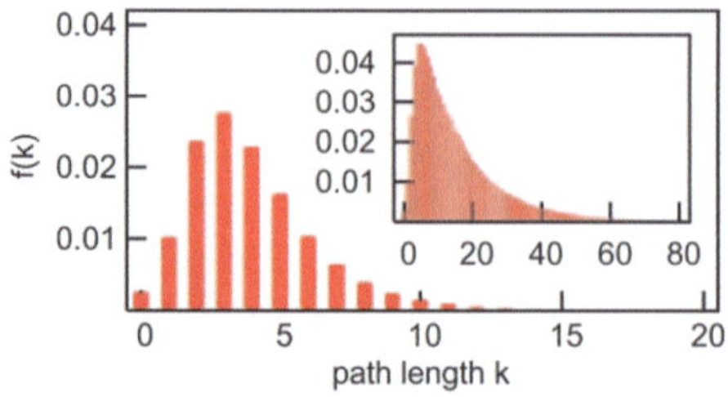


**Fig. 4.15** In each of 500, 000 trials, a source $s$ and target $t$ are chosen randomly; at each step, the message is forwarded from the current message-holder $u$ to the friend $v$ of $u$ geographically closest to $t$. If $d(v, t) > d(u, t)$, then the chain is considered to have failed. The fraction $f(k)$ of pairs in which the chain reaches $t$'s city in exactly $k$ steps is shown (12.78% chains completed; median 4, $\mu = 4.12$, $\sigma = 2.54$ for completed chains). (Inset) For 80.16% completed, median 12, $\mu = 16.74$, $\sigma = 17.84$; if $d(v, t) > d(u, t)$ then $u$ picks a random person in the same city as $u$ to pass the message to, and the chain fails only if there is no such person available.

$\approx 13\%$ of the trials, with a mean completed-chain length of slightly more than four (as shown in Fig. 4.15).

The authors conclude that, even under restrictive forwarding conditions, geographic information is sufficient to perform global routing in a significant fraction of cases. This simulated experiment may be taken as a lower bound on the presence of short discoverable paths, because only the on-average eight friends explicitly listed in each LiveJournal profile are candidates for forwarding. The routing algorithm was modified: an individual $u$ who has no friend geographically closer to the target instead forwards the message to a person selected at random from $u$'s city. Under this modification, chains complete 80% of the time, with median length 12 and mean length 16.74 (see Fig. 4.15). The completion rate is not 100% because a chain may still fail by landing at a location in which no inhabitant has a friend closer to the target. This modified experiment may be taken as an upper bound on completion rate, when the simulated individuals doggedly continue forwarding the message as long as any closer friend exists.

To closely examine the relationship between friendship and geographic distance, for each distance $\delta$, $P(\delta)$ denotes the proportion of pairs $u$, $v$ separated by distance $d(u, v) = \delta$ who are friends. As $\delta$ increases, it is observed that $P(\delta)$ decreases, indicating that geographic proximity indeed increases the probability of friendship (as shown in Fig. 4.16). However, for distances larger than $\approx 1,000$ km, the $\delta$-versus-$P(\delta)$ curve approximately flattens to a constant probability of friendship between people, regardless of the geographic distance between them. Figure 4.16 shows that $P(\delta)$ flattens to $P(\delta) \approx 5.0 \times 10^{-6}$ for large distances $\delta$; the background friendship probability $\epsilon$ dominates $f(\delta)$ for large separations $\delta$. It is thus estimated that $\epsilon$ is $5.0 \times 10^{-6}$ . This value can be used to estimate the proportion of friendships in the LiveJournal network that are formed by geographic and non-geographic processes. The probability of a non-geographic friendship between $u$ and $v$ is $\epsilon$, so on average $u$ will have $\approx 2.5$ non-geographic friends. An average person in the LiveJournal

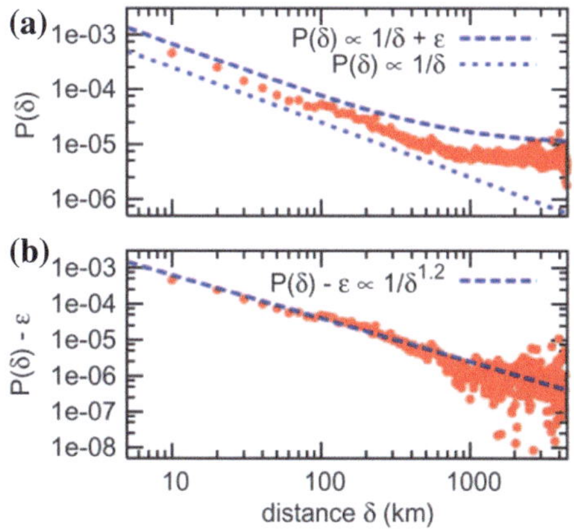


**Fig. 4.16** **a** For each distance $\delta$ , the proportion P($\delta$) of friendships among all pairs $u$, $v$ of LiveJournal users with $d(u, v) = \delta$ is shown. The number of pairs $u$,$v$ with $d(u, v) = \delta$ is estimated by computing the distance between 10, 000 randomly chosen pairs of people in the network. **b** The same data are plotted, correcting for the background friendship probability: plot distance $\delta$ versus $P(\delta) - 5.0 \times 10^{-6}$

network has eight friends, so $\approx 5.5$ of an average person's eight friends (69% of his or her friends) are formed by geographic processes. This statistic is aggregated across the entire network: no particular friendship can be tagged as geographic or non-geographic by this analysis; friendship between distant people is simply more likely (but not guaranteed) to be generated by the nongeographic process. However, this analysis does estimate that about two-thirds of LiveJournal friendships are geographic in nature. Figure 4.16 shows the plot of geographic distance $\delta$ versus the geographic-friendship probability $f(\delta) = P(\delta) - \epsilon$. The plot shows that $f(\delta)$ decreases smoothly as $\delta$ increases. This shows that any model of friendship that is based solely on the distance between people is insufficient to explain the geographic nature of friendships in the LiveJournal network.

Since, geographic distance alone is insufficient as the basis for a geographical model, this model uses rank as the key geographic notion: when examining a friend $v$ of $u$, the relevant quantity is the number of people who live closer to $u$ than $v$ does. Formally, the rank of $v$ with respect to $u$ is defined as given in Eq. 4.2.

$$rank_u(v) := |\{w : d(u, w) < d(u, v)\}| \tag{4.2}$$

Under the rank-based friendship model, the probability that $u$ and $v$ are geographic friends is modelled as in Eq. 4.3

$$Pr[u \rightarrow v] \alpha \frac{1}{rank_u(v)} \tag{4.3}$$

Under this model, the probability of a link from $u$ to $v$ depends only on the number of people within distance $d(u, v)$ of $u$ and not on the geographic distance itself; thus the non-uniformity of LiveJournal population density fits naturally into this framework.

The relationship between $rank_v(u)$ and the probability that $u$ is a friend of $v$ shows an approximately inverse linear fit for ranks up to $\approx 100,000$ (as shown in

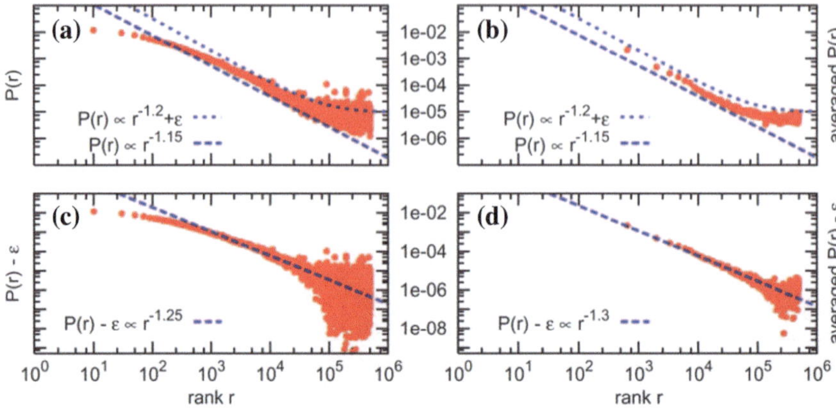


**Fig. 4.17** The relationship between friendship probability and rank. The probability $P(r)$ of a link from a randomly chosen source $u$ to the $r$th closest node to $u$, i.e, the node $v$ such that $rank_u(v) = r$, in the LiveJournal network, averaged over 10, 000 independent source samples. A link from $u$ to one of the nodes $S_\delta = \{v : d(u, v) = \delta\}$, where the people in $S_\delta$ are all tied for rank $r + 1, \ldots, r + |S_\delta|$, is counted as a $(\frac{1}{|S_\delta|})$ fraction of a link for each of these ranks. As before, the value of $\epsilon$ represents the background probability of a friendship independent of geography. **a** Data for every 20th rank are shown. **b** The data are averaged into buckets of size 1, 306: for each displayed rank $r$, the average probability of a friendship over ranks $\{r - 652, \ldots, r + 653\}$ is shown. **c** and **b** The same data are replotted (unaveraged and averaged, respectively), correcting for the background friendship probability: we plot the rank $r$ versus $P(r) - 5.0 \times 10^{-6}$

Fig. 4.17). An average person in the network lives in a city of population 1, 306. Thus in Fig. 4.17 the same data is shown where the probabilities are averaged over a range of 1, 306 ranks.

So, message passing in the real-world begins by making long geography-based hops as the message leaves the source and ends by making hops based on attributes other than geography. Thus there is a transition from geography-based to nongeography-based routing at some point in the process.

### 4.9.3 Human Wayfinding

Given a network of links between concepts of Wikipedia, [18] studied how more than 30000 trajectories from 9400 people find the shortest path from a given start to a given target concept following hyperlinks. Formally, they studied the game of *Wikispeedia* in which players (information seekers) are given two random articles with the aim to solve the task of navigating from one to the other by clicking as few hyperlinks as possible. However, the players are given no knowledge of the global structure and must rely solely on the local information they see on each page—the outgoing links connecting current articles to its neighbours—and on expectation about which articles are likely to be interlinked. The players are allowed to use the back button of the browser at any point in the game. This traversal from one webpage to another by information seekers is characterized as *human wayfinding*.

On first thought, it might obviously occur that each game of Wikispeedia is an instance of decentralized search. Therefore, employing a decentralized search algorithm will solve the problem. However, there is a subtle difference. In a decentralized search problem, each node works with local information and independently forwards the message to the next node, forfeiting control to the successor. While in Wikispeedia, although the information seeker has only local knowledge about the unknown network, she stays in control all the way and can thus form more elaborate strategies than in a multi-person scenario.

Human wayfinding is observed to take two approaches. The first approach is where players attempt to first find a *hub*. A hub is a high-degree node that is easily reachable from all over the graph and that has connections to many regions of this graph. Then they constantly decrease the conceptual distance to the target thereafter by following content features. While this strategy is sort of "playing it safe" and thus commonly preferred by most of the players, it is observed that this is not the most efficient. The other approach is to find the shortest paths between the articles while running the risk of repeatedly getting lost. This technique is a precarious one but is efficient, successful and thus particularly used by the top players.

This study identified aggregate strategies people use when navigating information spaces and derived insights which could be used in the development of automatically designing information spaces that humans find intuitive to navigate and identify individual links that could make the Wikipedia network easier to navigate.

Based on this study, we understand that although global information was unavailable, humans tend to be good at finding short paths. This could be because they possess vast amounts of background knowledge about the world, which they leverage to make good guesses about possible solutions. Does this mean that human-like high-level reasoning skills are really necessary for finding short paths?

In an attempt to answer this question, [17] designed a number of navigation agents that did not possess these skills, instead took decisions based solely on numerical features.

The agents were constrained by several rules to make them behave the same way humans would, thereby levelling the playing field. The agents could only use local node features independent of global information about the network. Only nodes visited so far, immediate neighbours, and the target may play a role in picking the next node. The user can only follow links from the current page or return to its immediate predecessor by clicking the back button. Jumping between two unconnected pages was not possible, even if they were both visited separately before.

The agent used the navigation algorithm given in Algorithm 6. Here, $s$ is the start node, $t$ is the target node and $V$ is the evaluation function. $V$ is used to score each neighbour $u'$ of the current node $u$ and is a function of $u$, $u'$ and $t$ only. Thus, $V(u'|u, t)$ captures the likelihood of $u$'s neighbour, $u'$ being closer to $t$ than $u$ is.

**Algorithm 6** Basic Navigation algorithm

```
procedure NAVIGATION(s,t,V)
    Let S and visited be empty stacks
    S.push(s)
    while S is not empty do
        u ← S.pop()
        visited.push(u)
        if u = t then
            return visited
        else if u is not in visited then
            for all neighbours u' of u in increasing order of V(u'|u, t) do
                S.push(u')
                if u' = t then
                    return
                end if
            end for
        end if
    end while
    return "No path between s and t exists"
end procedure
```

The following are the candidates for the evaluation $V$:

- Degree-based navigation (DBN): $V(u'|u,t) = out - degree(u')$
- Similarity-based navigation (SBN): $V(u'|u,t) = tf - idf(u',t)$
- Expected value navigation (EVN): $V(u'|u,t) = 1 - (1 - q_{u't})^{out-degree(u')}$
- Supervised learning to learn $V_i$ for every iteration $i$
- Reinforcement learning learns $Vi$ for every iteration $i$

The supervised and reinforcement learning were found to obtain the best results. With the exception of DBN, even the fairly simple agents were found to do well.

The study observed that agents find shorter paths than humans on average and therefore, no sophisticated background knowledge or high-level reasoning is required for navigating networks. However, humans are less likely to get totally lost during search because they typically form robust high-level plans with backup options, something automatic agents cannot do. Instead, agents compensate for this lack of smartness with increased thoroughness: since they cannot know what to expect, they always have to inspect all options available, thereby missing out on fewer immediate opportunities than humans, who focused on executing a premeditated plan, may overlook shortcuts. In other words, humans have a common sense expectation about what links may exist and strategize on the route to take before even making the first move. Following through on this premeditated plan, they might often just skim pages for links they already expect to exist, thereby not taking notice of shortcuts hidden in the abundant textual article contents. These deeper understanding of the world is the reason why their searches fail completely less often: instead of exact, narrow plans, they sketch out rough, high-level strategies with backup options that are robust to contingencies.

## 4.10 Small World Models

We have observed that random graphs have a low clustering and a low diameter, a regular graph has a high clustering and a high diameter. But, a real-world graph has a clustering value comparable with that of a regular graph but a diameter of the order of that of a random graph. This means that neither the random graph models nor a regular graph generator is the best model that can produce a graph with clustering and diameter comparable with those of real-world graphs. In this section, we will look at models that are capable of generating graphs that exhibit the small world property.

### *4.10.1 Watts–Strogatz Model*

In the Watts–Strogatz model, a generated graph has two kinds of edges, *local* and *long-range*. Start with a set $V$ of $n$ points spaced uniformly on a circle, and joins each point by an edge to each of its $k$ nearest neighbours, for a small constant $k$. These form the local edges which ensure the desired high value of clustering. But this still has a higher than desired diameter. In order to reduce the diameter, we introduce the long-range edges. First, add and remove edges to create shortcuts between remote parts of the graph. Next, for each edge with probability $p$, move the other end to a random vertex. This gives the small world property for the graph which is pictorially depicted in Fig. 4.18.

This Watts–Strogatz model provides insight on the interplay between clustering and small world. It helps capture the structure of many realistic networks and accounts

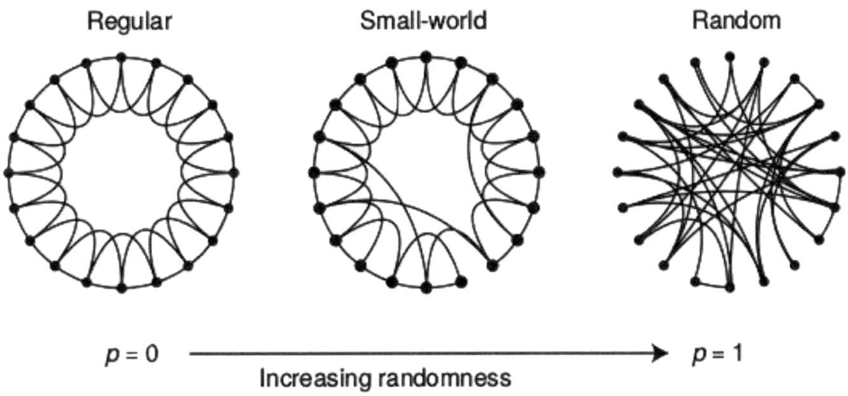


**Fig. 4.18** Depiction of a regular network proceeding first to a small world network and next to a random network as the randomness, $p$ increases

for the high clustering of real-world networks. However, this model fails to provide the correct degree distribution.

The Watts–Stogatz model having $O(|V|^{\frac{2}{3}})$ is a non-searchable graph.

### 4.10.2 Kleinberg Model

In this model, [8] begins with a set of nodes that are identified with a set of lattice points in a $n \times n$ square, $\{(i, j) : i \in \{1, 2, \ldots, n\}, j \in \{1, 2, \ldots, n\}\}$ and the lattice distance between two nodes $(i,j)$ and $(k,l)$ is the number of lattice steps between them $d((i, j), (k, l)) = |k - i| + |l - j|$. For a universal constant $p \geq 1$, node $u$ has a directed edge to every other node within lattice distance $p$. These are node $u$'s local contacts. For universal constants $q \geq 0$ and $r \geq 0$, we construct directed edges from $u$ to $q$ other nodes using independent random trials; the $i^{th}$ directed edge from $u$ has endpoint $v$ with probability proportional to $[d(u, v)]^{-r}$. These are node $u$'s long-range contacts. When $r$ is very small, the long range edges are too random to facilitate decentralized search (as observed in Sect. 4.10.1), when $r$ is too large, the long range edges are not random enough to provide the jumps necessary to allow small world phenomenon to be exhibited.

This model can be interpreted as follows: An individual lives in a grid and knows her neighbours in all directions for a certain number of steps, and the number of her acquaintances progressively decrease as we go further away from her.

The model gives the bounds for a decentralized algorithm in Theorems 6, 7 and 8.

**Theorem 6** *There is a constant $\alpha_0$, depending on p and q but independent of n, such that when $r = 0$, the expected delivery time of any decentralized algorithm is atleast $\alpha_0 n^{\frac{2}{3}}$*

As $n$ increases, decentralized algorithm performs best at $q$ closer and closer to 2 (Fig. 4.19). One way to look at why this value of 2 leads to best performance is that at this value, the long range edges are being formed in a way that is spread uniformly over all different scales of resolution. This allows people fowarding the message to consistently find ways of reducing their distance to the target, no matter the distance from it.

**Theorem 7** *There is a decentralized algorithm $\mathcal{A}$ and a constant $\alpha_2$, independent of n, so that when $r = 2$ and $p = q = 1$, the expected delivery time of $\mathcal{A}$ is atmost $\alpha_2(logn)^2$.*

When the long-range contacts are formed independent of the geometry of the grid (as is the case in Sect. 4.10.1), short chains will exist but the nodes will be unable to find them. When long-range contacts are formed by a process related to the geometry of the grid in a specific way, however, then the short chains will still form and the nodes operating with local knowledge will be able to construct them.

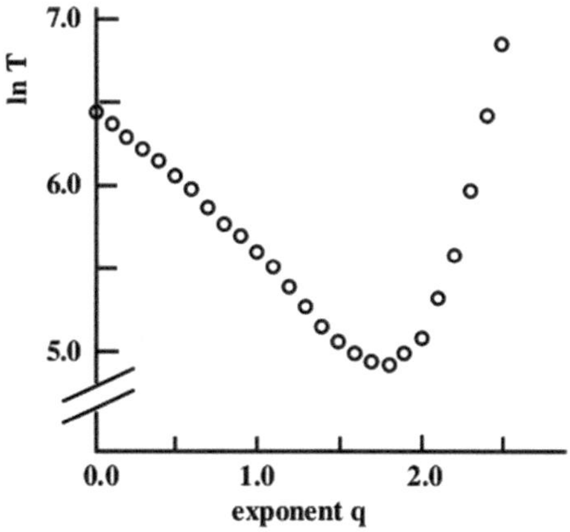


**Fig. 4.19** Log of decentralized search time as a function of the exponent

**Theorem 8** *1. Let $0 \leq r < 2$. There is a constant $\alpha_r$, depending on $p, q, r$ but independent of $n$, so that the expected delivery time of the decentralized algorithm is atleast $\alpha_r n^{\frac{2-r}{3}}$.*

2. *Let $r > 2$. There is a constant $\alpha_r$, depending on $p, q, r$ but independent of $n$, so that the expected delivery time of any decentralized algorithm is atleast $\alpha_r n^{\frac{r-2}{r-1}}$.*

Kleinberg's model is a searchable graph because its diameter is $O((log|V|)^2)$.

#### 4.10.2.1 Hierarchical Model

Consider a hierarchy using b-ary tree $T$ for a constant $b$. Let $V$ denote the set of leaves of $T$ and $n$ denote the size of $V$. For two leaves $v$ and $w$, $h(v, w)$ denotes the height of the least common ancestor of $v$ and $w$ in $T$ and $f(\cdot)$ determines the link probability. For each node $v \in V$, a random link to $w$ is created with probability proportional to $f(h(v, w))$, i.e, the probability of choosing $w$ is $f(h(v, w))/\sum_{x \neq v} f(h(v, x))$. $k$ links out of each node $v$ is created in this way, choosing endpoint $w$ each time independently and with repetitions allowed. This results in a graph $G$ on the set $V$. Here the out-degree is $k = clog^2 n$ for constant $c$. This process of producing $G$ is the *hierarchical model* with exponent $\alpha$ if $f(h)$ grows asymptotically like $b^{-\alpha h}$.

$$\lim_{h \to \infty} \frac{f(h)}{b^{-\alpha' h}} = 0 \; \forall \; \alpha' < \alpha \; and \; \lim_{h \to \infty} \frac{b^{-\alpha'' h}}{f(h)} = 0 \; \forall \; \alpha'' > \alpha$$

A decentralized algorithm has knowledge of the tree $T$, and knows the location of a target leaf that it must reach; however, it only learns the structure of $G$ as it visits nodes. The exponent $\alpha$ determines how the structures of $G$ and $T$ are related.

**Theorem 9** *1. There is a hierarchical model with exponent $\alpha = 1$ and polylogarithmic out-degree in which decentralized algorithm can achieve search time of $O(logn)$.*
*2. For every $\alpha \neq 1$, there is no hierarchical model with exponent $\alpha$ and polylogarithm out-degree in which a decentralized algorithm can achieve polylogarithm search time.*

#### 4.10.2.2 Group-Induced Model

A *group structure* consists of an underlying set of nodes and a collection of subsets of $V$. The collection of groups must include $V$ itself, and must satisfy the following two properties, for constants $\lambda < 1$ and $\beta > 1$.

1. If $R$ is a group of size $q \geq 2$ containing a node $v$, then there is a group $R' \subseteq R$ containing $v$ that is strictly smaller than $R$, but has size atleast $\lambda q$.
2. If $R_1, R_2, \ldots$ are groups that all have sizes atmost $q$ and all contain a common node $v$, then their union has size almost $\beta q$.

Given a group structure $(V, \{R_i\})$, and a monotone non-increasing function $f(\cdot)$, we generate a graph on $V$ in the following manner. For two nodes $v$ and $w$, $q(v, w)$ denotes the minimum size of the group containing both $v$ and $w$. For each node $v \in V$, we create a random link to $w$ with probability proportional to $f(q(v, w))$. Repeating this $k$ times independently yields $k$ links out of $v$. This is referred to as *group-induced model with exponent* $\alpha$ if $f(q)$ grows asymptotically like $q^{-\alpha}$.

$$\lim_{h\to\infty} \frac{f(q)}{q^{-\alpha}} = 0\ \forall\ \alpha' < \alpha\ and\ \lim_{h\to\infty} \frac{q^{-\alpha''}}{f(q)} = 0\ \forall\ \alpha'' > \alpha$$

A decentralized search algorithm in this network is given knowledge of the full group structure, and must follow links of $G$ to the designated target $t$.

**Theorem 10** *1. For every group structure, there is a group-induced model with exponent $\alpha = 1$ and polylogarithm out-degree in which a decentralized algorithm can achieve search time of $O(logn)$.*
*2. For every $\alpha < 1$, there is no group-induced model with exponent $\alpha$ and polylogarithm out-degree in which a decentralized algorithm can achieve polylogarithm search time.*

#### 4.10.2.3 Hierarchical Models with a Constant Out-Degree

To start with a hierarchical model and construct graphs with constant out-degree $k$, the value of $k$ must be sufficiently large in terms of other parameters of this model. To obviate the problem that $t$ itself may have no incoming links, the search problem is relaxed to finding a cluster of nodes containing $t$. Given a complete b-ary tree $T$, where $b$ is a constant, let $L$ denote the set of leaves of $T$ and $m$ denote the size of $L$. $r$ nodes are placed at each leaf of $T$, forming a set $V$ of $n = mr$ nodes total. A graph $G$ on $V$ is defined for a non-increasing function $f(\cdot)$, we create $k$ links out of each node $v \in V$, choosing $w$ as an endpoint with probability proportional to $f(h(v, w))$. Each set of $r$ nodes at a common leaf of $T$ is referred to as a *cluster* and the *resolution* of the hierarchical model is defined to be $r$.

A decentralized algorithm is given the knowledge of $T$, and a target node $t$. It must reach any node in the cluster containing $t$.

**Theorem 11** *1. There is a hierarchical model with exponent $\alpha = 1$, constant out-degree and polylogarithmic resolution in which a decentralized algorithm can achieve polylogarithmic search time.*
*2. For every $\alpha \neq 1$, there is no hierarchical model with exponent $\alpha$, constant out-degree and polylogarithmic resolution in which a decentralized algorithm can achieve polylogarithmic search time.*

The proofs for Theorems 9, 10 and 11 can be found in [9].

### *4.10.3 Destination Sampling Model*

Reference [14] describes an evolutionary model which by successively updating shortcut edges of a small-world graph generates configurations which exhibit the small world property.

The model defines $V$ as a set of vertices in a regular lattice and $E$ as the set of long-range (shortcut) edges between vertices in $V$. This gives a digraph $G(V, E)$. Let $G'$ be $G$ augmented with edges going both ways between each pair of adjacent vertices in lattice.

The configurations are generated in the following manner: Let $G_s = (V, E_s)$ be a digraph of shortcuts at time $s$ and $0 < p < 1$. Then $G_{s+1}$ is defined as:

1. Choose $y_{s+1}$ and $z_{s+1}$ uniformly from $V$.
2. If $y_{s+1} \neq z_{s+1}$ do a greedy walk in $G'_s$ from $y_s$ to $z_s$. Let $x_0 = y_{s+1}, x_1, \ldots, x_t = z_{s+1}$ denote the points of this walk.
2. For each $x_0, x_1, \ldots, x_{t-1}$ with atleast one shortcut, independently with probability $p$ replace a randomly chosen shortcut with one to $z_{s+1}$.

Updating shortcuts using this algorithm eventually results in a shortcut graph with greedy path-lengths of $O(log^2 n)$. $p$ serves to dissociate shortcut from a vertex with its neighbours. For this purpose, the lower the value of $p > 0$ the better, but very small values of $p$ will lead to slower sampling.

Each application of this algorithm defines a transition of Markov chain on a set of shortcut configurations. Thus for any $n$, the Markov chain is defined on a finite state space. Since this chain is irreducible and aperiodic, the chain converges to a unique stationary distribution.

## Problems

Download the *General Relativity and Quantum Cosmology* collaboration network available at https://snap.stanford.edu/data/ca-GrQc.txt.gz.

For the graph corresponding to this dataset (which will be referred to as *real world* graph), generate a small world graph and compute the following network parameters:

**33** Degree distribution

**34** Short path length distribution

**35** Clustering coefficient distribution

**36** WCC size distribution

**37** For each of these distributions, state whether or not the small world model has the same property as the real world graph

**38** Is the small world graph generator capable of generating graphs that are representative of real world graphs?

## References


1. Adamic, Lada, and Eytan Adar. 2005. How to search a social network. *Social Networks* 27 (3): 187–203.
2. Adamic, Lada A., Rajan M. Lukose, Amit R. Puniyani, and Bernardo A. Huberman. 2001. Search in power-law networks. *Physical Review E* 64 (4): 046135.
3. Beck, M., and P. Cadamagnani. 1968. The extent of intra-and inter-social group contact in the American society. *Unpublished manuscript, Stanley Milgram Papers, Manuscripts and Archives, Yale University*.
4. Dodds, Peter Sheridan, Roby Muhamad, and Duncan J. Watts. 2003. An experimental study of search in global social networks. *Science* 301 (5634): 827–829.
5. Horvitz, Eric, and Jure Leskovec. 2007. Planetary-scale views on an instant-messaging network. Redmond-USA: Microsoft research Technical report.
6. Killworth, Peter D., and H. Russell Bernard. 1978. The reversal small-world experiment. *Social Networks* 1 (2): 159–192.
7. Killworth, Peter D., Christopher McCarty, H. Russell Bernard, and Mark House. 2006. The accuracy of small world chains in social networks. *Social Networks* 28 (1): 85–96.
8. Kleinberg, Jon. 2000. The small-world phenomenon: An algorithmic perspective. In *Proceedings of the thirty-second annual ACM symposium on theory of computing*, 163–170. ACM.
9. Kleinberg, Jon M. 2002. Small-world phenomena and the dynamics of information. In *Advances in neural information processing systems*, 431–438.
10. Kleinfeld, Judith. 2002. Could it be a big world after all? the six degrees of separation myth. *Society* 12:5–2.
11. Korte, Charles, and Stanley Milgram. 1970. Acquaintance networks between racial groups: Application of the small world method. *Journal of Personality and Social Psychology* 15 (2): 101.

12. Liben-Nowell, David, Jasmine Novak, Ravi Kumar, Prabhakar Raghavan, and Andrew Tomkins. 2005. Geographic routing in social networks. *Proceedings of the National Academy of Sciences of the United States of America* 102 (33): 11623–11628.
13. Lin, Nan, Paul Dayton, and Peter Greenwald. 1977. The urban communication network and social stratification: A small world experiment. *Annals of the International Communication Association* 1 (1): 107–119.
14. Sandberg, Oskar, and Ian Clarke. 2006. The evolution of navigable small-world networks. arXiv:cs/0607025.
15. Travers, Jeffrey, and Stanley Milgram. 1967. The small world problem. *Phychology Today* 1 (1): 61–67.
16. Travers, Jeffrey, and Stanley Milgram. 1977. An experimental study of the small world problem. *Social Networks*, 179–197. Elsevier.
17. West, Robert, and Jure Leskovec. 2012. Automatic versus human navigation in information networks. *ICWSM*.
18. West, Robert, and Jure Leskovec. 2012. Human wayfinding in information networks. In *Proceedings of the 21st international conference on World Wide Web*, 619–628. ACM.

# Chapter 5
# Graph Structure of Facebook

Reference [2] explains the study of the social graph of the active users of the world's largest online social network, *Facebook*. The study mainly focused on computing the number of users and their friendships, degree distribution, path length, clustering and various mixing patterns. All calculations concerning this study were performed on Hadoop cluster with 2250 machines using Hadoop/Hive data analysis framework developed at Facebook. This social network is seen to display a broad range of unifying structural properties such as homophily, clustering, small-world effect, heterogeneous distribution of friends and community structure.

The graph of the entire social network of the active members of Facebook as of May 2011 is analysed in an anonymized form and the focus is placed on the set of active user accounts reliably corresponding to people. A user of Facebook is deemed as an active member if they logged into the site in the last 28 days from the time of measurement in May 2011 and had atleast one Facebook friend. The restriction to study only active users allows us to eliminate accounts that have been abandoned in the early stages of creation, and focus on accounts that plausibly represent actual individuals. This graphs precedes the existence of "subscriptions" and does not include "pages" that people may "like". According to this definition, the population of active Facebook users is 721 million at the time of measurement. The world's population at the time was 6.9 billion people which means that this graph includes roughly 10% of the Earth's inhabitants. There were 68.7 billion friendships in this graph, so the average Facebook user had around 190 Facebook friends.

The study also focuses on the subgraph of the 149 US Facebook users. The US Census Bureau for 2011 shows roughly 260 million individuals in the US over the age of 13 and therefore eligible to create a Facebook account. Therefore this social network includes more than half the eligible US population. This graph had 15.9 billion edges, so an average US user had 214 other US users as friends. Note that this average is higher than that of the global graph.

*Neighbourhood function*, denoted by $N_G(t)$ of a graph $G$ returns for each $t \in \mathbb{N}$, the number of pairs of vertices (x,y) such that $x$ has a path of length at most $x$ to $y$.



K. Raj P. M. et al., *Practical Social Network Analysis with Python*,
Computer Communications and Networks,
https://doi.org/10.1007/978-3-319-96746-2_5

It provides data about how fast the "average ball" around each vertex expands. It measures what percentile of vertex pairs are within a given distance. Although, the diameter of a graph can be wildly distorted by the presence of a single ill- connected path in some peripheral region of the graph, the neighbourhood function and the average path length are thought to robustly capture the distances between pairs of vertices. From this function, it is possible to derive the distance distribution which gives for each $t$, the fraction of reachable pairs at a distance of exactly $t$.

## 5.1 HyperANF Algorithm

The HyperANF algorithm [1] is a new tool for accurately studying the distance distribution of large graphs. It is a diffusion-based algorithm that is able to approximate quickly the neighbourhood functions of very large graphs. It is based on the observation that $B(x, r)$, the ball of radius $r$ around the vertex $x$ satisfies

$$B(x, r) = \cup_{x \to y} B(y, r-1) \cup \{x\}$$

Since $B(x, 0) = \{x\}$, we can compute each $B(x, r)$ incrementally using sequential scans of graph, i.e, scans in which we go in turn through the successor list of each vertex. The problem is that during the scan we need to access randomly the sets $B(x, r-1)$ (the sets $B(x, r)$ can be just saved on disk on a update file and reloaded later). The space needed for such sets would be too large to be kept in main memory. However, HyperANF represents these sets in an approximate way, using *HyperLogLog* counters, which are a kind of dictionaries that can answer questions related to size. Each such counter is made of a number of small *registers*. A register keeps track of the maximum number of trailing zeros of the values of a good hash function applied to the elements of a sequence of vertices: the number of distinct elements in the sequence is proportional to $2^M$. A technique called *stochastic averaging* is used to divide the stream into a number of substreams, each analysed by a different register. The result is then computed by aggregating suitably the estimation from each register.

The main performance challenge to solve is, how to quickly compute the HyperLogLog counter associated to a union of balls, each represented by a HyperLogLog counter: HyperANF uses an algorithm based on word-level parallelism that makes the computation very fast, and a carefully engineered implementation exploits multicore architectures with a linear speedup in the number of cores. Another important feature of HyperANF is that it uses a *systolic approach* to avoid recomputing balls that do not change during an iteration. This approach is fundamental to be able to compute the entire distance distribution.

The results of a run of HyperANF at the $t^{th}$ iteration is the estimation of the neighbourhood function in $t$.

$$\hat{N_G}(t) = \sum_{0 \leq i < |V|} X_{i,t}$$

where $X_{i,t}$ denotes the HyperLogLog counter that counts the vertices reached by vertex $i$ in $t$ steps.

## 5.2 Iterative Fringe Upper Bound (iFUB) Algorithm

HyperANF cannot provide exact results about the diameter. However, the number of steps of a run is necessarily a lower bound for the diameter. To compute the exact diameter, a highly parallel version of this iFUB algorithm [1] was implemented.

The idea behind this algorithm is as follows: consider some vertex $x$, and find by breadth-first search a vertex $y$ farthest from $x$. Now, find a vertex $z$ farthest from $y$ by which $d(y, z)$ gives us a very good lower bound on the diameter. Then, consider a vertex $c$ halfway between $y$ and $z$. This vertex $c$ is in the middle of the graph, so if $h$ is the eccentricity of $c$, $2h$ is expected to be a good upper bound for the diameter. If lower and upper bounds match, we are done. Otherwise, we consider the fringe: the vertices at distance exactly $h$ from $c$. If $M$ is the maximum of eccentricities of the vertices in fringe, $max\{2(h-1), M\}$ is a new upper bound, and $M$ is a new lower bound. We then iterate the process by examining fringes closer to the root until the bounds match. The implementation uses a multicore breadth first search: the queue of vertices at distance $d$ is segmented into small blocks handled by each core. At the end of a round, we have computed the queue of vertices at distance $d+1$.

## 5.3 Spid

Measures the dispersion of degree distribution. Spid, an acronym for "shortest-paths index of dispersion", is defined as the variance-to-mean ratio of the distance distribution. It is sometimes referred to as the webbiness of a social network. Networks with spid greater than one should be considered web-like whereas networks with spid less than one should be considered properly social.

The intuition behind this measure is that proper social networks strongly favour short connections, whereas in the web, long connections are not uncommon. The correlation between spid and average distance is inverse, i.e, larger the average distance, smaller is the spid.

The spid of the Facebook graph is 0.09 thereby confirming that it is a proper social network.

## 5.4 Degree Distribution

The degree distribution was computed by performing several HyperANF runs on the graph, obtaining estimate of the values of the neighbourhood function with relative standard deviation at most 58%. These neighbourhood functions were computed on a single 24-core machine with 72 GiB of RAM and 1 TiB of disk space, using the HyperANF algorithm, averaging across 10 runs.

Figure 5.1 shows the degree distribution of the global and the US Facebook graph. We observe that it is monotonically decreasing, except for a small anomaly near 20 friends. This kink is due to forces within the Facebook product to encourage the low friend count individuals in particular to gain more friends until they reach 20 friends. The distribution shows a clear cut-off at 5000 friends, a limit imposed on the number of friends by Facebook at the time of measurement. Since 5000 is nowhere near the number of Facebook users, each user is clearly friends with a vanishing fraction of the Facebook population, making these social relationships sparse.

From Fig. 5.1, we observe that most individuals have a moderate number of friends, less than 200, while a much smaller population have many hundreds or even thousands of friends. There is a small population of users who have an abnormally high degree than the average user. The distribution is clearly right-skewed with high variance but there is a substantial curvature exhibited in the distribution on the log–log scale. This curvature is somewhat surprising because empirical measurements of networks have claimed that the degree distributions follow a power law. Thus, strict power laws are inappropriate for this degree distribution.

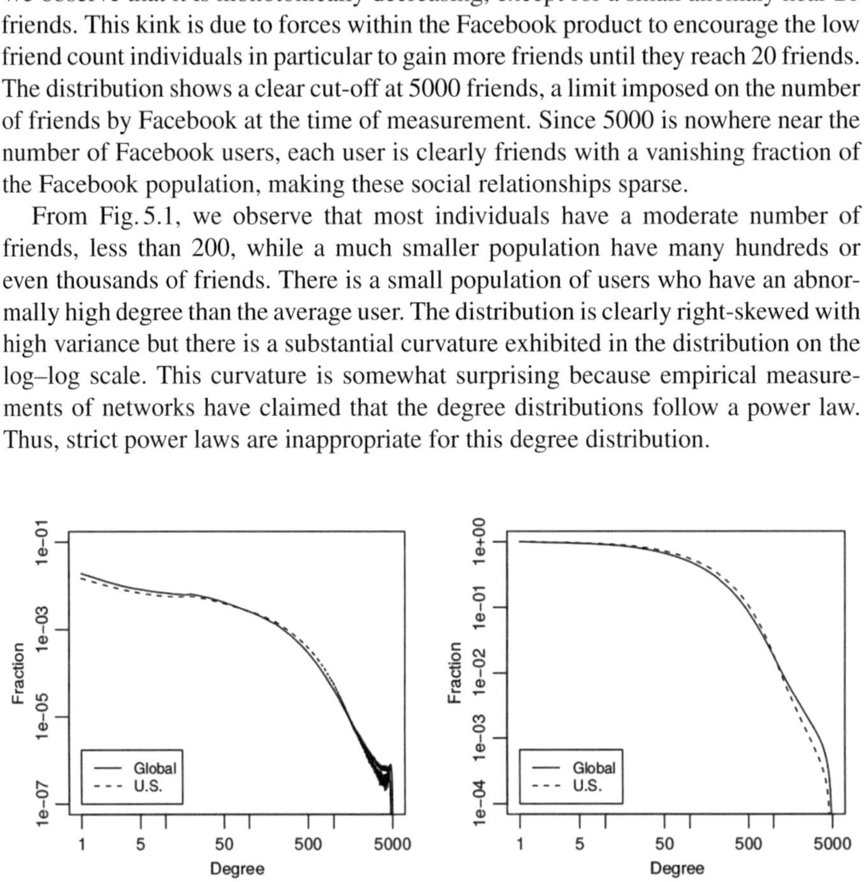


**Fig. 5.1** Degree distribution of the global and US Facebook active users, alongside its CCDF

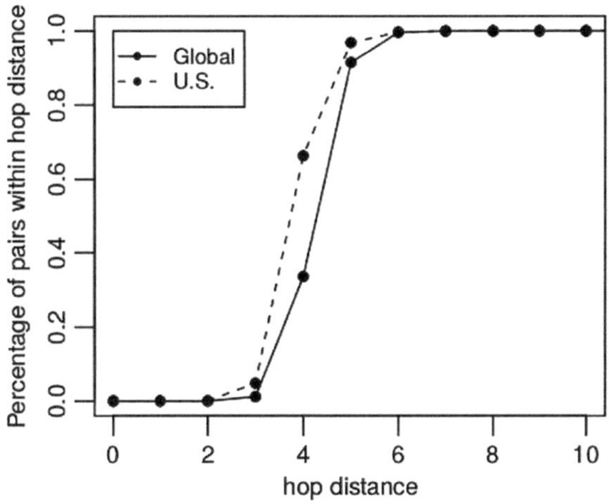


**Fig. 5.2** Neighbourhood function showing the percentage of users that are within $h$ hops of one another

## 5.5 Path Length

The goal in studying the distance distribution is the identification of interesting statistical parameters that can be used to tell proper social networks from other complex networks such as web graphs. Distance distribution is one such interesting global feature that makes it possible to reject probabilistic models even when they match local features such as in-degree distribution.

The Facebook graph does not have paths between all pairs of vertices. It consists of one large connected component and therefore the neighbourhood function is representative of an overwhelming majority of pair of vertices. Figure 5.2 shows the neighbourhood function computed on the graph. The average distance between users was 4.7 for global users and 4.3 for US users, thus confirming the six degrees of separation. What is more interesting, is that since the results show 3.74 intermediaries, this gives a "four degrees of separation". 92% of all pairs of FB users were within 5 degrees of separation, 99.6% were within 6 degrees. For US, 96% were within 5 degrees and 99.7% were within 6 degrees.

## 5.6 Component Size

Figure 5.3 shows the distribution of component sizes on log–log scale. While there are many connected components, most of these components are extremely small. The second largest component has just over 2000 individuals, whereas the largest component consists of 99.91% of the network. This giant component comprises the vast majority of active Facebook users with atleast one friend. So not only are the average path lengths between individuals short, these social connections exist between nearly everyone on Facebook.

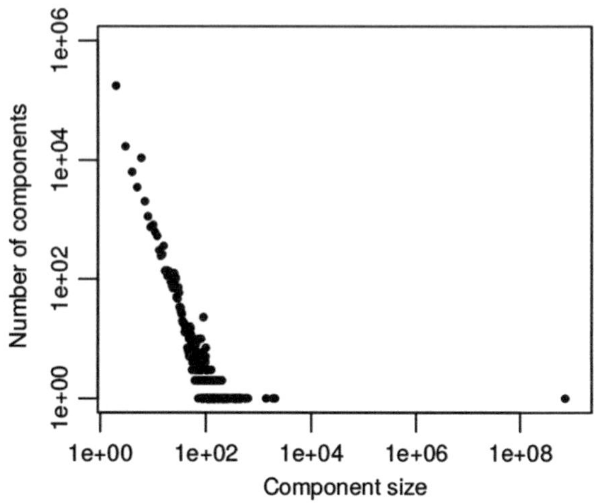


**Fig. 5.3** Distribution of component sizes on log–log scale

This component structure was analysed using the *Newman–Zipf* (NZ) algorithm. The NZ algorithm is a type of *Union-Find* algorithm with path compression which records the component structure dynamically as edges are added to the network that begins completely empty of edges. When all the edges are added, the algorithm has computed the component structure of the network. This algorithm does not require that the edges must be retained in memory. The algorithm is applied to the Facebook graph on a single computer with 64GB of RAM by streaming over a list of edges.

## 5.7 Clustering Coefficient and Degeneracy

Neighbourhood graph for user $i$, also called the *ego* or 1-*ball* graph is the graph-induced subgraph consisting of users who are friends with user $i$ and friendship between these users. However, user $i$ is not included in their own neighbourhoods.

Figure 5.4 shows the clustering coefficient and the degeneracy on log–log scale. The clustering coefficient decreases monotonically with degree. In particular, the clustering coefficient drops rapidly for users with close to 5000 friends, indicating that these users are likely using Facebook for less coherent social purposes and befriending users more indiscriminately.

Having observed such large clustering coefficients, the degeneracy of the graph was measured to study the sparsity of neighbourhood graphs. Formally, the *degeneracy* of an undirected graph is the largest $k$ for which the graph has a non-empty $k$-core. The $k$-*core* of a graph is the maximal subgraph in which all the vertices have degree atleast $k$, i.e, the subgraph formed by iteratively removing all the vertices of degree less than $k$ until convergence. Figure 5.4 depicts the average degeneracy as an increasing function of user degree. From this, we find that even though the graph

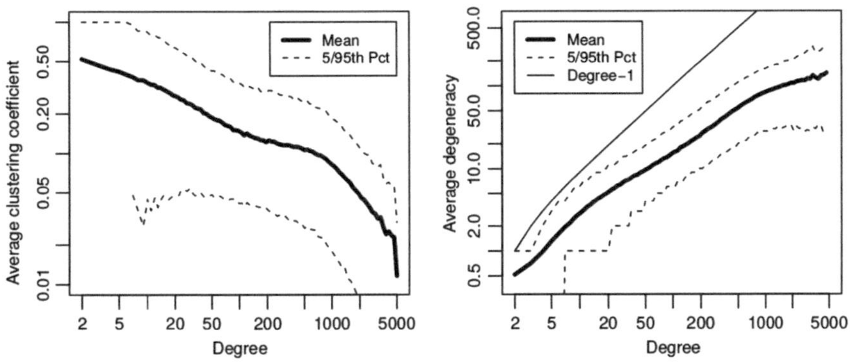


**Fig. 5.4** Clustering coefficient and degeneracy as a function of degree on log–log scale

is sparse as a whole, when users accumulate sizeable friend counts, their friendships are far more indiscriminate and instead center around sizeable dense cores.

## 5.8 Friends-of-Friends

The friends-of-friends, as the name suggests, denotes the number of users that are within two hops of an initial user. Figure 5.5 computes the average counts of both the unique and non-unique friends-of-friends as a function of the degree. The *non-unique friends-of-friends* count corresponds to the number of length 2 paths starting at an initial vertex and not returning to that vertex. The *unique friends-of-friends*

**Fig. 5.5** Average number of unique and non-unique friends-of-friends as a function of degree

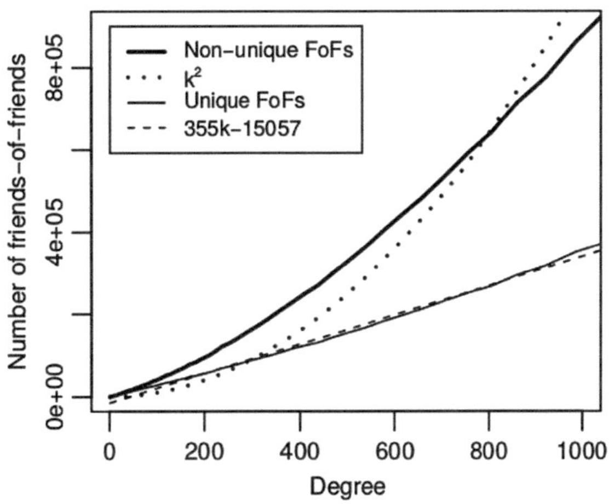

count corresponds to the number of unique vertices that can be reached at the end of a length 2 path.

A naive approach to counting friends-of-friends would assume that a user with $k$ friends has roughly $k^2$ non-unique friends-of-friends, assuming that their friends have roughly the same friend count as them. The same principle could also apply to estimating the number of unique friends-of-friends. However, the number of unique friends-of- friends grows very close to linear, and the number of non-unique friends-of-friends grows only moderately faster than linear. While the growth rate may be slower than expected, as Fig. 5.5 illustrates, until a user has more than 800 friends the absolute amounts are unexpectedly large: a user with 100 friends has 27500 unique friends-of-friends and 40300 non-unique friends-of-friends. This is significantly more than $100 \times 99 = 9900$ non-unique friends-of-friends we would have expected if our friends had roughly the same number of friends as us.

## 5.9 Degree Assortativity

The number of friendships in your local network neighbourhood depends on the number of friends of your friends. It is observed that your neighbour's degree is correlated with your own degree: it tends to be large when your degree is large, and small when your degree is small. This is called *degree assortativity*. Figure 5.6 depicts the degree assortativity and this explains the more than expected friends behaviour of the previous section.

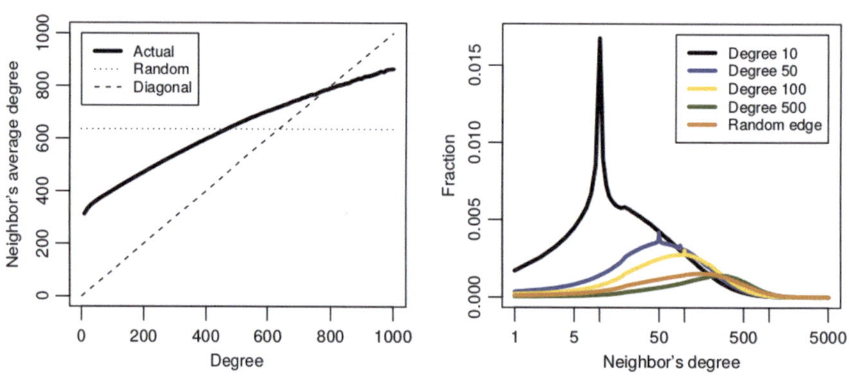


**Fig. 5.6** Average neighbour degree as a function of an individual's degree, and the conditional probability $p(k'|k)$ that a randomly chosen neighbour of an individual with degree $k$ has degree $k'$

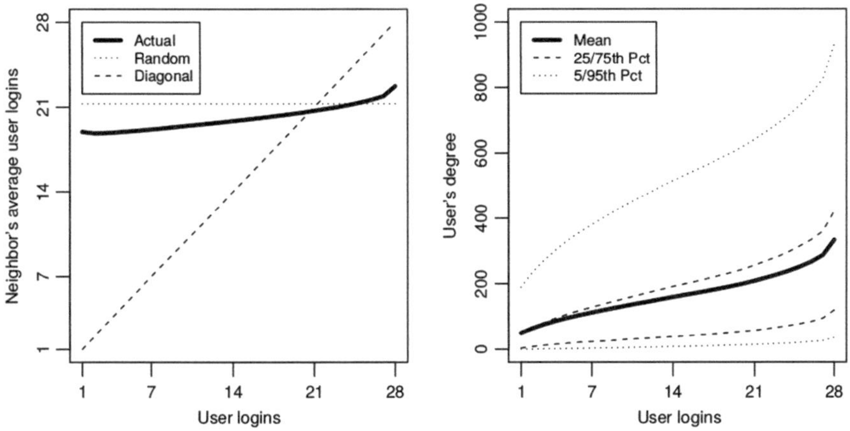


**Fig. 5.7** Neighbor's logins versus user's logins to Facebook over a period of 28 days, and a user's degree versus the number of days a user logged into Facebook in the 28 day period

## 5.10 Login Correlation

Figure 5.7 shows the correlation calculation of the number of days users logged in during the 28-day window of the study. The definition of a random neighbour of vertices with trait $x$ is to first select a vertex with trait $x$ in proportion to their degree and select an edge connected to that vertex uniformly at random, i.e, we give each edge connected to vertices with trait $x$ equal weight. From Fig. 5.7, it is evident that similar to degree's assortativity property, login also shows a correlation between that of an individual with neighbours'.

This correlation phenomena is best explained as follows: a Facebook user provides and receives content through status updates, links, videos, photos, etc to and from friends, and hence may be motivated to login if they have more friends. So, a user who logs in more generally has more friends on Facebook and vice versa. So, since your friends have more friends than you do, they also login to Facebook more than you do.

## 5.11 Other Mixing Patterns

The study later focused on the effects of age, gender and country of origin on friendships.

### *5.11.1 Age*

To understand the friendship patterns among individuals with different ages, we compute $p(t'|t)$ of selecting a random neighbour of individuals with age $t$ who has

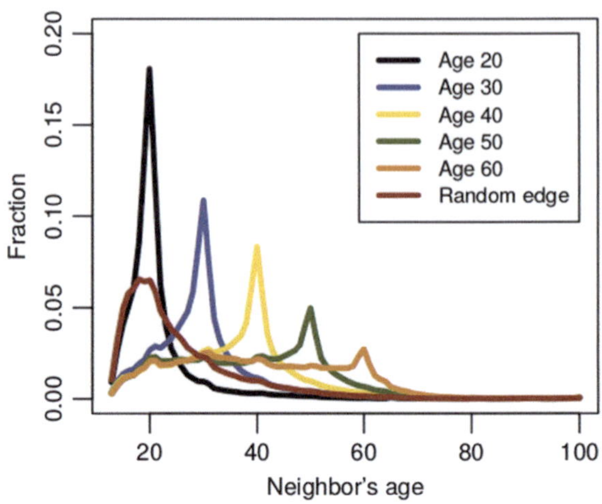


**Fig. 5.8** Distribution $p(t'|t)$ of ages $t'$ for the neighbours of users with age $t$

age $t'$. A random neighbour means that each edge connected to a user with age $t$ is given equal probability of being followed. Figure 5.8 shows that the resulting distribution is not merely a function of the magnitude of age difference $|t - t'|$ as might naively be expected, and instead are asymmetric about a maximum value of $t' = t$. Unsurprisingly, a random neighbour is most likely to be the same age as you. Younger individuals have most of their friends within a small age range while older individuals have a much wider range.

### 5.11.2 Gender

By computing $p(g'|g)$, we get the probability that a random neighbour of individuals with gender $g$ has gender $g'$ where $M$ denotes male and $F$ denotes female. The Facebook graph gives us the following probabilities, $p(F|M) = 0.5131$, $p(M|M) = 0.4869$, $p(F|F) = 0.5178$ and $p(M|F) = 0.4822$. By these computations, a random neighbour is more likely to be a female. There are roughly 30 million fewer active female users on Facebook with average female degree (198) larger than the average male degree (172) with $p(F) = 0.5156$ and $p(M) = 0.4844$. Therefore, we have $p(F|M) < p(F) < p(F|F)$ and $p(M|F) < p(M) < p(M|M)$. However, the difference between these probabilities is extremely small thereby giving a minimal effect on the preference for same gender friendships on Facebook.

### 5.11.3 Country of Origin

The obvious expectation is that an individual will have more friends from the same country of origin than from outside that country, and data shows that 84.2% of edges are within countries. So, the network divides fairly cleanly along country lines into network clusters or communities. This division can be quantified using *modularity*, denoted by $Q$, which is the fraction of edges within communities in a randomized version of the network that preserves the degree for each individual, but is otherwise random. The computed value of $Q = 0.7486$ which is quite large and indicates a strongly modular network structure at the scale of countries. Figure 5.9 visualizes this structure displayed as a heatmap of the number of edges between 54 countries where active Facebook user population exceeds a million users and is more than 50% of internet-enabled population. The results show a intuitive grouping according to geography. However, other groupings not based on geography include combination of UK, Ghana and South Africa which reflect links based on strong historical ties.

The complete list of countries is provided in Table 5.1.

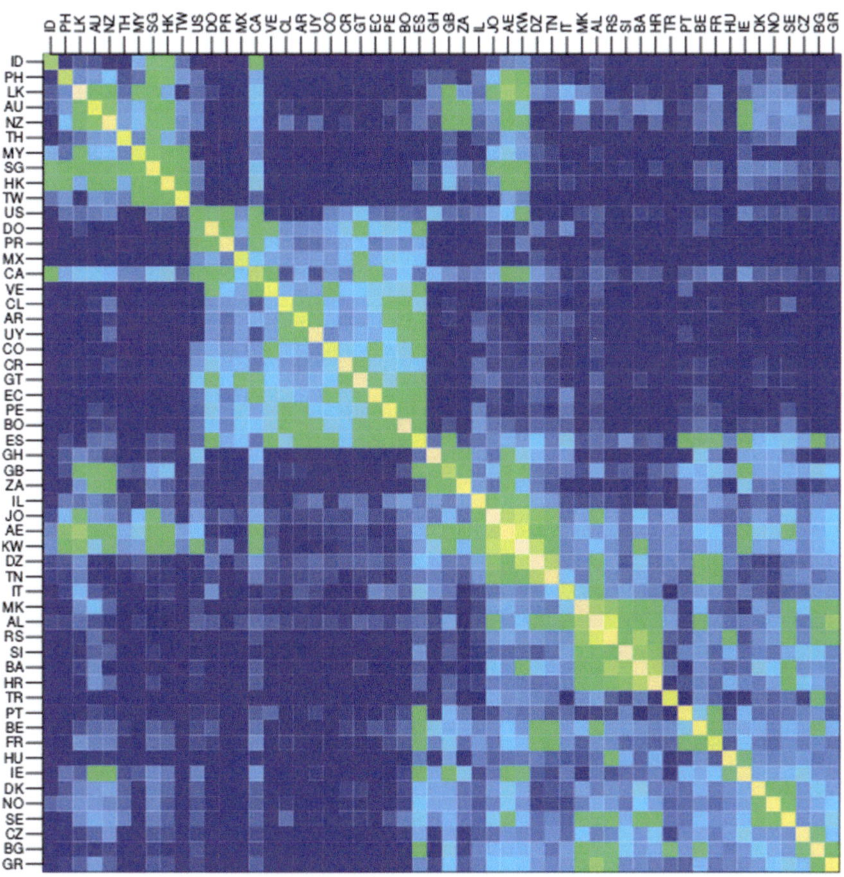


**Fig. 5.9** Normalized country adjacency matrix as a heatmap on a log scale. Normalized by dividing each element of the adjacency matrix by the product of the row country degree and column country degree

**Table 5.1** Countries with their codes

| Country | Code |
|---|---|
| Indonesia | ID |
| Philipines | PH |
| Sri Lanka | LK |
| Australia | AU |
| New Zealand | NZ |
| Thailand | TH |
| Malaysia | MY |
| Singapore | SG |
| Hong Kong | HK |
| Taiwan | TW |
| United States | US |
| Dominican Republic | DO |
| Puerto Rico | PR |
| Mexico | MX |
| Canada | CA |
| Venezuela | VE |
| Chile | CL |
| Argentina | AR |
| Uruguay | UY |
| Colombia | CO |
| Costa Rica | CR |
| Guatemala | GT |
| Ecuador | EC |
| Peru | PE |
| Bolivia | BO |
| Spain | ES |
| Ghana | GH |
| United Kingdom | GB |
| South Africa | ZA |
| Israel | IL |
| Jordan | JO |
| United Arab Emirates | AE |
| Kuwait | KW |
| Algeria | DZ |
| Tunisia | TN |
| Italy | IT |
| Macedonia | MK |

(continued)

**Table 5.1** (continued)

| | |
|---|---|
| Albania | AL |
| Serbia | RS |
| Slovenia | SI |
| Bosnia and Herzegovina | BA |
| Croatia | HR |
| Turkey | TR |
| Portugal | PT |
| Belgium | BE |
| France | FR |
| Hungary | HU |
| Ireland | IE |
| Denmark | DK |
| Norway | NO |
| Sweden | SE |
| Czech Republic | CZ |
| Bulgaria | BG |
| Greece | GR |

# Appendix

## Problems

Download the *Friendster* undirected social network data available at https://snap.stanford.edu/data/com-Friendster.html.

This network consists of 65 million nodes and 180 million edges. The world's population in 2012 was 7 billion people. This means that the network has 1% of the world's inhabitants.

For this graph, compute the following network parameters:

**39** Degree distribution

**40** Path length distribution

**41** WCC size distribution

**42** Clustering coefficient distribution

**43** k-core node size distribution

**44** Average friends-of-friends distribution

**45** Average neighbour degree distribution

## References

1. Backstrom, Lars, Paolo Boldi, Marco Rosa, Johan Ugander, and Sebastiano Vigna. 2012. Four degrees of separation. In *Proceedings of the 4th Annual ACM Web Science Conference*, 33–42. ACM.
2. Ugander, Johan, Brian Karrer, Lars Backstrom, and Cameron Marlow. 2011. The anatomy of the facebook social graph. arXiv:1111.4503.

# Chapter 6
# Peer-To-Peer Networks

Peer-To-Peer (P2P) overlay networks are distributed systems in nature, without any hierarchical organization or centralized control. Peers form self-organizing networks that are overlayed on the Internet Protocol (IP) networks, offering a mix of various features such as robust wide-area routing architecture, efficient search of data items, selection of nearby peers, redundant storage, permanence, hierarchical naming, trust and authentication, anonymity, massive scalability and fault tolerance. These systems go beyond services offered by client-server systems by having symmetry in roles where a client may also be a server. It allows access to its resources by other systems and supports resource-sharing, which requires fault-tolerance, self-organization and massive scalability properties. Unlike Grid systems, P2P networks do not arise from the collaboration between established and connected groups of systems and without a more reliable set of resources to share. All being said, the core operation in a P2P network is the efficient location of data items.

These networks are deliberately designed in a decentralized manner, such that global search is impossible.

Figure 6.1 shows an abstract P2P overlay architecture, illustrating the components in the communications framework. The communication framework specifies a fully-distributed, cooperative network design with peers building a self-organizing system.

There are two classes of P2P infrastructure: *Structured* and *Unstructured*. Structured P2P networks are tightly controlled and content are placed not at random peers but at specified locations that will make subsequent queries more efficient. Content Addressable Network (CAN), Tapestry, Chord, Pastry, Kademlia and Viceroy are some of the commonly known Structured networks. Unstructured P2P networks organize peers in a random graph in flat or hierarchical manners and use flooding or random walks or expanding-ring Time-To-Live (TTL) search, etc on the graph



K. Raj P. M. et al., *Practical Social Network Analysis with Python*,
Computer Communications and Networks,
https://doi.org/10.1007/978-3-319-96746-2_6

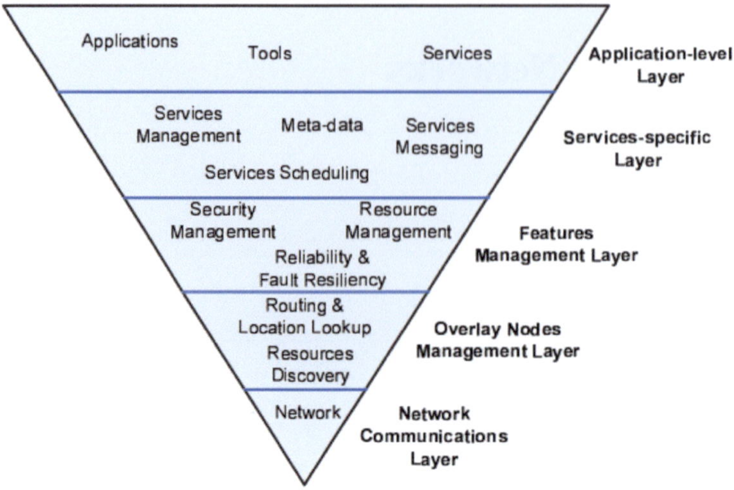


**Fig. 6.1** Abstract P2P network architecture

to query content stored by overlay peers. Each peer visited will evaluate the query locally on its own content, and will support complex queries. Freenet, Gnutella, Fastrack/KaZaA, BitTorrent and Overnet/eDonkey2000 are instances of Unstructured networks.

Reference [2] gives a detailed comparison of these P2P networks. In this chapter we will take a close look at the Chord and the Freenet P2P networks.

## 6.1 Chord

Chord [3] is a distributed lookup protocol that addresses the problem of efficiently locating the node that stores a particular data item in a structured P2P application. Given a key, it maps the key onto a node. A key is associated with each data item and key/data item pair is stored at the node to which the key maps. Chord is designed to adapt efficiently as nodes join and leave the network dynamically.

The Chord software takes the form of a library to be linked with the client and server applications that use it. The application interacts with Chord in two ways: First, Chord provides *key* algorithm that yields IP address of the node responsible for the key. Next, the Chord software on each node notifies the application of changes in the set of keys that the node is responsible for. This allows the application to move the corresponding values to new homes when new node joins.

Chord uses *consistent hashing*. In this algorithm, each node and key has a $m$-bit identifier. One has to ensure that $m$ is large enough to make the probability of two nodes or keys hashing to the same identifier negligible. The keys are assigned to nodes as follows: The identifiers are ordered in an identifier circle modulo $2^m$. Key

$k$ is assigned to the first node whose identifier is equal to or follows $k$. This node is called the *successor* node of key $k$, denoted by $successor(k)$. If the identifiers are represented as a circle of numbers from 0 to $2^{m-1}$, then $successor(k)$ is the first node clockwise from $k$. This tends to balance the load, since each node receives roughly the same number of keys and involves relatively little movement of keys when nodes join and leave the system. In a $N$-node system, each node maintains information of $O(logN)$ other nodes and resolves all lookups via $O(logN)$ messages to the other nodes. To maintain consistent hashing mapping when a node $n$ joins the network, certain keys previously assigned to $n$'s successor now become assigned to $n$. When $n$ leaves the network, all of its assigned keys are reassigned to $n$'s successor.

Each node $n$, maintains a routing table with atmost $m$ entries, called the *finger table*. The $i$th entry in a table at node $n$ contains entry of the first node $s$, that succeeds $n$ by atleast $2^{i-1}$ on the identifier circle, i.e, $s = successor(n + 2^{i-1})$ where $1 \leq i \leq m$ (and all arithmetic is modulo $2^m$). Node $s$ is the $i$ 4th finger of node $n$. This finger table scheme is designed for two purposes: First, each node stores information about only a small number of other nodes and knows more about nodes closely following it than the nodes far away. Next, the node's finger table generally does not contain enough information to determine the success of an arbitrary key $k$.

If $n$ does not know the successor of key $k$, then it finds the node whose ID is closer than its own to $k$. That node will know more about identifier circle in region of $k$ than $n$ does. Thus, $n$ searches its finger table for node $j$ whose ID immediately precedes $k$, and asks $j$ for the node it knows whose ID is closest to $k$. By repeating this process, $n$ learns about nodes with IDs closer to $k$.

In a dynamic network where the nodes can join and leave at any time, to preserve the ability to locate every key in the network, each node's successor must be correctly maintained. For fast lookups, the finger tables must be correct. To simplify this joining and leaving mechanisms, each node maintains a *predecessor pointer*. A node's predecessor pointer contains Chord identifier and IP address of the immediate predecessor of this node, and can be used to walk counter-clockwise around the identifier circle. To preserve this, Chord performs the following tasks when a node $n$ joins the network: First, it initializes the predecessor and fingers of the node $n$. Next, it updates the fingers and predecessors of the existing nodes to reflect the addition of $n$. Finally, it notifies the application software so that it can transfer state associated keys that node $n$ is now responsible for.

## 6.2 Freenet

Freenet [1] is an unstructured P2P network application that allows the publication, replication and retrieval of data while protecting the anonymity of both the authors and the readers. It operates as a network of identical nodes that collectively pool their storage space to store data files and cooperate to route requests to the most likely physical location of data. The files are referred to in a location-independent manner, and are dynamically replicated in locations near requestors and deleted from locations where there is no interest. It is infeasible to discover the true origin or destination of a file passing through the network, and difficult for a node operator to be held responsible for the actual physical contents of his or her node.

The adaptive peer-to-peer network of nodes query one another to store and retrieve data files, which are named by location-independent keys. Each node maintains a datastore which it makes available to the network for reading and writing, as well as a dynamic routing table containing addresses of their immediate neighbour nodes and the keys they are thought to hold. Most users run nodes, both for security from hostile foreign nodes and to contribute to the network's storage capacity. Thus, the system is a cooperative distributed file system with location independence and transparent lazy replication.

The basic model is that the request for keys are passed along from node to node through a chain of proxy requests in which each node makes a local decision about where to send the request next, in the style of IP routing. Since the nodes only have knowledge of their immediate neighbours, the routing algorithms are designed to adaptively adjust routes over time to provide efficient performance while using only local knowledge. Each request is identified by a pseudo-unique random number, so that nodes can reject requests they have seen before, and a hops-to-live limit which is decremented at each node, to prevent infinite chains. If a request is rejected by a node, then the immediately preceding node chooses a different node to forward to. The process continues until the request is either satisfied or exceeds its hops-to-live. The result backtracks the chain to the sending node.

No privileges among the nodes, thereby preventing hierarchy or a central point of failure. Joining the network is simply a matter of first discovering the address of one or more existing nodes and then starting to send messages.

To retrieve a file, a user must first obtain or calculate its key (calculation of the key is explained in [1]). Then, a request message is sent to his or her own node specifying that key and a hops-to-live value. When a node receives a request, it first checks its own store for the file and returns it if found, together with a note saying it was the source of the data. If not found, it looks up the nearest key in its routing table to the key requested and forwards the request to the corresponding node. If that request is ultimately successful and returns with the data, the node will pass the data back to the user, cache the file in its own datastore, and create a new entry in its routing table associating the actual data source with the requested key. A subsequent request for the same key will be immediately satisfied by the user's node. To obviate the security issue which could potentially be caused by maintaining a table of data sources, any node can unilaterally decide to change the reply message to claim itself or another arbitrarily chosen node as the data source.

If a node cannot forward a request to its preferred node, the node having the second-nearest key will be tried, then the third-nearest, and so on. If a node runs out of candidates to try, it reports failure back to its predecessor node, which will then try its second choice, etc. In this manner, a request operates as a steepest-ascent hill-climbing search with backtracking. If the hops-to-live limit is exceeded, a failure result is propagated back to the original requestor without any further nodes being tried. As nodes process requests, they create new routing table entries for previously unknown nodes that supplies files, thereby increasing connectivity.

File insertions work in the same manner as file requests. To insert a file, a user first calculates a file key and then sends an insert message to his or her node specifying the proposed key and a hops-to-live value (this will determine the number of nodes to store it on). When a node receives an insert message, it first checks its own store to see if the key is already taken. If the key exists, the node returns the existing file as if a request has been made for it. This notifies the user of a collision. If the key is not found, the node looks up the nearest key in its routing table to the key proposed and forward the insert to the corresponding node. If that insert also causes a collision and returns with the data, the node will pass the data back to the upstream inserter and again behave as if a request has been made. If the hops-to-live limit is reached without a key collision being detected, a success message will be propagated back to the original inserter. The user then sends the data to insert, which will be propagated along the path established by the initial query and stored in each node along the way. Each node will also create an entry in its routing table associating the inserter with the new key. To avoid the obvious security problem, any node along the way can arbitrarily decide to change the insert message to claim itself or another arbitrarily-chosen node as the data source. If a node cannot forward an insert to its preferred node, it uses the same backtracking approach as was used while handling requests.

Data storage is managed as a least recently used cache (LRU) approach by each node, in which data items are kept stored in decreasing order by the time of most recent request, or time of insert, if an item has never been requested. When a new file arrives, which would cause the datastore to exceed the designated size, the least recently used files are evicted in order until there is space. Once a particular file is dropped from all the nodes, it will no longer be available in the network. Files are encrypted to the extent that node operators cannot access its contents.

When a new node intends to join the network, it chooses a random seed and sends an announcement message containing its address and the hash of that seed to some existing node. When a node receives a new node announcement, it generates a random seed, XORs that with the hash it received and hashes the result again to create a commitment. It then forwards this new hash to some randomly chosen node. This forwarding continues until the hops-to-live of the announcement runs out. The last node to receive the announcement just generates a seed. Now all the nodes in the chain reveal their seeds and the key of the new node is assigned as the XOR of all the seeds. Checking the commitments enables each node to confirm that everyone revealed their seeds truthfully. This yields a consistent random key which each node as an entry for this new node in the routing table.

A key factor in the identification of a small-world network is the existence of a scale-free power-law distribution of the links within the network, as the tail of such distributions provides the highly connected nodes needed to create short paths. Figure 6.2 shows the degree distribution of the Freenet network. Except for one point, it seems to follow a power-law. Therefore, Freenet seems to exhibit power-law.

Reference [4] observed that the LRU cache replacement had a steep reduction in the hit ratio with increasing load. Based on intuition from the small-world models

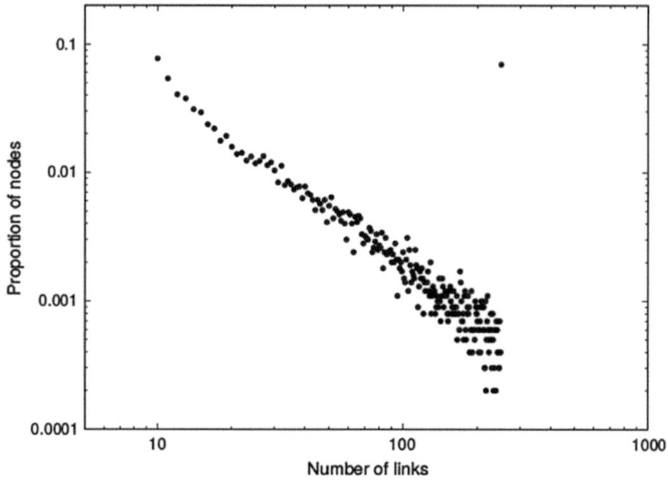


**Fig. 6.2** Degree distribution of the freenet network

they proposed an enhanced-clustering cache replacement scheme for use in place of LRU. This replacement scheme forced the routing tables to resemble neighbour relationships in a small-world acquaintance graph and improved the request hit ratio dramatically while keeping the small average hops per successful request comparable to LRU.

## Problems

In this exercise, the task is to evaluate a decentralized search algorithm on a network where the edges are created according to a hierarchical tree structure. The leaves of the tree will form the nodes of the network and the edge probabilities between two nodes depends on their proximity in the underlying tree structure.

P2P networks can be organized in a tree hierarchy, where the root is the main software application and the second level contains the different countries. The third level represents the different states and the fourth level is the different cities. There could be several more levels depending on the size and structure of the P2P network. Nevertheless, the final level are the clients.

Consider a situation where client $A$ wants a file that is located in client $B$. If $A$ cannot access $B$ directly, $A$ may connect to a node $C$ which is, for instance, in the same city and ask $C$ to access the file instead. If $A$ does not have access to any node in the same city as $B$, it may try to access a node in the same state. In general, $A$ will attempt to connect to the node "closest" to $B$.

In this problem, there are two networks: one is the observed network, i.e, the edge between P2P clients and the other is the hierarchical tree structure that is used to generated the edges in the observed network.

For this exercise, we will use a complete, perfectly balanced $b$-ary tree $T$ (each node has $b$ children and $b \geq 2$), and a network whose nodes are the leaves of $T$. For any pair of network nodes $v$ and $w$, $h(v, w)$ denotes the distance between the nodes and is defined as the height of the subtree $L(v, w)$ of $T$ rooted at the lowest common ancestor of $v$ and $w$. The distance captures the intuition that clients in the same city are more likely to be connected than, for example, in the same state.

To model this intuition, generate a random network on the leaf nodes where for a node $v$, the probability distribution of node $v$ creating an edge to any other node $w$ is given by Eq. 6.1

$$p_v(w) = \frac{1}{Z} b^{-h(v,w)} \tag{6.1}$$

where $Z = \sum_{w \neq v} b^{-h(v,w)}$ is a normalizing constant.

Next, set some parameter $k$ and ensure that every node $v$ has exactly $k$ outgoing edges, using the following procedure. For each node $v$, sample a random node $w$ according to $p_v$ and create edge $(v, w)$ in the network. Continue this until $v$ has exactly $k$ neighbours. Equivalently, after an edge is added from $v$ to $w$, set $p_v(w)$ to 0 and renormalize with a new $Z$ to ensure that $\sum_w p(w) = 1$. This results in a $k$-regular directed network.

Now experimentally investigate a more general case where the edge probability is proportional to $b^{-\alpha h(v,w)}$. Here $\alpha > 0$ is a parameter in our experiments.

Consider a network with the setting $h(T) = 10$, $b = 2$, $k = 5$, and a given $\alpha$, i.e, the network consists of all the leaves in a binary tree of height 10; the out degree of each node is 5. Given $\alpha$, create edges according to the distribution described above.

**46** Create random networks for $\alpha = 0.1, 0.2, \ldots, 10$. For each of these networks, sample 1000 unique random $(s, t)$ pairs $(s \neq t)$. Then do a decentralized search starting from $s$ as follows. Assuming that the current node is $s$, pick its neighbour $u$ with smallest $h(u, t)$ (break ties arbitrarily). If $u = t$, the search succeeds. If $h(s, t) > h(u, t)$, set $s$ to $u$ and repeat. If $h(s, t) \leq h(u, t)$, the search fails.

For each $\alpha$, pick 1000 pairs of nodes and compute the average path length for the searches that succeeded. Then draw a plot of the average path length as a function of $\alpha$. Also, plot the search success probability as a function of $\alpha$.

## References

1. Clarke, Ian, Oskar Sandberg, Brandon Wiley, and Theodore W. Hong. 2001. Freenet: A distributed anonymous information storage and retrieval system. In *Designing privacy enhancing technologies*, 46–66. Berlin: Springer.

2. Lua, Eng Keong, Jon Crowcroft, Marcelo Pias, Ravi Sharma, and Steven Lim. 2005. A survey and comparison of peer-to-peer overlay network schemes. *IEEE Communications Surveys & Tutorials* 7 (2): 72–93.
3. Stoica, Ion, Robert Morris, David Liben-Nowell, David R. Karger, M. Frans Kaashoek, Frank Dabek, and Hari Balakrishnan. 2003. Chord: A scalable peer-to-peer lookup protocol for internet applications. *IEEE/ACM Transactions on Networking (TON)* 11 (1): 17–32.
4. Zhang, Hui, Ashish Goel, and Ramesh Govindan. 2002. Using the small-world model to improve freenet performance. In *INFOCOM 2002. Twenty-first annual joint conference of the IEEE computer and communications societies. Proceedings. IEEE*, vol. 3, 1228–1237. IEEE.

# Chapter 7
# Signed Networks

In many online social applications, users express positive or negative attitudes or opinions in two ways:

- Through actions. Eg: One user giving a "like" or a "rating".
- Through text. Eg: User "comments" and "reviews".

These user expressions result in a *signed network*. A signed network is defined as a network whose edges are associated with an explicit sign. More formally, for a given link $(u, v)$ between vertices $u$ and $v$ in this signed network, the *sign* of this edge denoted by, $s(u, v)$ is defined to be either positive or negative depending on whether it expresses a positive or negative attitude from the generator of the link to the recipient. Although this definition is in the purview of directed signed networks, this also applies to the undirected case.

Positive edges between vertices signify amity while negative edges signify enmity.

The user expressions are more commonly known as *user evaluations*. They reflect the overall levels of status in the community, i.e, the extent of users' past contributions or achievements and serve a crucial purpose in the functioning of social applications, by directing users toward content that is highly favoured, and (where applicable) enabling the formation of cohorts of highly trusted users who guide the operation of the site.

## 7.1 Theory of Structural Balance

According to this theory, a triad is said to be *balanced* if and only if all three of these edges are positive or exactly one of them is. In other words, a triad is balanced if the sign of the product of the links equals one. This property is called the *structural balance property*.



K. Raj P. M. et al., *Practical Social Network Analysis with Python*,
Computer Communications and Networks,
https://doi.org/10.1007/978-3-319-96746-2_7

Therefore a triad that does satisfy the structural balance property is called an *unbalanced* triad.

A balanced triad therefore fulfils the adage:

- "The friend of my friend is my friend".
- "The enemy of my enemy is my friend".
- "The enemy of my friend is my enemy".
- "The friend of my enemy is my enemy".

Figures 7.1, 7.2, 7.3 and 7.4 are instances of two balanced and two unbalanced triads respectively.

A graph in which all possible triads satisfy the structural balance property is called a balanced graph and one which does not is called an unbalanced graph.

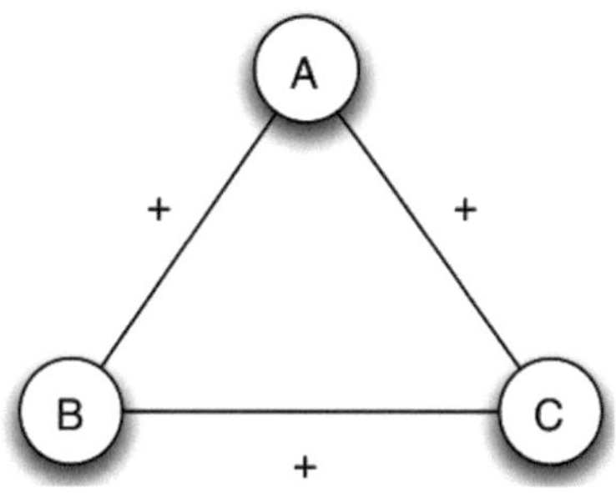


**Fig. 7.1** *A*, *B* and *C* are all friends of each other. Therefore this triad ($T_3$) by satisfying structural balance property is balanced

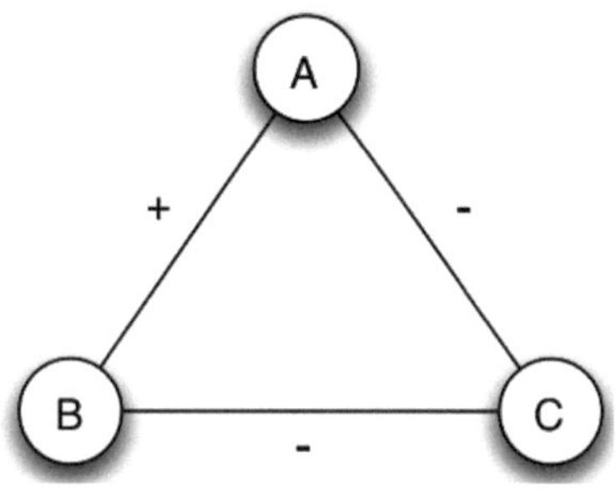


**Fig. 7.2** *A* and *B* are friends. However, both of them are enemies of *C*. Similar to Fig. 7.1, this triad ($T_1$) is balanced

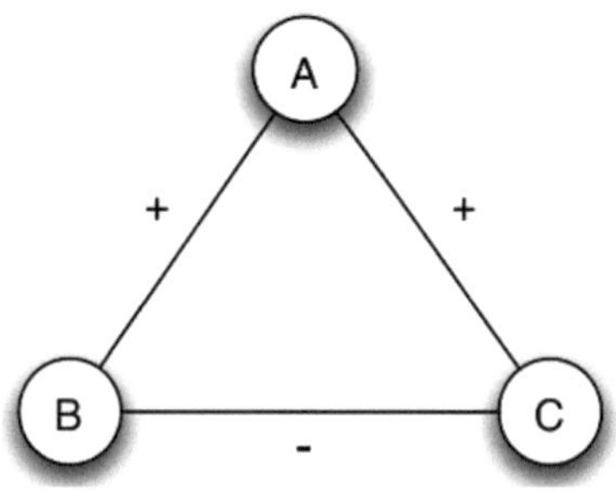


**Fig. 7.3** *A* is friends with *B* and *C*. However, *B* and *C* are enemies. Therefore the triad ($T_2$) by failing to satisfy the structural balance property is unbalanced

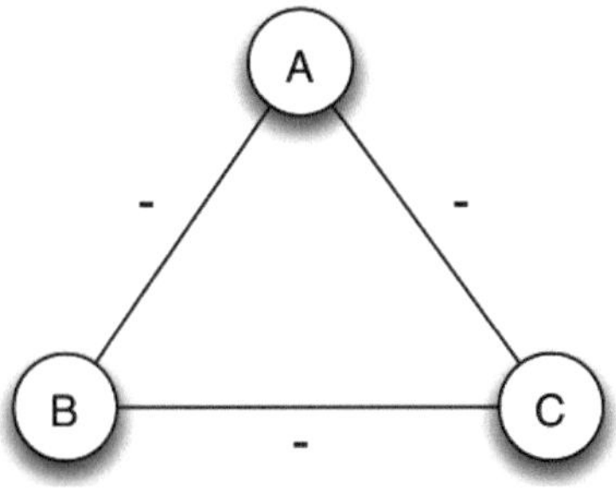


**Fig. 7.4** $A$, $B$ and $C$ are all enemies of one another. Similar to Fig. 7.3, the triad ($T_0$) is unbalanced

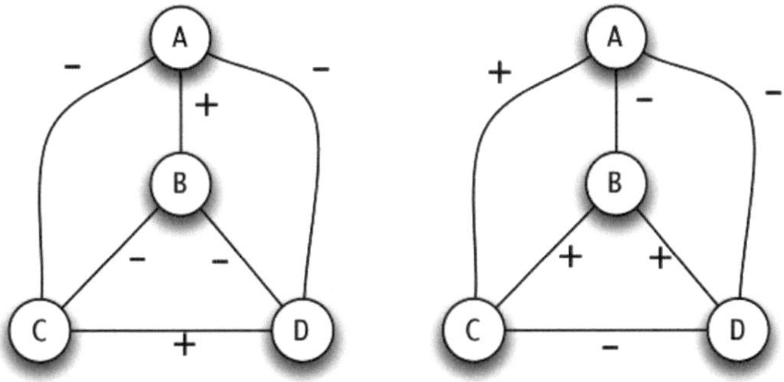


**Fig. 7.5** A balanced (left) and an unbalanced (right) graph

Figure 7.5 depicts a balanced and an unbalanced graph. The graph to the left is balanced because all of the triads $A,B,C$; $A,B,D$; $B,C,D$ and $A,C,D$ satisfy the structural balance property. However, the graph to the right is unbalanced because the triads $A,B,C$ and $B,C,D$ do not satisfy the structural balance property.

This leads to the *balance theorem* which states that if a labelled complete graph is balanced, then either all pairs of its vertices are friends (this state is referred as "paradise" [3]) , or else the nodes can be divided into two groups, $X$ and $Y$, such that every pair of vertices in $X$ are friends of each other, every pair of vertices in $Y$ are friends of each other, and everyone in $X$ is the enemy of everyone in $Y$ (this state is called "bipolar" [3]). Reference [6] reformulated this theorem to include multiple groups $X$, $Y$, ..., $Z$, such that every pair of vertices in $X$, $Y$ or $Z$ are friends of each other, and everyone in different groups are enemies of one another.

Reference [6] also made an argument that a triad where all edges bear a negative sign is inherently balanced, therefore giving a *weak structural balance property*. This property says that there is no triad such that the edges among them consist of exactly two positive edges and one negative edge.

Reference [11] found a closed-form expression for faction membership as a function of initial conditions which implies that the initial amount of friendliness in large

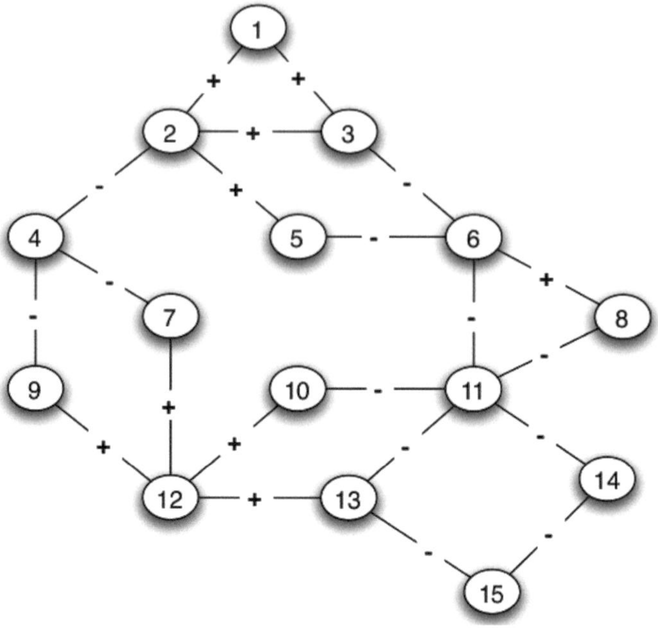


**Fig. 7.6** A signed graph

social networks (started from random initial conditions) determines whether they will end up as a paradise or a pair of bipolar sets.

Although identifying whether or not a graph is balanced merely involves determining whether or not all of its triads satisfy the structural balance property, this is a rather convoluted approach. A simpler approach is as follows: Consider the signed graph shown in Fig. 7.6. To determine whether or not this graph is balanced, we follow the procedure given below:

1. Identify the *supernodes*. Supernodes are defined as the connected components where each pair of adjacent vertices have a positive edge. If the entire graph forms one supernode, then the graph is balanced. If there is a vertex that cannot be part of any supernode, then this vertex is a supernode in itself. Figure 7.7 depicts the supernodes of Fig. 7.6. Here, we see that the vertices 4, 11, 14 and 15 are supernodes by themselves.
2. Now beginning at a supernode we assign each of the supernodes to groups $X$ or $Y$ alternatively. If every adjacent connected pair of supernodes can be placed in different groups, then the graph is said to be balanced. If such a placement is not possible, then the graph is unbalanced. Figure 7.6 is unbalanced because, if we consider a simplified graph of the supernodes (Fig. 7.8), then there are two ways to bipartition these vertices starting from the vertex $A$: either $A$, $C$, $G$ and $E$ are assigned to $X$ with $B$, $D$ and $F$ assigned to $Y$ or $A$, $F$, $D$ and $B$ are assigned to $X$ with $E$, $G$ and $C$ assigned to $Y$. In the first case, $A$ and $E$ are placed in the same

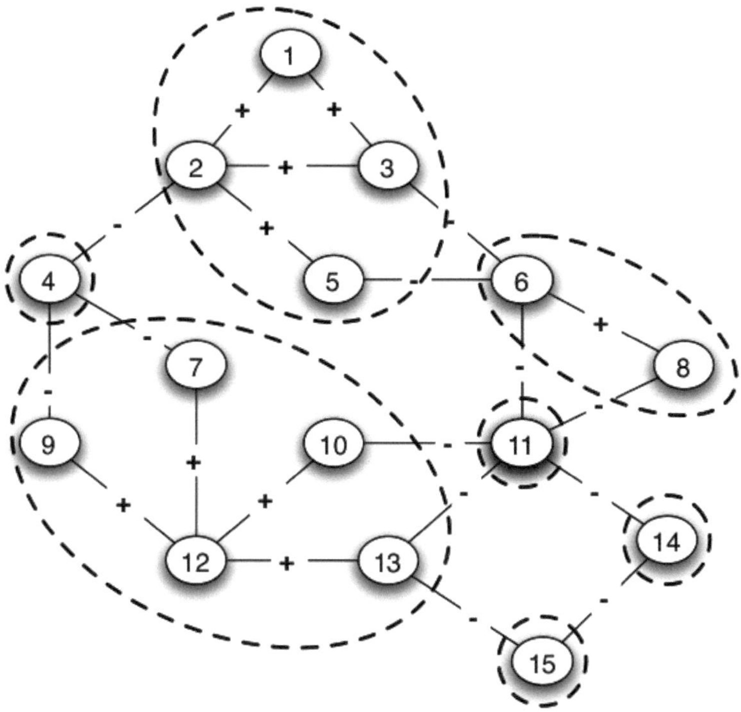


**Fig. 7.7** Supernodes of the graph in Fig. 7.6

**Fig. 7.8** A simplified labelling of the supernodes for the graph in Fig. 7.6

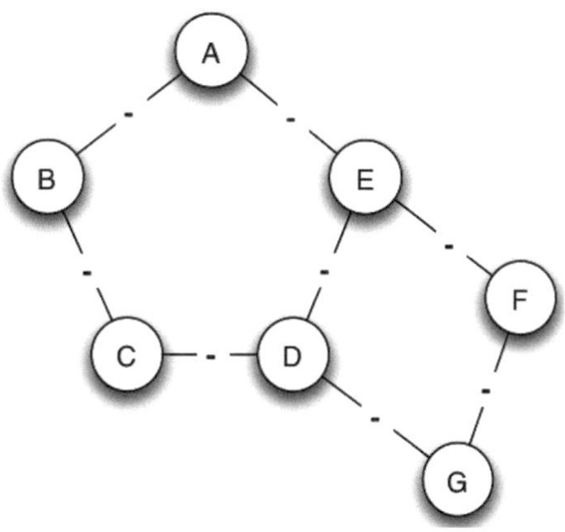


group while in the next case, $A$ and $B$ are assigned to the same group. Since this is the case no matter which of the vertices we start from, this graph is unbalanced.

This procedure however shows that the condition for a graph to be balanced is very strict. Such a strict condition almost never applies in real case scenarios.

Alternatively, we come up with an *approximate balanced graph* condition. According to this condition, let $\epsilon$ be any number such that $0 \leq \epsilon < \frac{1}{8}$, and define $\delta = (\epsilon)^{\frac{1}{3}}$. If atleast $1 - \epsilon$ of all triangles in a labelled completed graph are balanced, then either

1. there is a set consisting of atleast $1 - \delta$ of the vertices in which atleast $1 - \delta$ of all the pairs are friends, or else
2. the vertices can be divided into two groups, $X$ and $Y$, such that
   a. atleast $1 - \delta$ of the pairs in $X$ are friends of one another
   b. atleast $1 - \delta$ of the pairs in $Y$ are friends of one another, and
   c. atleast $1-\delta$ of the pairs with one end in $X$ and the other end in $Y$ are enemies.

## 7.2 Theory of Status

The theory of status for signed link formation is based on an implicit ordering of the vertices, in which a positive $s(u, v)$ indicates that $u$ considers $v$ to have higher status, while a negative $s(u, v)$ indicates that $u$ considers $v$ to have lower status.

## 7.3 Conflict Between the Theory of Balance and Status

Consider the situation where $A$ has a positive edge to $B$ and $B$ has a positive edge to $C$. If $C$ forms an edge to $A$, what should be the sign of this edge? The theory of balance would suggest a positive sign to satisfy the structural balance, while the theory of status would say that since $A$ regards $B$ as having a higher status and $B$ regards $C$ as having a higher status, $C$ should regard $A$ as having lower status and thus assign a negative sign to the link. Therefore, the theory of balance and status are at odds with one another.

One must keep in mind that the balance theory disregards the direction of the edges in the graph, while the status theory considers the edge's direction while making predictions.

In an attempt to investigate this conflict [10] studied three signed social network datasets: the trust networks of the Epinions website, where users can indicate their trust or distrust of reviews; the Slashdot blog, where users can like or dislike comments; and the Wikipedia adminship voting network where users can vote for or against the promotion of another. The statistics of the dataset is as shown in Table 7.1.

Table 7.2 tabulates the number of all the balanced and unbalanced triads in each of these datasets. Let $p$ denote the fraction of positive edges in the network, $T_i$ denote the type of the triad, $|T_i|$ denote the number of $T_i$, and $p(T_i)$ denote the fraction of triads $T_i$, computed as $p(T_i) = T_i/\Delta$ where $\Delta$ denotes the total number of triads. Now, we shuffle the signs of all the edges in the graph (keeping the fraction $p$ of positive edges the same), and we let $p_0(T_i)$ denote the expected fraction of triads that are of type $T_i$ after this shuffling.

**Table 7.1** Dataset statistics

| | Epinions | Slashdot | Wikipedia |
|---|---|---|---|
| Nodes | 119, 217 | 82, 144 | 7, 118 |
| Edges | 841, 200 | 549, 202 | 103, 747 |
| + edges | 85.0% | 77.4% | 78.7% |
| − edges | 15.0% | 22.6% | 21.2% |
| Triads | 13, 375, 407 | 1, 508, 105 | 790, 532 |

**Table 7.2** Dataset statistics

| $T_i$ | $\|T_i\|$ | $p(T_i)$ | $p_0(T_i)$ | $s(T_i)$ |
|---|---|---|---|---|
| | | Epinions | | |
| $T_3$+++ | 11, 640, 257 | 0.870 | 0.621 | 1881.1 |
| $T_1$+−− | 947, 855 | 0.071 | 0.055 | 249.4 |
| $T_2$++− | 698, 023 | 0.052 | 0.321 | −2104.8 |
| $T_0$−−− | 89, 272 | 0.007 | 0.003 | 227.5 |
| | | Slashdot | | |
| $T_3$+++ | 1, 266, 646 | 0.840 | 0.464 | 926.5 |
| $T_1$+−− | 109, 303 | 0.072 | 0.119 | −175.2 |
| $T_2$++− | 115, 884 | 0.077 | 0.406 | −823.5 |
| $T_0$−−− | 16, 272 | 0.011 | 0.012 | −8.7 |
| | | Wikipedia | | |
| $T_3$+++ | 555, 300 | 0.702 | 0.489 | 379.6 |
| $T_1$+−− | 163, 328 | 0.207 | 0.106 | 289.1 |
| $T_2$++− | 63, 425 | 0.080 | 0.395 | −572.6 |
| $T_0$−−− | 8, 479 | 0.011 | 0.010 | 10.8 |

If $p(T_i) > p_0(T_i)$, then triads of type $T_i$ are over-represented in the data relative to chance; if $p(T_i) < p_0(T_i)$, then they are under-represented. To measure how significant this over- or under-representation is, we define the *surprise* $s(T_i)$ to be the number of standard deviations by which the actual quantity of type-$T_i$ triads differs from the expected number under the random-shuffling model. This surprise is formally computed as given in Eq. 7.1

$$s(T_i) = (T_i - E[T_i])/\sqrt{\Delta p_0(T_i)(1 - p_0(T_i))} \tag{7.1}$$

where $E[T_i]$ is the expected number of triads $T_i$ computed as $E[T_i] = p_0(T_i)\Delta$.

Table 7.2 shows that $T_3$ is heavily over-represented (40% in all three datasets) and $T_2$ is heavily under-represented (75% in Epinions and Slashdot, 50% in Wikipedia).

The overall fraction of positive signs that a user creates, considering all her links, is referred to as her *generative baseline* and the overall fraction of positive signs in the links a user receives as her *receptive baseline*.

There is the question of *joint positive endorsement*—if a node $X$ links positively to each of the two nodes $A$ and $B$, and $A$ now forms a link to $B$, should there be an expected elevation in the probability of the link being positive, or a reduced probability of the link being positive? Balance theory would predict a positive link because $A$ and $B$ are both friends of $X$, they must be friends of one another. Status theory, on the other hand, would make two contradictory predictions. From the viewpoint of $B$, since she has received a positive evaluation from $X$, she is more likely than not to have above-average status. Therefore, $A$ should more likely have a positive link to $B$. However, from the perspective of $A$, since she has also been positively evaluated by $X$, she is more likely than not to have above-average status. Therefore, $A$ is less likely to have a positive link to $B$. In other words, status theory predicts that the evaluation will lie between $A$'s generative baseline and $B$'s receptive baseline.

To deal with these contrasting predictions, a *contextualized link* (c-link) is defined. The c-link is a triple $(A,B;X)$ which evaluates the sign of a link between $A$ and $B$ after each of $A$ and $B$ already has a link either to or from $X$. This gives 16 distinct possible combinations depending on the direction and sign of the link between $A$ and $X$, and $B$ and $X$. These 16 c-links labelled $t_1$ to $t_{16}$ are as shown in Fig. 7.9.

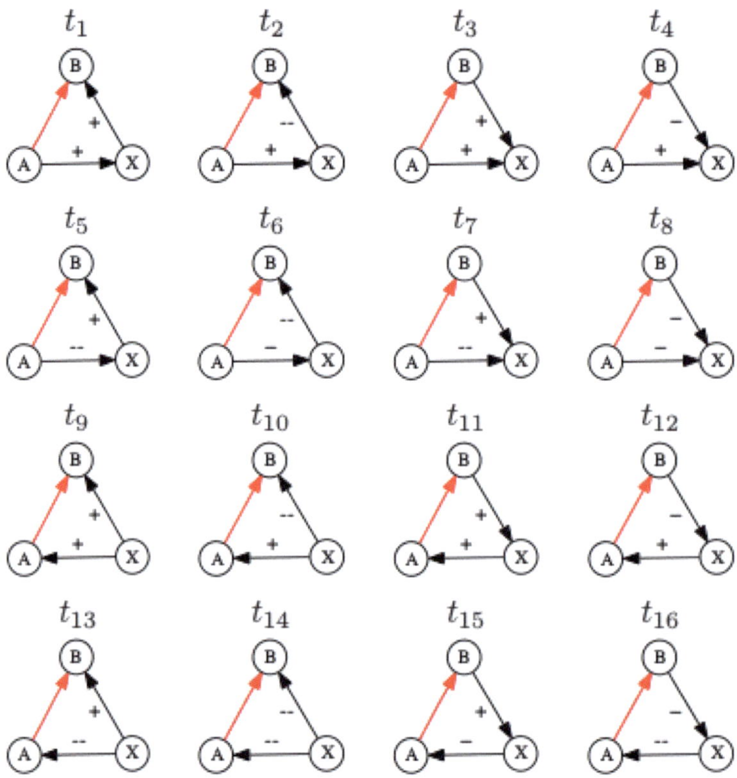

Fig. 7.9 All contexts $(A,B;X)$ where the red edge closes the triad

Consider a particular type $t$ of c-link and suppose $(A_1,B_1;X_1)$, $(A_2,B_2;X_2)$, ..., $(A_k,B_k;X_k)$ are all instances of this type $t$ of c-link in the data. The generative baseline for this type $t$ is defined as the sum of the generative baselines of all vertices $A_i$. This gives the *generative surprise*, $s_g(t)$ for this type $t$ to be the number of standard deviations by which the actual number of $A_i - B_i$ edges in the data differs above or below this generative baseline. On similar lines, the definitions for the receptive baseline and the *receptive surprise*, $s_r(t)$.

To quantify the statuses of each of the users in a c-link, we start with $X$ having a status value of 0. If $X$ links positively to $A$, or $A$ links negatively to $X$, then $A$ gets a status value of 1, otherwise, $A$ is assigned a status of $-1$. The same applies to $B$. The generative surprise for type $t$ is said to be *consistent with status* if $B$'s status has the same sign as the generative surprise: in this case, high-status recipients $B$ receive more positive evaluations than would be expected from the generative baseline of the user $A$ producing the link. Similarly, the receptive surprise for type $t$ is consistent with status if $A$'s status has the opposite sign from the receptive surprise: high-status generators of links $A$ produce fewer positive evaluations than would be expected from the receptive baseline of the user $B$ receiving the link.

Similarly, balance is said to consistent with generative surprise for a particular c-link type if the sign of the generative surprise is equal to the sign of the edge as predicted by balance. Analogously, balance is consistent with receptive surprise for a particular c-link type if the sign of the receptive surprise is equal to the sign of the edge as predicted by balance.

Figure 7.10 shows that the prediction of status with respect to both the generative and receptive surprise perform much better against the data that the predictions of structural balance. This gives us some interesting insights. First, we observe that one of the two c-link types where status is inconsistent with generative surprise is the $t_3$ configuration. This suggests that when such conditions arise, users of the systems may be relying on balance-based reasoning more than status-based reasoning. In addition, it shows that balance theory is a reasonable approximation to the structure of signed networks when they are viewed as undirected graphs, while status theory better captures many of the properties when the networks are viewed in more detail as directed graphs that grow over time.

To understand the boundary between the balance and status theories and where they apply, it is interesting to consider a particular subset of these networks where the directed edges are used to create reciprocating relationships. Figure 7.11 shows that users treat each other differently in the context of reciprocating interactions than when they are using links to refer to others who do not link back.

To consider how reciprocation between $A$ and $B$ is affected by the context of $A$ and $B$'s relationships to third nodes $X$, suppose that an $A$-$B$ link is part of a directed triad in which each of $A$ and $B$ has a link to or from a node $X$. Now, $B$ reciprocates the link to $A$. As indicated in Fig. 7.12, we find that the $B$-$A$ link is significantly more likely to have the same sign as the $A$-$B$ link when the original triad on $A$-$B$-$X$ (viewed as an undirected triad) is structurally balanced. In other words, when the initial $A$-$B$-$X$ triad is unbalanced, there is more of a latent tendency for $B$ to "reverse the sign" when she links back to $A$.

| $t_i$ | count | $P(+)$ | $s_g$ | $s_r$ | $B_g$ | $B_r$ | $S_g$ | $S_r$ |
|---|---|---|---|---|---|---|---|---|
| $t_1$ | 178,051 | 0.97 | 95.9 | 197.8 | ✓ | ✓ | ✓ | ✓ |
| $t_2$ | 45,797 | 0.54 | -151.3 | -229.9 | ✓ | ✓ | ✓ | ∘ |
| $t_3$ | 246,371 | 0.94 | 89.9 | 195.9 | ✓ | ✓ | ∘ | ✓ |
| $t_4$ | 25,384 | 0.89 | 1.8 | 44.9 | ∘ | ∘ | ✓ | ✓ |
| $t_5$ | 45,925 | 0.30 | 18.1 | -333.7 | ∘ | ✓ | ✓ | ✓ |
| $t_6$ | 11,215 | 0.23 | -15.5 | -193.6 | ∘ | ∘ | ✓ | ✓ |
| $t_7$ | 36,184 | 0.14 | -53.1 | -357.3 | ✓ | ✓ | ✓ | ✓ |
| $t_8$ | 61,519 | 0.63 | 124.1 | -225.6 | ✓ | ∘ | ✓ | ✓ |
| $t_9$ | 338,238 | 0.82 | 207.0 | -239.5 | ✓ | ∘ | ✓ | ✓ |
| $t_{10}$ | 27,089 | 0.20 | -110.7 | -449.6 | ✓ | ✓ | ✓ | ✓ |
| $t_{11}$ | 35,093 | 0.53 | -7.4 | -260.1 | ∘ | ∘ | ✓ | ✓ |
| $t_{12}$ | 20,933 | 0.71 | 17.2 | -113.4 | ∘ | ✓ | ✓ | ✓ |
| $t_{13}$ | 14,305 | 0.79 | 23.5 | 24.0 | ∘ | ∘ | ✓ | ✓ |
| $t_{14}$ | 30,235 | 0.69 | -12.8 | -53.6 | ∘ | ∘ | ✓ | ∘ |
| $t_{15}$ | 17,189 | 0.76 | 6.4 | 24.0 | ∘ | ∘ | ∘ | ✓ |
| $t_{16}$ | 4,133 | 0.77 | 11.9 | -2.6 | ✓ | ∘ | ✓ | ∘ |
| | | | Number of correct predictions | | 8 | 7 | 14 | 13 |

**Fig. 7.10** Surprise values and predictions based on the competing theories of structural balance and status

| Epinions | Count | Probability |
|---|---|---|
| $P(+\|+)$ | 38,415 | 0.969 |
| $P(-\|+)$ | 1,204 | 0.031 |
| $P(+\|-)$ | 1,192 | 0.692 |
| $P(-\|-)$ | 560 | 0.308 |
| **Wikipedia** | Count | Fraction |
| $P(+\|+)$ | 2,509 | 0.945 |
| $P(-\|+)$ | 145 | 0.055 |
| $P(+\|-)$ | 193 | 0.706 |
| $P(-\|-)$ | 80 | 0.294 |

**Fig. 7.11** Given that the first edge was of sign $X$, $P(Y \mid X)$ gives the probability that reciprocated edge is of sign $Y$

## Transition of an Unbalanced Network to a Balanced One

A large signed network whose signs were randomly assigned was almost surely unbalanced. This currently unbalanced network had to evolve to a more balanced state with nodes changing their signs accordingly. Reference [3] studied how a unbalanced network transitions to a balanced one and focused on any human tendencies being exhibited.

They considered *local triad dynamics* (LTD) wherein every update step chooses a triad at random. If this triad is balanced, $T_1$ or $T_3$, no evolution occurs. If the triad is unbalanced, $T_0$ or $T_2$, the sign of one of the links is changed as follows:

| **Epinions** | Triads | $P$(RSS) | $P(+\|+)$ | $P(-\|-)$ |
|---|---|---|---|---|
| Balanced | 348,538 | 0.929 | 0.941 | 0.688 |
| Unbalanced | 74,860 | 0.788 | 0.834 | 0.676 |
| **Wikipedia** | Triads | $P$(RSS) | $P(+\|+)$ | $P(-\|-)$ |
| Balanced | 53,973 | 0.912 | 0.934 | 0.336 |
| Unbalanced | 13,542 | 0.661 | 0.878 | 0.195 |

**Fig. 7.12** Edge reciprocation in balanced and unbalanced triads. *Triads*: number of balanced/unbalanced triads in the network where one of the edges was reciprocated. $P(RSS)$: probability that the reciprocated edge is of the same sign. $P(+ \mid +)$: probability that the positive edge is later reciprocated with a plus. $P(- \mid -)$: probability that the negative edge is reciprocated with a minus

$T_2 \rightarrow T_3$ occurs with probability $p$, $T_2 \rightarrow T_1$ occurs with probability $1 - p$, while $T_0 \rightarrow T_1$ occurs with probability 1. After an update step, the unbalanced triad becomes balanced but this could cause a balanced triad that shares a link with this target to become unbalanced. These could subsequently evolve to balance, leading to new unbalanced triads.

They show that for $p < \frac{1}{2}$, LTD quickly drives an infinite network to a quasi-stationary dynamic state. As $p$ passes through a critical value of $\frac{1}{2}$, the network undergoes a phase transition to a paradise state. On the other hand, a finite network always reaches a balanced state. For $p < \frac{1}{2}$, this balanced state is bipolar and the time to reach this state scales faster than exponentially with network size. For $p \geq \frac{1}{2}$, the final state is paradise. The time to reach this state scales algebraically with $N$ when $p = \frac{1}{2}$, and logarithmically in $N$ for $p > \frac{1}{2}$.

They also investigated *constrained triad dynamics* (CTD). A random link was selected, and the sign of this link was changed if the total number of unbalanced triads decreases. If the total number of unbalanced triads is conserved in an update, then the update occurs with probability $\frac{1}{2}$. Updates that would increase the total number of unbalanced triads are not allowed. On average each link is changed once in a unit of time. A crucial outcome of this is that a network is quickly driven to a balanced state in a time that scales as $lnN$ .

What is most important with user evaluations is to determine what are the factors that drive one's evaluations and how a composite description that accurately reflects the aggregate opinion of the community can be created. The following are some of the studies that focus on addressing this problem.

Reference [12] designed and analysed a large-scale randomized experiment on a social news aggregation Web site to investigate whether knowledge of such aggregates distorts decision-making . Prior ratings were found to create significant bias in individual rating behaviour, and positive and negative social influences were found to create asymmetric herding effects. Whereas negative social influence inspired users to correct manipulated ratings, positive social influence increased the likelihood of positive ratings by 32% and created accumulating positive herding that increased final ratings by 25% on average. This positive herding was topic-dependent and affected by whether individuals were viewing the opinions of friends or enemies. A mixture of changing opinion and greater turnout under both manipulations together with a natural tendency to up-vote on the site combined to create the herding effects.

Reference [13] studied factors in how users give ratings in different contexts, i.e, whether they are given anonymously or under one's own name and whether they are displayed publicly or held confidentially. They investigated on three datasets, Amazon.com reviews, Epinions ratings, and CouchSurfing.com trust and friendship networks, which were found to represent a variety of design choices in how ratings are collected and shared. The findings indicate that ratings should not be taken at face value, but rather that one should examine the context in which they were given. Public, identified ratings tend to be disproportionately positive, but only when the ratee is another user who can reciprocate.

Reference [1] studied *YahooAnswers* (YA) which is a large and diverse question answer community, acting not only as a medium for knowledge sharing, but as a place to seek advice, gather opinions, and satisfy one's curiosity about things which may not have a single best answer. The fact about YA that sets it apart from others is that participants believe that anything from the sordid intricacies of celebrities' lives to conspiracy theories is considered knowledge, worthy of being exchanged. Taking advantage of the range of user behaviour in YA, several aspects of question-answer dynamics were investigated. First, content properties and social network interactions across different YA categories (or topics) were contrasted. It was found that the categories could be clustered according to thread length and overlap between the set of users who asked and those who replied. While, discussion topics or topics that did not focus on factual answers tended to have longer threads, broader distributions of activity levels, and their users tended to participate by both posing and replying to questions, YA categories favouring factual questions had shorter thread lengths on average and users typically did not occupy both a helper and asker role in the same forum. It was found that the ego-networks easily revealed YA categories where discussion threads, even in this constrained question-answer format, tended to dominate. While many users are quite broad, answering questions in many different categories, this was of a mild detriment for specialized, technical categories. In those categories, users who focused the most (had a lower entropy and a higher proportion of answers just in that category) tended to have their answers selected as best more often. Finally, they attempted to predict best answers based on attributes of the question and the replier. They found that just the very basic metric of reply length, along with the number of competing answers, and the track record of the user, was most predictive of whether the answer would be selected. The number of other best answers by a user, a potential indicator of expertise, was predictive of an answer being selected as best, but most significantly so for the technically focused categories.

Reference [8] explored *CouchSurfing*, an application which enables users to either allow other users to sleep in their couch or sleep on someone else's couch. Due to security and privacy concerns, this application heavily depends on reciprocity and trust among these users. By studing the surfing activities, social networks and vouch networks, they found the following: First, CouchSurfing is a community rife with generalized reciprocity, i.e, active participants take on the role of both hosts and surfers, in roughly equal proportion. About a third of those who hosted or surfed are in the giant strongly connected component, such that one couch can be reached from any other by following previous surfs. Second, the high degree of activity and reciprocity is enabled by a reputation system wherein users vouch for one another. They found that connections that are vouched, or declared trustworthy can best be predicted based on the direct interaction between the two individuals: their friendship degree, followed by the overall experience from surfing or hosting with the other person, and also how the two friends met. However, global measures that aim to propagate trust, such as PageRank, are found to be poor predictors of whether an edge is vouched. Although such metrics may be useful in assigning overall reputation scores to individuals, they are too diffuse to predict specifically whether one individual will vouch for another. Finally, the analysis revealed a high rate of vouching: about a quarter of all edges that can be vouched are, as are a majority of highly active users. While this could be reflection of a healthy web of trust, there are indications that vouches may be given too freely. The main reason behind this high rate of vouching may be its public nature. It can be awkward for friends to not give or reciprocate a vouch, even if privately they have reservations about the trustworthiness of the other person.

## 7.4 Trust in a Network

Reference [7] proposed and analysed algorithms to develop a web of trust that would allow users to express trust of other users, and in return would apply the entire web of relationships and trusts to help a user assess the likely quality of information before acting on it. Through such a web of trust, a user can develop an opinion of another user without prior interaction.

The first issue was that webs of trust tend to be relatively "sparse": every user has expressed trust values for only a handful of other users. The problem is to determine trust values for the remaining user pairs using only those which are explicitly specified.

Assume a universe of $n$ users, each of whom may optionally express some level of trust and distrust for any other user. These entries will be partitioned into two matrices, let $T$ be the matrix of trusts; $t_{ij}$ is the trust that user $i$ holds for user $j$. Similarly, let $D$ be the matrix of distrusts. Both $t_{ij}$ and $d_{ij}$ lie between 0 and 1. From these matrices the intent is to predict an unknown trust/distrust value between any two users, using the entries available in the trust and distrust matrices. Now, let matrix $B$ represent a set of beliefs that we initially hold about the world, i.e, $B_{ij}$ might be $i$'s trust of $j$, $i$'s distrust of $j$, or any of the possible combinations.

### 7.4.1 Atomic Propagations

The atomic propagations are a "basis set" of techniques by which the system may infer that one user should trust or distrust another. The set is constructed so that any inference regarding trust should be expressible as a combination of elements of this set. The basis set is as follows:

1. *Direct propagation*: If $B_{ij} = 1$, i.e, $i$ trusts $j$ and $B_{jk} = 1$, i.e, $j$ trusts $k$, then we could conclude that $B_{ik} = 1$, i.e, $i$ trusts $k$. This operation is referred to as direct propagation since the trust propagated directly along an edge. Such direct propagations are represented as a matrix $M$ such that all conclusions expressible by these direct propagation can be read from the matrix $B \cdot M$. The appropriate matrix $M$ to encode direct propagation is simply $B$ itself: in this case $B \cdot M = B^2$, which is the matrix of all length-2 paths in the initial belief graph. Thus, $B$ itself is the operator matrix that encodes the direct propagation basis element.
2. *Co-citation*: If $B_{i_1 j_1} = 1$, $B_{i_1 j_2} = 1$ and $B_{i_2 j_2} = 1$, i.e, $i_1$ trusts $j_1$ and $j_2$, and $i_2$ trusts $j_2$, then we conclude that $i_2$ should also trust $j_1$. Here, $B \cdot M = BB^T B$ will capture all beliefs that are inferable through a single co-citation. The sequence $B^T B$ can be viewed as a backward-forward step propagating $i_2$'s trust of $j_2$ backward to $i_1$, then forward to $j_1$. Therefore, the operator $M$ for this atomic propagation is $B^T B$.
3. *Transpose trust*: Here $i$'s trust of $j$ causes $j$ to develop some level of trust towards $i$. In this case, $M = B^T$.
4. *Trust coupling*: When both $i$ and $j$ trust $k$, this implies that $i$ trusts $j$. This makes $M = BB^T$.

If $\alpha = (\alpha_1, \alpha_2, \alpha_3, \alpha_4)$ is a vector representing weights for combining these four atomic propagation schemes. Then all these atomic propagations can be captured into a single combined matrix $C_{B,\alpha}$ based on a belief matrix $B$ and a weight vector $\alpha$ as follows:

$$C_{B,\alpha} = \alpha_1 B + \alpha_2 B^T B + \alpha_3 B^T + \alpha_4 BB^T$$

$C_{B,\alpha}$ is a matrix whose $ij$th entry describes how beliefs should flow from $i$ to $j$ via an atomic propagation step; if the entry is 0, then nothing can be concluded in an atomic step about $i$'s views on $j$.

### 7.4.2 Propagation of Distrust

Let $k \in \mathbb{Z}^+$, and $P^{(k)}$ be a matrix whose $ij$th entry represents the propagation from $i$ to $j$ after $k$ atomic propagations. The following are three models defined on $B$ and $P(k)$ for the propagation of trust and distrust, given initial trust and distrust matrices $T$ and $D$ respectively:

1. *Trust only*: By completely disregarding distrust scores and propagating only the trust scores, we get: $B = T$ and $P^{(k)} = C^{(k)}_{B,\alpha}$.
2. *One-step distrust*: When a user distrusts someone, they discount all their judgements. Therefore, distrust propagates only one step, giving us: $B = T$ and $P^{(k)} = C_{B,\alpha} \cdot (T - D)$.
3. *Propagated distrust*: When trust and distrust both propagate together, we get: $B = T - D$ and $P^{(k)} = C^{(k)}_{B,\alpha}$.

### 7.4.3 Iterative Propagation

The end goal is to produce a final matrix $F$ that has the trust or distrust between any pair of users in this universe. There are two approaches to computing $F$ from the sequence of propagations:

1. *Eigenvalue propagation*(EIG): If $K \in \mathbb{Z}$, then $F = P^{(K)}$.
2. *Weighted linear combinations*(WLC): If $\gamma$ is a discount factor that is smaller than the largest eigenvalue of $C_{B,\alpha}$ and $K \in \mathbb{Z}$, then $F = \sum_{k=1}^{K} \gamma^k \cdot P^{(k)}$.

### 7.4.4 Rounding

The next problem encountered was that of converting a continuous value into a discrete one ($\pm 1$). There were the following three ways of accomplishing this rounding:

1. *Global rounding*: This rounding tries to align the ratio of trust to distrust values in $F$ to that in the input $M$. In the row vector $F_i$, $i$ trusts $j$ if and only if $F_{ij}$ is within the top $\tau$ fraction of entries of the vector $F_i$. This threshold $\tau$ is chosen based on the overall relative fractions of trust and distrust in the input.
2. *Local rounding*: Here, we account for the trust/distrust behavior of $i$. The conditions for $F_{ij}$ and $\tau$ are same as the previous definition.
3. *Majority rounding*: This rounding intends to capture the local structure of the original trust and distrust matrix. Consider the set $J$ of users on whom $i$ has expressed either trust or distrust. If $J$ is a set of labelled examples using which we are to predict the label of a user $j$, $j \notin J$. We order $J$ along with $j$ according to the entries $F_{ij'}$ where $j' \in J \cup \{j\}$. At the end of this, we have an ordered sequence of trust and distrust labels with the unknown label for $j$ embedded in the sequence at a unique location. From this, we predict the label of $j$ to be that of the majority of the labels in the smallest local neighbourhood surrounding it where the majority is well-defined.

## Epinions

For this study, the Epinions web of trust was constructed as a directed graph consisting of 131, 829 nodes and 841, 372 edges, each labelled either trust or distrust. Of these labelled edges, 85.29% were labelled trust; we interpret trustto be the real value +1.0 and distrust to be −1.0.

The combinations of atomic propagations, distrust propagations, iterative propagations and rounding methods gave 81 experimental schemes. To determine whether any particular algorithm can correctly induce the trust or distrust that $i$ holds for $j$, a single trial edge $(i, j)$ is masked from the truth graph, and then each of the 81 schemes is asked to guess whether $i$ trusts $j$. This trial was performed on 3, 250 randomly masked edges for each of the 81 schemes, resulting in 263, 000 total trust computations, and depicted in Fig. 7.13. In this table, $\epsilon$ denotes the prediction error of an algorithm and a given rounding method, i.e., $\epsilon$ is the fraction of incorrect predictions made by the algorithm.

The trust edges in the graph outnumber the distrust edges by a huge margin: 85 versus 15. Hence, a naive algorithm that always predicts "trust" will incur a prediction error of only 15%. Nevertheless, the results are first reported for prediction on

| Iteration | $\alpha$ | Propagation | Global round. | | Local round. | | Maj. round. | |
|---|---|---|---|---|---|---|---|---|
| | | | $\epsilon$ | $\epsilon_S$ | $\epsilon$ | $\epsilon_S$ | $\epsilon$ | $\epsilon_S$ |
| EIG | $e_1$ | Trust only | 0.153 | 0.500 | 0.123 | 0.399 | 0.077 | 0.175 |
| | | One-step distrust | 0.119 | 0.251 | 0.108 | 0.223 | 0.067 | 0.162 |
| | | Prop. distrust | 0.365 | 0.452 | 0.368 | 0.430 | 0.084 | 0.206 |
| | $e_2$ | Trust only | 0.153 | 0.500 | 0.114 | 0.365 | 0.080 | 0.190 |
| | | One-step distrust | 0.097 | 0.259 | 0.087 | 0.234 | 0.066 | 0.159 |
| | | Prop. distrust | 0.149 | 0.380 | 0.121 | 0.279 | 0.080 | 0.187 |
| | $e^*$ | Trust only | 0.153 | 0.500 | 0.107 | 0.336 | 0.077 | 0.180 |
| | | One-step distrust | 0.096 | 0.253 | 0.086 | 0.220 | 0.064 | 0.147 |
| | | Prop. distrust | 0.110 | 0.284 | 0.101 | 0.238 | 0.079 | 0.180 |
| WLC, $\gamma = 0.5$ | $e_1$ | Trust only | 0.153 | 0.500 | 0.123 | 0.390 | 0.189 | 0.163 |
| | | One-step distrust | 0.093 | 0.231 | 0.083 | 0.205 | 0.098 | 0.205 |
| | | Prop. distrust | 0.102 | 0.221 | 0.098 | 0.199 | 0.121 | 0.295 |
| | $e_2$ | Trust only | 0.153 | 0.500 | 0.113 | 0.354 | 0.074 | 0.174 |
| | | One-step distrust | 0.088 | 0.254 | 0.080 | 0.231 | 0.093 | 0.187 |
| | | Prop. distrust | 0.126 | 0.336 | 0.100 | 0.252 | 0.076 | 0.177 |
| | $e^*$ | Trust only | 0.153 | 0.500 | 0.108 | 0.340 | 0.078 | 0.159 |
| | | One-step distrust | 0.086 | 0.247 | 0.076 | 0.217 | 0.092 | 0.190 |
| | | Prop. distrust | 0.087 | 0.237 | 0.079 | 0.203 | 0.074 | 0.162 |
| WLC, $\gamma = 0.9$ | $e_1$ | Trust only | 0.153 | 0.500 | 0.123 | 0.391 | 0.132 | 0.152 |
| | | One-step distrust | 0.102 | 0.241 | 0.092 | 0.216 | 0.069 | 0.171 |
| | | Prop. distrust | 0.111 | 0.238 | 0.106 | 0.211 | 0.101 | 0.227 |
| | $e_2$ | Trust only | 0.153 | 0.500 | 0.113 | 0.356 | 0.078 | 0.184 |
| | | One-step distrust | 0.092 | 0.260 | 0.082 | 0.235 | 0.071 | 0.173 |
| | | Prop. distrust | 0.134 | 0.355 | 0.106 | 0.261 | 0.078 | 0.188 |
| | $e^*$ | Trust only | 0.153 | 0.500 | 0.107 | 0.337 | 0.075 | 0.169 |
| | | One-step distrust | 0.091 | 0.253 | 0.082 | 0.222 | 0.072 | 0.171 |
| | | Prop. distrust | 0.091 | 0.254 | 0.081 | 0.209 | 0.078 | 0.177 |

**Fig. 7.13** Prediction of the algorithms. Here, $e^* = (0.4, 0.4, 0.1, 0.1)$, $K = 20$

randomly masked edges in the graph, as it reflects the underlying problem. However, to ensure that the algorithms are not benefiting unduly from this bias, the largest balanced subset of the 3, 250 randomly masked trial edges are taken such that half the edges are trust and the other half are distrust—this is done by taking all the 498 distrust edges in the trial set as well as the 498 randomly chosen trust edges from the trial set. Thus, the size of this subset $S$ is 996. The prediction error in $S$ is called $\epsilon_S$. The naive prediction error on $S$ would be 50%.

They found that even a small amount of information about distrust (rather than information about trust alone) can provide tangibly better judgements about how much user $i$ should trust user $j$, and that a small number of expressed trusts/distrust per individual can allow prediction of trust between any two people in the system with surprisingly high accuracy.

## 7.5 Perception of User Evaluation

Reference [5] reasoned that the evaluation of an opinion is fundamentally different from reasoning about the opinion itself: instead of say,"What did Y think of X?", look at, "What did Z think of Y's opinion of X?". For this study, they picked *Amazon.com*, one of the largest online e-commerce providers whose website includes not just product reviews contributed by users, but also evaluations of the helpfulness of these reviews. Here, each review comes with both a *star rating*—the number of stars it assigns to the product—and a *helpfulness vote*—the information that $a$ out of $b$ people found the review itself helpful.

A dataset consisting of over 4 million book reviews of roughly 675, 000 books on Amazon's US site, as well as smaller but comparably- sized corpora from Amazon's UK, Germany, and Japan sites were used. Of these reviews, more than 1 million received atleast 10 helpfulness votes each.

The following four hypothesis were considered:

1. *The conformity hypothesis*: This hypothesis holds that a review is evaluated as more helpful when its star rating is closer to the consensus star rating for the product.
2. *The individual-bias hypothesis*: According to this hypothesis, when a user considers a review, she will rate it more highly if it expresses an opinion that she agrees with. However, one might expect that if a diverse range of individuals apply this rule, then the overall helpfulness evaluation could be hard to distinguish from one based on conformity.
3. *The brilliant-but-cruel hypothesis*: This hypothesis arises from the argument that "negative reviewers are perceived as more intelligent, competent, and expert than positive reviewers."
4. *The quality-only straw-man hypothesis*: There is the possibility that helpfulness is being evaluated purely based on the textual content of the reviews, and that these non-textual factors are simply correlates of textual quality.

The *helpfulness ratio* of a review is defined to be the fraction of evaluators who found it to be helpful (in other words, it is the fraction $\frac{a}{b}$ when $a$ out of $b$ people found the review helpful). The *product average* for a review of a given product is defined to be the average star rating given by all reviews of that product. Figure 7.14 shows that the median helpfulness ratio of reviews decreases monotonically as a function of the absolute difference between their star rating and the product average. This is consistent with the conformity hypothesis: reviews in aggregate are deemed more helpful when they are close to the product average. However, to assess the brilliant-but-cruel hypothesis, we must look not at the absolute difference between a review's star rating and its product average, but at the signed difference, which is positive or negative depending on whether the star rating is above or below the average. Figure 7.15 shows that not only does the median helpfulness as a function of signed difference fall away on both sides of 0; it does so asymmetrically: slightly negative reviews are punished more strongly, with respect to helpfulness evaluation, than slightly positive reviews. This is at odds with both the brilliant-but-cruel hypothesis as well as the conformity hypothesis.

To investigate the oddity, we group products by the variance of the star ratings assigned to it by all its reviews, and perform the signed-difference analysis on sets of products having fixed levels of variance. Figure 7.16 shows that the effect of signed difference to the average changes smoothly but in a complex fashion as the variance increases. The role of variance can be summarized as follows.

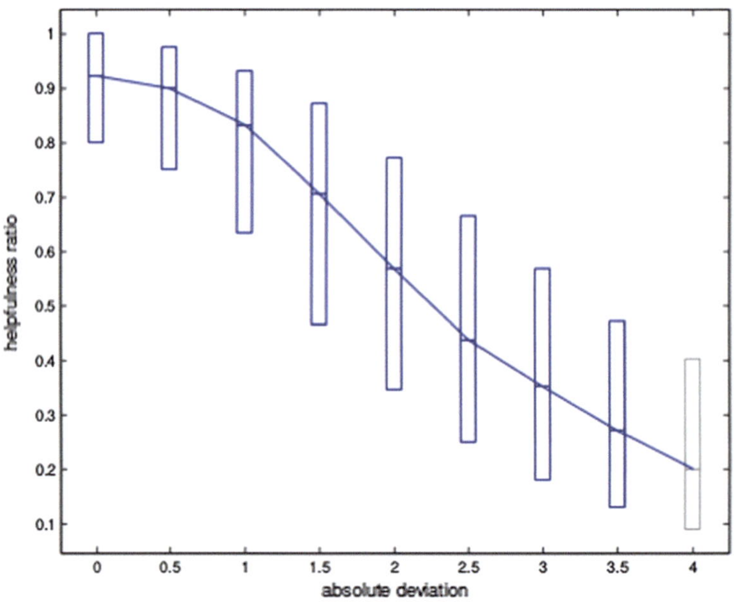


**Fig. 7.14** Helpfulness ratio declines with the absolute value of a review's deviation from the computed star average. The line segments within the bars indicate the median helpfulness ratio; the bars depict the helpfulness ratio's second and third quantiles. Grey bars indicate that the amount of data at that $x$ value represents 0.1% or less of the data depicted in the plot

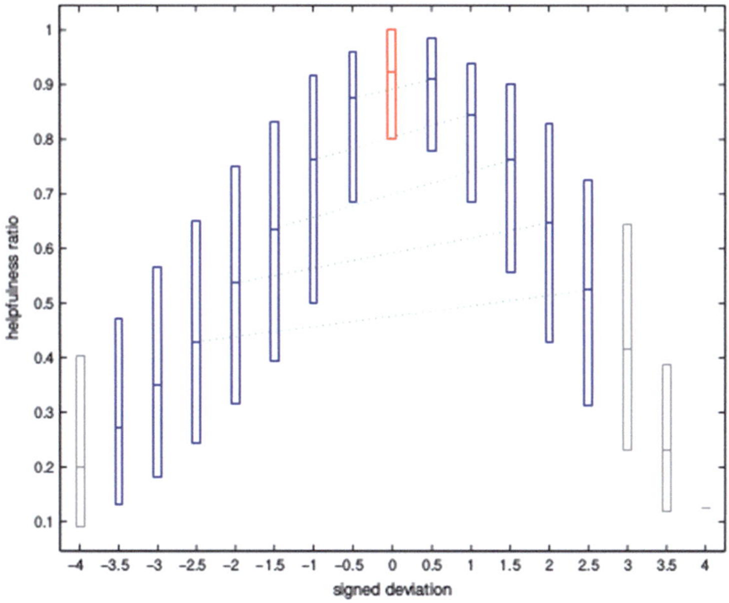


**Fig. 7.15** Helpfulness ratio as a function of a review's signed deviation

- When the variance is very low, the reviews with the highest helpfulness ratios are those with the average star rating.
- With moderate values of the variance, the reviews evaluated as most helpful are those that are slightly above the average star rating.
- As the variance becomes large, reviews with star ratings both above and below the average are evaluated as more helpful than those that have the average star rating (with the positive reviews still deemed somewhat more helpful).

This is a clear indication that variance is a key factor that any hypothesis needs to incorporate.

For a given review, let the *computed product-average star rating* be the average star rating as computed over all reviews of that product in the dataset.

To investigate straw-man quality-only hypothesis, we must review the text quality. To avoid the subjectiveness that may be involved when human evaluators are used, a machine learning algorithm is trained to automatically determine the degree of helpfulness of each review. For $i, j \in \{0, 0.5, \ldots, 3.5\}$ where $i < j, i \succ j$ when the helpfulness ratio of reviews, with absolute deviation $i$ is significantly larger than for reviews with absolute deviation $j$.

Reference [5] explains a model that can explain the observed behaviour.

We evaluate the robustness of the observed social-effects phenomena by comparing review data from three additional different national Amazon sites: Amazon.co.uk (UK), Amazon.de (Germany) and Amazon.co.jp (Japan). The Japanese data exhibits a left hump that is higher than the right one for reviews with high variance, i.e.,

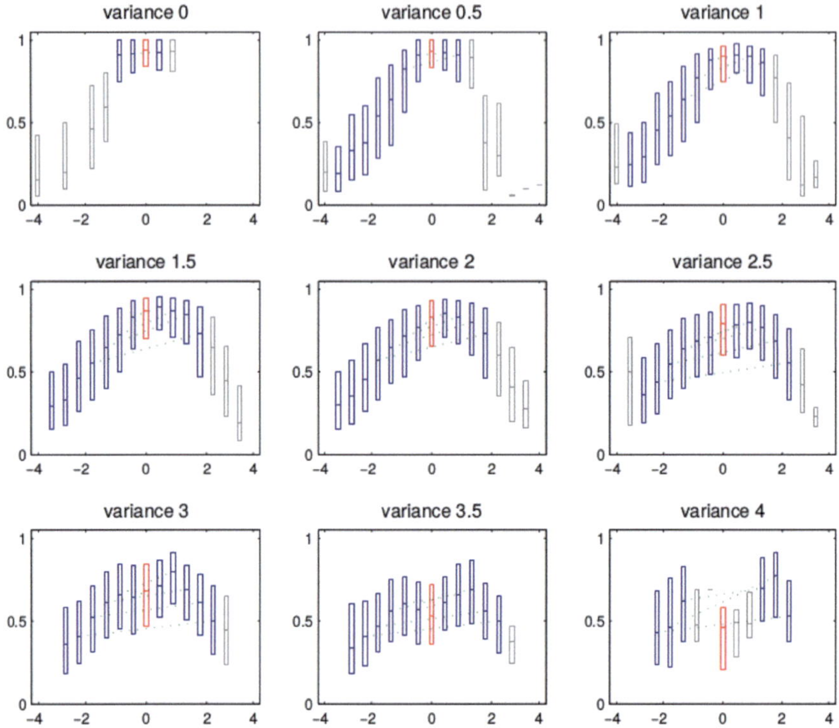


**Fig. 7.16** As the variance of the star ratings of reviews for a particular product increases, the median helpfulness ratio curve becomes two-humped and the helpfulness ratio at signed deviation 0 (indicated in red) no longer represents the unique global maximum

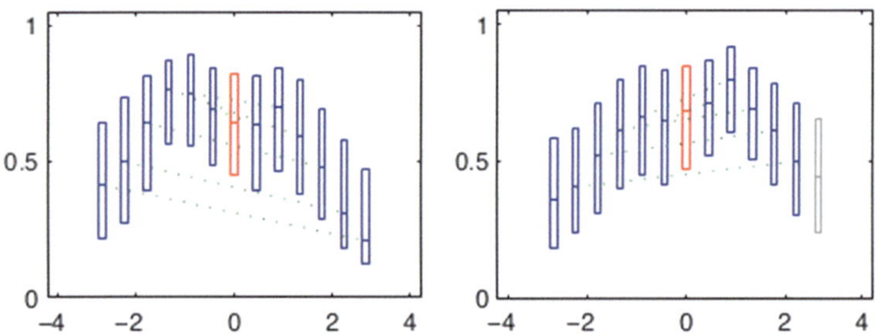

**Fig. 7.17** Signed deviations vs. helpfulness ratio for variance = 3, in the Japanese (left) and U.S. (right) data. The curve for Japan has a pronounced lean towards the left

reviews with star ratings below the mean are more favored by helpfulness evaluators than the respective reviews with positive deviations (Fig. 7.17).

They found that the perceived helpfulness of a review depends not just on its content but also in subtle ways on how the expressed evaluation relates to other evaluations of the same product.

## 7.6 Effect of Status and Similarity on User Evaluation

Some of the most commonly found social applications that greatly rely on these user evaluations are.

- *Wikipedia* is a collaboratively authored free encyclopedia. Active users can be nominated for promotion to admin privilege status. Once nominated, a public deliberation process begins and other Wikipedia users cast either positive, negative, or neutral votes on the candidate. Votes are public, signed by the voter, and timestamped. After enough time has passed, a Wikipedia official reviews the votes and discussion and decides whether the election was successful or not. A public record of the election is archived online. Table 7.3 tabulates a public record of election from English, German, French and Spanish Wikipedias.
- *Stack Overflow* is a popular question-answering site for programmers. Users post questions and answers, and can upvote or downvote other users' questions and answers. Heavily upvoted answers are prominently displayed on the question page, and heavily upvoted questions are publicized on the site. There is a visible reputation system that assigns a score to each user on the site. Users gain/lose reputation by receiving upvotes/downvotes on the content they produce. Users cannot downvote freely; it costs them a small amount of reputation to do so. There were 1.1 M questions, 3.2 M answers, and 7.5 M votes (1.8 M on questions, 5.7 M on answers) from the site's inception in 2008–2011. 93.4% of the votes are positive, and for each vote we know the identity of the voter and the time it occurred. Who voted on what is not publicly displayed on the site. Questions are annotated with tags describing relevant topics. There are 31 K unique tags and 3.6 M tag events.
- *Epinions* is an online reviewing site where users can review products and rate each others' reviews. Our dataset has 132 K users, 1.5 M reviews, and 13.6 M ratings of those reviews (on a scale of 1–5 stars). The ratings are overwhelming positive (78% are 5-star ratings), so we call a 5-star rating a "positive" evaluation and all others "negative".

The question is: "When multiple people all provide evaluations of the same "target" person, how to create a composite description of these evaluations that accurately reflects some type of cumulative opinion of the community?" In an attempt to answer this question, [2] found that similarity in the characteristics of two users—such as the extent to which their contributions to the site have involved similar content, or have

**Table 7.3** Wikipedia statistics. $N$ = number of votes, $P_0(+)$ = baseline fraction of positive votes, $U$ = number of users

| Wikipedia language | $N$ | $P_0(+)$ | $U$ |
|---|---|---|---|
| English | 119489 | 74.5% | 10558 |
| German | 78647 | 67.7% | 3560 |
| French | 22534 | 78.0% | 1552 |
| Spanish | 8641 | 83.4% | 917 |

involved interactions with a common set of other users—can affect the evaluation one user provides of another. They also found how the interaction of similarity and status can produce strong effects, and that evaluations are less status-driven when users are more similar to each other; and evaluations are particularly low among users of roughly equal status.

They describe user $A$ evaluating a user $B$ as shorthand either for a direct evaluation of $B$ herself, or for an indirect evaluation via content that $B$ has authored.

The authors have defined the following two notions of similarity.

- Users are represented by the "actions" they take. By action, we mean editing an article on Wikipedia, asking or answering a question on Stack Overflow, and rating a review on Epinions. Let user $u$'s *binary action vector* be a vector of length $M$ (where $M$ is the number of all possible actions a user can take) with a 1 in the $i$th position if $u$ took action $i$ at least once, and 0 otherwise. The similarity between users $u$ and $v$ is then the cosine between their respective binary action vectors: $s(u, v) = \frac{u_a \cdot v_a}{||u_a|| \cdot ||v_a||}$ (where $u_a$ is $u$'s binary action vector). If either $||u_a|| = 0$ or $||v_a|| = 0$ (either $u$ or $v$ hasn't taken any actions), then we say $s(u, v)$ is undefined and exclude it from calculations. A user's action vector changes over time as they make more actions. Whenever we compute the similarity $s(E, T)$ between an evaluator $E$ and a target $T$, we use the action vectors corresponding to the time at which $E$ evaluated $T$. This is called the *content similarity*.
- A user is characterized by a vector of other users that a user has evaluated and define similarity between two users as the cosine between their corresponding binary evaluation vectors. This is called the *social similarity*.

### 7.6.1 Effect of Similarity on Evaluation

The investigation on how similarity affected the probability of a positive evaluation gave the following results. On Wikipedia the probability of a positive evaluation grows with the content as well as social similarity between the evaluator and the target. On average, overlapping interests with the target make it more likely that an evaluator will cast a positive vote. Figure 7.18 shows the probability of a positive vote as a function of the cosine between the evaluator and target binary edit vectors (averaging over all values of $\Delta$). The monotonically-increasing, diminishing- returns relationship between them is clearly present. For ease of presentation, Wikipedia plots are restricted to English Wikipedia for the remainder of this section. The results are similar across all Wikipedia datasets, except where explicitly stated.

On Stack Overflow, the effect of similarity on evaluations is more nuanced. The more similar an evaluator-target pair is, the more likely the evaluation is positive. But in contrast to Wikipedia, the strength of this relationship depends on which notion of similarity is used. The similarity on tags is a measure of content similarity and the similarity on evaluations is a measure of social similarity. Figure 7.19 plots the fraction of positive evaluations as a function of these two measures of similarity.

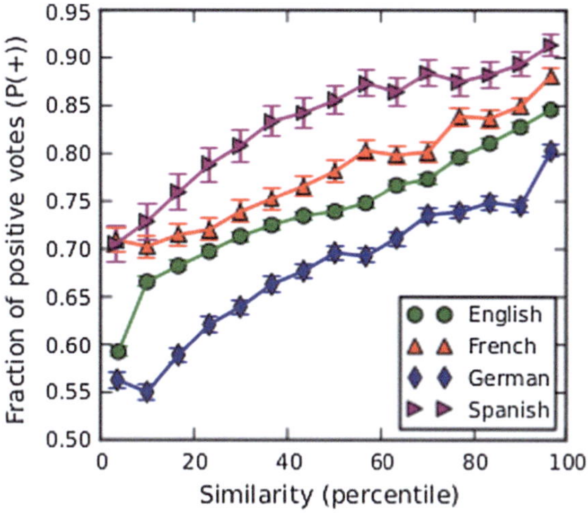


**Fig. 7.18** Probability of a positive evaluation ($P(+)$) as a function of the similarity (binary cosine) between the evaluator and target edit vectors ($s(e, t)$) in Wikipedia

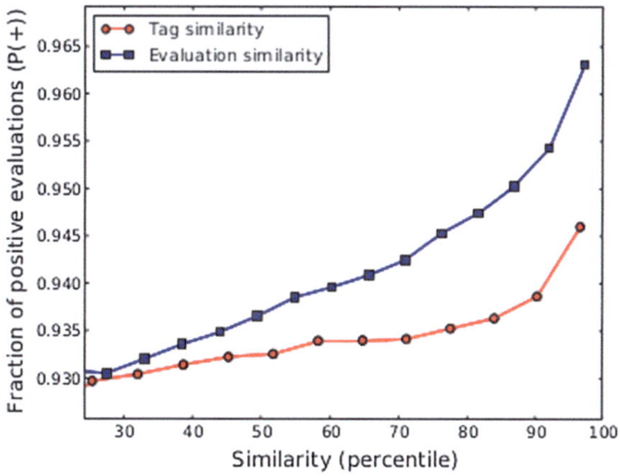


**Fig. 7.19** Probability of $E$ positively evaluating $T$ as a function of similarity in Stack Overflow

Since the scale of the cosine values are different for the two measures, we normalize by their respective cumulative distribution functions so that we compare percentiles instead of raw values on the x-axis. We find that $P(+)$ increases with tag-similarity very gradually for most of the data (from the 25th to the 80th percentile, $P(+)$ only increases by 0.5%, a relative gain of 7%). But for evaluation-similarity, $P(+)$ is higher than it is for tag-similarity (except for $s = 0$) and rises much more significantly (for the same range, $P(+)$ increases 1.5%, a relative gain of 21%—3 times as much). This suggests that the social orbits users travel in influence evaluations much more than the topics they're interested in. Similar effects were found for content similarity on Epinions while social similarity turns out to be too sparse to be meaningful in Epinions.

### 7.6.2 *Effect of Status on Evaluation*

A user's status, or standing in the community, is a function of the community's perception of her contributions. User $u$'s status, denoted as $\sigma_u$, at time $t$ is defined as the number of actions $u$ has taken before time $t$ (i.e. the number of non-zero entries in her corresponding binary action vector $u_a$ at time $t$). Thus the status, on Wikipedia is the total number of edits made by a user $u$ before time $t$; on Stack Overflow, the total number of questions asked and answers; and on Epinions, the number of ratings given.

The *differential status*, $\Delta = \sigma_E - \sigma_T$ compare the evaluator's status with the target's status. It was observed that if an evaluator and target have similar action profiles, the vote varies less with their status difference than if the evaluator and target operate in different domains. This is shown in Fig. 7.20, where $P(+)$ is plotted as a function of $\Delta$ for different levels of similarity in English Wikipedia.

The trend is somewhat similar on Stack Overflow as depicted in Fig. 7.21 for $P(+)$ versus $\Delta$ plot. When $\Delta > 0$, the picture is qualitatively the same as in Wikipedia: the higher the similarity, the higher $P(+)$ is. But for $\Delta < 0$, the situation is very different: the similarity curves are in the opposite order from before: evaluators with low similarity to the higher-status targets (since $\Delta < 0$) are more positive than evaluators with high similarity. This is due to a particular property of Stack Overflow's reputation system, in which it costs a user a small amount of reputation to downvote a question or answer (issue a negative evaluation). This creates a dis-

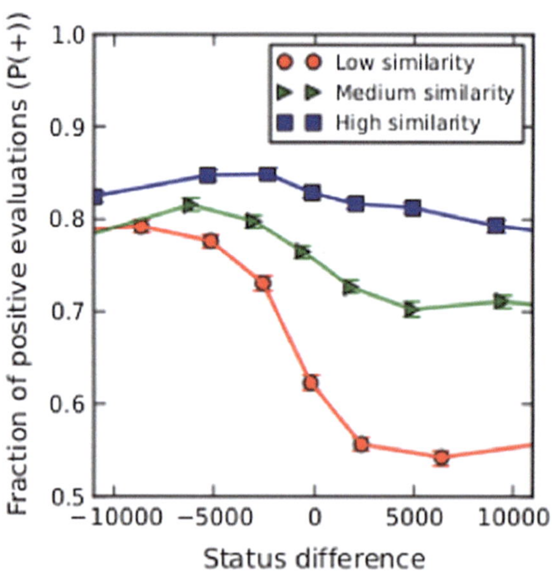


**Fig. 7.20** Probability of $E$ voting positively on $T$ as a function of $\Delta$ for different levels of similarity in English Wikipedia

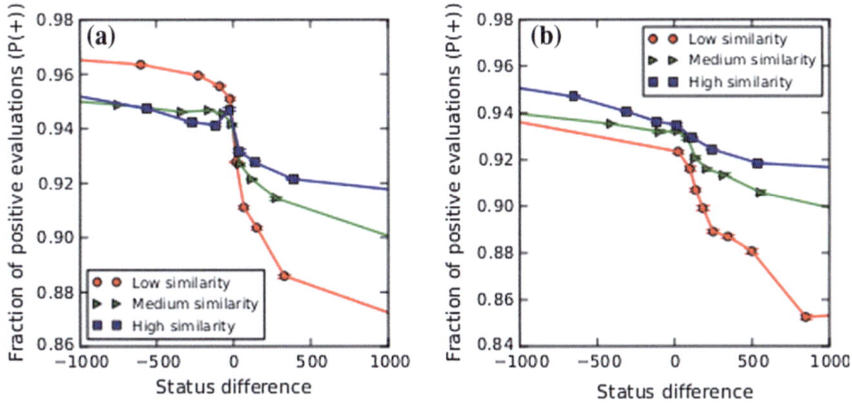


**Fig. 7.21** Probability of $E$ voting positively on $T$ as a function of $\Delta$ for different levels of similarity on Stack Overflow for **a** all evaluators **b** no low status evaluators

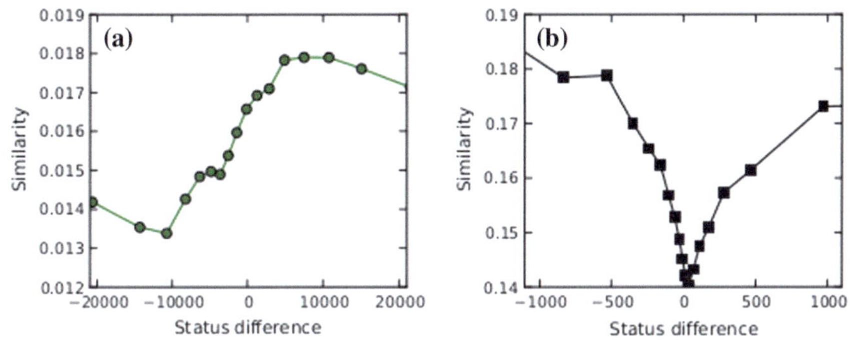


**Fig. 7.22** Similarity between $E$ and $T$ pairs as a function of $\Delta$ for **a** English Wikipedia and **b** Stack Overflow

incentive to downvote which is most strongly felt by users with lower reputation scores (which correlates with our measure of status on Stack Overflow). When the low-status evaluators ($\sigma_E < 100$), this effect disappears and the overall picture looks the same as it does on Wikipedia.

In Wikipedia elections, we find that the evaluator's similarity to the target depends strongly on $\Delta$ while this does not happen on Stack Overflow or Epinions. This is shown in Fig. 7.22.

Figure 7.23 plots the fraction of positive evaluations $P(+)$ against the target's status $\sigma_T$ within several narrow $\Delta$ ranges on Stack Overflow. If the status difference is really how users compare their status against others, then we would expect that these curves are approximately flat, because this would imply that for pairs separated by $\Delta$, evaluation positivity does not depend on what their individual statuses are, and that the level of these constant curves depends on $\Delta$, so that different $\Delta$ values result in different evaluation behaviour. However, $\Delta$ does not control the result well for

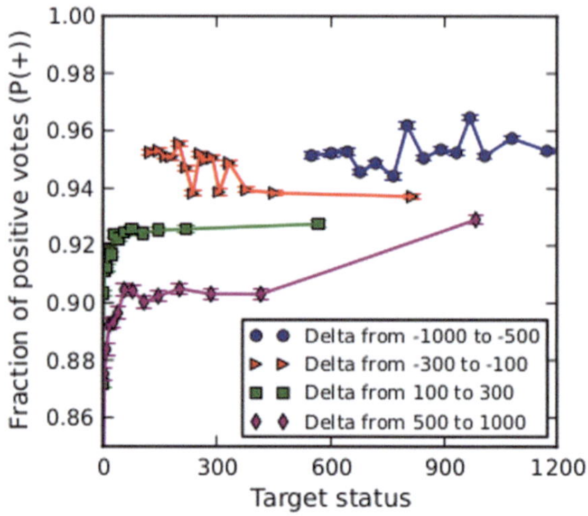


**Fig. 7.23** Probability of $E$ positively evaluating $T$ versus $\sigma_T$ for various fixed levels of $\Delta$ in Stack Overflow

extremely low target status values, where evaluators are much more negative than just the difference in status would otherwise suggest. This is because the poor quality of targets with low status overwhelms the difference in status between evaluator and target. Thus absolute status, and not differential status, is the main criterion evaluators use to evaluate very low-status targets.

## *7.6.3 Aggregate User Evaluation*

At small positive $\Delta$, there appears to be a "dip" and subsequent rebound in Fig. 7.24. This suggests that users are particularly harsh on each other when they have approximately the same status. However, this is at odds with the findings in the previous subsection that users who are similar in other dimensions tend to be more positive toward each other.

When we examine $P(+)$ as a function of $\Delta$, we are aggregating over the two different regimes of user evaluations. In the previous subsection, we showed that evaluation behaviour is qualitatively different for low-status targets. Since most evaluators in the data have relatively low status, this implies that most evaluations in the absolute status evaluation regime will have small positive $\Delta$ values. And since these evaluations are much more negative than those made in the relative status regime, this can cause a dip slightly to the right of 0. This explains the anomaly in the case of Stack Overflow and Epinions but in the case of Wikipedia, the dip persists even when we eliminate targets of low status. The high similarity between evaluator and target, and the observation that higher-status evaluators are more similar to the target than lower-status evaluators are contribute to this non-monotonicity in Wikipedia.

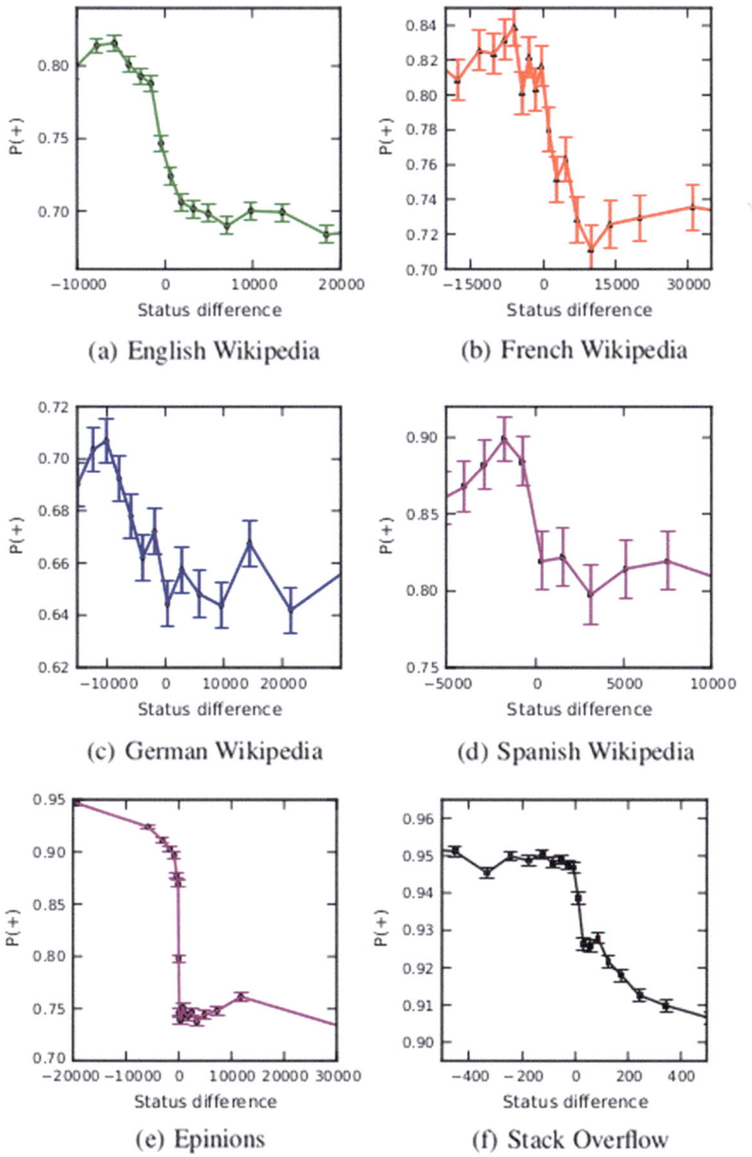


(a) English Wikipedia (b) French Wikipedia

(c) German Wikipedia (d) Spanish Wikipedia

(e) Epinions (f) Stack Overflow

**Fig. 7.24** Dip in various datasets

### 7.6.4 Ballot-Blind Prediction

The problem of ballot-blind prediction is formally defined as follows. Knowing only the first few users $A_1$, $A_2$, ..., $A_k$ who evaluate another user $B$ and their attributes (similarity to $B$ and relative status)—but not the actual evaluations—can we make accurate predictions about the outcome of the election? The crucial point being that we do not have access to the evaluations provided by $A_1, A_2, \ldots, A_k$, but only to their attributes as individuals relative to user $B$. In other words, can we infer an audience's approval or disapproval of a piece of content purely from the makeup of the audience.

Here, we focus on predicting administrator promotion on Wikipedia from the early voters, without looking at the sign of their votes. Just by looking at properties of the first few voters who show up (and importantly, their similarity with the candidate up for election), we attempt to predict whether the election succeeds or not.

Formally, a Wikipedia adminship election $(T, \omega, R)$ is specified by a target (or candidate) $T$ , a set of ordered votes $\omega$, and a result $R\epsilon\{+1, -1\}$ denoting whether $T$ was promoted or not. Each vote $v_i \epsilon \omega$ is a tuple $(E_i, s_i, t_i)$ where $E_i$ is the evaluator, $s_i \epsilon\{+1, -1\}$ denotes whether the vote is positive or negative (disregarding neutral votes), and $t_i$ is the time when $E_i$ cast the vote. The votes are sorted by time, so $t_1 < t_2 < \cdots < t_m$ , where $m$ is the number of votes cast in the election. The task is to predict $R$ from the first $k$ votes $v_1, \ldots, v_k$ (without looking at the sign $s_i$ of each vote) using the similarity and status of the evaluators relative to the target.

In English Wikipedia, the data consisted of approximately 120, 000 votes made by approximately 7, 600 unique voters across 3, 422 elections on 2, 953 distinct candidates. (The number of elections exceeds the number of distinct candidates since some candidates go up for election more than once). $k = 5$ is used in the experiments. The performance is evaluated using accuracy on *leave-one-out cross-validation*, where the model is trained on the entire dataset minus one example and is tested on the example for every example in the dataset.

For each vote $v_i$ , the identity of the evaluator $E_i$, her similarity $s(E_i, T)$ with the target, her status $\sigma_{E_i}$, and the status difference $\Delta_i = \sigma_{E_i} - \sigma_T$ between her and the target. *Positivity* is voter $i$'s historical fraction of positive votes $P_i$ (excluding the current vote, since this the value to be predicted). If $i$ has no other votes in the dataset, their positivity is defined to be the global positivity across the entire dataset (the overall fraction of positive votes across all voters).

Two classes of features were used:

- Simple Summary Statistics (**S**) of the status and similarity of the target and the evaluators: $log(\sigma_T)$, mean similarity $\overline{s} = \sum_{i=1}^{k} \frac{s(v_i,T)}{k}$ and $\overline{\Delta} = \sum_{i=1}^{k} \frac{(\sigma_{E_i} - \sigma_T)}{k}$.
- $\Delta$-s space is divided into four quadrants as shown in Fig. 7.25, divided by $\Delta = 0$ and a similarity value that roughly splits the evaluations into two equally-sized buckets. This gives us four features where each simply counts the number of voters coming from a particular $\Delta$-s quadrant.

Three baselines were formulated:

- **B1**: A logistic regression classifier that uses the 4 features of $\Delta$-s quadrants and the **S** statistics.
- **B2**: The probability of voter $E_i$ voting positively (without considering his relation to the candidate). The probability of user $E_i$ voting positively $P(E_i = 1)$ is

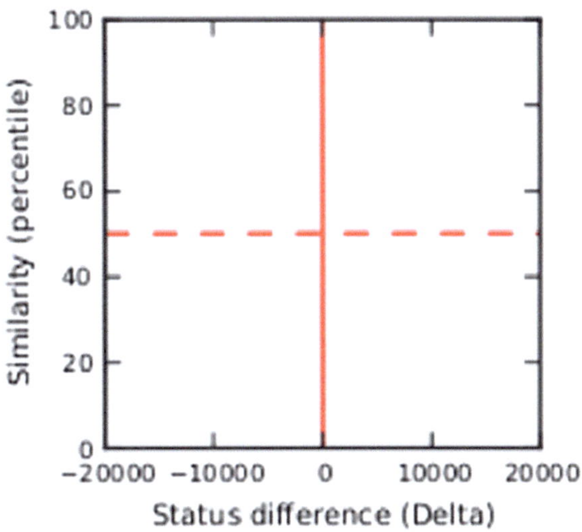


**Fig. 7.25** The Delta-similarity half-plane. Votes in each quadrant are treated as a group

estimated as the empirical fraction $E_i$'s votes that are positive. The estimated fraction of positive votes in an election is simply the average $\frac{1}{k}\sum_{i=1}^{k} P_i$ of the first $k$ voters.

- **GS**: The "gold-standard" represents the best possible performance that can be achieved. It "cheats" by examining the values of actual votes themselves ($s_i$, for $i \leq k$), computes the empirical fraction of positive votes and learns the optimal threshold to predict the election outcome.

The methods developed were:

- **M1**: M1 models the probability that $E_i$ votes positively as $P(E_i = 1) = P_i + d(\Delta_i, s_i)$, where $P_i$ is $E_i$'s positivity, and $d(\Delta_i, s_i)$ is the average deviation of the fraction of positive votes in the $\Delta_i$, $s_i$ bucket compared to the overall fraction of positive votes across the entire dataset. The average $P(E_i = 1)$ for $i = 1 \ldots k$ is computed and then made threshold for prediction.
- **M2**: $P(E_i = 1)$ is modelled as $P(E_i = 1) = \alpha \cdot P_i(\Delta_i, s_i) + (1 - \alpha) \cdot d(\Delta_i, s_i)$. $\alpha$ between 0.6 and 0.9 is used for computation.

Figure 7.26 plots the classification accuracy for the models on English Wikipedia as well as German Wikipedia (French and Spanish Wikipedia were very similar to the German results). Here, the prior refers to the accuracy of random guessing.

These results demonstrate that without even looking at the actual votes, it is possible to derive a lot of information about the outcome of the election from a small prefix of the evaluators. Very informative implicit feedback could be gleaned from a small sampling of the audience consuming the content in question, especially if previous evaluation behaviour by the audience members is known.

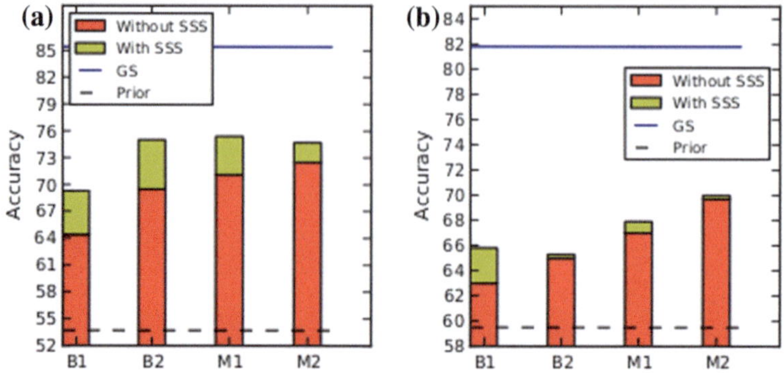


**Fig. 7.26** Ballot-blind prediction results for **a** English Wikipedia **b** German Wikipedia

## 7.7 Predicting Positive and Negative Links

Reference [9] investigated relationships in Epinions, Slashdot and Wikipedia. They observed that the signs of links in the underlying social networks can be predicted with high accuracy using generalized models. These models are found to provide insight into some of the fundamental principles that drive the formation of signed links in networks, shedding light on theories of balance and status from social psychology. They also suggest social computing applications by which the attitude of one user towards another can be estimated from evidence provided by their relationships with other members of the surrounding social network.

The study looked at three datasets.

- The trust network of Epinions data spanning from the inception of the site in 1999 until 2003. This network contained $119,217$ nodes and $841,000$ edges, of which 85.0% were positive. $80,668$ users received at least one trust or distrust edge, while there were $49,534$ users that created at least one and received at least one signed edge. In this network, $s(u, v)$ indicates whether $u$ had expressed trust or distrust of user $v$.
- The social network of the technology-related news website Slashdot, where $u$ can designate $v$ as either a "friend" or "foe" to indicate $u$'s approval or disapproval of $v$'s comments. Slashdot was crawled Slashdot in 2009 to obtain its network of $82,144$ users and $549,202$ edges of which 77.4% are positive. $70,284$ users received at least one signed edge, and there were $32,188$ users with non-zero in- and out-degree.
- The network of votes cast by Wikipedia users in elections for promoting individuals to the role of admin. A signed link indicated a positive or negative vote by one user on the promotion of another. Using the January 2008 complete dump of Wikipedia page edit history all administrator election and vote history data was extracted. This gave $2,794$ elections with $103,747$ total votes and $7,118$ users participating in the elections. Out of this total, $1,235$ elections resulted in a successful promotion,

while 1, 559 elections did not result in the promotion of the candidate. The resulting network contained 7, 118 nodes and 103, 747 edges of which 78.7% are positive. There were 2, 794 nodes that received at least one edge and 1, 376 users that both received and created signed edges. $s(u, v)$ indicates whether $u$ voted for or against the promotion of $v$ to admin status.

In all of these networks the background proportion of positive edges is about the same, with ≈80% of the edges having a positive sign.

The aim was to answer the question: "How does the sign of a given link interact with the pattern of link signs in its local vicinity, or more broadly throughout the network? Moreover, what are the plausible configurations of link signs in real social networks?" The attempt is to infer the attitude of one user towards another, using the positive and negative relations that have been observed in the vicinity of this user. This becomes particularly important in the case of recommender systems where users' pre-existing attitudes and opinions must be deliberated before recommending a link. This involves predicting the sign of the link to be recommended before actually suggesting this.

This gives us the *edge sign prediction* problem. Formally, given a social network with signs on all its edges, but the sign on the edge from node $u$ to node $v$, denoted $s(u, v)$, has been "hidden". With what probability can we infer this sign $s(u, v)$ using the information provided by the rest of the network? In a way, this problem is similar to the problem of *link prediction*.

## 7.7.1 Predicting Edge Sign

Given a directed graph $G = (V, E)$ with a sign (positive or negative) on each edge, let $s(x, y)$ denote the sign of the edge $(x, y)$ from $x$ to $y$, i.e, $s(x, y) = 1$ when the sign of $(x, y)$ is positive, $-1$ when the sign is negative, and 0 when there is no directed edge from $x$ to $y$. In cases where we are interested in the sign of edge $(x, y)$ regardless of its direction, we write $\overline{s}(x, y) = 1$ when there is a positive edge in one of the two directions $(x, y)$ or $(y, x)$, and either a positive edge or no edge in the other direction. We write $\overline{s}(x, y) = -1$ analogously when there is a negative edge in one of these directions, and either a negative edge or no edge in the other direction. We write $\overline{s}(x, y) = 0$ in all other cases (including when there are edges $(x, y)$ and $(y, x)$ with opposite signs, though this is in fact rare). For different formulations, we will suppose that for a particular edge $(u, v)$, the sign $s(u, v)$ or $\overline{s}(u, v)$ is hidden and that we are trying to infer it.

There are two classes of features. The first class of features, based on degree, is as follows. As we are interested in predicting the sign of the edge from $u$ to $v$, we consider outgoing edges from $u$ and incoming edges to $v$. $d^+_{in}(v)$ and $d_in^-(v)$ denotes the number of incoming positive and negative edges to $v$, respectively. Similarly, $d^+_{out}(u)$ and $d^-_{out}(u)$ denotes the number of outgoing positive and negative edges from $u$, respectively. $C(u, v)$ denotes the total number of common neighbours of $u$

and $v$ in an undirected sense, i.e, the number of nodes $w$ such that $w$ is linked by an edge in either direction with both $u$ and $v$. $C(u, v)$ is sometimes also referred to as the embeddedness of the edge $(u, v)$. In summary, the features in this class are: $d_{in}^{+}(v)$, $d_{in}^{-}(v)$, $d_{out}^{+}(u)$, $d_{out}^{-}(u)$, $C(u, v)$, together with the total out-degree of $u$ and the total in-degree of $v$, which are $d_{out}^{+}(u)+d_{out}^{-}(u)$ and $d_{in}^{+}(v)+d_{in}^{-}(v)$ respectively.

For the second class of feature, we consider each triad involving the edge $(u, v)$, consisting of a node $w$ such that $w$ has an edge either to or from $u$ and also an edge either to or from $v$. Since, the edge between $w$ and $u$ can be in either direction and of either sign, and the edge between $w$ and $v$ can also be in either direction and of either sign; this leads to $2 \times 2 \times 2 \times 2 = 16$ distinct possibilities. Each of these 16 triad types may provide different evidence about the sign of the edge from $u$ to $v$, some favouring a negative sign and others a positive sign. All of this is encoded in a 16-dimensional vector specifying the number of triads of each type that $(u, v)$ is involved in.

Logistic regression was applied to learn the sign of an edge based on these 23 features. The full dataset containing 80% positive edges are first used. Next, a balanced dataset was created with equal numbers of positive and negative edges, so that random guessing yields a 50% correct prediction rate. The classification accuracy is shown in Fig. 7.27, for different levels of minimum embeddedness ($E_m$).

The coefficients provided by logistic regression when associated with each feature suggests how the feature is being used by the model to provide weight for or against a positive edge sign. Specifically, we say that a *theory of triad types* is a function

$$f : \{types\ \tau\} \rightarrow \{+1, -1, 0\}$$

which specifies for each triad type $\tau$ whether it constitutes evidence for a positive $(u, v)$ edge ($f(\tau) = +1$), evidence for a negative $(u, v)$ edge ($f(\tau) = -1$), or whether it offers no evidence ($f(\tau) = 0$).

For studying balance, we see that if $w$ forms a triad with the edge $(u, v)$, then $(u, v)$ should have the sign that causes the triangle on $u$, $v$, $w$ to have an odd number of positive signs, regardless of edge direction. In other words, $f_{balance}(\tau) = \bar{s}(u, w)\bar{s}(v, w)$. In order to determine $f_{status}(\tau)$, we first flip the directions of the edges between $u$ and $w$ and between $v$ and $w$, so that they point from $u$ to $w$ and from $w$ to $v$; we flip the signs accordingly as we do this. We then define $f_{status}(\tau)$ to be the sign of $s(u, w) + s(w, v)$. The accuracy of predicting signs considering these balance and status coefficients is depicted in Fig. 7.28. Here, *StatusLrn* and *BalanceLrn* denote the coefficients learned via logistic regression. The coefficients from $\{-1, 0, +1\}$ provided by balance, weak balance and status are denoted by *BalanceDet*, *WeakBalDet* and *StatusDet* respectively.

Next the following handwritten heuristic predictors were considered:

- *Balance heuristic* (Balance): For each choice of the sign of $(u, v)$, some of the triads it participates in will be consistent with balance theory, and the rest of the triads will not. We choose the sign for $(u, v)$ that causes it to participate in a greater number of triads that are consistent with balance.

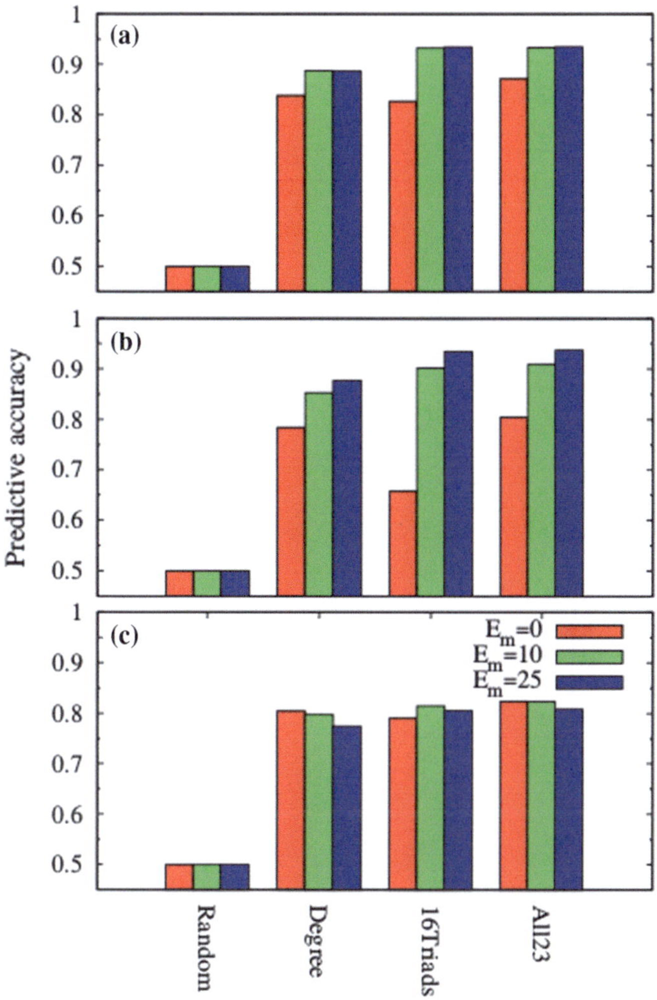


**Fig. 7.27** Accuracy of predicting the sign of an edge based on the signs of all the other edges in the network in **a** Epinions, **b** Slashdot and **c** Wikipedia

- *Status heuristic* (StatDif): An estimate of a node $x$'s status is $\sigma_x = d_{in}^+(x) + d_{out}^-(x) - d_{out}^+(x) - d_{in}^-(x)$. This gives $x$ status benefits for each positive link it receives and each negative link it generates, and status detriments for each negative link it receives and each positive link it generates. We then predict a positive sign for $(u, v)$ if $\sigma_u \leq \sigma_v$, and a negative sign otherwise.
- *Out-degree heuristic* (OutSign): We predict the majority sign based on the signs given by the edge initiator $u$, i.e, we predict a positive sign if $d_{out}^+(u) \geq d_{out}^-(u)$.
- *In-degree heuristic* (InSign): We predict the majority sign based on the signs received by the edge target $v$, i.e, we predict a poisitive sign if $d_{in}^+(u) \geq d_{in}^-(v)$.

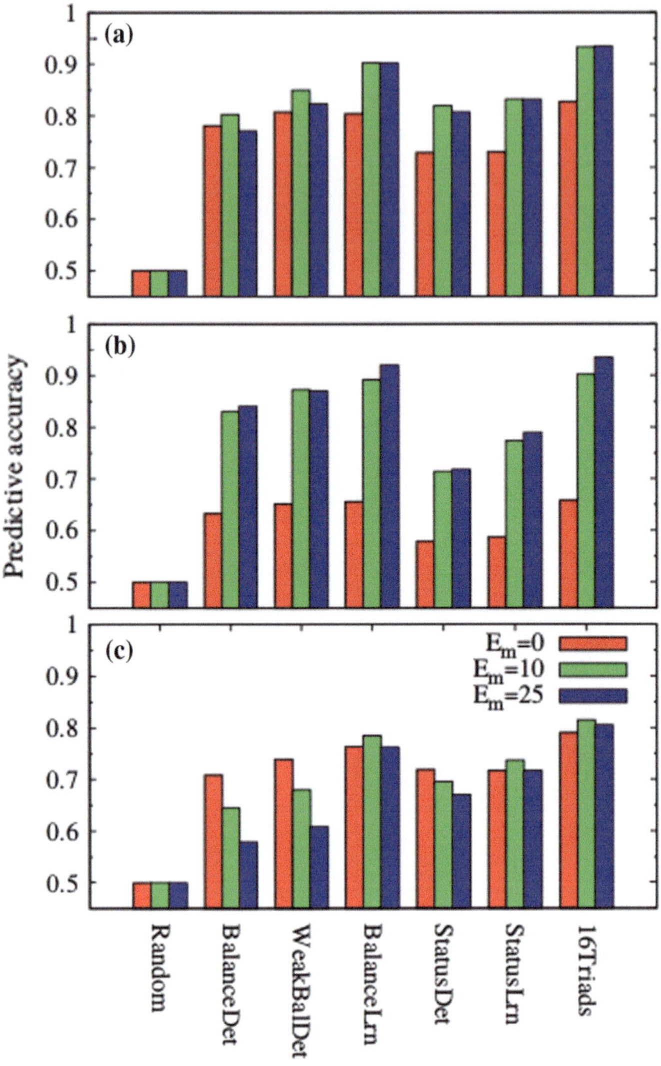


**Fig. 7.28** Accuracy of predicting the sign of an edge based on the signs of all the other edges in the network in **a** Epinions, **b** Slashdot and **c** Wikipedia

These predictors are plotted in Fig. 7.29 as a function of embeddedness.

In addition to sign prediction, the study focused at whether information about negative links can be helpful in addressing questions that concern purely positive links, i.e, given a pair $u$ and $v$, is there a positive link between $u$ and $v$? If so, how much performance is improved if the negative links in the network are also visible. In other words, how useful is it to know where a person's enemies are, if we want to predict the presence of additional friends? The study found that negative links can be

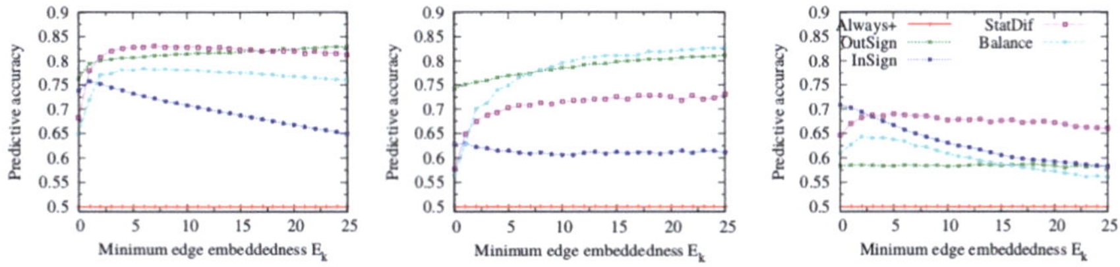


**Fig. 7.29** Accuracy for handwritten heuristics as a function of minimum edge embeddedness

a powerful source of additional information for a task such as this. This type of result helps to argue that positive and negative links in online systems should be viewed as tightly related to each other, rather than as distinct non-interacting features of the system.

Reference [4] studied *Essembly.com*, a "fiercely non-partisan social network" that allows members to post resolves reflecting controversial opinions. Members can then vote on these resolves, using a four-point scale: *Agree*, *Lean Agree*, *Lean Against*, or *Against*. Users can only vote once per resolve, and all their votes are viewable by other members, forming an ideological profile. Instead of a plain "friend request", this social network apart allows users to form three semantically distinct but overlapping types of connections: *friend request*, *ally request*: a person who shares the same ideologies as the person being requested, and *nemesis request*: a person who has opposite ideologies to the person being requested. They found that users are affected differently by their friends, allies and nemesis, indicating that people use these distinct connections for different purposes.

They conclude that social applications that encourage online socialization and registration of users' "friends" may compel people to add as "friends" people whom they know only superficially or who don't hold much influence over them. Therefore, the use of this friends network to make recommendations or to influence users may then be diminished. Therefore, sites seeking to exploit the influence exerted by friends in changing behaviour or making recommendations should provide multiple classes of friendship. The closer a user is to recommending friends, the stronger the persuasion is likely to be.

## Problems

Download the signed *Epinions* social network dataset available at https://snap.stanford.edu/data/soc-sign-epinions.txt.gz.

Consider the graph as undirected and compute the following:

**47** Calculate the count and fraction of triads of each type in this network.

**48** Calculate the fraction of positive and negative edges in the graph. Let the fraction of positive edges be $p$. Assuming that each edge of a triad will independently be assigned a positive sign with probability $p$ and a negative sign with probability $1 - p$, calculate the probability of each type of triad.

**49** Now, analyse a simple generative model of signed networks by running simulations of the dynamic process on small networks in the following manner. Create a complete network on 10 nodes. For each edge, choose a sign with uniform probability. Run this dynamic process for a million iterations. Repeat this process 100 times. What fraction of these networks are balanced?

## References

1. Adamic, Lada A., Jun Zhang, Eytan Bakshy, and Mark S. Ackerman. 2008. Knowledge sharing and Yahoo answers: Everyone knows something. In *Proceedings of the 17th international conference on World Wide Web*, 665–674. ACM.
2. Anderson, Ashton, Daniel Huttenlocher, Jon Kleinberg, and Jure Leskovec. 2012. Effects of user similarity in social media. In *Proceedings of the fifth ACM international conference on Web search and data mining*, 703–712. ACM.
3. Antal, Tibor, Pavel L. Krapivsky, and Sidney Redner. 2005. Dynamics of social balance on networks. *Physical Review E* 72(3):036121.
4. Brzozowski, Michael J., Tad Hogg, and Gabor Szabo. 2008. Friends and foes: Ideological social networking. In *Proceedings of the SIGCHI conference on human factors in computing systems*, 817–820. ACM.
5. Danescu-Niculescu-Mizil, Cristian, Gueorgi Kossinets, Jon Kleinberg, and Lillian Lee. 2009. How opinions are received by online communities: A case study on Amazon. com helpfulness votes. In *Proceedings of the 18th international conference on World Wide Web*, 141–150. ACM.
6. Davis, James A. 1963. Structural balance, mechanical solidarity, and interpersonal relations. *American Journal of Sociology* 68 (4): 444–462.
7. Guha, Ramanthan, Ravi Kumar, Prabhakar Raghavan, and Andrew Tomkins. 2004. Propagation of trust and distrust. In *Proceedings of the 13th international conference on World Wide Web*, 403–412. ACM.
8. Lauterbach, Debra, Hung Truong, Tanuj Shah, and Lada Adamic. 2009. Surfing a web of trust: Reputation and reciprocity on couchsurfing. com. In *2009 International conference on computational science and engineering (CSE'09)*, vol. 4, 346–353. IEEE.
9. Leskovec, Jure, Daniel Huttenlocher, and Jon Kleinberg. 2010. Predicting positive and negative links in online social networks. In *Proceedings of the 19th international conference on World Wide Web*, 641–650. ACM.
10. Leskovec, Jure, Daniel Huttenlocher, and Jon Kleinberg. 2010. Signed networks in social media. In *Proceedings of the SIGCHI conference on human factors in computing systems*, 1361–1370. ACM.
11. Marvel, Seth A., Jon Kleinberg, Robert D. Kleinberg, and Steven H. Strogatz. 2011. Continuous-time model of structural balance. *Proceedings of the National Academy of Sciences* 108 (5): 1771–1776.
12. Muchnik, Lev, Sinan Aral, and Sean J. Taylor. 2013. Social influence bias: A randomized experiment. *Science* 341(6146):647–651.
13. Teng, ChunYuen, Debra Lauterbach, and Lada A. Adamic. 2010. I rate you. You rate me. Should we do so publicly? In *WOSN*.

# Chapter 8
# Cascading in Social Networks

Cascades are periods during which individuals in a population exhibit herd-like behaviour because they are making decisions based on the actions of other individuals rather than relying on their own information about the problem. Cascades are often regarded as a specific manifestation of the robust yet fragile nature of many complex systems: a system may appear stable for long periods of time and withstand many external shocks, then suddenly and apparently inexplicably exhibit a large cascade [17].

## 8.1 Decision Based Models of Cascade

Consider the following coordination game that helps to better understand decision based cascading. Consider a situation in a social network where every node has to decide between two possible behaviours, $A$ and $B$. If nodes $v$ and $w$ are neighbours, then it would be of mutual benefit if both of them adopted the same behaviour. The possible payoffs between the players and the behaviours are as follows: if both $v$ and $w$ adopt behaviour $A$, they each get a payoff of $a > 0$; if they both adopt $B$, they each get a payoff of $b > 0$; and if they adopt opposite behaviours, then they each get a payoff of 0. This is better illustrated in the payoff matrix given in Table 8.1.

Each node $v$ is faced with the choice of adopting a certain behaviour taking into consideration the payoffs it will receive from each of its neighbour. Figure 8.1 shows node $v$'s predicament. In the figure, $p$ fraction of $v$'s neighbours adopt behaviour $A$, while $(1 - p)$ fraction have behaviour $B$. So if $d$ denotes the degree of $v$, then $v$ will receive a payoff of $pda$ if it adopts behaviour $A$, and $v$ will receive a payoff of $(1 - p)db$ if it adopts behaviour $B$. Therefore, $A$ is a better choice if



K. Raj P. M. et al., *Practical Social Network Analysis with Python*,
Computer Communications and Networks,
https://doi.org/10.1007/978-3-319-96746-2_8

**Table 8.1** A-B coordination game payoff matrix

| | *A* | *B* |
|---|---|---|
| *A* | *a*,*a* | 0,0 |
| *B* | 0,0 | *b*,*b* |

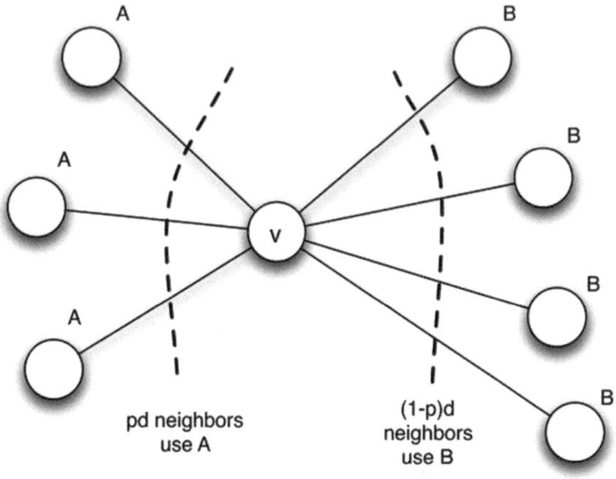


**Fig. 8.1** $v$ must choose between behaviours $A$ and $B$ based on its neighbours behaviours

$$pda \geq (1-p)db \tag{8.1}$$

Rearranging the terms in Eq. 8.1, we get

$$p \geq \frac{b}{a+b} \tag{8.2}$$

If we denote the right had side term as $q$ ($q = \frac{b}{a+b}$), then $q$ can be called the *threshold*. This gives us the *threshold rule*: if atleast a $q$ fraction of $v$'s neighbours adopt a specific behaviour, then in terms of payoff, it is beneficial for $v$ to also adopt this behaviour.

In the long run, this behaviour adoption leads to one of the following states of equilibria. Either everyone adopts behaviour $A$, or everyone adopts behaviour $B$. Additionally, there exists a third possibility where nodes adopting behaviour $A$ coexist with nodes adopting behaviour $B$. In this section, we will understand the network circumstances that will lead to one of these possibilities.

Assume a network where every node initially has behaviour $B$. Let a small portion of the nodes be *early adopters* of the behaviour $A$. These early adopters choose $A$ for reasons other than those guiding the coordination game, while the other nodes operate within the rules of the game. Now with every time step, each of these nodes following $B$ will adopt $A$ based on the threshold rule. This adoption will cascade until one of the two possibilities occur: Either all nodes eventually adopt $A$ leading

**Fig. 8.2** Initial network where all nodes exhibit the behaviour $B$

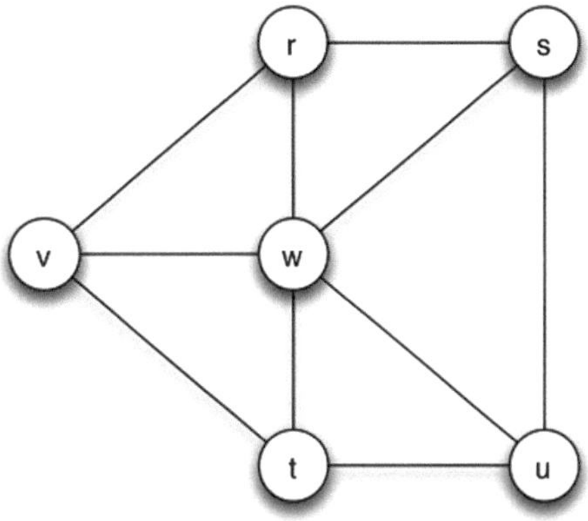


**Fig. 8.3** Nodes $v$ and $w$ are initial adopters of behaviour $A$ while all the other nodes still exhibit behaviour $B$

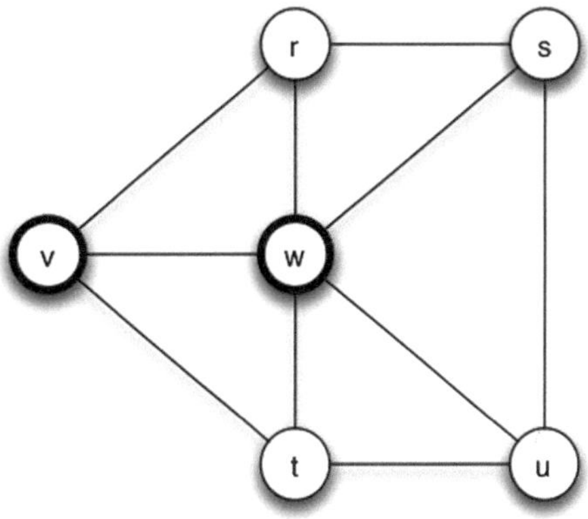


to a *complete cascade*, or an impasse arises between those adopting $A$ and the ones adopting $B$ forming a *partial cascade*.

Figures 8.2, 8.3, 8.4 and 8.5 all show an example of a complete cascade. In this network, let the payoffs be $a = 4$ and $b = 5$, and the initial adopters be $v$ and $w$. Assuming that all the nodes started with behaviour $B$. In the first time step, $q = \frac{5}{9}$ but $p = \frac{2}{3}$ for the nodes $r$ and $t$, and $p = \frac{1}{3}$ for the nodes $s$ and $u$. Since the $p$ for nodes $r$ and $t$ is greater than $q$, $r$ and $t$ will adopt $A$. However, the $p$ for nodes $s$ and $u$ is less than $q$. Therefore these two nodes will not adopt $A$. In the second time step, $p = \frac{2}{3}$ for the nodes $s$ and $u$. $p$ being greater than $q$ cause the remaining two nodes to adopt the behaviour, thereby causing a complete cascade.

Figures 8.6, 8.7 and 8.8 illustrate a partial cascade. Similar to the complete cascade depiction, we begin with a network where all the nodes exhibit behaviour $B$ with payoffs $a = 3$ and $b = 2$. The nodes 7 and 8 are the initial adopters, and $q = \frac{2}{5}$. In the first step, node 5 with $p = \frac{2}{3}$ and node 10 with $p = \frac{1}{2}$ are the only two nodes that can change behaviour to $A$. In the second step, node 4 has $p = \frac{2}{3}$ and node 9 has $p = \frac{1}{1}$, causing them to switch to $A$. In the third time step, node 6 with $p = \frac{2}{3}$

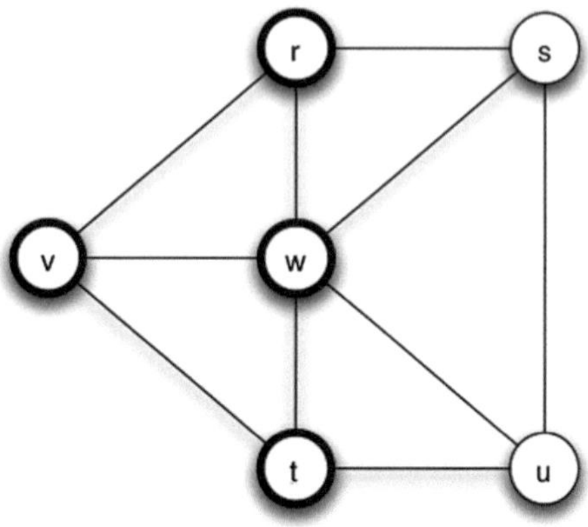


**Fig. 8.4** First time step where $r$ and $t$ adopt behaviour $A$ by threshold rule

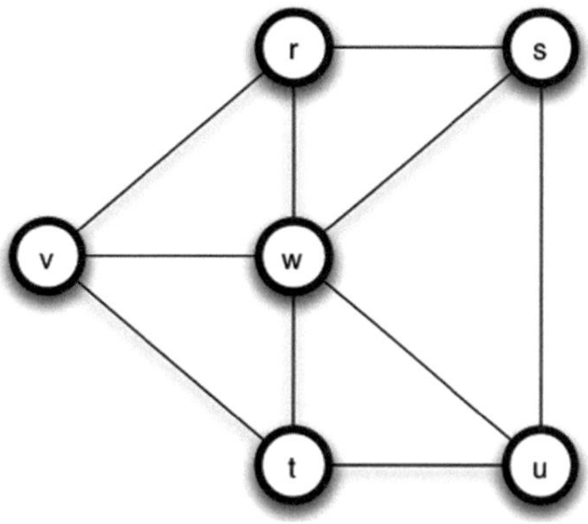


**Fig. 8.5** Second time step where $s$ and $u$ adopt behaviour $A$ also by threshold rule

adopts $A$. Beyond these adoptions, there are no possible cascades leading to a partial cascade of behaviour $A$.

There are two ways for a partial cascade to turn into a complete cascade. The first way is for the payoff of one of the behaviours to exceed the other. In Fig. 8.6, if the payoff $a$ is increased, then the whole network will eventually switch to $A$. The other way is to coerce some critical nodes of one of the behaviours to adopt the other. This would restart the cascade, ending in a complete cascade in favour of the coerced behaviour. In Fig. 8.6, if nodes 12 and 13 were forced to adopt $A$, then this would lead to a complete cascade. Instead, if 11 and 14 were coerced to switch, then there would be no further cascades.

Partial cascades are caused due to the fact that the spread of a new behaviour can stall when it tries to break into a tightly-knit community within the network, i.e, homophily can often serve as a barrier to diffusion, by making it hard for innovations to arrive from outside densely connected communities. More formally, consider a set of initial adopters of behaviour $A$, with a threshold of $q$ for nodes in the remaining network to adopt behaviour $A$. If the remaining network contains a cluster of density greater than $1 - q$, then the set of initial adopters will not cause a complete cascade.

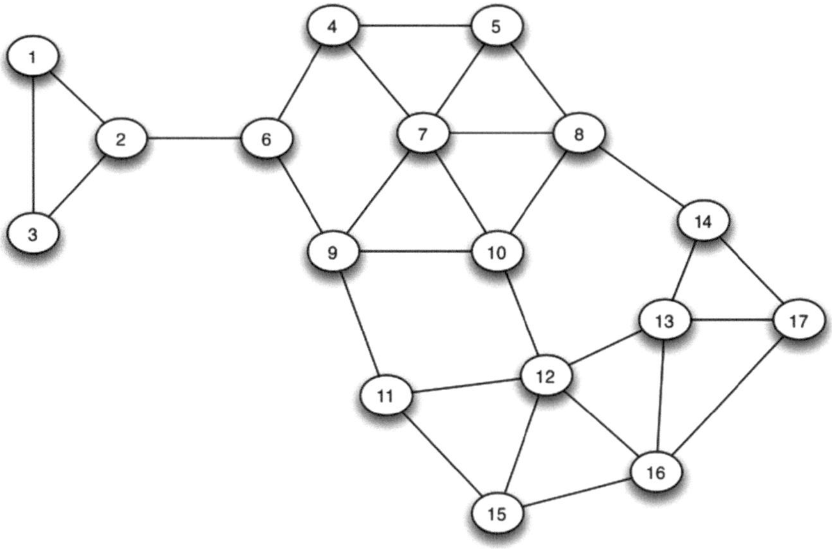


**Fig. 8.6** Initial network where all nodes have behaviour *B*

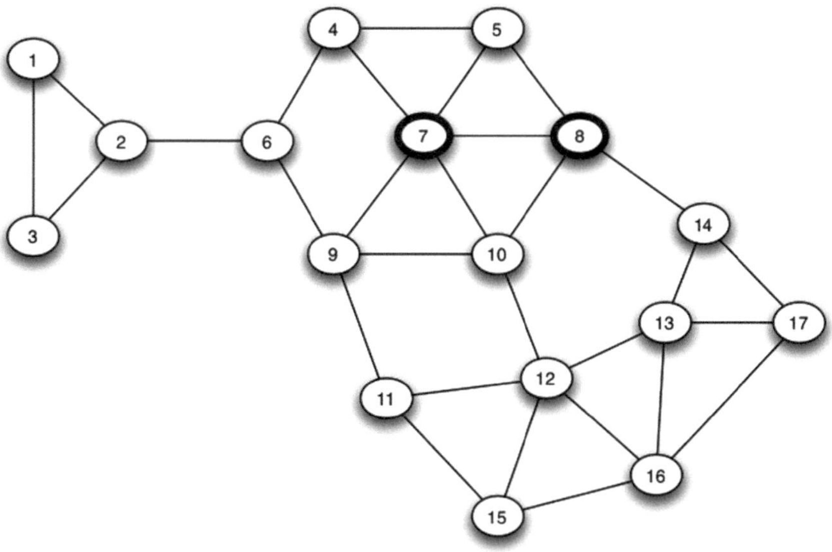


**Fig. 8.7** Nodes 7 and 8 are early adopters of behaviour *A* while all the other nodes exhibit *B*

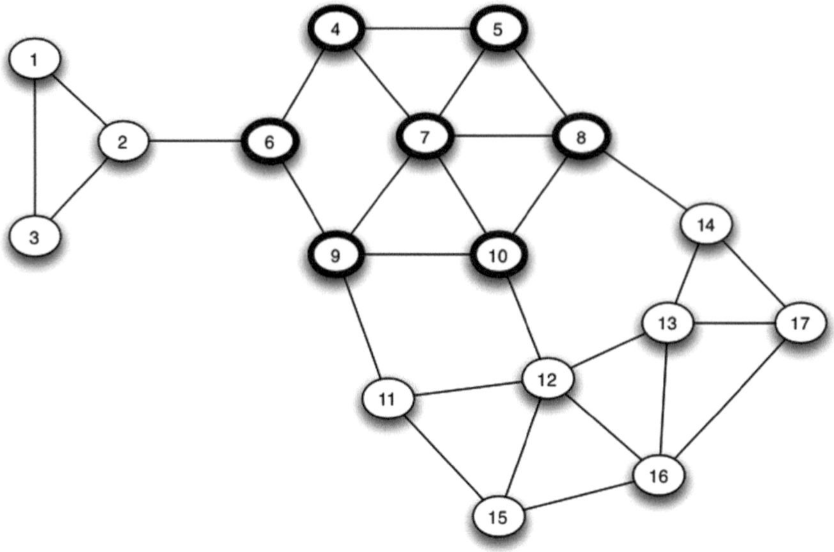


**Fig. 8.8** After three time steps there are no further cascades

**Table 8.2** Coordination game for node specific payoffs

| | $A$ | $B$ |
|---|---|---|
| $A$ | $a_v, a_w$ | $0, 0$ |
| $B$ | $0, 0$ | $b_v, b_w$ |

Whenever a set of initial adopters does not cause a complete cascade with threshold $q$, the remaining network must contain a cluster of density greater than $1 - q$.

The above discussed models work on the assumption that the payoffs that each adopter receives is the same, i.e, $a$ for each adopter of $A$ and $b$ for each adopter of $B$. However, if we consider the possibility of node specific payoff, i.e, every node $v$ receives a payoff $a_v$ for adopting $A$ and payoff $b_v$ for taking $B$. So the payoff matrix in such a coordination game is as shown in Table 8.2.

On the same lines as the previous coordination game we arrive at the Eq. 8.3

$$p \geq \frac{b_v}{a_v + b_v} \tag{8.3}$$

Here, we can define $q_v = \frac{b_v}{a_v+b_v}$ as the *personal threshold* of $v$. So, this will give a *personal threshold rule* whereby $v$ will take the behaviour adopted by atleast $q_v$ of its neighbours.

### 8.1.1 Collective Action

Collective action problems are those where an activity produces benefit only if enough people participate. Situations such as protest against a repressive regime work only with collective action. If only a handful of demonstrators staged a protest, these protesters would simply be arrested and thereby end the revolt. Instead if a large group were mobilised, the government would be weakened and everyone including the demonstrators would benefit. However, this large group will assemble if and only if every individual in the group is assured of the fact that the number of other protesters being present is greater than this individual's personal threshold. In other words, the success of this demonstration is incumbent upon the *common knowledge* of all of these protesters, i.e, among the protesters in this group, each protester knows that a number greater than their personal threshold is going to be mobilised, each protester knows that every protester knows it, each protester knows that every protester knows that each of the protesters know it, and so on indefinitely. The various forms of mass media and social network applications usually help people achieve this common knowledge. Additionally, it is observed that although a large fraction of a group are in support of a radical idea, most believe that they are in a small minority and it is way too risky for them to get involved. This phenomenon is termed as *pluralistic ignorance*. To maintain a state of pluralistic ignorance by preventing the spread of common knowledge, is the reason why governments usually curb the freedom of press during protests and why repressive governments work so hard towards achieving censorship.

### 8.1.2 Cascade Capacity

The cascade capacity is defined with respect to an infinite network as the largest threshold at which a finite set of nodes can cause a complete cascade.

Consider a network with infinite nodes where each node is connected to a finite set of these nodes. Let a finite set $S$ of these nodes have behaviour $A$ while the rest of the network exhibits behaviour $B$. In each time step $t$, each of these nodes initially exhibiting behaviour $B$ adopt $A$ based on their threshold. So, the cascade capacity of this network is the largest value of $q$ for which $S$ can cause complete cascade.

First, let us consider what happens if the network is an infinite path. Even if just one node in this network is an early adopter of $A$ while all other nodes exhibit $B$, a value of $q \leq \frac{1}{2}$ is sufficient for a complete cascade while $q > \frac{1}{2}$ fails to do so. Therefore in the case of an infinite path, the cascade capacity is $\frac{1}{2}$.

Next, we will look at an infinite grid as shown in Fig. 8.9. Let the nine nodes in black be the early adopters of behaviour $A$ while the other nodes exhibit behaviour $B$. Here, if the threshold $q \leq \frac{3}{8}$ then there will be a complete cascade. First the nodes $c, i, h$ and $n$ will adopt $A$, followed by $b, d, f, g, j, k, m$ and $o$, and then the others. Thus, the cascade capacity of this network is $\frac{3}{8}$.

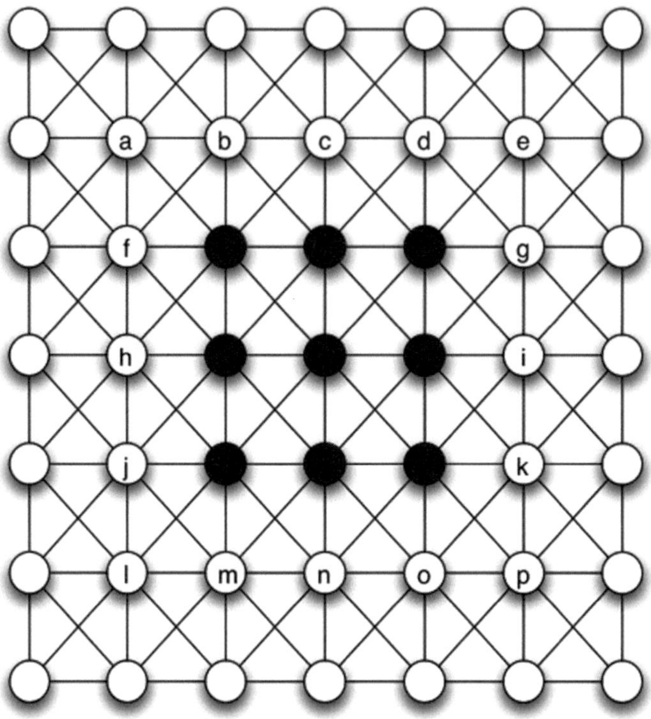


**Fig. 8.9** An infinite grid with 9 early adopters of behaviour $A$ while the others exhibit behaviour $B$

### *8.1.3 Co-existence of Behaviours*

Reference [9] sought to understand how a new technology $A$ might spread through a social network of individuals who are currently users of technology $B$, and how diffusion works when there exist a group of these individuals who can manage both $A$ and $B$ (*bilingual*).

Suppose there are two instant messenger (IM) systems $A$ and $B$, which are not interoperable, i.e, users must be on the same system in order to communicate. There is a social network $G$ on the users, indicating who wants to talk to whom, and the endpoints of each edge $(v, w)$ play a coordination game with possible strategies $A$ or $B$: if $v$ and $w$ each choose IM system $B$, then they they each receive a payoff of $q$; if they each choose IM system $A$, then they they each receive a payoff of $1 - q$; and if they choose opposite systems, then they each receive a payoff of 0. $A$ becomes the "better" technology if $q < \frac{1}{2}$, in the sense that $A - A$ payoffs would then exceed $B - B$ payoffs, while $A$ is the "worse" technology if $q > \frac{1}{2}$.

If all nodes initially play $B$, and a small number of nodes begin adopting strategy $A$ instead, the best response would be to switch to $A$ if enough of a user's neighbours have already adopted $A$. As this unfolds, cascading will occur where either all nodes

**Table 8.3** Payoff matrix

| | $A$ | $B$ | $AB$ |
|---|---|---|---|
| $A$ | $1-q, 1-q$ | $0, 0$ | $1-q, 1-q-c$ |
| $B$ | $0, 0$ | $q, q$ | $q, q-c$ |
| $AB$ | $1-q-c, 1-q$ | $q-c, q$ | $max(q, 1-q)-c, max(q, 1-q)-c$ |

switch to $A$, or there will exist a state of co-existence where some users use $A$, others use $B$, with no interoperability between these two groups.

However, we see that the real-world contains examples where co-existence occurs. Windows coexisting with Mac OS, or Android coexisting with iOS. The point of interest is that these coexisting groups are not completely isolated. There exists a region of overlap between these groups, i.e, there are certain users who are able to use both of the choices and thus act as the bridge between the groups.

Considering that our IM system becomes as follows. Users can choose among three strategies, $A$, $B$ and $AB$ (in which both $A$ and $B$ are used). An adopter of $AB$ gets to use, on an edge-by-edge basis, whichever of $A$ or $B$ yields higher payoffs in each interaction. However, $AB$ has to pay a fixed cost $c$ for being bilingual. The payoffs now become as shown in Table 8.3.

Let us consider that $G$ is infinite and each node has a degree $\Delta \in \mathbb{N}$. The per-edge cost for adopting $AB$ is defined as $r = c/\Delta$.

Reference [9] found that for values of $q$ close to but less than $\frac{1}{2}$, strategy $A$ can cascade on the infinite line if $r$ is sufficiently small or sufficiently large, but not if $r$ takes values in some intermediate interval. In other words, strategy $B$ (which represents the worse technology, since $q < \frac{1}{2}$) will survive if and only if the cost of adopting $AB$ is calibrated to lie in this middle interval. The explanation for this is as follows:

- When $r$ is very small, it is cheap for nodes to adopt $AB$ as a strategy, and so $AB$ spreads through the whole network. Once $AB$ is everywhere, the best-response updates cause all nodes to switch to $A$, since they get the same interaction benefits without paying the penalty of $r$.
- When $r$ is very large, nodes at the interface, with one $A$ neighbour and one $B$ neighbour, will find it too expensive to choose $AB$, so they will choose $A$ (the better technology), and hence $A$ will spread step-by-step through the network.
- When $r$ takes an intermediate value, a node with one $A$ neighbour and one $B$ neighbour, will find it most beneficial to adopt $AB$ as a strategy. Once this happens, the neighbour who is playing $B$ will not have sufficient incentive to switch, and the updates make no further progress. Hence, this intermediate value of $r$ allows a "boundary" of $AB$ to form between the adopters of $A$ and the adopters of $B$.

Therefore, the situation facing $B$ is this: if it is too permissive, it gets invaded by $AB$ followed by $A$; if it is too inflexible, forcing nodes to choose just one of $A$ or $B$, it gets destroyed by a cascade of direct conversions to $A$. But if it has the right balance in the value of $r$, then the adoptions of $A$ come to a stop at a boundary where nodes adopt $AB$.

Reference [9] also shows that when there are three competing technologies, two of these technologies have an incentive to adopt a limited "strategic alliance", partially increasing their interoperability to defend against a new entrant.

## *8.1.4 Cascade Capacity with Bilinguality*

Here, we will look at the following question: Given an infinite network with three possible behaviours, $A$, $B$ and $AB$, and payoff values of $a$ for adopting $A$, $b$ for adopting $B$ and $max(a, b)$ for adopting $AB$ with an incurred cost $c$ for bilinguality; what is the largest threshold at which a finite set adopting $A$ can cause a complete cascade when the rest of the network adopts $B$?

In the case of an infinite path, instead of looking at it in the perspective of a sequence of time steps, we will look at what a certain node will do when it is faced with the choice between different behaviours from each of its neighbour.

### 8.1.4.1 Choice between *A* and *B*

We look at the graph in Fig. 8.10 where $w$ is sandwiched between a neighbour with behaviour $A$ and neighbour adopting behaviour $B$.

Here, $w$ receives a payoff of $a$ if it chooses $A$; it receives a payoff of 1 for choosing $B$; and a payoff of $a + 1 - c$ for adopting $AB$. The logical thing for $w$ is to adopt the behaviour that gives it the highest payoff. The $a - c$ plot in Fig. 8.11 gives us a simpler way to look at the payoffs. These lines intersect at (1, 1) and gives six regions. We see that $A$ is the best strategy in two of these regions, $B$ is the best in two of them, and $AB$ is the best in other two.

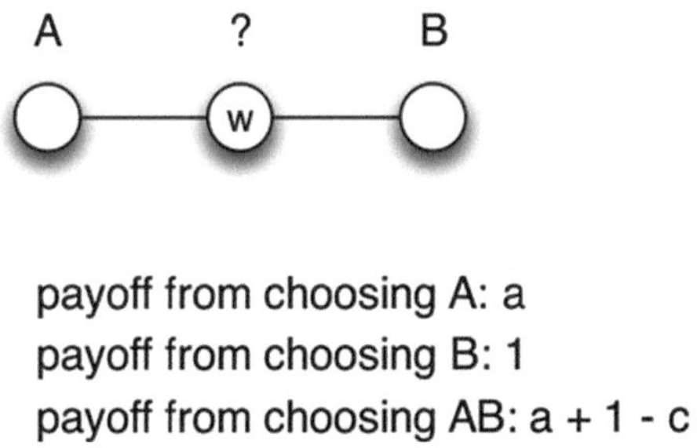


**Fig. 8.10** The payoffs to node $w$ on an infinite path with neighbours exhibiting behaviour $A$ and $B$

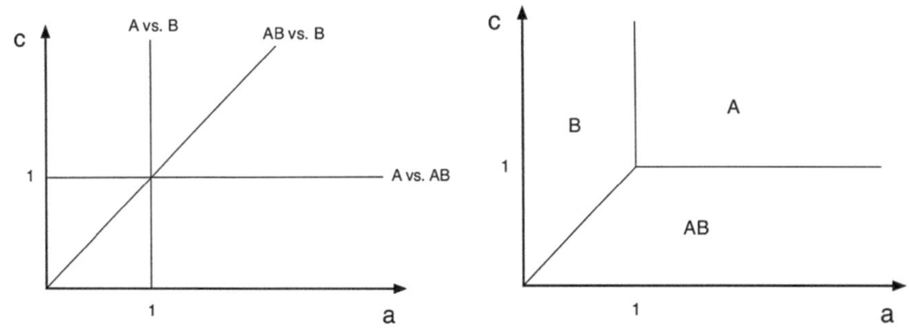


(a) *Lines showing break-even points between strategies.* (b) *Regions defining the best choice of strategy.*

**Fig. 8.11** By dividing the a-c plot based on the payoffs, we get the regions corresponding to the different choices

**Fig. 8.12** The payoffs to node $w$ on an infinite path with neighbours exhibiting behaviour $AB$ and $B$

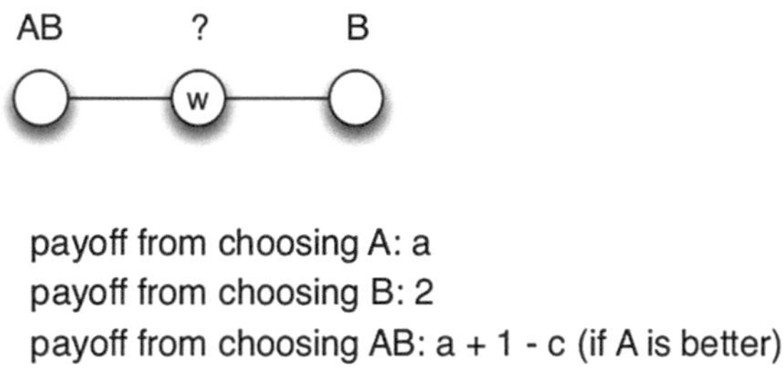


#### 8.1.4.2 Choice Between $AB$ and $B$

The graph in Fig. 8.12 gives us the situation where $w$ is placed between a node with behaviour $AB$ and another exhibiting $B$.

If $a < 1$, then $B$ will provide $w$ with the highest payoff regardless of the value of $c$. Instead, let $a \geq 1$ and $b = 2$ (if $w$ adopts behaviour $B$, it can interact with both of its neighbours). Similar to the case where $w$ was sandwiched between neighbours exhibiting $A$ and $B$, $a - c$ plot as shown in Fig. 8.13 simplifies the view of the payoffs. This $a - c$ plot shows a diagonal line segment from the point $(1, 0)$ to the point $(2, 1)$. To the left of this line segment, $B$ wins and the cascade stops. To the left of this line segment, $AB$ wins—so $AB$ continues spreading to the right, and behind this wave of $AB$'s, nodes will steadily drop $B$ and use only $A$.

Figure 8.14 summarises the possible cascade outcomes based on the values of $a$ and $c$. The possibilities are: (i) $B$ is favoured by all nodes outside the initial adopter set, (ii) $A$ spreads directly without help from $AB$, (iii) $AB$ spreads for one step beyond the initial adopter set, but then $B$ is favoured by all nodes after that, (iv) $AB$ spreads indefinitely to the right, with nodes subsequently switching to $A$.

Models are developed to understand systems where users are faced with alternatives and the costs and benefits of each depend on how many others choose which alternative. This is further complicated when the idea of a "threshold" is introduced.

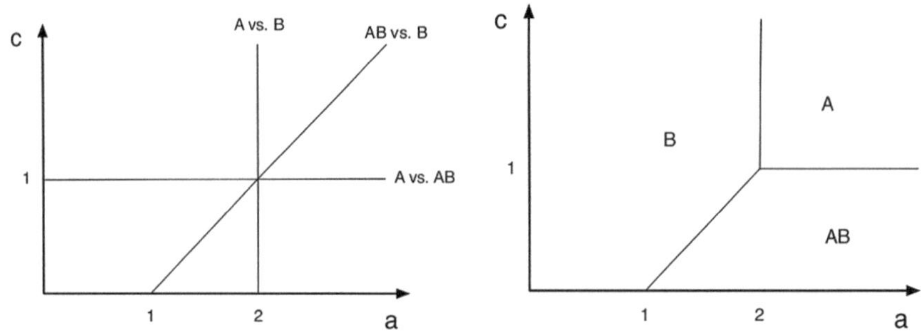


(a) *Lines showing break-even points between strategies.* (b) *Regions defining the best choice of strategy.*

**Fig. 8.13** The a-c plot shows the regions where $w$ chooses each of the possible strategies

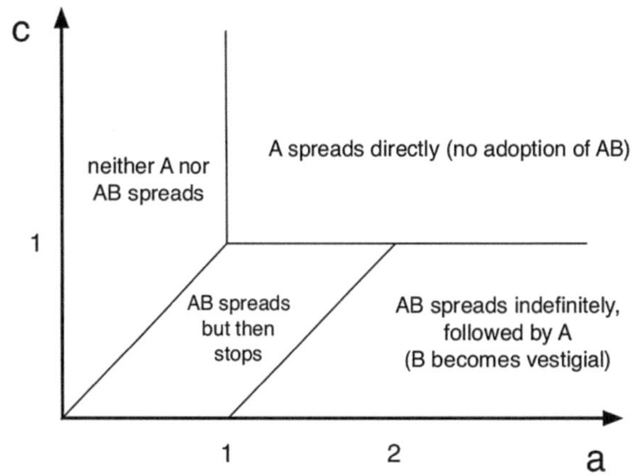


**Fig. 8.14** The plot shows the four possible outcomes for how $A$ spreads or fails to spread on the infinite path, indicated by this division of the $(a, c)$-plane into four regions

The threshold is defined as the proportion of neighbours who must take a decision so that adoption of the same decision by the user renders the net benefits to exceed the net costs for this user.

Reference [8] aimed to present a formal model that could predict, from the initial distribution of thresholds, the final proportion of the users in a system making each of the two decisions, i.e, finding a state of equilibrium. Let the threshold be $x$, the frequency distribution be $f(x)$, and the cumulative distribution be $F(x)$. Let the proportion of adopters at time $t$ be denoted by $r(t)$. This process is described by the difference equation $r(t+1) = F[r(t)]$. When the frequency distribution has a simple form, the difference equation can be solved to give an expression for $r(t)$ at any value of $t$. Then, by setting $r(t+1) = r(t)$, the equilibrium outcome can be found. However, when the functional form is not simple, the equilibrium must be computed by forward recursion. Graphical observation can be used to compute the equilibrium points instead of manipulating the difference equations. Let's start with the fact that we know $r(t)$. Since $r(t+1) = F[r(t)]$, this gives us $r(t+1)$. Repeating this process we find the point $r_e$ at $F[r_e] = r_e$. This is illustrated in Fig. 8.15.

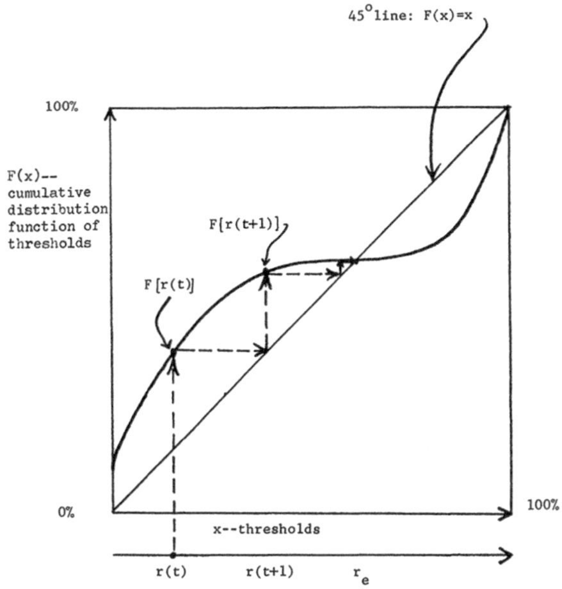


**Fig. 8.15** Graphical method of finding the equilibrium point of a threshold distribution

**Table 8.4** Symmetric payoff matrix

| | 0 | 1 |
|---|---|---|
| 0 | $u(0, 0), u(0, 0)$ | $u(0, 1), u(1, 0)$ |
| 1 | $u(1, 0), u(0, 1)$ | $u(1, 1), u(1, 1)$ |

Consider an infinite population of players. Each player interacts with some finite subset of the population and must choose one of two actions (0 and 1) to play against all neighbours. Let $\Gamma(x)$ denote the set of neighbours of $x$. There exists a critical number $0 \leq q \leq 1$ such that action 1 is the best response for a player if at least proportion $q$ of the neighbours plays 1. The *payoff* of a player is denoted as $u(a, a')$ if the player chooses the action $a$ and the neighbour chooses the action $a'$. This payoff function gives the symmetric payoff matrix shown in Table 8.4.

Action 1 is best response for some player exactly if the probability assigned is at least

$$q = \frac{u(0, 0) - u(1, 0)}{(u(0, 0) - u(1, 0)) + (u(1, 1) - u(0, 1))} \tag{8.4}$$

This changes the payoff matrix to as tabulated in Table 8.5.

A *configuration* $s$ is the assignment of actions for each of the players in the population. Given a configuration $s$, player $x$'s best response is to choose an action which maximises the sum of the payoffs from the interactions with each of the neighbours. Thus action $a$ is the best response to configuration $s$ for player $x$, i.e, $a \epsilon b(s, x)$, if Eq. 8.5 is satisfied.

**Table 8.5** Symmetric payoff matrix parametrized by critical probability $q$

| | 0 | 1 |
|---|---|---|
| 0 | $q, q$ | $0, 0$ |
| 1 | $0, 0$ | $1-q, 1-q$ |

$$\sum_{y \epsilon \Gamma(x)} u(a, s(y)) \geq \sum_{y \epsilon \Gamma(x)} u(1-a, s(y)) \tag{8.5}$$

*Contagion* is said to occur if one action can spread from a finite set of players to the whole population. There is a *contagion threshold* such that the contagion occurs if and only if the payoff parameter $q$ is less than this contagion threshold. A group of players is said to be $p$-cohesive if every member of that group has at least proportion $p$ of the neighbours within the group. Reference [13] shows that the contagion threshold is the smallest $p$ such that every "large" group (consisting of all but a finite sets of players) contains an infinite, $(1-p)$-cohesive, subgroup. Additionally, the contagion threshold is the largest $p$ such that it is possible to label players so that, for any player with a sufficiently high label, proportion at least $p$ of the neighbours has a lower label.

Contagion is most likely to occur if the contagion threshold is close to its upper bound of $\frac{1}{2}$. Reference [13] shows that the contagion threshold will be close to $\frac{1}{2}$ if two properties hold. First, there is *low neighbour growth*: the number of players who can be reached in $k$ steps grows less than exponentially in $k$. This will occur if there is a tendency for players' neighbours' neighbours to be their own neighbours. Second, the local interaction system must be sufficiently uniform, i.e, there is some number $\alpha$ such that for all players a long way from some core group, roughly proportion $\alpha$ of their neighbours are closer to the core group.

Reference [1] deals with a polling game on a directed graph. At round 0, the vertices of a subset $W_0$ are coloured white and all the other vertices are coloured black. At each round, each vertex $v$ is coloured according to the following rule. If at a round $r$, the vertex $v$ has has more than half of its neighbours coloured $c$, then at round $r+1$, the vertex $v$ will be coloured $c$. If at round $r$, the vertex $v$ has the vertex $v$ has exactly half of its neighbours coloured white and the other half coloured black, then this is said to be a tie. In this case, $v$ is coloured at round $r+1$ by the same colour it had at round $r$. If at a finite round $r$, all the vertices are white, then $W_0$ is said to be a *dynamic monopoly* or *dynamo*. The paper proves that for $n \in \mathbb{N}$, there exists a graph with more than $n$ vertices and with a dynamo of 18 vertices. In general, a dynamo of size $O(1)$ (as a function of the number of vertices) is sufficient.

Reference [4] performed a study to understand the strength of weak ties versus the strong ties. They found that the strength of weak ties is that they tend to be long—they connect socially distant locations. Moreover, only a few long ties are needed to give large and highly clustered populations the "degrees of separation" of a random network, in which simple contagions, like disease or information, can rapidly diffuse. It is tempting to regard this principle as a lawful regularity, in part because it justifies generalization from mathematically tractable random graphs to the structured networks that characterize patterns of social interaction. Nevertheless, our research cautions against uncritical generalization. Using Watts and Strogatz's original model of a small world network, they found that long ties do not always facilitate the spread of complex contagions and can even preclude diffusion entirely if nodes have too few common neighbours to provide multiple sources of confirmation or reinforcement. While networks with long, narrow bridges are useful for spreading information about an innovation or social movement, too much randomness can be inefficient for spreading the social reinforcement necessary to act on that information, especially as thresholds increase or connectedness declines.

An informational cascade occurs when it is optimal for an individual, having observed the actions of those ahead of him, to follow the behaviour of the preceding individual without regard to his own information. Reference [2] modelled the dynamics of imitative decision processes as informational cascades and showed that at some stage a decision maker will ignore his private information and act only on the information obtained from previous decisions. Once this stage is reached, her decision is uninformative to others. Therefore, the next individual draws the same inference from the history of past decisions; thus if her signal is drawn independently from the same distribution as previous individuals', this individual also ignores her own information and takes the same action as the previous individual. In the absence of external disturbances, so do all later individuals.

The origin of large but rare cascades that are triggered by small initial shocks is a phenomenon that manifests itself as diversely as cultural fads, collective action, the diffusion of norms and innovations, and cascading failures in infrastructure and organizational networks. Reference [17] presented a possible explanation of this phenomenon in terms of a sparse, random network of interacting agents whose decisions are determined by the actions of their neighbours according to a simple threshold rule. Two regimes are identified in which the network is susceptible to very large cascades also called global cascades, that occur very rarely. When cascade propagation is limited by the connectivity of the network, a power law distribution of cascade sizes is observed. But when the network is highly connected, cascade propagation is limited instead by the local stability of the nodes themselves, and the size distribution of cascades is bimodal, implying a more extreme kind of instability that is correspondingly harder to anticipate. In the first regime, where the distribution of network neighbours is highly skewed, it was found that the most connected nodes were far more likely than average nodes to trigger cascades, but not in the second regime. Finally, it was shown that heterogeneity plays an ambiguous role in determining a system's stability: increasingly heterogeneous thresholds make the system more vulnerable to global cascades; but an increasingly heterogeneous degree distribution makes it less vulnerable.

To understand how social networks affect the spread of behavior, [3] juxtaposed several hypothesis. One popular hypothesis stated that networks with many clustered ties and a high degree of separation will be less effective for behavioural diffusion than networks in which locally redundant ties are rewired to provide shortcuts across the social space. A competing hypothesis argued that when behaviours require social reinforcement, a network with more clustering may be more advantageous, even if the network as a whole has a larger diameter. To really understand the phenomenon, the paper investigated the effects of network structure on diffusion by studying the spread of health behaviour through artificially structured online communities. Individual adoption was found to be much more likely when participants received social reinforcement from multiple neighbours in the social network. The behaviour spread farther and faster across clustered-lattice networks than across corresponding random networks.

Reference [5] called the propagation requiring simultaneous exposure to multiple sources of activation, *multiplex propagation*. This paper found that the effect of random links makes the propagation more difficult to achieve.

## 8.2 Probabilistic Models of Cascade

These cascades primarily refer to epidemic diseases which are contagious and pass from one person to another. These epidemics can either spread through the population at an alarming rate or persist quietly for a long time. In a manner of speaking, the cascade of diseases is similar to the cascade of behaviours. Both of these travel from person to person. However, this is where the similarities end. Behaviour adoption depends on the decision of a person whether or not to switch to that behaviour. On the other hand, a person's decision is moot in the case of the spread of diseases. Only the susceptibility of a person plays a factor in epidemics.

The spread of diseases from one to another can be visualized through a *contact network*. A network where every node is a person and an edge between people if they come in contact with one another which makes it possible for disease to spread. Contact networks are used not only to study the spread of fast-moving diseases in plants and animals but also to track the spread of malicious software through communication networks.

The pathogen and the network are closely intertwined: for different diseases affecting the same population, depending on the transmission medium these diseases may have different rates of spreading. Air-borne diseases would spread faster and over a larger area, infecting a large fraction of the population in very little time. Whereas, a disease requiring some form of physical contact may not spread as fast and may not be able to infect as many individuals when compared to other forms of transmission. A similar case exists in the case of malicious software. A software that can infect any device running a particular operating system, for example, will spread at a rate faster than one requiring a more specific form of access, such as being connected to the same network or being at a certain distance from another infected physical device.

The cascading process in epidemics is more random than that used in modelling behaviour because in each stage of contact there is a certain probability associated with whether or not the disease will be spread. To understand such random behaviour, there exist several models which are discussed as follows.

### 8.2.1 Branching Process

This is the simplest model which works in the following steps:

- *First wave*: Suppose that a disease carrier enters a population. She will transmit the disease to every person she meets independently with probability $p$. Let's suppose she met $k$ people. These $k$ individuals form the first wave of the epidemic and some of them may be infected, while others may not.
- *Second wave*: Now, each of these $k$ individuals in the first wave meet with $k$ different people. This results in $k \cdot k = k^2$ people. Each individual infected in the first wave infects each person in the second wave independently with probability $p$.
- *Subsequent waves*: Further waves are formed in a similar manner where each person in the preceding wave meets with $k$ different people and transmits the infection independently with probability $p$.

The contact network in Fig. 8.16 illustrates the transmission of an epidemic. In this tree network, the root node represents the disease carrier. The first wave is represented by this root node's child nodes. Each of these child nodes denote the parent nodes for the second wave. The set of nodes in every subsequent depth depict each wave.

Figure 8.17 depicts a contact network where the probability of infection is high. This leads the disease to become widespread and multiply at every level, possibly reaching a level where all nodes are infected. In stark contrast, Fig. 8.18 signifies a contact network where the probability is low. This causes the disease to infect fewer and fewer individuals at every level until it completely vanishes.

### 8.2.2 Basic Reproductive Number

The basic reproductive number, denoted by $R_0$, is defined as the expected number of new cases of the disease caused by a single individual. In the branching process discussed in Sect. 8.2.1, since each individual meets $k$ new people and infects each with probability $p$, the basic reproductive number is $pk$.

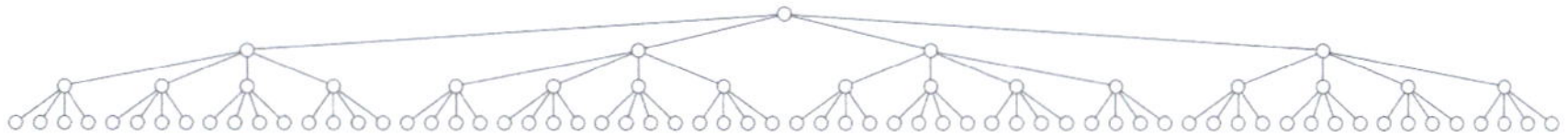

**Fig. 8.16** Contact network for branching process

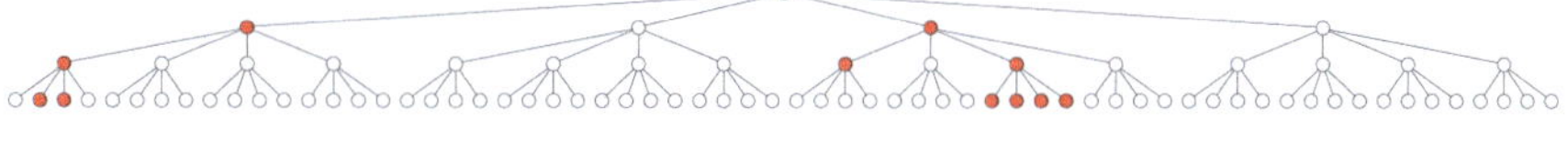

**Fig. 8.17** Contact network for branching process where high infection probability leads to widespread

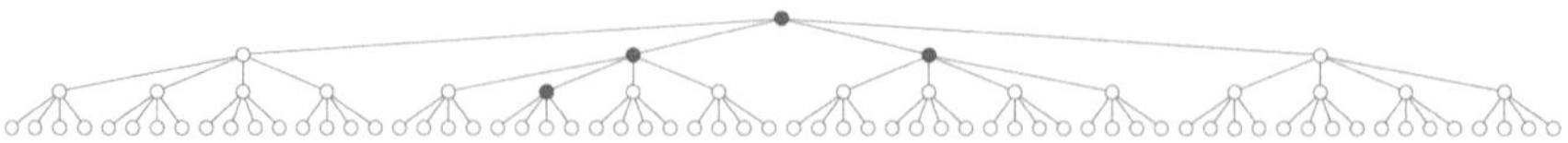

**Fig. 8.18** Contact network for branching process where low infection probability leads to the disappearance of the disease

Let $q_n$ denote the probability that the epidemic survives for atleast $n$ waves, i.e, that some individual in the $n$th level of the tree becomes infected. Let $q^*$ be the limit of $q_n$ as $n$ goes to infinity. In other words, we can call this term $q^*$ the *probability of persistence*.

#### 8.2.2.1 Expected Number of Infected Individuals in the Branching Process

The number of individuals at level $n$ of this tree is $k^n$. Let $X_n$ be a random variable equal to the number of infected individuals at this level $n$. For each individual at level $n$, let $Y_{nj}$ be a random variable equal to 1 if $j$ is infected, and equal to 0 otherwise. Then

$$X_n = Y_{n1} + Y_{n2} + \cdots + Y_{nm} \tag{8.6}$$

where $m = k^n$. By linearity of expectation.

$$E[X_n] = E[Y_{n1} + Y_{n2} + \cdots + Y_{nm}] = E[Y_{n1}] + E[Y_{n2}] + \cdots + E[Y_{nm}] \tag{8.7}$$

Now, $E[Y_{nj}] = 1 \cdot P[Y_{nj} = 1] + 0 \cdot P[Y_{nj} = 0] = P[Y_{nj} = 1]$, i.e, the expectation of each $Y_{nj}$ is the probability of that individual $j$ getting infected.

Individual $j$ at depth $n$ gets infected when each of the $n$ contacts leading from the root to $j$ successfully transmit the disease. Since each contact transmits the disease independently with probability $p$, individual $j$ is infected with probability $p^n$. Therefore, $E[Y_{nj}] = p^n$. This leads us to conclude that

$$E[X_n] = p^n k^n = (pk)^n = R_0^n \tag{8.8}$$

#### 8.2.2.2 Formula for $q_n$

This quantity $q_n$ depends on three quantities: the number of contacts per individual $k$, the contagion probability $p$, and the level of the tree $n$. A direct formula for $q_n$ is difficult to formulate, but it is easier to express $q_n$ in terms of $q_{n-1}$.

Let us consider the following situation: Starting from the root node, the disease spreads through the root's first contact $j$ and then continues to transmit down to $n$ levels in the part of the tree reachable through $j$. For this to happen, it would first require $j$ to catch the disease from the root, which will happen with probability $p$.

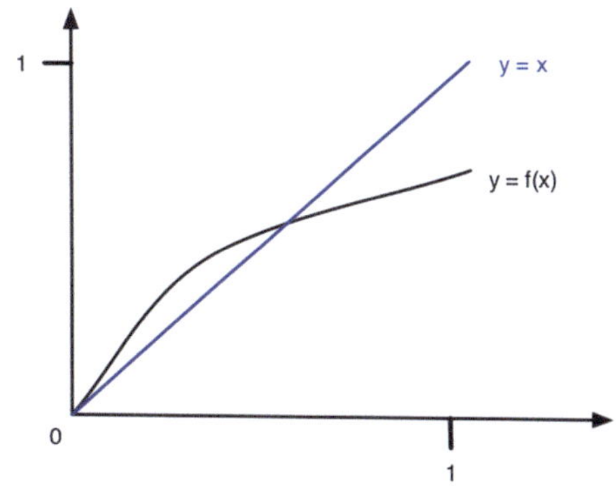


**Fig. 8.19** Repeated application of $f(x) = 1 - (1 - px)^k$

Once $j$ has contracted the pathogen, $j$ analogously becomes the root of its tree. Now the disease will persists through this tree containing $n-1$ levels, accessible by $j$ with probability $q_{n-1}$ (by definition of $q_{n-1}$). This means that the situation will occur with probability $pq_{n-1}$. In other words, the situation will fail with probability $1 - pq_{n-1}$. Now, this gives the probability of failure for the disease to persist through the tree accessible by $j$. Since, the root node has $k$ contacts in all, each of these contacts will fail with probability $1 - pq_{n-1}$. Since they're independent, the probability that they all fail is $(1 - pq_{n-1})^k$. But this is also $1 - q_n$, since by definition of $q_n$, the quantity $1 - q_n$ is exactly the probability that the disease fails to persist to $n$ levels. Therefore

$$1 - q_n = (1 - pq_{n-1})^k \implies q_n = 1 - (1 - pq_{n-1})^k \tag{8.9}$$

Since the root is infected, we can take $q_0 = 1$ by considering that the root is at level 0. From here, we can compute $q_1, q_2, \ldots$. However, this does not tells us the value of $q_n$ as $n$ tends to infinity.

Let $f(x) = 1 - (1 - px)^k$. Then, we can write $q_n = f(q_{n-1})$. Figure 8.19 shows the plot of $f(x)$ for the values $1, f(1), f(f(1)), \ldots$ obtained by repeated application of $f$.

The derivative of $f$ is $f'(x) = pk(1 - px)^k$. Now $f'(0) = pk = R_0$. From the figure, we can conclude that when $R_0 > 1$, $q^* > 0$ and $q^* = 0$ when $R_0 < 1$.

In summary, if $R_0 < 1$, then with probability 1, the disease dies out after a finite number of waves, i.e, $q^* = 0$. If $R_0 > 1$, then with probability greater than 0 the disease persists by infecting atleast one person in each wave, i.e, $q^* > 0$.

So in situations requiring us to contain an epidemic, we have to either quarantine individuals, which will reduce $k$, or take additional measures such as improving sanitation, which could bring down the value of $p$.

### 8.2.3 SIR Epidemic Model

In this epidemic model, each individual goes through the following three stages during the course of the epidemic:

- *Susceptible* (S): Before the individual has caught the disease, it is susceptible to infection from its neighbours.
- *Infected* (I): Once the individual has caught the disease, it is infected and has some probability of infecting each of its susceptible neighbours.
- *Removed* (R): After the individual has experienced the full infectious period, it is removed from the network because it no longer poses a threat of future infection.

The SIR model is defined as follows: Given a directed graph representing the contact network where an edge between $u$ and $v$ indicates that if $u$ becomes infected, then the disease could spread to $v$. Each individual in this network can go through the Susceptible-Infected-Removed cycle. To control the progress of the epidemic, the model has the following two parameters: $p$ is the probability of the spread of infection and $t_I$ indicates the length of the infection.

The model progresses in the following manner: Initially, a finite set of these nodes are in state $I$ while all the others are in state $S$. Each node $v$ that is in this state $I$ remains infectious for a fixed number of steps $t_I$. During these $t_I$ time steps, $v$ can infect its susceptible neighbour with probability $p$. After $t_I$ time steps, the node $v$ moves to state $R$ and can neither infect any other susceptible node nor get infected by any other node.

However, this model is only applicable for diseases which individuals can only contract once in their lifetime such as chicken pox, small pox, etc. The node gets removed from the network because it has gained lifetime immunity. When dealing with diseases such as cholera, typhoid, jaundice, etc, which can recur in individuals, such models cannot be used.

Additionally, this model makes the assumption that the probability of an infection spreading from an infected individual to a susceptible one is uniform throughout with probability $p$. This assumption rarely works in the real-world. The probability of disease spreading depends on the duration and intensity of contact between an infected and a susceptible individual. To account for this, we modify the model to have the probability $p_{u,v}$ between node $u$ and $v$. Higher the probability, greater the intensity of contact.

### 8.2.4 SIS Epidemic Model

This is a model which is useful for diseases that can be contracted by individuals multiple times. In this model, there are only two states: *Susceptible* and *Infected*. There is no *Removed* state. Instead, an infected individual returns to the susceptible state once she is done with the infectious state. The mechanics of the SIS model is similar to the SIR model except that in the latter model, after $t_I$ time steps, an infected node moves to state $R$, but in the former model, the infected node moves to state $S$. Like the SIR model, this model can also have varying probability of infection.

The SIS model may be considered the same as the SIR model if we consider that a node $u$ infected at time step $t$ is different from the same node $u$ infected at time step $t'$. A network that represents the same nodes at different time steps is called a *time-expanded network*.

The qualitative difference between a SIR model and a SIS model is that in the former model, the disease kind of "burns" through the network because nodes once infected move to the removed state after $t_I$ time steps and cannot be reinfected. However, in the latter model, the disease can persist for a very long time infecting an individual multiple times. The only point when the disease vanishes from the network by this model, is when no individual possess the pathogen.

### 8.2.5 SIRS Epidemic Model

Measles and certain sexually transmitted diseases show a certain property of oscillation, i.e, these diseases confer a temporary period of immunity on the infected individuals. To accommodate this phenomenon, we build a model that combines the elements of the SIS and the SIR model. In this model after $t_I$ time steps, i.e, after the infected node has recovered, the node moves to the $R$ state for $t_R$ time steps. After $t_R$ time steps, the node returns to the $S$ state.

### 8.2.6 Transient Contact Network

There are certain other diseases such as HIV/AIDS which progress over many years, and its course is heavily dependent on the contact network. There is a possibility of multiple contacts at a certain period of time which can affect the progression of the disease. Additionally, these contacts so not necessarily last through the whole course of the epidemic, thereby making the contact transient. To keep track of this transience, we will associate with every edge in this contact network the time period during which it was possible for the disease to have been transmitted from one node to the other. Figure 8.20 illustrates a transient network where the time period of contact is associate with each edge.

#### 8.2.6.1 Concurrency

In certain situations it is not just the timing of the contacts that matter but the pattern of timing also which can influence the severity of the epidemic. A timing pattern of particular interest is concurrency. A person is involved in concurrent partnerships if

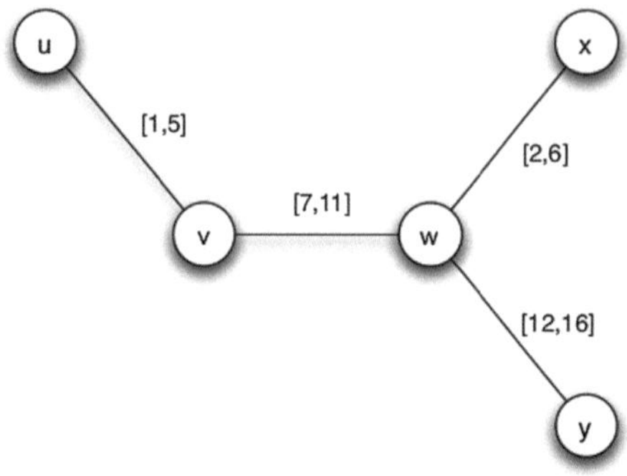


**Fig. 8.20** A contact network where each edge has an associated period of time denoting the time of contact between the connected vertices

she has multiple active partnerships that overlap in time. These concurrent patterns cause the disease to circulate more vigorously through the network and enable any node with the disease to spread it to any other.

Reference [7] proposed a model which when given as input the social network graph with the edges labelled with probabilities of influence between users could predict the time by which a user may be expected to perform an action.

## 8.3 Cascading in Twitter

Reference [16] analysed the ways in which hashtags spread on the network of Twitter users. The network contains a directed edge from user $u$ to user $v$ if $u$ includes "@$v$" in atleast $t$ tweets for some threshold $t$. The *neighbour set* of a user $u$ is the the set of other users to whom $u$ has an edge. As users in $u$'s neighbour set each mentioned a given hashtag $H$ in a tweet for the first time, this paper looked at the probability that $u$ would first mention it as well. Looking at all the users $u$ who have not yet mentioned $H$, but for whom $k$ neighbors have; $p(k)$ is defined to be the fraction of such users who mentioned $H$ before a $(k+1)$st neighbour did so. In other words, $p(k)$ is the fraction of users who adopt the hashtag directly after their $k$th exposure to it, given that they hadn't yet adopted it. Figure 8.21 shows a plot of $p(k)$ as a function of $k$ for the 500 most mentioned hashtags in the dataset. Such a curve is called an *exposure* or *influence* curve. It can be observed that the curve peaks relatively early on and then declines.

*Stickiness* is defined as the probability that a piece of information will pass from a person who knows or mentions it to a person who is exposed to it. It is computed as the maximum value of $p(k)$. *Persistence* is defined as the relative extent to which repeated exposures to a piece of information continue to have significant marginal effects on its adoption.

To understand how these exposure curves vary across different kinds of hashtags, the 500 most-mentioned hashtags were classified according to their topic. Then the curves $p(k)$ were averaged separately within each category and their shapes were

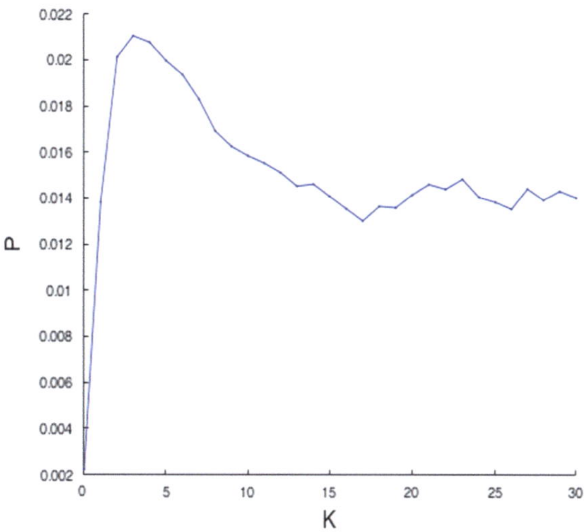


**Fig. 8.21** Exposure curve for top 500 hashtags

compared. Many of the categories had $p(k)$ curves that did not differ significantly in shape from the average, but unusual shapes for several important categories were found. First, for political hashtags, the persistence had a significantly larger value than the average - in other words, successive exposures to a political hashtag had an unusually large effect relative to the peak. In contrast, Twitter idiom hastags - a kind of hashtag that will be familiar to Twitter users in which common English words are concatenated together to serve as a marker for a conversational theme (e.g. #cantlivewithout, #dontyouhate, #iloveitwhen, and many others, including concatenated markers for weekly Twitter events such as #musicmonday and #followfriday). In such cases, the stickiness was high, but the persistence was unusually low; if a user didn't adopt an idiom after a small number of exposures, the marginal chance they did so later fell off quickly.

Next, the paper looks at the overall structure of interconnections among the initial adopters of a hashtag. For this, the first $m$ individuals to mention a particular hashtag $H$ were taken, and the structure of the subgraph $G_m$ induced on these first $m$ mentioners were studied. In this structural context, it was found that political hashtags exhibited distinctive features - in particular, the subgraphs $G_m$ for political hashtags $H$ tended to exhibit higher internal degree, a greater density of triangles, and a large of number of nodes not in $G_m$ who had significant number of neighbors in it.

In the real-world there are multiple pieces of information spreading through the network simultaneously. These pieces of information do not spread in isolation, independent of all other information currently diffusing in the network. These pieces sometimes cooperate while in other times compete with one another. Reference [14] explains a statistical model that allows for this competition as well as cooperation of different contagions in information diffusion. Competing contagions decrease each other's probability of spreading, while cooperating contagions help each other in being adopted throughout the network. It was observed that the sequence in which the contagions were exposed to a person played a role in the effect of a particular contagion $X$. Thus all possible sequences of contagions have to be considered. This model was evaluated on 18,000 contagions simultaneously spreading through the Twitter network. It learnt how different contagions interact with each other and then uses these interactions to more accurately predict the diffusion of a contagion through the network. The following summary for the effects of contagions was learnt:

- A user is exposed to a certain contagion $u_1$. Whether or not she retweets it, this contagion influences her.
- This user is next exposed to another contagion $u_2$. If $u_2$ is more infectious than $u_1$, the user shifts focus from $u_1$ to $u_2$.
- On the other hand, if $u_2$ is less infectious than $u_1$, then the user will still be influenced by $u_1$ instead of switching to $u_2$. However, one of two things can happen:
  - If $u_2$ is highly related to $u_1$ in content, then the user will be more receptive of $u_2$ and this will increase the infection probability of $u_2$.
  - If $u_2$ is unrelated to $u_1$, then the user is less receptive of $u_2$ and the infection probability is decreased.

Moreover, the model also provided a compelling hypothesis for the principles that govern content interaction in information diffusion. It was found that contagions have an adversely negative (suppressive) effect on less infectious contagions that are of unrelated content or subject matter, while at the same time they can dramatically increase the infection probability of contagions that are less infectious but are highly related in subject matter. These interactions caused a relative change in the spreading probability of a contagion by 71% on the average. This model provides ways in which promotion content could strategically be placed to encourage its adoption, and also ways to suppress previously exposed contagions (such as in the case of fake news).

Information reaches people not only through ties in online networks but also through offline networks. Reference [15] devised such a model where a node can receive information through both offline as well as online connections. Using the Twitter data in [14], they studied how information reached the nodes of the network. It was discovered that the information tended to "jump" across the network, which could only be explained as an effect of an unobservable external influence on the network. Additionally, it was found that only about 71% of the information volume in Twitter could be attributed to network diffusion, and the remaining 29% was due to external events and factors outside the network.

### Cascades in Recommendations

Reference [11] studied information cascades in the context of recommendations, and in particular studied the patterns of cascading recommendations that arise in large social networks. A large person-to-person recommendation network from a online retailer consisting of four million people who made sixteen million recommendations on half a million products were investigated. During the period covered by the dataset, each time a person purchased a book, DVD, video, or music product, she was given the option of sending an e-mail message recommending the item to friends. The first recipient to purchase the item received a discount, and the sender received a referral credit with monetary value. A person could make recommendations on a product only after purchasing it. Since each sender had an incentive for making effective referrals, it is natural to hypothesize that this dataset is a good source of cascades. Such a dataset allowed the discovery of novel patterns: the distribution of cascade sizes is approximately heavy-tailed; cascades tend to be shallow, but occasional large bursts of propagation can occur. The cascade sub-patterns revealed mostly small tree-like subgraphs; however differences in connectivity, density, and the shape of cascades across product types were observed. It was observed that the frequency of different cascade subgraphs was not a simple consequence of differences in size or density; rather, there were instances where denser subgraphs were more frequent than sparser ones, in a manner suggestive of properties in the underlying social network and recommendation process. The relative abundance of different cascade subgraphs suggested subtle properties of the underlying social network and recommendation process.

Reference [10] analysed blog information to find out how blogs behave and how information propagates through the *Blogspace*, the space of all blogs. There findings are summarized as follows: The decline of a post's popularity was found to follow a power law with slope $\approx -1.5$. The size of the cascades, size of blogs, in-degrees and out-degrees all follow a power law. Stars and chains were the basic components of cascades, with stars being more common. A SIS model was found to generate cascades that match very well the real cascades with respect to in-degree distribution and cascade size distribution.

Reference [6] developed a generative model that is able to produce the temporal characteristics of the Blogspace. This model $\mathbb{ZC}$ used a 'zero-crossing' approach based on a random walk, combined with exploration and exploitation.

Reference [12] analysed a large network of mass media and blog posts to determine how sentiment features of a post affect the sentiment of connected posts and the structure of the network itself. The experiments were conducted on a graph containing nearly 8 million nodes and 15 million edges. They found that (i) the nodes are not only influenced by their immediate neighbours but also by its position within a cascade and that cascade's characteristics., (ii) deep cascades lead complex but predictable lives, (iii) shallow cascades tend to be objective, and (iv) sentiment becomes more polarized as depth increases.

## Problems

Generate the following two graphs with random seed of 10:

**50** An Erdös-Rényi undirected random graph with 10000 nodes and 100000 edges.

**51** A preferential attachment graph with 10000 nodes with out-degree 10.

Let the nodes in each of these graphs have IDs ranging from 0 to 9999.

Assume that the graphs represent the political climate of an upcoming election between yourself and a rival with a total of 10000 voters. If most of the voters have already made up their mind: 40% will vote for you, 40% for your rival, and the remaining 20% are undecided. Let us say that each voter's support is determined by the last digit of their node ID. If the last digit is 0, 2, 4 or 6, the node supports you. If the last digit is 1, 3, 5 or 7, the node supports your rival. And if the last digit is 8 or 9, the node is undecided.

Assume that the loyalties of the ones that have already made up their minds are steadfast. There are 10 days to the election and the undecided voters will choose their candidate in the following manner:

1. In each iteration, every undecided voter decides on a candidate. Voters are processed in increasing order of node ID. For every undecided voter, if the majority of their friends support you, they now support you. If the majority of their friends support your rival, they now support your rival.
2. If a voter has equal number of friends supporting you and your rival, support is assigned in an alternating fashion, starting from yourself. In other words, the first tie leads to support for you, the second tie leads to support for your rival, the third for you, the fourth for your rival, and so on.
3. When processing the updates, the values from the current iteration are used.
4. There are 10 iterations of the process described above. One happening on each day.
5. The 11th day is the election day, and the votes are counted.

**52** Perform these configurations and iterations, and compute who wins in the first graph, and by how much? Similarly, compute the votes for the second graph.

Let us say that you have a total funding of Rs. 9000, and you have decided to spend this money by hosting a live stream. Unfortunately, only the voters with IDs 3000–3099. However, your stream is so persuasive that any voter who sees it will immediately decide to vote for you, regardless of whether they had decided to vote for yourself, your rival, or where undecided. If it costs Rs. 1000 to reach 10 voters in sequential order, i.e, the first Rs. 1000 reaches voters 3000–3009, the second Rs. 1000 reaches voters 3010–3019, and so on. In other words, the total of Rs. $k$ reaches voters with IDs from 3000 to $3000 + k/100 - 1$. The live stream happens before the 10 day period, and the persuaded voters never change their mind.

**53** Simulate the effect of spending on the two graphs. First, read in the two graphs again and assign the initial configurations as before. Now, before the decision process, you purchase Rs. $k$ of ads and go through the decision process of counting votes.

For each of the two social graphs, plot Rs. $k$ (the amount you spend) on the x-axis (for values k = 1000, 2000, ..., 9000) and the number of votes you win by on the y-axis (that is, the number of votes for youself less the number of votes for your rival). Put these on the same plot. What is the minimum amount you can spend to win the election in each of these graphs?

Instead of general campaigning, you decide to target your campaign. Let's say you have a posh Rs. 1000 per plate event for the high rollers among your voters (the people with the highest degree). You invite high rollers in decreasing order of their degree, and your event is so spectacular that any one who comes to your event is instantly persuaded to vote for you regardless of their previous decision. This event happens before the decision period. When there are ties between voters of the same degree, the high roller with lowest node ID gets chosen first.

**54** Simulate the effect of the high roller dinner on the two graphs. First, read in the graphs and assign the initial configuration as before. Now, before the decision process, you spend Rs. $k$ on the fancy dinner and then go through the decision process of counting votes.

For each of the two social graphs, plot Rs. $k$ (the amount you spend) on the x-axis (for values $k = 1000, 2000, \ldots, 9000$) and the number of votes you win by on the y-axis (that is, the number of votes for yourself less the number of votes for your rival). What is the minimum amount you can spend to win the election in each of the two social graphs?

Assume that a mob has to choose between two behaviours, riot or not. However, this behaviour depends on a threshold which varies from one individual to another, i.e, an individual $i$ has a threshold $t_i$ that determines whether or not to participate. If there are atleast $t_i$ individuals rioting, then $i$ will also participate, otherwise $i$ will refrain from the behaviour.

Assuming that each individual has full knowledge of the behaviour of all the other nodes in the network. In order to explore the impact of thresholds on the final number of rioters, for a mob of $n$ individuals, the histogram of thresholds $N = (N_0, \ldots, N_{n-1})$ is defined, where $N_l$ expresses the number of individuals that have threshold $l \in [n]$. For example, $N_0$ is the number of people who riot no matter what, $N_1$ is the number of people who will riot if one person is rioting, and so on.

Let $T$ = [1, 1, 1, 1, 1, 4, 1, 0, 4, 1, 1, 1, 1, 1, 1, 1, 0, 0, 0, 1, 0, 4, 0, 1, 4, 0, 1, 1, 1, 4, 0, 1, 1, 1, 1, 0, 0, 0, 0, 1, 1, 0, 0, 1, 0, 0, 0, 0, 1, 1, 0, 0, 4, 1, 1, 4. 1, 4, 0, 1, 0, 1, 1, 1, 0, 4, 0, 1, 0, 1, 0, 0, 0, 1, 0, 1, 1, 1, 0, 1, 0, 0, 0, 1, 1, 1, 1, 1, 0, 4, 0, 4, 0, 0, 1, 1, 1, 4, 0, 4, 0] be the vector of thresholds of 101 rioters.

**55** For this threshold vector, compute the histogram $N$.

**56** Using the $N$ calculated in Problem 55, compute its cumulative histogram $[N] = (N_{[1]}, \ldots, N_{[n-1]})$, where $N_{[k]} = \sum_{l=0}^{k} N_l$. Plot the cumulative histogram and report the final number of rioters.

## References


1. Berger, Eli. 2001. Dynamic monopolies of constant size. *Journal of Combinatorial Theory, Series B* 83 (2): 191–200.

2. Bikhchandani, Sushil, David Hirshleifer, and Ivo Welch. 1992. A theory of fads, fashion, custom, and cultural change as informational cascades. *Journal of Political Economy* 100 (5): 992–1026.
3. Centola, Damon. 2010. The spread of behavior in an online social network experiment. *Science* 329 (5996): 1194–1197.
4. Centola, Damon, and Michael Macy. 2007. Complex contagions and the weakness of long ties. *American Journal of Sociology* 113 (3): 702–734.
5. Centola, Damon, Víctor M. Eguíluz, and Michael W. Macy. 2007. Cascade dynamics of complex propagation. *Physica A: Statistical Mechanics and its Applications* 374 (1): 449–456.
6. Goetz, Michaela, Jure Leskovec, Mary McGlohon, and Christos Faloutsos. 2009. Modeling blog dynamics. In *ICWSM*.
7. Goyal, Amit, Francesco Bonchi, and Laks V.S. Lakshmanan. 2010. Learning influence probabilities in social networks. In *Proceedings of the third ACM international conference on Web search and data mining*, 241–250. ACM.
8. Granovetter, Mark. 1978. Threshold models of collective behavior. *American Journal of Sociology* 83 (6): 1420–1443.
9. Immorlica, Nicole, Jon Kleinberg, Mohammad Mahdian, and Tom Wexler. 2007. The role of compatibility in the diffusion of technologies through social networks. In *Proceedings of the 8th ACM conference on Electronic commerce*, 75–83. ACM.
10. Leskovec, Jure, Mary McGlohon, Christos Faloutsos, Natalie Glance, and Matthew Hurst. 2007. Patterns of cascading behavior in large blog graphs. In *Proceedings of the 2007 SIAM international conference on data mining*, 551–556. SIAM
11. Leskovec, Jure, Ajit Singh, and Jon Kleinberg. 2006. Patterns of influence in a recommendation network. In *Pacific-Asia conference on knowledge discovery and data mining*, 380–389. Berlin: Springer.
12. Miller, Mahalia, Conal Sathi, Daniel Wiesenthal, Jure Leskovec, and Christopher Potts. 2011. Sentiment flow through hyperlink networks. In *ICWSM*.
13. Morris, Stephen. 2000. Contagion. *The Review of Economic Studies* 67 (1): 57–78.
14. Myers, Seth A., and Jure Leskovec. 2012. Clash of the contagions: Cooperation and competition in information diffusion. In *2012 IEEE 12th international conference on data mining (ICDM)*, 539–548. IEEE.
15. Myers, Seth A., Chenguang Zhu, and Jure Leskovec. 2012. Information diffusion and external influence in networks. In *Proceedings of the 18th ACM SIGKDD international conference on Knowledge discovery and data mining*, 33–41. ACM.
16. Romero, Daniel M., Brendan Meeder, and Jon Kleinberg. 2011. Differences in the mechanics of information diffusion across topics: idioms, political hashtags, and complex contagion on twitter. In *Proceedings of the 20th international conference on World wide web*, 695–704. ACM.
17. Watts, Duncan J. 2002. A simple model of global cascades on random networks. *Proceedings of the National Academy of Sciences* 99 (9): 5766–5771.

# Chapter 9
# Influence Maximisation

The influence maximization problem is a long running problem with significant amount of literature dedicated to solving this problem. Given a directed social network with influence weights on edges and a number $k$, find $k$ seed nodes such that activating them leads to the maximum expected number of activated nodes, according to a propagation model. In this chapter, we learn that this problem is a NP-hard problem with an approximation giving at best a 63% optimal solution.

## 9.1 Viral Marketing

Marketing is one of the crucial aspects of an organisation because this department is tasked with determining which potential customers to market to. The traditional idea was that if the expected profits from the customer were greater than the cost of marketing to her, then this customer was marketed to. The limitation of this idea is that it believes each customer's decision to be independent of others. However, this is rarely the case. In reality, each customer's decision is based on friends, acquaintances and other buyers. Taking this into account, each customer has two kinds of values. (i) *Intrinsic value* from the profits that can be obtained from a customer, (ii) *Network value* from the profits that can be obtained from her influences, each of their influences, and so on. So if the marketing costs exceed the expected profits from the customer's intrinsic value but can be more than paid up for from her network value, then it is worth marketing to this customer. This marketing strategy that taps on the network value of customers and thereby inexpensively promoting a product by marketing primarily to those with the strongest influence in the market is called *viral marketing*. This dependency of one's decision on that of the people she's connected to makes viral marketing potentially more profitable than direct marketing.



K. Raj P. M. et al., *Practical Social Network Analysis with Python*,
Computer Communications and Networks,
https://doi.org/10.1007/978-3-319-96746-2_9

Reference [4] sought to answer the following question: Suppose that we have data on a social network, with estimates for the extent to which individuals influence one another, and we would like to market a new product that we hope will be adopted by a large fraction of the network. If we can initially targeting a few "influential" members of the network using incentives, we can trigger a cascade of influence by which friends will recommend the product to other friends, and many individuals will ultimately try it. But how should we choose the few key individuals to use for seeding this process? In the search for the solution, a model was developed to compute each customer's probability of buying a product as a function of both the intrinsic value and the network value to optimize the choice of customers to market to, as well as estimating the optimum customer acquisition cost. The framework was applied to marketing movies using the publicly available *EachMovie* database of 2.8 million movie ratings. Reference [12] later modified this work and applied the framework to study the *Epinions* social network application.

Let us say that $X = \{X_1, \ldots, X_n\}$ be the set of $n$ potential customers, $X_i$ be a boolean variable that takes the value 1 if customer $i$ buys the marketed product and 0 otherwise, and $N_i = \{X_{i,1}, \ldots, X_{i,n_i}\} \subseteq X - \{X_i\}$ be the neighbours of $X_i$ each of whom can directly influence $X_i$. Let the product be described by a set of attributes $Y = \{Y_1, \ldots, Y_m\}$. Let $M_i$ be a variable representing the marketing action that is taken by customer $i$, i.e, either $M_i$ could be 1 if customer $i$ was offered a discount and 0 if not, or $M_i$ could be a continuous variable indicating the amount of discount offered, or a nominal variable indicating which of the several possible actions was taken.

Let $M = \{M_1, \ldots, M_n\}$ represent the *marketing plan* containing the marketing actions for each of the $n$ potential customers.

$$\begin{aligned} P(X_i|X - \{X_i\}, Y, M) &= P(X_i|N_i, Y, M) \\ &= \beta_i P_0(X_i|Y, M_i) + (1 - \beta_i) P_N(X_i|N_i, Y, M) \end{aligned} \tag{9.1}$$

where $P_0(X_i|Y, M_i)$ is $X_i$'s internal probability of purchasing the marketed product. $P_N(X_i|N_i, Y, M)$ is the effect that $X_i$'s neighbours have on him. $0 \leq \beta_i \leq 1$ measures how self-reliant $X_i$ is.

$$P_N(X_i|N_i, Y, M) = \sum_{X_j \in N_i} w_{ij} X_j \tag{9.2}$$

where $w_{ij}$ represents how much customer $i$ is influenced by her neighbour $j$, with $w_{ij} \geq 0$ and $\sum_{X_j \in N_i} w_{ij} = 1$. $w_{ij} = 0$ if $j \notin N_i$.

Combining Eqs. 9.1 and 9.2, we get

$$P(X_i = 1|N_i, Y, M) = \beta_i P_0(X_i = 1|Y, M_i) + (1 - \beta_i) \sum_{X_j \in N_i} w_{ij} X_j \tag{9.3}$$

For calculating the optimal marketing plan for a product that has not yet been introduced to the market, we compute

$$P(X_i = 1|Y, M) = \sum_{\tilde{N} \in C(N_i)} P(X_i = 1|\tilde{N}, Y, M) P(\tilde{N}|Y, M) \tag{9.4}$$

where $C(N_i)$ is the set of all possible configurations of $N_i$ and hence $\tilde{N}$ is a set of neighbour state assignments.

Substituting Eq. 9.4 in Eq. 9.3, we get

$$\begin{aligned} P(X_i = 1|Y, M) = & \sum_{\tilde{N} \in C(N_i)} \beta_i P_0(X_i = 1|Y, M_i) P(\tilde{N}|Y, M) \\ & + \sum_{\tilde{N}} (1 - \beta_i) \sum_{X_j \in N_i} w_{ij} \tilde{N}_j P(\tilde{N}|Y, M) \end{aligned} \tag{9.5}$$

where $N_j$ is the value of $X_j$ specified by $\tilde{N}$. $P_0(X_i = 1|Y, M_i)$ is independent of $\tilde{(N)}$, so the first term simplifies to it. The summation order in the second term is swapped, and it is zero whenever $\tilde{N}_j$ is zero. This leads to

$$P(X_i = 1|Y, M) = \beta_i P_0(X_i = 1|Y, M_i) + (1 - \beta_i) \sum_{X_j \in N_i} w_{ij} P(X_j = 1|Y, M) \tag{9.6}$$

The goal is to find the marketing plan that maximises profit. Assume that $M$ is a boolean vector, $c$ is the cost of marketing to a customer, $r_0$ is the revenue from selling to the customer if no marketing action is performed, and $r_1$ is the revenue if marketing is performed. $r_0$ and $r_1$ is the same unless marketing action includes offering a discount. Let $f_i^1(M)$ be the result of setting $M_i$ to 1 and leaving the rest of $M$ unchanged, and similarly for $f_i^0(M)$. The *expected lift in profit* from marketing to customer $i$ in isolation is then

$$\begin{aligned} ELP_i^1(Y, M) = & \\ & r_1 P(X_i = 1|Y, f_i^1(M)) \\ & - r_0 P(X_i = 1|Y, f_i^0(M)) - c \end{aligned} \tag{9.7}$$

This equation gives the intrinsic value of the customer. Let $M_0$ be the null vector. The *global lift in profit* that results from a particular choice $M$ of customers to market to is then

$$ELP(Y, M) = \sum_{i=1}^{n} [r_i P(X_i = 1|Y, M) - r_0 P(X_i = 1|Y, M_0) - c_i] \tag{9.8}$$

where $r_i = r_1$ if $M_i = 1$, $r_i = r_0$ if $M_i = 0$, and $|M|$ is the number of ones in $M$. The total value of a customer is computed as $ELP(Y, f_i^1(M)) - ELP(Y, f_i^0(M))$. The network value is the difference between her total and intrinsic values.

Let $0 \leq z \leq 1$ be a marketing action where $z = 0$ when no marketing action is performed. Let $c(z)$ be the cost of performing the action and $r(z)$ be the revenue obtained if the product is purchased. Let $f_i^z(M)$ be the result of setting $M_i$ to $z$ and leaving the rest of $M$ unchanged. The expected lift in profit from performing marketing action $z$ on customer $i$ in isolation is then

$$\begin{aligned} ELP_i^z(Y, M) = r(z)P(X_i = 1|Y, f_i^z(M)) \\ - r(0)(X_i = 1|Y, f_i^0(M)) - c(z). \end{aligned} \tag{9.9}$$

The global lift in profit is

$$ELP(Y, M) = \sum_{i=1}^{n} [r(M_i)P(X_i = 1|Y, M) - r(0)P(X_i = 1|Y, M_0) - c(M_i)]. \tag{9.10}$$

To find the optimal $M$ that maximises $ELP$, we must try all possible combinations of assignments to its components. However, this is intractable, [4] proposes the following approximate procedures:

- *Single pass*: For each $i$, set $M_i = 1$ if $ELP(Y, f_i^1(M_0)) > 0$ and set $M_i = 0$ otherwise.
- *Greedy search*: Set $M = M_0$. Loop through the $M_i$'s setting each $M_i$ to 1 if $ELP(Y, f_i^1(M)) > ELP(Y, M)$. Continue looping until there are no changes in a complete scan of the $M_i$'s.
- *Hill climbing search*: Set $M = M_0$. Set $M_{i_1} = 1$ where $i_1 = argmax_i \{ELP(Y, f_i^1(M))\}$. Now, set $M_{i_2} = 1$ where $i_2 = argmax_i \{ELP(Y, f_i^1(f_i^1(M)))\}$. Repeat until there is no $i$ for which setting $M_i = 1$ increases $ELP$.

The effect that marketing to a person has on the rest of the network is independent of the marketing actions to other customers. From a customer's network effect, we can directly compute whether he is worth marketing to. Let the $\Delta_i(Y)$ be the network effect of customer $i$ for a product with attributes $Y$. It is defined as the total increase in probability of purchasing in the network (including $X_i$) that results from a unit change in $P_0(X_i)$:

$$\Delta_i(Y) = \sum_{j=1}^{N} \frac{\partial P(X_j = 1|Y, M_0)}{\partial P(X_i = 1|Y, M_i)} \tag{9.11}$$

Since $\Delta_i(Y)$ is the same for any $M$, we define it for $M = M0$. Reference [4] calculates $\Delta_i(Y)$ as

$$\Delta_i(Y) = \sum_{j=1}^{n} w_{ji}\Delta_j(Y) \tag{9.12}$$

$\Delta_i(Y)$ is initially set to 1 for all $i$, then recursively re-calculated using Eq. 9.12 until convergence. $\Delta P_i(z, Y)$ is defined to be the immediate change in customer $i$'s probability of purchasing when he is marketed to with marketing action $z$:

$$\begin{aligned} &\Delta P_i(z, Y) = \\ &\qquad \beta_i[P_0(X_i = 1|Y, M_i = z) - P_0(X_i = 1|Y, M_i = 0)] \end{aligned} \tag{9.13}$$

From Eq. 9.11, and given that $P(X_j = 1|Y, M_0)$ varies linearly with $P(X_j = 1|Y, M_i)$, the change in the probability of purchasing across the entire network is then

$$\begin{aligned} \sum_{j=1}^{n} \Delta P(X_j = 1|Y, M_0) &= \Delta_i(Y) \cdot \Delta P_0(X_i = 1|Y, M_i) \\ &= \Delta_i(Y) \cdot \Delta P_i(z, Y) \end{aligned} \tag{9.14}$$

So the total lift in profit becomes

$$\begin{aligned} &ELP^z_{i,total}(Y, M) = \\ &\qquad r(0)[(\Delta_i(Y) - 1) \cdot \Delta P_i(z, Y)] \\ &\qquad + [r(z)P(X_i = 1|Y, f_i^z(M)) - r(0)P(X_i = 1|Y, M)] \\ &\qquad - c(z) \end{aligned} \tag{9.15}$$

This approximation is exact when $r(z)$ is constant, which is the case in any marketing scenario that is advertising-based. When this is the case, the equation simplifies to:

$$\begin{aligned} &ELP^z_{i,total}(Y, M) \\ &\qquad = r[(\Delta_i(Y) - 1) \cdot \Delta P_i(z, Y)] + r[\Delta P_i(z, Y)] - c(z) \\ &\qquad = r\Delta_i(Y) \cdot \Delta P_i(z, Y) - c(z) \end{aligned} \tag{9.16}$$

With Eq. 9.16, we can directly estimate customer $i$'s lift in profit for any marketing action $z$. To find the $z$ that maximises the lift in profit, we take the derivative with respect to $z$ and set it equal to zero, resulting in:

$$r\Delta_i(Y)\frac{d\Delta P_i(z, Y)}{dz} = \frac{dc(z)}{dz} \tag{9.17}$$

Assume $\Delta P_i(z, Y)$ is differentiable, this allows us to directly calculate the $z$ which maximises $ELP^z_{i,total}(Y, M)$ which is the optimal value for $M_i$ in the $M$ that maximizes $ELP(Y, M)$. Hence, from the customers network effects, $\Delta_i(Y)$, we can directly calculate the optimal marketing plan.

Collaborative filtering systems were used to identify the items to recommend to customers. In these systems, users rate a set of items, and these ratings are used to recommend other items that the user might be interested in. The quantitative collaborative filtering algorithm proposed in [11] was used in this study. The algorithm predicts a user's rating of an item as the weighted average of the ratings given by similar users, and recommends these items with high predicted ratings.

These methodologies were applied on the problem of marketing movies using the *EachMovie* collaboration filtering database. EachMovie contains 2.8 million ratings of 1628 movies by 72916 users between 1996 and 1997 by the eponymous recommendation site. EachMovie consists of three databases: one contains the ratings (on a scale of zero to five), one contains the demographic information, and one containing information about the movies. The methods with certain modifications were applied to the *Epinions* dataset.

In summary, the goal is to market to a good customer. Although in a general sense, the definition of good is a subjective one, this paper uses the following operating definitions. A good customer is one who satisfies the following conditions: (i) Likely to give the product a high rating, (ii) Has a strong weight in determining the rating prediction for many of her neighbours, (iii) Has many neighbours who are easily influenced by the rating prediction they receive, (iv) Will have high probability of purchasing the product, and thus will be likely to actually submit a rating that will affect her neighbours, (v) has many neighbours with the aforementioned four characteristics, (vi) will enjoy the marketed movie, (vii) has many close friends, (viii) these close friends are easily swayed, (ix) the friends will very likely see this movie, and (x) has friends whose friends have these properties.

## 9.2 Approximation Algorithm for Influential Identification

Reference [8] found that the optimization problem of selecting the most influential nodes is NP-hard. The paper instead proposes an approximation algorithm. Using an analysis framework based on submodular functions, the paper showed that a natural greedy strategy obtains a solution that is provably within 63% of optimal for several classes of models.

Consider a directed graph $G$ which represents a social network. Each node is either *active* or *inactive* depending on whether or not this node is an adopter of an innovation or product. We will look at how the node progresses from being inactive to active. The switch in the other direction can be made easily. Roughly, a node $v$ is initially inactive. As time unfolds, more and more of $v$'s neighbours become active. At some point, this may cause $v$ to become active, and this decision may in turn trigger further decisions by nodes to which $v$ is connected.

Here, the *linear threshold model* is used to look at the cascading process. A node $v$ is influenced by each neighbour $w$ according to a weight $b_{v,w}$ such that $\sum_{w \ neighbour \ of \ v} b_{v,w} \leq 1$. Each node $v$ chooses a threshold $\theta_v$ uniformly at random from the interval $[0, 1]$ which represents the weighted fraction of $v$'s neighbours that must become active in order for $v$ to become active. Given a random choice of thresholds, and an initial set of active nodes $A_0$ with all other nodes inactive, the diffusion process unfolds deterministically in discrete steps. In step $t$, all nodes that were active in step $t-1$ remain active, and we activate any node $v$ for which the total weight of its active neighbours is atleast $\theta_v$, such that

$$\sum_{w \ active \ neighbour \ of \ v} b_{v,w} \geq \theta_v \tag{9.18}$$

Additionally, the *independent cascade model* is also considered sometimes. This model also starts with an initial active set of nodes $A_0$, and the process unfolds in discrete steps according to the following randomized rule. When node $v$ first becomes active in step $t$, it is given a single chance to activate each currently inactive neighbour $w$. It succeeds with probability $p_{v,w}$. If $v$ succeeds, then $w$ will become active in step $t+1$. Whether or not $v$ succeeds, it cannot make any further attempts to activate $w$ in subsequent rounds. This process runs until no more activations are possible.

We define the *influence* of a set of nodes $A$, denoted by $\sigma(A)$, as the expected number of active nodes at the end of the process. We need to find for a given value of $k$, a $k$-node set of maximum influence. It is NP-hard to determine the optimum for influence maximisation and an approximation can be done to a factor of $(1 - \frac{1}{e} - \epsilon)$ where $e$ is the base of the natural logarithm and $\epsilon$ is any positive real number. This gives a performance guarantee of approximately 63%. The algorithm that achieves this performance guarantee is a natural greedy hill-climbing strategy. Additionally, the paper shows that this approximation algorithm can be applied to the models proposed in [4, 12].

Consider a function $f(\cdot)$ that maps subsets of a finite ground set $U$ to non-negative real numbers. $f$ is said to be *submodular* if it satisfies a natural self-diminishing property: the marginal gain from adding an element to a set $S$ is atleast as high as the marginal gain from adding the same element to a superset of $S$. Formally, a submodular function satisfies Eq. 9.19.

$$f(S \cup \{v\}) - f(S) \geq f(T \cup \{v\}) - f(T) \tag{9.19}$$

for all elements $v$ and all pairs of sets $S \subseteq T$. There is one particular property of submodular functions that is of specific interest to the paper.

**Theorem 12** *For a non-negative integer, monotone submodular function $f$, let $S$ be a set of size $k$ obtained by selecting elements one at a time, each time choosing an element that provides the largest marginal increase in the function value. Let $S^*$ be a* *set that maximises the value of $f$ over all $k$-element sets. Then $f(S) \geq (1-\frac{1}{e}) \cdot f(S^*)$, i.e, $S$ provides a $(1-\frac{1}{e})$-approximation.*

This property can be extended to show that for any $\epsilon > 0$, there is a $\gamma > 0$ such that by using $(1+\gamma)$-approximate values for the function to be optimized, a $(1-\frac{1}{e}-\epsilon)$-approximation.

Further it is assumed that each node $v$ has an associated non-negative weight $w_v$ which tells us how important it is that $v$ be activated in the final outcome. If $B$ denotes the set activated by the process with initial activation $A$, then the weighted influence function $\sigma_w(A)$ is defined to be the expected value over outcomes $B$ of the quantity $\sum\limits_{v \in B} w_v$.

The paper proves the following theorems:

- **Theorem 13** *For an arbitrary instance of the independent cascade model, the resulting influence function $\sigma(\cdot)$ is submodular.*
- **Theorem 14** *For an arbitrary instance of the linear threshold model, the resulting influence function $\sigma(\cdot)$ is submodular.*
- **Theorem 15** *A node $x$ ends up active if and only if there is a path from some node in $A$ to $x$ consisting of live edges.*
- **Theorem 16** *For a given targeted set $A$, the following two distributions over sets of nodes are the same:*

1. *The distribution over active sets obtained by running the linear threshold model to completion starting from $A$.*
2. *The distribution over sets reachable from $A$ via live-edge paths, under the random selection of live edges defined above.*

- **Theorem 17** *The influence maximization problem is NP-hard for the independent cascade model.*
- **Theorem 18** *The influence maximization problem is NP-hard for the linear threshold model.*

This approximation algorithm was tested on the collaboration graph obtained from co-authorships in the high-energy physics theory section of the e-print arXiv publications. This collaboration graph contains a node for each researcher who has atleast one paper with co-author(s) in the arXiv database. For each paper with two or more authors, an edge was inserted for each pair of authors (single-author papers were ignored). The resulting graph had 10748 nodes, and edges between about 53000 pairs of nodes.

The algorithm was compared in three different models of influence. In the linear threshold model, if nodes $u$ and $v$ have $c_{u,v}$ parallel edges between them, and degrees $d_u$ and $d_v$, the edge $(u, v)$ was assigned the weight $\frac{c_{u,v}}{d_v}$ and the edge $(v, u)$ is given the weight $\frac{c_{u,v}}{d_u}$. In the independent cascade model, a uniform probability of $p$ was assigned to each edge, choosing 1 and 10% in separate trials. If nodes $u$ and $v$ have $c_{u,v}$ edges, $u$ has a chance of $p$ to activate $v$, i.e, $u$ has total probability of $1-(1-p)^{c_{u,v}}$ of activating $v$ once it becomes active. A special case of the independent cascade model termed as "weighted cascade" was studied wherein each edge from node $u$ to $v$ was assigned probability $\frac{1}{d_v}$ of activating $v$.

The greedy algorithm was compared with heuristics based on degree centrality, distance centrality and a crude baseline of choosing random nodes to target. The degree centrality involves choosing nodes in order of decreasing degrees, the distance centrality chooses nodes in order of increasing average distance to other nodes in the network.

For computing $\sigma(A)$, the process was simulated 10000 times for each targeted set, re-choosing thresholds or edge outcomes pseudo-randomly from [0, 1] every time.

Figures 9.1, 9.2, 9.3, 9.4 show the performance of the algorithms in the linear model, weight cascade model, independent cascade model with probabilities 1 and 10% respectively. It is observed that the greedy algorithm clearly surpasses the other heuristics.

From these results, the paper proposes a broader framework that generalizes these models. The *general threshold model* is proposed. A node $v$'s decision to become active can be based on an arbitrary monotone function of the set of neighbours of $v$ that are already active. Thus, associated with $v$ is a *monotone threshold function* $f_v$ that maps subsets of $v$'s neighbour set to real numbers in [0, 1], subject to the condition that $f_v(\phi) = 0$. Each node $v$ initially chooses $\theta_v$ uniformly at random from the interval [0, 1]. Now, however, $v$ becomes active in step $t$ if $f_v(S) \geq \theta_v$ , where $S$ is the set of neighbours of $v$ that are active in step $t-1$. Thus, the linear threshold model is a special case of this general threshold model in which each threshold function has the form $f_v(S) = \sum_{u \in S} b_{v,u}$ for parameters $b_{v,u}$ such that $\sum_{u\ neighbour\ of\ v} b_{v,u} \leq 1$.

The independent cascade model is generalized to allow the probability that $u$ succeeds in activating a neighbour $v$ to depend on the set of $v$'s neighbours that

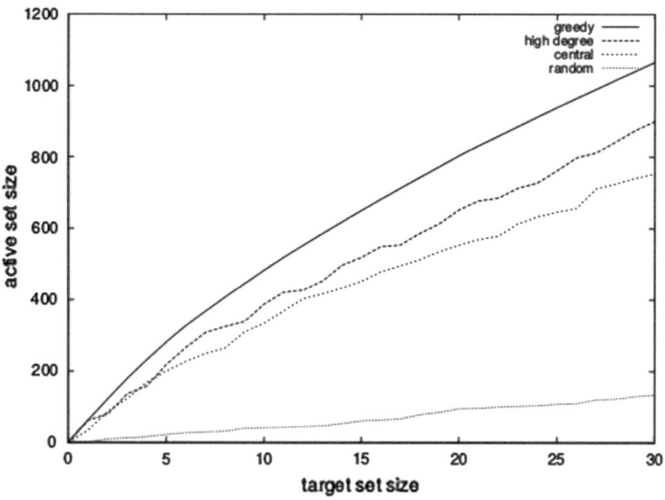


**Fig. 9.1** Results for the linear threshold model

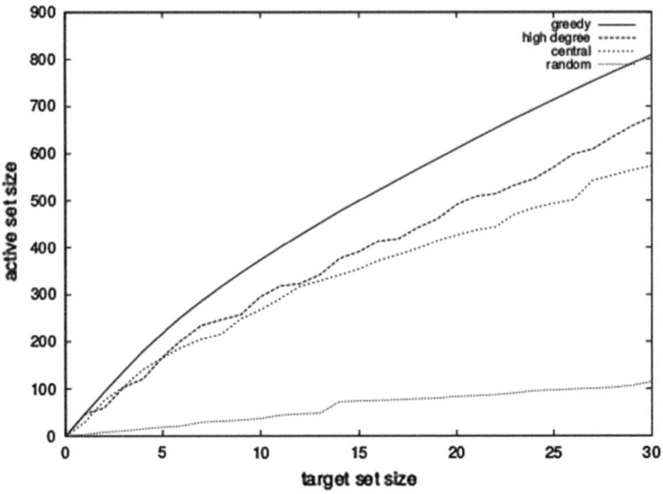


**Fig. 9.2** Results for the weight cascade model

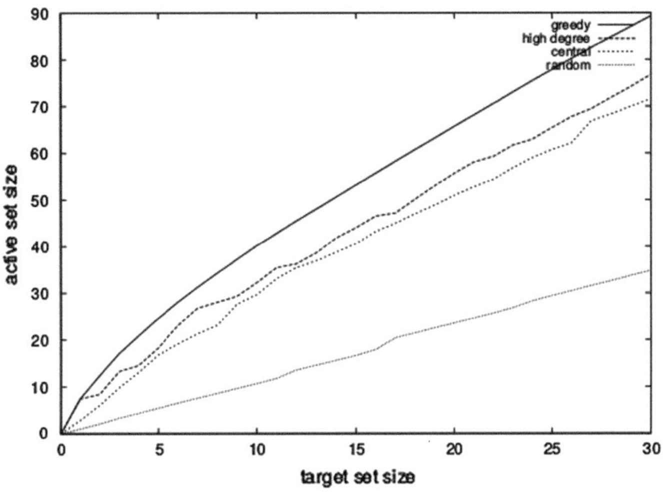


**Fig. 9.3** Results for the independent cascade model with probability 1%

have already tried. This uses an *incremental function* $p_v(u, S) \in [0, 1]$, where $S$ and $u$ are disjoint subsets of $v$'s neighbour set. A general cascade process works by analogy with the independent case: in the general case, when $u$ attempts to activate $v$, it succeeds with probability $p_v(u, S)$, where $S$ is the set of neighbours that have already tried (and failed) to activate $v$. The independent cascade model is the special case where $p_v(u, S)$ is a constant $p_{u,v}$, independent of $S$. The cascade models of interest are only those defined by incremental functions that are order-independent in the following sense: if neighbours $u_1, u_2, \ldots, u_l$ try to activate $v$, then the probability

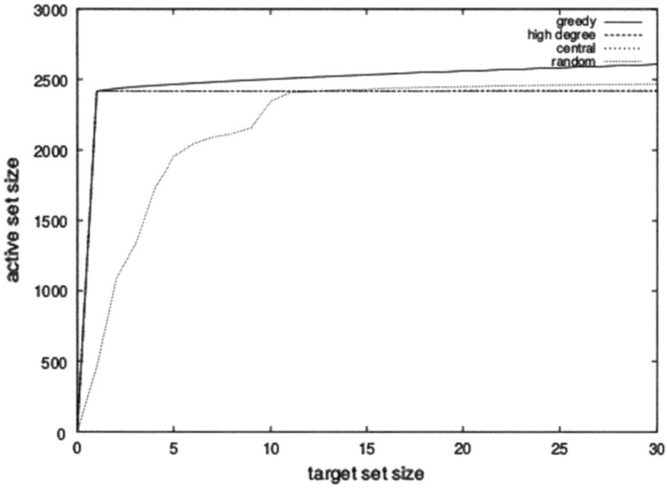


**Fig. 9.4** Results for the independent cascade model with probability 10%

that $v$ is activated at the end of these $l$ attempts does not depend on the order in which the attempts are made.

These two models are equivalent and there is a way to convert between them. First, consider an instance of the general threshold model with threshold functions $f_v$ . To define an equivalent cascade model, we need to understand the probability that an additional neighbour $u$ can activate $v$, given that the nodes in a set $S$ have already tried and failed. If the nodes in $S$ have failed, then node $v$'s threshold $\theta_v$ must be in the range $\theta_v \in (f_v(S), 1]$. However, subject to this constraint, it is uniformly distributed. Thus, the probability that a neighbour $u \notin S$ succeeds in activating $v$, given that the nodes in $S$ have failed, is as given in Eq. 9.20.

$$p_v(u, S) = \frac{f_v(S \cup \{u\}) - f_v(S)}{1 - f_v(S)} \tag{9.20}$$

So the cascade process with these functions is equivalent to the original threshold process.

Conversely, consider a node $v$ in the cascade model, and a set $S = \{u_1, \ldots, u_k\}$ of its neighbours. Assume that the nodes in $S$ try to activate $v$ in the order $u_1, \ldots, u_k$, and let $S_i = \{u_1, \ldots, u_i\}$. Then the probability that $v$ is not activated by this process is by definition $\prod_{i=1}^{k}(1 - p_v(u_i, S_{i-1}))$. Recall that we assumed that the order in which the $u_i$ try to activate $v$ does not affect their overall success probability. Hence, this value depends on the set $S$ only, and we can define $f_v(S) = \prod_{i=1}^{k}(1 - p_v(u_i, S_{i-1}))$. Analogously, one can show that this instance of the threshold model is equivalent to the original cascade process.

The paper also proposed a *triggering model*, where each node $v$ independently chooses a random "triggering set" $T_v$ according to some distribution over subsets of its neighbours. To start the process, we target a set $A$ for initial activation. After this initial iteration, an inactive node $v$ becomes active in step $t$ if it has a neighbour in its chosen triggering set $T_v$ that is active at time $t-1$. (Thus, $v$'s threshold has been replaced by a latent subset of $T_v$ of neighbours whose behaviour actually affects $v$).

**Theorem 19** *Whenever the threshold functions $f_v$ at every node are monotone and submodular, the resulting influence function $\sigma(\cdot)$ is monotone and submodular as well.*

Reference [10] presented an optimization in selecting new seeds, which is referred to as the "Cost-Effective Lazy Forward" (CELF) scheme. This CELF optimization uses the submodularity property of the influence maximization objective to greatly reduce the number of evaluations on the influence spread of vertices. Their experimental results demonstrate that CELF optimization could achieve as much as 700 times speedup in selecting seed vertices.

Reference [2] designed schemes to combine with the CELF optimisation to improve the greedy algorithms of [8], and proposed a *degree discount* heuristics with influence spreads to replace the degree and distance centrality heuristics of [8]. The advantage of these new heuristics is their speed. The algorithm using this degree discount has order of $O(klogn + m)$ when compared to the greedy algorithm which has $O(knRm)$. Here $n$ denotes the number of vertices, $m$ denotes the number of edges, $k$ is the number of elements in the $k$-set of influentials, and $R$ is the number of simulations. These schemes when applied to the independent cascade model showed a completion time of only a few milliseconds, which is less than one-millionth of the time of the fastest greedy algorithm. Additionally, they also show a good influence spread performance. The developed algorithms were tested on the same datasets as used in [8].

However these heuristics developed in [2] apply only to the independent cascade model and not to the independent cascade model. Reference [3] developed the LDAG algorithm for this latter model. In this model, a local DAG is computed for each vertex $v$ and the influence to $v$ is restricted to within this DAG structure. To select local DAGs that could cover a significant portion of influence propagation, a fast greedy algorithm of adding nodes into the local DAG of a node $v$ one by one was proposed such that the individual influence of these nodes to $v$ is larger than a threshold parameter $\theta$. After constructing the local DAGs, the greedy approach of selecting seeds that provide the maximum incremental influence spread with a fast scheme of updating incremental influence spread of every node was combined. This combined fast local DAG construction and fast incremental influence update make the LDAG algorithm very efficient. This algorithm was found to perform much faster than the greedy algorithm at a fraction of its completion time. However, finding the optimal LDAG is still NP-hard.

Reference [6] proposed *SIMPATH*, an algorithm under the linear cascade model that addresses the drawbacks found in [8] using several optimisations. The paper proves that in the linear threshold model which says the spread of a set of nodes can be calculated as the sum of spreads of each node in the set on appropriate induced subgraphs. SIMPATH builds on the CELF optimization. However, instead of using expensive MC simulations to estimate the spread, the spread is computed by enumerating the simple paths starting from the seed nodes. Although the problem of enumerating simple paths is #P-hard, majority of the influence flows within a small neighbourhood, since probabilities of paths diminish rapidly as they get longer. Thus, the spread can be computed accurately by enumerating paths within a small neighbourhood. A parameter $\eta$ is proposed to control the size of the neighbourhood that represents a direct trade-off between accuracy of spread estimation and running time. Two novel optimizations were proposed to reduce the number of spread estimation calls made by SIMPATH . The first one, called the *VERTEX COVER OPTIMIZATION*, cuts down on the number of calls made in the first iteration, thus addressing a key weakness of the simple greedy algorithm that is not addressed by CELF. Since the spread of a node can be computed directly using the spread of its out-neighbors, in the first iteration, a vertex cover of the graph is first constructed and the spread only for these nodes is obtained using the spread estimation procedure. The spread of the rest of the nodes is derived from this. This significantly reduces the running time of the first iteration. Next, it is observed that as the size of the seed set grows in subsequent iterations, the spread estimation process slows down considerably. Another optimization called *LOOK AHEAD OPTIMIZATION* which addresses this issue and keeps the running time of subsequent iterations small is proposed. Specifically, using a parameter $l$, it picks the top-$l$ most promising seed candidates in the start of an iteration and shares the marginal gain computation of those candidates. The paper concludes by showing through extensive experiments on four real datasets that the SIMPATH algorithm is more efficient, consumes less memory and produces seed sets with larger spread of influence than LDAG. Indeed, among all the settings we tried, the seed selection quality of SIMPATH is quite close to the simple greedy algorithm.

Reference [9] studied the contrasting behaviour between cascading models and viral marketing by analysing a person-to-person recommendation network, consisting of 4 million people who made 16 million recommendations on half a million products. This network was retrieved from an online retailer's incentivised viral marketing program. The website gave discounts to customers recommending any of its products to others, and then tracked the resulting purchases and additional recommendations. Although, it is assumed in epidemic models such as SIRS model that individuals have equal probability of being infected every time they interact, the paper observed that the probability of infection decreases with repeated interaction. This means that providing excessive incentives for customers to recommend products could backfire by weakening the credibility of the very same links they are trying to take advantage of.

Cascading models also often assume that individuals either have a constant probability of 'converting' every time they interact with an infected individual [5], or that they convert once the fraction of their contacts who are infected exceeds a threshold [7]. In both cases, an increasing number of infected contacts results in an increased likelihood of infection. Instead, it was found that the probability of purchasing a product increases with the number of recommendations received, but quickly saturated to a constant and relatively low probability. This meant that individuals are often impervious to the recommendations of their friends, and resist buying items that they do not want.

In network-based epidemic models, extremely highly connected individuals play a very important role. For example, in needle sharing and sexual contact networks these nodes become the "super-spreaders" by infecting a large number of people. But these models assume that a high degree node has as much of a probability of infecting each of its neighbours as a low degree node does. In contrast, it was found that there are limits to how influential high degree nodes are in the recommendation network. As a person sends out more and more recommendations past a certain number for a product, the success per recommendation declines. This indicates that individuals have influence over a few of their friends, but not everybody they know.

A simple stochastic model was also presented that allowed for the presence of relatively large cascades for a few products, but reflects well the general tendency of recommendation chains to terminate after just a short number of steps. Aggregating such cascades over all the products, a highly disconnected network was obtained, where the largest component grew over time by aggregating typically very small but occasionally fairly large components. It was observed that the most popular categories of items recommended within communities in the largest component reflected differing interests between these communities. A model which showed that these smaller and more tightly knit groups tended to be more conducive to viral marketing was presented.

The characteristics of product reviews and effectiveness of recommendations was found to vary by category and price. A small fraction of the products accounted for a large proportion of the recommendations. Although not quite as extreme in proportions, the number of successful recommendations also varied widely by product. Still, a sizeable portion of successful recommendations were for a product with only one such sale—hinting at a long tail phenomenon.

Thus viral marketing was found to be, in general, not as epidemic as one might have hoped. Marketers hoping to develop normative strategies for word-of-mouth advertising should analyze the topology and interests of the social network of their customers.

By investigating the attributes and relative influence of 1.6 million Twitter users by tracking 74 million diffusion events that took place on the Twitter follower graph over a two month interval in 2009, [1] found that although individuals who have been influential in the past and who have many followers are indeed more likely to be influential in the future, this intuition is correct only on average. Although it is the most cost-effective approach for marketing, we have learnt that finding these influentials is NP-hard. Instead, they propose that under certain circumstances it was effective to find the "ordinary influencers", individuals who exert average, or even less-than-average influence. However, these results were based on statistical modelling of observational data and thus do not imply causality. It is quite possible, for example, that content seeded by outside sources— e.g., marketers—may diffuse quite differently than content selected by users themselves. Likewise, while a wide range of possible cost functions was considered, other assumptions about costs are certainly possible and may lead to different conclusions. Nevertheless, these finding regarding the relative efficacy of ordinary influencers is consistent with previous theoretical work [14] that has also questioned the feasibility of word-of-mouth strategies that depend on triggering "social epidemics" by targeting special individuals.

Reference [13] show that even when given access to individuals' costs, no mechanism that offers uniform rewards can approximate the optimal solution within a factor better than $\Omega(\frac{logn}{loglogn})$. The paper introduces *incentive compatible mechanisms* which take each users' true private information and use it to identify and reward the subset of initial adopters. Thereby developing incentive compatible mechanisms that compare favourably against the optimal influence maximization solution. The experiments used Facebook network data that had almost a million nodes and over 72 million edges, together with a representative cost distribution that was obtained by running a simulated campaign on Amazon's Mechanical Turk platform.

## References

1. Bakshy, Eytan, J.M. Hofman, W.A. Mason, and D.J. Watts. 2011. Everyone's an influencer: quantifying influence on twitter. In *Proceedings of the fourth ACM international conference on Web search and data mining*, 65–74. ACM.
2. Chen, Wei, Yajun Wang, and Siyu Yang. 2009. Efficient influence maximization in social networks. In *Proceedings of the 15th ACM SIGKDD international conference on Knowledge discovery and data mining*, 199–208. ACM.
3. Chen, Wei , Yifei Yuan, and Li Zhang. 2010. Scalable influence maximization in social networks under the linear threshold model. In *2010 IEEE 10th international conference on data mining (ICDM)*, 88–97. IEEE.
4. Domingos, Pedro, and Matt Richardson. 2001. Mining the network value of customers. In *Proceedings of the seventh ACM SIGKDD international conference on Knowledge discovery and data mining*, 57–66. ACM.
5. Goldenberg, Jacob, Barak Libai, and Eitan Muller. 2001. Talk of the network: A complex systems look at the underlying process of word-of-mouth. *Marketing Letters* 12 (3): 211–223.
6. Goyal, Amit, Wei Lu, and Laks V.S. Lakshmanan. 2011. Simpath: An efficient algorithm for influence maximization under the linear threshold model. In *2011 IEEE 11th international conference on data mining (ICDM)*, 211–220. IEEE.
7. Granovetter, Mark S. 1977. The strength of weak ties. In *Social networks*, 347–367. Elsevier.
8. Kempe, David, Jon Kleinberg, and Éva Tardos. 2003. Maximizing the spread of influence through a social network. In *Proceedings of the ninth ACM SIGKDD international conference on Knowledge discovery and data mining*, 137–146. ACM.
9. Leskovec, Jure, Lada A. Adamic, and Bernardo A. Huberman. 2007. The dynamics of viral marketing. *ACM Transactions on the Web (TWEB)* 1 (1): 5.
10. Leskovec, Jure, Andreas Krause, Carlos Guestrin, Christos Faloutsos, Jeanne Van Briesen, and Natalie Glance. 2007. Cost-effective outbreak detection in networks. In *Proceedings of the 13th ACM SIGKDD international conference on Knowledge discovery and data mining*, 420–429. ACM.
11. Resnick, Paul, Neophytos Iacovou, Mitesh Suchak, Peter Bergstrom, and John Riedl. Grouplens: An open architecture for collaborative filtering of netnews. In *Proceedings of the 1994 ACM conference on computer supported cooperative work*, 175–186. ACM.

12. Richardson, Matthew, and Pedro Domingos. 2002. Mining knowledge-sharing sites for viral marketing. In *Proceedings of the eighth ACM SIGKDD international conference on knowledge discovery and data mining*, 61–70. ACM.
13. Singer, Yaron. 2012. How to win friends and influence people, truthfully: Influence maximization mechanisms for social networks. In *Proceedings of the fifth ACM international conference on web search and data mining*, 733–742. ACM.
14. Watts, Duncan J., and Peter Sheridan Dodds. 2007. Influentials, networks, and public opinion formation. *Journal of Consumer Research* 34 (4): 441–458.

# Chapter 10
# Outbreak Detection

Outbreak detection is the task of detecting outbreaks in networks, where given a network and a dynamic process spreading over this network, we have to select a set of nodes to detect this process as effectively as possible. Multiple situations fall under these settings. Consider a city water distribution network, delivering water to households via pipes and junctions. Accidental or malicious intrusions can cause contaminants to spread over the network, and we want to select a few locations (pipe junctions) to install sensors, in order to detect these contaminations as quickly as possible. Next, if we have a social network of interactions between people, we want to select a small set of people to monitor, so that any disease outbreak can be detected early, when very few people are infected.

In the domain of blogs, bloggers publish posts and use hyper-links to refer to other bloggers' posts and content on the web. Each post is time stamped, so the spread of information on the Blogspace can be observed. In this setting, we want to select a set of blogs which are most up to date, i.e, our goal is to select a small set of blogs which "catch" as many cascades as possible.

## 10.1 Battle of the Water Sensor Networks

Following the terrorist attacks of September 11, 2001, in the United States, awareness for possible attacks on the water grid has increased dramatically. The most feared of all the threats to the water supply system is the deliberate chemical or biological contaminant injection, due to both the uncertainty of the type of injected contaminant and its consequences, and the uncertainty of the time and location of the injection. An online contaminant monitoring system is considered as a major opportunity to



K. Raj P. M. et al., *Practical Social Network Analysis with Python*,
Computer Communications and Networks,
https://doi.org/10.1007/978-3-319-96746-2_10

protect against the impacts of a deliberate contaminant intrusion. To develop the infrastructure required to efficiently run this monitoring system, the *Battle of the Water Sensor Networks* (BWSN) competition was undertaken as part of the 8th Annual Water Distribution Systems Analysis Symposium, Cincinnati, Ohio, August 27–29, 2006.

The following four quantitative design objectives were used for evaluation:

### 10.1.1 Expected Time of Detection ($Z_1$)

For a particular contamination, the time of detection by a sensor is defined as the elapsed time from the start of the contamination event to the first identified presence of a non-zero contaminant concentration. The time of first detection $t_j$, refers to the $j$th sensor location. The time of detection (or detection time (DT)) for the sensor network for a particular contamination, $t_d$, is the minimum among all the sensors present in the design

$$t_d = min_j t_j \tag{10.1}$$

The objective function to be minimized is the expected value computed over the assumed probability distribution of the contaminations

$$Zi = E(t_d) \tag{10.2}$$

where $E(t_d)$ denotes the mathematical expectation of the minimum detection time $t_d$. Undetected events have no detection times.

### 10.1.2 Expected Population Affected Prior to Detection ($Z_2$)

For a specific contamination, the population affected is a function of the ingested contaminant mass. The assumptions are that no mass is ingested after detection and that all mass ingested during undetected events is not counted. For a particular contamination, the mass ingested by any individual at a network node $i$ is

$$M_i = \varphi \Delta t \sum_{k=1}^{N} c_{ik} \rho_{ik} \tag{10.3}$$

where $\varphi$ denotes the mean amount of water consumed by an individual (L/day/person), $\Delta t$ is the evaluation time step (days), $c_{ik}$ is the contaminant concentration for node $i$ at time step $k$ (mg/L), $\rho_{ik}$ is the dose rate multiplier for node $i$ and time step $k$, and $N$ is the number of evaluation time steps prior to detection. The series $\rho_{ik}, k = 1, \ldots, N$

has a mean of 1 and is intended to model the variation in ingestion rate throughout the day. It is assumed that the ingestion rate varies with the water demand rate at the respective node, thus

$$\rho_{ik} = q_{ik}/\overline{q_i} \; \forall \, k \in N \tag{10.4}$$

where $q_{ik}$ is the water demand for time step $k$ and node $i$, and $q_i$ is the average water demand at node $i$.

A dose-response model is used to express the probability that any person ingesting mass $M_i$ will be infected

$$R_i = \Phi\{\beta log_{10}[(M_i/W)/D_{50}]\} \tag{10.5}$$

where $R_i$ is the probability that a person who ingests contaminant mass $M_i$ will become infected, $\beta$ is called the Probit slope parameter, $W$ is the average body mass (kg/person), $D_{50}$ is the dose that would result in a 0.5 probability of being infected (mg/kg), and $\Phi$ is the standard normal cumulative distribution function.

The population affected (PA), $P_a$, for a particular contamination is calculated as

$$P_a = \sum_{i=1}^{V} R_i P_i \tag{10.6}$$

where $P_i$ is the population assigned to node $i$ and $V$ is the total number of nodes. The objective function to be minimized is the expected value of $P_a$ computed over the assumed probability distribution of contamination events

$$Z_2 = E(P_a) \tag{10.7}$$

where $E(P_a)$ denotes the mathematical expectation of the affected population $P_a$.

### *10.1.3 Expected Consumption of Contaminated Water Prior to Detection ($Z_3$)*

$Z_3$ is the expected volume of contaminated water consumed prior to detection.

$$Z_3 = E(V_d) \tag{10.8}$$

where $V_d$ denotes the total volumetric water demand that exceeds a predefined hazard concentration threshold $C$; and $E(V_d)$ is the mathematical expectation of $V_d$.

### 10.1.4 Detection Likelihood ($Z_4$)

Given a sensor network design, the detection likelihood (DL) is estimated by

$$Z_4 = \frac{1}{S} \sum_{r=1} Sd_r \tag{10.9}$$

where $d_r = 1$ if contamination scenario $r$ is detected, and zero otherwise; and $S$ denotes the total number of the contaminations considered.

### 10.1.5 Evaluation

A methodology for evaluating a given sensor design should comply with two basic requirements: (i) it should be objective, and (ii) it should assess a design regardless of the method used to receive it.

To accomplish this the utility developed comprised of two steps: (i) generation of a matrix of contamination injection events in either of two mechanisms: random, using Monte Carlo-type simulations selected by the user; or deterministic, injection at each node each 5 min, and (ii) evaluation of $Z_i (i = 1, \ldots, 4)$ according to the matrix of contamination injection events constructed in Stage 1.

This utility was distributed to all participants prior to the BWSN for testing both the networks.

Thus, the goal of the BWSN was to objectively compare the solutions obtained using different approaches to the problem of placing five and 20 sensors for two real water distribution systems of increasing complexity and for four derivative cases, taking into account the aforementioned four design objectives. Fifteen contributions were received from academia and practitioners.

Reference [5] provides a summary of these contributions and concludes that due to the presence of four different objective functions, BWSN is a multi-objective problem. In a multi-objective context the goal is to find, from all the possible feasible solutions, the set of non-dominated solutions, where a non-dominated solution is optimal in the sense that there is no other solution that dominates it (i.e, there is no other solution that is better than that solution with respect to all objectives). This leads to two observations: (i) comparisons can be made on the $Z_i (i = 1, 2, 3)$ versus $Z_4$ domains, and (ii) a unique single optimal solution cannot be identified, thus a "winner" cannot be declared. It should also be emphasized in this context that alternate comparison methods could have been employed, thus there is no claim that the adopted comparison approach is better in an absolute sense than an alternative methodology. However, this assessment provides indications of breadth and similarity of findings, as desired using different mathematical algorithms.

This competition found that general guidelines cannot be set. Engineering judgment and intuition alone are not sufficient for effectively placing sensors, and these need to be supported by quantitative analysis. The analysis has shown that sensors do not need to be clustered and that placing sensors at vertical assets (sources, tanks, and pumps) is not a necessity. In fact, most of the designs have not placed sensors at vertical assets. In some cases, there were considerable similarities where the same nodes (or nodes at a immediate vicinity) were selected by many of the methodologies.

## 10.2 Cost-Effective Lazy Forward Selection Algorithm

Of all the sensor designs contributed to the BWSN, one of the interesting ones was [3]. Reference [4] explains in detail the algorithm behind the near optimal sensor placements. Outbreak detection objectives are found to exhibit the property of submodularity. In the previous chapter, we have learnt that problems having these submodularity properties can be solved using the hill-climbing approach. The *CELF* algorithm presented in this paper are a factor of 700 times faster than this greedy algorithm. References [2, 3] further detail the results in support of the algorithm presented in this paper.

The paper proves that the objective functions described in the previous section are submodular and by exploiting this property, an efficient approximation algorithm was proposed.

Detection of outbreaks essentially involves strategically planting *sensors* on a subset $A$ of nodes in a graph $G = (V, E)$ which will trigger an alarm to indicate that an outbreak has been detected. However, these sensors are expensive with each sensor $s$ having an associated non-negative cost $c(s)$ and a reward $R(s)$. Thus, the total cost of all the sensors, $c(A)$ is $c(A) = \sum_{s \in A} c(s)$ which must not exceed a total budget of $B$ which is the maximum amount that can be spent on the sensors. The goal is to solve the optimisation function

$$max_{A \subseteq V} R(A) \; subject \; to \; c(A) \leq B \tag{10.10}$$

An event $i \in I$ from set $I$ of contaminants originates from a node $s' \in V$, and spreads through the network, affecting other nodes. Eventually, it reaches a monitored node $s \in A \subseteq V$ and gets detected. Depending on the time of detection $t = T(i, s)$, and the impact on the network before the detection, a penalty $\pi_i(t)$. The goal is to minimize the expected penalty over all possible contaminants $i$:

$$\pi(A) = \sum_i P(i)\pi_i(T(i, A)) \tag{10.11}$$

where for $A \subseteq V$, $T(i, A) = min_{s \in A} T(i, s)$ is the time until event $i$ is detected by one of the sensors in $A$, and $P$ is a given probability distribution over the events.

$\pi_i(t)$ is assumed to be monotonically nondecreasing in $t$, i.e, late detection are never preferred if they can be avoided. Also $T(i, \phi) = \infty$, and set $\pi_i(\infty)$ to some maximum penalty incurred for not detecting event $i$.

Instead of maximising the penalty $\pi(A)$, the paper considers penalty reduction, $R_i(A) = \pi_i(\infty) - \pi_i(T(i, A))$ and the expected penalty reduction

$$R(A) = \sum_i P(i)R_i(A) = \pi(\phi) - \pi(A) \tag{10.12}$$

which describes the expected reward received from placing sensors.

For the DL function, $\pi_i(t) = 0$ and $\pi_i(\infty) = 1$, i.e, no penalty is incurred if the outbreak is detected in finite time, otherwise the incurred penalty is 1. For the DT measure, $\pi_i(t) = min(t, T_{max})$, where $T_{max}$ is the time horizon. The PA criterion has $\pi_i(t)$ is the size of the cascade $i$ at time $t$, and $\pi_i(\infty)$ is the size of the cascade at the end of the horizon.

The penalty reduction function $R(A)$ has several properties: First, $R(\phi) = 0$, i.e, we do not reduce the penalty if we do not place any sensors. Second, $R$ is non-decreasing, i.e, $R(A) \leq R(B)\ \forall\ A \subseteq B \subseteq V$. So, adding sensors can only decrease the penalty. Finally, $\forall\ A \subseteq B \subseteq V$ and sensors $s \in V \setminus B$, $R(A \cup \{s\}) - R(A) \geq R(B \cup \{s\}) - R(B)$, i.e, $R$ is submodular.

To solve the outbreak detection problem, we will have to simultaneously optimize multiple objective functions. Then, each $A$ is $R(A) = (R_1(A), \ldots, R_m(A))$. However, there can arise a situation where $A_1$ and $A_2$ are incomparable, i.e, $R_1(A_1) > R_1(A_2)$, but $R_2(A_1) > R_2(A_2)$. So, we hope for *Pareto-optimal solutions*. $A$ is said to be Pareto-optimal, if there does not exist $A'$ such that $R_i(A') \geq R_i(A) \forall i$, and $R_j(A') > R_j(A)$ for some $j$. One approach to finding such Pareto-optimal solutions is *scalarization*. Here, one picks positive weights $\lambda_1 > 0, \ldots, \lambda_m > 0$, and optimizes the objective $R(A) = \sum_i \lambda_i R_i(A)$. Any solution maximising $R(A)$ is guaranteed to be Pareto-optimal, and by varying the weights $\lambda_i$, different Pareto-optimal solutions can be obtained.

If we consider that every node has equal cost (i.e., unit cost, $c(s) = 1$ for all locations $s$), then the greedy algorithm starts with $A_0 = \phi$, and iteratively, in step $k$, adds the location $s_k$ which maximizes the *marginal gain*

$$s_k = argmax_{s \in V \setminus A_{k-1}} R(A_{k-1} \cup s) - R(A_{k-1}) \tag{10.13}$$

The algorithm stops, once it has selected $B$ elements. For this unit cost case, the greedy algorithm is proved to achieve atleast 63% optimal score (Chap. 9). We will refer to this algorithm as the *unit cost algorithm*.

In the case where the nodes non-constant costs, the greedy algorithm that iteratively adds sensors until the budget is exhausted can fail badly, since a very expensive sensor providing reward $r$ is preferred over a cheaper sensor providing reward $r - \epsilon$. To avoid this, we modify Eq. 10.13 to take costs into account

$$s_k = argmax_{s \in V \setminus A_{k-1}} \frac{R(A_{k-1} \cup s) - R(A_{k-1})}{c(s)} \tag{10.14}$$

So the greedy algorithm picks the element maximising the benefit/cost ratio. The algorithm stops once no element can be added to the current set $A$ without exceeding the budget. Unfortunately, this intuitive generalization of the greedy algorithm can perform arbitrarily worse than the optimal solution. Consider the case where we have two locations, $s_1$ and $s_2$ , $c(s_1) = \epsilon$ and $c(s_2) = B$. Also assume we have only one contaminant $i$, and $R(s_1) = 2\epsilon$, and $R(s_2) = B$. Now, $R((s_1) - R(\phi))/c(s_1) = 2$, and $R((s_2) - R(\phi))/c(s_2) = 1$. Hence the greedy algorithm would pick $s_1$. After selecting $s_1$, we cannot afford $s_2$ anymore, and our total reward would be $\epsilon$. However, the optimal solution would pick $s_2$, achieving total penalty reduction of $B$. As $\epsilon$ goes to 0, the performance of the greedy algorithm becomes arbitrarily bad. This algorithm is called the *benefit-cost greedy algorithm*.

The paper proposes the Cost-Effective Forward selection (CEF) algorithm. It computes $A_{GCB}$ using the benefit-cost greedy algorithm and $A_{GUC}$ using the unit-cost greedy algorithm. For both of these, CEF only considers elements which do not exceed the budget $B$. CEF then returns the solution with higher score. Even though both solutions can be arbitrarily bad, if $R$ is a non-decreasing submodular function with $R(\phi) = 0$. Then we get Eq. 10.15.

$$max\{R(A_{GCB}), R(A_{GUC})\} \geq \frac{1}{2}\left(1 - \frac{1}{e}\right) max_{A,c(A) \leq B} R(A) \tag{10.15}$$

The running time of CEF is $O(B|V|)$. The approximation guarantees of $(1 - \frac{1}{e})$ and $\frac{1}{2}(1 - \frac{1}{e})$ in the unit and non- constant cost cases are offline, i.e, we can state them in advance before running the actual algorithm. Online bounds on the performance can be found through arbitrary sensor locations. For $\hat{A} \subseteq V$ and each $s \in V \setminus \hat{A}$, let $\delta_s = R(\hat{A} \cup \{s\}) - R(\hat{A})$. Let $r_s = \delta_s/c(s)$, and let $s_1, \ldots, s_m$ be the sequence of locations with $r_s$ in decreasing order. Let $k$ be such that $C = \sum_{i=1}^{k-1} c(s_i) \leq B$ and $\sum_{i=1}^{k} c(s_i) > B$. Let $\lambda = (B - C)/c(s_k)$, then we get Eq. 10.16.

$$max_{A,c(A) \leq B} R(A) \leq R(\hat{A}) + \sum_{i=1}^{k-1} \delta_{s_i} + \lambda \delta_{s_k} \tag{10.16}$$

This computes how far away $\hat{A}$ is from the optimal solution. This is found to give a 31% bound.

Most outbreaks are sparse, i.e, affect only a small area of network, and hence are only detected by a small number of nodes. Hence, most nodes $s$ do not reduce the penalty incurred by an outbreak, i.e, $R_i(s) = 0$. However, this sparsity is only present when penalty reductions are considered. If for each sensor $s \in V$ and contaminant $i \in I$ we store the actual penalty $\pi_i(s)$, the resulting representation is not sparse. By representing the penalty function $R$ as an inverted index, which allows fast lookup of the penalty reductions by sensor $s$, the sparsity can be exploited. Therefore, the penalty reduction can be computed as given in Eq. 10.17.

$$R(A) = \sum_{i:i \; detected \; by \; A} P(i) max_{s \in A} R_i(\{s\}) \tag{10.17}$$

Even if we can quickly evaluate the score $R(A)$ of any $A$, we still need to perform a large number of these evaluations in order to run the greedy algorithm. If we select $k$ sensors among $|V|$ locations, we roughly need $k|V|$ function evaluations. We can exploit submodularity further to require far fewer function evaluations in practice. Assume we have computed the marginal increments $\delta_s(A) = R(A \cup \{s\}) - R(A)$ (or $\delta_s(A)/c(s)$) for all $s \in V \setminus A$. As our node selection $A$ grows, the marginal increments $\delta_{s'}$ (and $\delta_{s'}/c(s)$) (i.e., the benefits for adding sensor $s'$) can never increase: For $A \subseteq B \subseteq V$, it holds that $\delta_s(A) \geq \delta_s(B)$. So instead of recomputing $\delta_s \equiv \delta_s(A)$ for every sensor after adding $s'$ (and hence requiring $|V| - |A|$ evaluations of $R$), we perform lazy evaluations: Initially, we mark all $\delta_s$ as invalid. When finding the next location to place a sensor, we go through the nodes in decreasing order of their $\delta_s$. If the $\delta_s$ for the top node $s$ is invalid, we recompute it, and insert it into the existing order of the $\delta_s$ (e.g., by using a priority queue). In many cases, the recomputation of $\delta_s$ will lead to a new value which is not much smaller, and hence often, the top element will stay the top element even after recomputation. In this case, we found a new sensor to add, without having re-evaluated $\delta_s$ for every location $s$. The correctness of this lazy procedure follows directly from submodularity, and leads to far fewer (expensive) evaluations of $R$. This is called the lazy greedy algorithm CELF (Cost-Effective Lazy Forward selection). This is found to have a factor 700 improvement in speed compared to CEF.

### *10.2.1 Blogspace*

A dataset having 45000 blogs with 10.5 million posts and 16.2 million links was taken. Every cascade has a single starting post, and other posts recursively join by linking to posts within the cascade, whereby the links obey time order. We detect cascades by first identifying starting post and then following in-links. 346, 209 non-trivial cascades having at least 2 nodes were discovered. Since the cascade size distribution is heavy-tailed, the analysis was limited to only cascades that had at least 10 nodes. The final dataset had 17, 589 cascades, where each blog participated in 9.4 different cascades on average.

Figure 10.1 shows the results when PA function is optimized. The offline and the online bounds can be computed regardless of the algorithm used. CELF shows that we are at 13.8% away from optimal solution. In the right, we have the performance using various objective functions (from top to bottom: DL, DT, PA). DL increases the fastest, which means that one only needs to read a few blogs to detect most of the

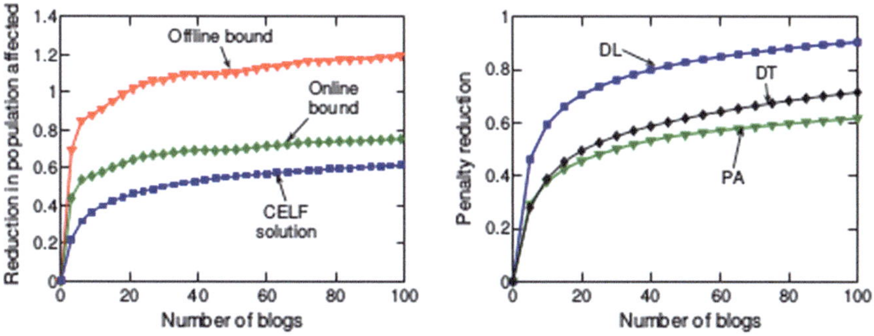


**Fig. 10.1** (Left) Performance of CELF algorithm and off-line and on-line bounds for PA objective function. (Right) Compares objective functions

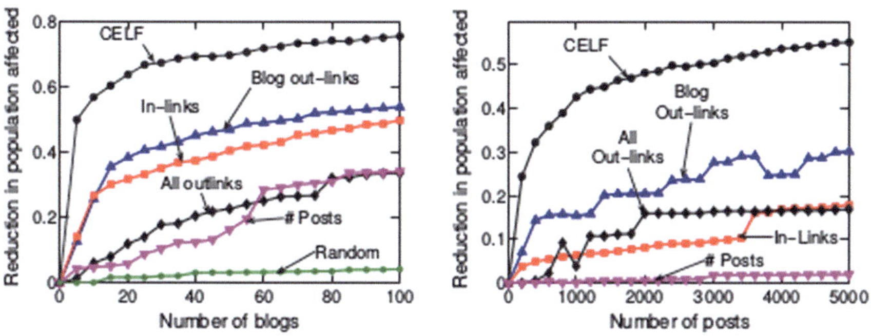


**Fig. 10.2** Heuristic blog selection methods. (Left) unit cost model, (Right) number of posts cost model

cascades, or equivalently that most cascades hit one of the big blogs. However, the population affected (PA) increases much slower, which means that one needs many more blogs to know about stories before the rest of population does.

In Fig. 10.2, the CELF method is compared with several intuitive heuristic selection techniques. The heuristics are: the number of posts on the blog, the cumulative number of out-links of blog's posts, the number of in-links the blog received from other blogs in the dataset, and the number of out-links to other blogs in the dataset. CELF is observed to greatly outperform the other methods. For the figure in the right, given a budget of $B$ posts, we select a set of blogs to optimize PA objective. For the heuristics, a set of blogs to optimize chosen heuristic was selected, e.g., the total number of in-links of selected blogs while still fitting inside the budget of $B$ posts. Again, CELF outperforms the next best heuristics by 41%.

### 10.2.2 Water Networks

In this water distribution system application, the data and rules introduced by the Battle of Water Sensor Networks (BWSN) challenge was used. Both the small network on 129 nodes (BWSN1), and a large, realistic, 12, 527 node distribution network (BWSN2) provided as part of the BWSN challenge were considered. In addition a third water distribution network (NW3) of a large metropolitan area in the United States was considered. The network (not including the household level) contains 21, 000 nodes and 25, 000 pipes (edges). The networks consist of a static description (junctions and pipes) and dynamic parameters (time-varying water consumption demand patterns at different nodes, opening and closing of valves, pumps, tanks, etc).

In the BWSN challenge, the goal is to select a set of 20 sensors, simultaneously optimizing the objective functions DT, PA and DL. To obtain cascades a realistic disease model was used, which depends on the demands and the contaminant concentration at each node. In order to evaluate these objectives, the EPANET simulator was used, which is based on a physical model to provide realistic predictions on the detection time and concentration of contaminant for any possible contamination event. Simulations of 48 h length, with 5 min simulation timesteps were considered. Contaminations can happen at any node and any time within the first 24 h, and spread through the network according to the EPANET simulation. The time of the outbreak is important, since water consumption varies over the day and the contamination spreads at different rates depending on the time of the day. Altogether, a set of 3.6 million possible contamination scenarios were considered, each of which were associated with a "cascade" of contaminant spreading over the network.

Figure 10.3 presents the CELF score, the off-line and on-line bounds for PA objective on the BWSN2 network. On the right is shown CELF's performance on all 3 objective functions.

Figure 10.4 shows two 20 sensor placements after optimizing DL and PA respectively on BWSN2. When optimizing the population affected (PA), the placed sen-

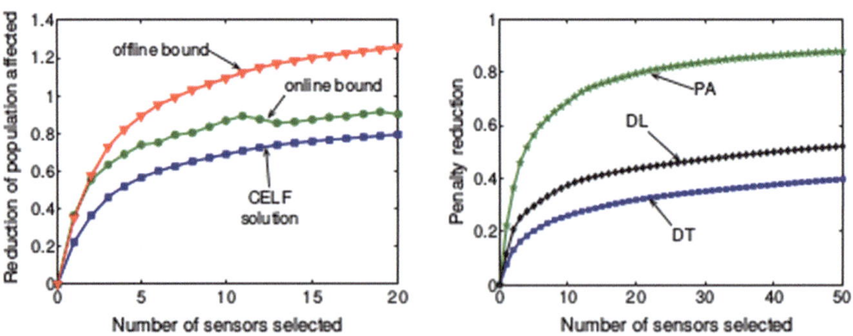


**Fig. 10.3** (Left) CELF with offline and online bounds for PA objective. (Right) Different objective functions

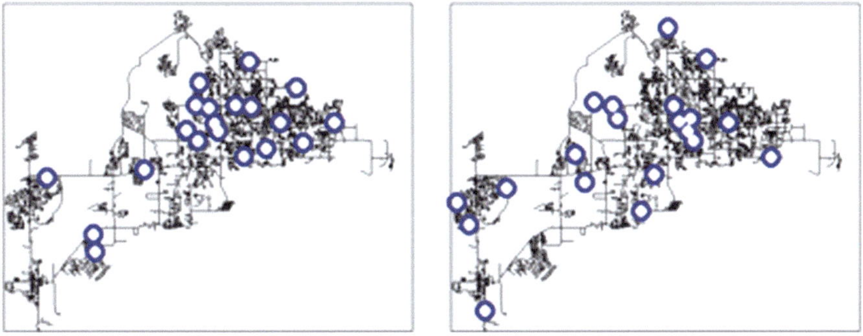

**Fig. 10.4** Water network sensor placements: (Left) when optimizing PA, sensors are concentrated in high population areas. (Right) when optimizing DL, sensors are uniformly spread out

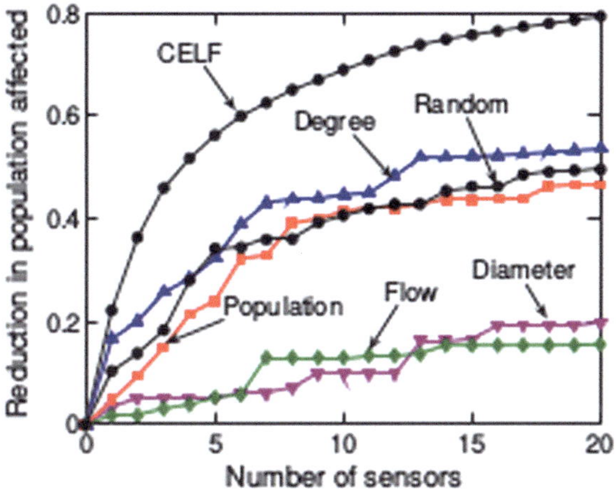


**Fig. 10.5** Solutions of CELF outperform heuristic approaches

sors are concentrated in the dense high-population areas, since the goal is to detect outbreaks which affect the population the most. When optimizing the detection likelihood, the sensors are uniformly spread out over the network. Intuitively this makes sense, since according to BWSN challenge, outbreaks happen with same probability at every node. So, for DL, the placed sensors should be as close to all nodes as possible.

Figure 10.5 shows the scores achieved by CELF compared with several heuristic sensor placement techniques, where the nodes were ordered by some "goodness" criteria, and then the top nodes were picked for the PA objective function. The following criteria were considered: population at the node, water flow through the node, and the diameter and the number of pipes at the node. CELF outperforms the best heuristic by 45%.

Reference [1] proposed the *CELF++* algorithm which the paper showed as being 35–55% faster than CELF. Here $\sigma_S$ denotes the spread of seed set $S$. A heap $Q$ is maintained with nodes corresponding to users in the network. The node of $Q$

corresponding to user $u$ stores a tuple of the form $< u.mg1, u.prev\_best, u.mg2, u.flag >$, where $u.mg1 = \delta_u(S)$ which is the marginal gain of $u$ w.r.t the current seed set $S$, $u.prev\_best$ is the node that has the maximal marginal gain among all the users examined in the current iteration before user $u$, $u.mg2 = \delta_u(S \cup \{prev\_best\})$, and $u.flag$ is the iteration number when $u.mg1$ was last updated. The idea is that if the node $u.prev\_best$ is picked as a seed in the current iteration, the marginal gain of $u$ w.r.t $(S \cup \{prev\_best\})$ need not be recomputed in the next iteration. In addition to computing $\Delta_u(S)$, it is not necessary to compute $\Delta_u(S \cup \{prev\_best\})$ from scratch. The algorithm can be implemented in an efficient manner such that both $\Delta_u(S)$ and $\Delta_u(S \cup \{prev\_best\})$ are evaluated simultaneously in a single iteration of Monte Carlo simulation (which typically contains $10,000$ runs).

The variables $S$ is used to denote the current seed set, last seed to track the ID of the last seed user picked by the algorithm, and $cur\_best$ to track the user having the maximum marginal gain w.r.t $S$ over all users examined in the current iteration. The algorithm starts by building the heap $Q$ initially. Then, it continues to select seeds until the budget $k$ is exhausted. As in CELF, the root element $u$ of $Q$ is looked at and if $u.flag$ is equal to the size of the seed set, we pick $u$ as the seed as this indicates that $u.mg1$ is actually $\Delta_u(S)$. The optimization of CELF++ is that we update $u.mg1$ without recomputing the marginal gain. Clearly, this can be done since $u.mg2$ has already been computed efficiently w.r.t the last seed node picked. If none of the above cases applies, we recompute the marginal gain of $u$.

Reference [6] indicate that uniform immunization programmes undertaken are unsatisfactory in curtailing the spread of epidemics. Instead they show results which indicate that targeted immunization achieve the lowering of epidemics. The targeting of just the most connected individuals is found to raise the tolerance to infections in the whole population by a dramatic factor. An instance of this is provided by the spread of computer viruses. Even after the virus is detected and corresponding patches are developed, it still has a large lifetime. A similar situation persists in the case of sexually transmitted diseases where instead of uniform immunization, the approach must be to identify "superseeders", the set of the promiscuous individuals who are key in the spread of the infection.

## Problems

Download the *DBLP* collaboration network dataset at https://snap.stanford.edu/data/bigdata/communities/com-dblp.ungraph.txt.gz.

This exercise is to explore how varying the set of initially infected nodes in a SIR model can affect how a contagion spreads through a network. We learnt in Sect. 8.2.3 that under the SIR model, every node can be either susceptible, infected, or recovered and every node starts off as either susceptible or infected. Every infected neighbour of a susceptible node infects the susceptible node with probability $\beta$, and infected nodes can recover with probability $\delta$. Recovered nodes are no longer susceptible and cannot be infected again. The pseudocode is as given in Algorithm 7.

**Algorithm 7** SIR model

```
procedure SIRMODEL(G(V, E), I)                    ▷ I is initial set of infected nodes
    S ← V \ I                                                    ▷ susceptible nodes
    R ← φ                                                          ▷ recovered nodes
    while I ≠ φ do
        S′ ← φ                                           ▷ nodes no longer susceptible
        I′ ← φ                                                ▷ newly infected nodes
        J′ ← φ                                             ▷ nodes no longer infected
        R′ ← φ                                               ▷ newly recovered nodes
        for each node u ∈ V do
            if u ∈ S then
                for each (u, v) ∈ E with v ∈ I do
                    With probability β: S′ ← S′ ∪ {u}, I′ ← I′ ∪ {u}
                    break
                end for
            else if u ∈ I then
                With probability δ: J′ ← J′ ∪ {u}, R′ ← R′ ∪ {u}
            end if
        end for
        S ← S \ S′
        I ← (I ∪ I′) \ J′
        R ← R ∪ R′
    end while
end procedure
```

**57** Implement the SIR model in Algorithm 7 and run 100 simulations with $\beta = 0.05$ and $\delta = 0.5$ for each of the following three graphs:

1. The graph for the network in the dataset (will be referred to as the *real world* graph).
2. An Erdös-Rényi random graph with the same number of nodes and edges as the real world graph. Set a random seed of 10.
3. A preferential attachment graph with the same number of nodes and expected degree as the real world graph. Set a random seed of 10.

For each of these graphs, initialize the infected set with a single node chosen uniformly at random. Record the total percentage of nodes that became infected in each simulation. Note that a simulation ends when there are no more infected nodes; the total percentage of nodes that became infected at some point is thus the number of recovered nodes at the end of your simulation divided by the total number of nodes in the network.

**58** Repeat the above process, but instead of selecting a random starting node, infect the node with the highest degree. Compute the total percentage of nodes that became infected in each simulation.

**59** Repeat the experiments by initialising the infected set to be 10 random nodes and the top 10 highest degree nodes, respectively. Calculate the total percentage of nodes that became infected in each simulation.

## References

1. Goyal, Amit, Wei Lu, and Laks V.S. Lakshmanan. 2011. Celf++: Optimizing the greedy algorithm for influence maximization in social networks. In *Proceedings of the 20th international conference companion on World wide web*, 47–48. ACM.
2. Krause, Andreas, and Carlos Guestrin. 2005. A note on the budgeted maximization of submodular functions. 2005.
3. Krause, Andreas, Jure Leskovec, Carlos Guestrin, Jeanne VanBriesen, and Christos Faloutsos. 2008. Efficient sensor placement optimization for securing large water distribution networks. *Journal of Water Resources Planning and Management* 134 (6): 516–526.
4. Leskovec, Jure, Andreas Krause, Carlos Guestrin, Christos Faloutsos, Jeanne VanBriesen, and Natalie Glance. 2007. Cost-effective outbreak detection in networks. In *Proceedings of the 13th ACM SIGKDD international conference on Knowledge discovery and data mining*, 420–429. ACM.
5. Ostfeld, Avi, James G. Uber, Elad Salomons, Jonathan W. Berry, William E. Hart, Cindy A. Phillips, Jean-Paul Watson, Gianluca Dorini, Philip Jonkergouw, Zoran Kapelan, et al. 2008. The battle of the water sensor networks (BWSN): A design challenge for engineers and algorithms. *Journal of Water Resources Planning and Management* 134 (6): 556–568.
6. Pastor-Satorras, Romualdo, and Alessandro Vespignani. 2002. Immunization of complex networks. *Physical Review E* 65 (3): 036104.

# Chapter 11
# Power Law

An interesting question to ask is, which are the *popular* websites? Although popularity may be considered an elusive term with a lot of varying definitions, here we will restrict ourselves by taking a snapshot of the Web and counting the number of in-links to websites and using this a measure of the site's popularity.

Another way of looking at this is as follows: As a function of $k$, what fraction of sites on the Web have $k$ in-links? Since larger values of $k$ indicate greater popularity, this should give us the popularity distribution of the Web.

On first thought, one would guess that the popularity would follow a *normal* or *Gaussian* distribution, since the probability of observing a value that exceeds the mean by more than $c$ times the standard deviation decreases exponentially in $c$. *Central Limit Theorem* supports this fact because it states that if we take any sequence of small independent random quantities, then in the limit their sum (or average) will be distributed according to the normal distribution. So, if we assume that each website decides independently at random whether to link to any other site, then the number of in-links to a given page is the sum of many independent random quantities, and hence we'd expect it to be normally distributed. Then, by this model, the number of pages with $k$ in-links should decrease exponentially in $k$, as $k$ grows large.

However, we learnt in Chap. 2 that this is not the case. The fraction of websites that have $k$ in-links is approximately proportional to $1/k^2$ (the exponent is slightly larger than 2). A function that decreases as $k$ to some fixed power, such as $1/k^2$, is called a *power law*; when used to measure the fraction of items having value $k$, it says, that it's possible to see very large values of $k$.

Mathematically, a quantity $x$ obeys a power law if it is drawn from a probability distribution given by Eq. 11.1

$$p(x) \propto x^{-\alpha} \tag{11.1}$$



K. Raj P. M. et al., *Practical Social Network Analysis with Python*,
Computer Communications and Networks,
https://doi.org/10.1007/978-3-319-96746-2_11

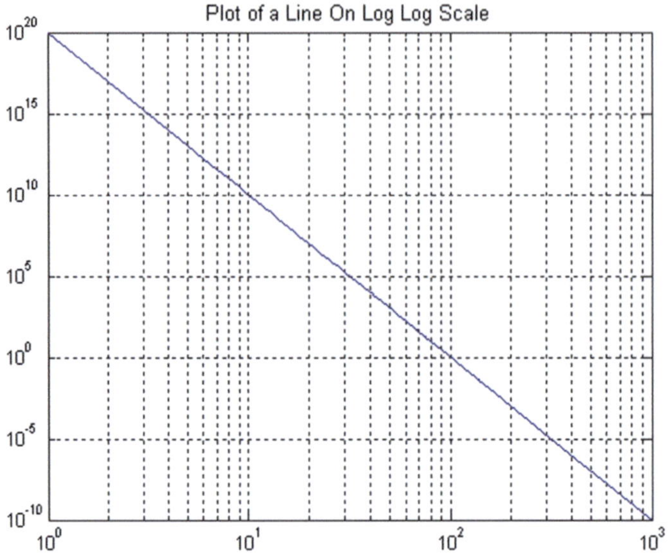


**Fig. 11.1** A log-log plot exhibiting a power law

where $\alpha$ is a constant parameter of the distribution known as the *exponent* or *scaling* parameter.

Going back to the question of popularity, this means that extreme imbalances with very large values are likely to arise. This is true in reality because there are a few websites that are greatly popular while compared to others. Additionally, we have learnt in previous chapters that the degree distributions of several social network applications exhibit a power law.

We could say that just as the normal distribution is widespread among natural sciences settings, so is the case of power law when the network in question has a popularity factor to it.

One way to quickly check if a dataset exhibits a power-law distribution is to generate a "log-log" plot, i.e, if we want to see if $f(k)$ follows a power law, we plot $log(f(k))$ as a function of $logk$. If this plot has an approximately straight line whose exponent can be read from the slope (as shown in Fig. 11.1), then the dataset follows a power law.

However, [5] argues against this practise of determining whether or not a dataset follows a power law. The paper found that such straight-line behaviour was a necessary but by no means sufficient condition for true power-law behaviour. Instead a statistically principled set of techniques were presented that allow for the validation and quantification of power laws. Properly applied, these techniques can provide objective evidence for or against the claim that a particular distribution follows a power law.

In practice, few empirical phenomena obey power laws for all values of $x$. More often the power law applies only for values greater than some minimum $x_{min}$. In such cases we say that the tail of the distribution follows a power law.

Broadly, the steps to verify power-law exhibition by a dataset is as follows:

1. Estimate the parameters $x_{min}$ and $\alpha$ of the power-law model using maximum likelihood estimation (MLE) techniques.
2. Calculate the goodness-of-fit between the data and the power law. If the resulting p-value is greater than 0.1 the power law is a plausible hypothesis for the data, otherwise it is rejected.
3. Compare the power law with alternative hypotheses via a likelihood ratio test. For each alternative, if the calculated likelihood ratio is significantly different from zero, then its sign indicates whether the alternative is favoured over the power-law model or not. Other established and statistically principled approaches for model comparison, such as a fully Bayesian approach [9], a cross-validation approach [17], or a minimum description length approach [8] can also be used instead.

The power law has several moniker in various fields. It goes by the term Lotka distribution for scientific productivity [15], Bradford law for journal use [4], Pareto law of income distribution [16] and the Zipf law for literary word frequencies.

## 11.1 Power Law Random Graph Models

Reference [1] proposed a set of random graph models which exhibit power law in its degree distributions. The four models are given as follows:

### *11.1.1 Model A*

Model A is the basic model which the subsequent models rely upon. It starts with no nodes and no edges at time step 0. At time step 1, a node with in-weight 1 and out-weight 1 is added. At time step $t+1$, with probability $1-\alpha$ a new node with in-weight 1 and out-weight 1 is added. With probability $\alpha$ a new directed edge $(u, v)$ is added to the existing nodes. Here the origin $u$ is chosen with probability proportional to the current out-weight $w_{u,t}^{out} \overset{\text{def}}{=} 1 + \delta_{u,t}^{out}$ and the destination $v$ is chosen with probability proportional to the current in-weight $w_{v,t}^{in} \overset{\text{def}}{=} 1 + \delta_{v,t}^{in}$. $\delta_{u,t}^{out}$ and $\delta_{v,t}^{in}$ denote the out-degree of $u$ and the in-degree of $v$ at time $t$, respectively.

The total in-weight (out-weight) of graph in model A increases by 1 at a time step. At time step $t$, both total in-weight and total out-weight are exactly $t$. So the probability that a new edge is added onto two particular nodes $u$ and $v$ is exactly as given in Eq. 11.2.

$$\alpha \frac{(1+\delta_{u,t}^{out})(1+\delta_{v,t}^{in})}{t^2} \tag{11.2}$$

### 11.1.2 Model B

Model B is a slight improvement of Model A. Two additional positive constant $\gamma^{in}$ and $\gamma^{out}$ are introduced. Different powers can be generated for in-degrees and out-degrees. In addition, the edge density can be independently controlled.

Model B starts with no node and no edge at time step 0. At time step 1, a node with in-weight $\gamma^{in}$ and out-weight $\gamma^{out}$ is added. At time step $t+1$, with probability $1-\alpha$ a new node with in-weight $\gamma^{in}$ and out-weight $\gamma^{out}$ is added. With probability $\alpha$ a new directed edge $(u, v)$ is added to the existing nodes. Here the origin $u$ (destination $v$) is chosen proportional to the current out-weight $w_{u,t}^{out} \stackrel{\text{def}}{=} \gamma^{out} + \delta_{u,t}^{out}$ while the current in-weight $w_{v,t}^{in} \stackrel{\text{def}}{=} \gamma^{in} + \delta_{v,t}^{in}$. $\delta_{u,t}^{out}$ and $\delta_{v,t}^{in}$ denote the out-degree of $u$ and the in-degree of $v$ at time $t$, respectively.

In model B, at time step $t$ the total in-weight $w_t^{in}$ and the out-weight $w_t^{out}$ of the graph are random variables. The probability that a new edge is added onto two particular nodes $u$ and $v$ is as given in Eq. 11.3.

$$\alpha \frac{(\gamma^{out}+\delta_{u,t}^{out})(\gamma^{in}+\delta_{v,t}^{in})}{w_t^{in} w_t^{out}} \tag{11.3}$$

### 11.1.3 Model C

Now we consider Model C, this is a general model with four specified types of edges to be added.

Assume that the random process of model C starts at time step $t_0$. At $t = t_0$, we start with an initial directed graph with some vertices and edges. At time step $t > t_0$, a new vertex is added and four numbers $m^{e,e}$, $m^{n,e}$, $m^{e,n}$, $m^{n,n}$ are drawn according to some probability distribution. Assuming that the four random variables are bounded, we proceed as follows:

- Add $m^{e,e}$ edges randomly. The origins are chosen with the probability proportional to the current out-degree and the destinations are chosen proportional to the current in-degree.
- Add $m^{e,n}$ edges into the new vertex randomly. The origins are chosen with the probability proportional to the current out-degree and the destinations are the new vertex.
- Add $m^{n,e}$ edges from the new vertex randomly. The destinations are chosen with the probability proportional to the current in-degree and the origins are the new vertex.

- Add $m^{n,n}$ loops to the new vertex.

Each of these random variables has a well-defined expectation which we denote by $\mu^{e,e}$, $\mu^{n,e}$, $\mu^{e,n}$, $\mu^{n,n}$, respectively. We will show that this general process still yields power law degree distributions and the powers are simple rational functions of $\mu^{e,e}$, $\mu^{n,e}$, $\mu^{e,n}$, $\mu^{n,n}$.

### 11.1.4 Model D

Model A, B and C are all power law models for directed graphs. Here we describe a general undirected model which we denote by Model D. It is a natural variant of Model C. We assume that the random process of model C starts at time step $t_0$. At $t = t_0$, we start with an initial undirected graph with some Vertices and edges. At time step $t > t_0$, a new vertex is added and three numbers $m^{e,e}$, $m^{n,e}$, $m^{n,n}$ are drawn according to some probability distribution. We assume that the three random variables are bounded. Then we proceed as follows:

- Add $m^{e,e}$ edges randomly. The vertices are chosen with the probability proportional to the current degree.
- Add $m^{e,n}$ edges randomly. One vertex of each edge must be the new vertex. The other one is chosen with the probability proportional to the current degree.
- Add $m^{n,n}$ loops to the new vertex.

## 11.2 Copying Model

Reference [3] proposed the following model to generate graphs that exhibit power law. Consider a directed graph which grows by adding single edges at discrete time steps. At each such step a vertex may or may not also be added. Let multiple edges and loops be allowed. More precisely, let $\alpha$, $\beta$, $\gamma$, $\delta_{in}$ and $\delta_{out}$ be non-negative real numbers, with $\alpha + \beta + \gamma = 1$. Let $G_0$ be any fixed initial directed graph, for example a single vertex without edges, and let $t_0$ be the number of edges of $G_0$. We set $G(t_0) = G_0$, so at time step $t$ the graph $G(t)$ has exactly $t$ edges, and a random number $n(t)$ of vertices. In what follows, to choose a vertex $v$ of $G(t)$ according to $d_{out} + \delta_{out}$ means to choose $v$ so that $P(v = v_i)$ is proportional to $d_{out}(v_i) + \delta_{out}$, i.e., so that $P(v = v_i) = (d_{out}(v_i) + \delta_{out})/(t + \delta_{out}n(t))$. To choose $v$ according to $d_{in} + \delta_{in}$ means to choose $v$ so that $P(v = v_i) = (d_{in}(v_i) + \delta_{in})/(t + \delta_{in}n(t))$. Here $d_{out}(v_i)$ and $d_{in}(v_i)$ are the out-degree and in-degree of $v_i$, measured in the graph $G(t)$.

For $t \geq t_0$ we form $G(t + 1)$ from $G(t)$ according to the following rules:

1. With probability $\alpha$, add a new vertex $v$ together with an edge from $v$ to an existing vertex $w$, where $w$ is chosen according to $d_{in} + \delta_{in}$.

2. With probability $\beta$, add an edge from an existing vertex $v$ to an existing vertex $w$, where $v$ and $w$ are chosen independently, $v$ according to $d_{out} + \delta_{out}$, and $w$ according to $d_{in} + \delta_{in}$.
3. With probability $\gamma$, add a new vertex $w$ and an edge from an existing vertex $v$ to $w$, where $v$ is chosen according to $d_{out} + \delta_{out}$.

The probabilities $\alpha$, $\beta$ and $\gamma$ clearly should add up to one. We will also assume that $\alpha + \gamma > 0$. When considering the web graph we take $\delta_{out} = 0$; the motivation is that vertices added under the final step correspond to web pages which purely provide content - such pages never change, are born without out-links and remain without out-links. Vertices added under the first step correspond to usual pages, to which links may be added later. If we take $\delta_{in} = 0$ in addition to $\delta_{out} = 0$, this gives a model in which every page not in $G_0$ has either no in-links or no out-links. A non-zero value of $\delta_{in}$ corresponds to insisting that a page is not considered part of the Web until something points to it, typically one of the big search engines. We include the parameter $\delta_{out}$ to make the model symmetric with respect to reversing the directions of edges (swapping $\alpha$ with $\gamma$ and $\delta_{in}$ with $\delta_{out}$), and because we expect the model to be applicable in contexts other than that of the web graph.

This model allows loops and multiple edges; there seems no reason to exclude them. However, there will not be very many, so excluding them would not significantly affect the conclusions.

Reference [7] studied how power law was exhibited in the demand for products and how companies could operate based on this exhibition to improve the size and quality of service provided to their patronage. Companies that have limited inventory space have to opt for operating on only those products that are at the top of the distribution, so as to remain in the competition. On the other hand, there exist companies called "infinite-inventory" spaced who are capable of servicing all products no matter how low their demand. This way the companies can profit by catering to all kinds of customers and earn from selling products their limited spaced competitors could not.

## 11.3 Preferential Attachment Model

Reference [2] found that a common problem with the Erdös-Rényi (Chap. 3) and the Watts-Strogatz (Chap. 4) model is that the probability of finding a highly connected vertex (,i.e, a large $k$, where $k$ denotes the degree of the vertex) decreases exponentially with $k$, thus vertices with large connectivity are practically absent. In contrast, the power-law tail characterizing $P(k)$ for the studied networks indicates that highly connected (large $k$) vertices have a large chance of occurring, dominating the connectivity.

This is attributed to two properties of the real-world networks that are not incorporated in either of these models. First, both of these models begin with a fixed number of vertices which does not change. However, this is rarely the case in real-world networks, where this number varies. Second, the models assume that the probability that two vertices are connected is uniform and random. In contrast, real-world networks exhibit preferential attachment. So, the probability with which a new vertex connects to the existing vertices is not uniform, but there is a higher probability to be linked to a vertex that already has a large number of connections.

This scale-free model was thus proposed to deal with these two issues. Scale-free in the sense that the frequency of sampling (w.r.t. the growth rate) is independent of the parameter of the resulting power law graphs. This model is found to show properties resembling those of real-world networks. To counter the first issue, starting with a small number $m_0$ of vertices, at every time step a new vertex is added with $m \leq m_0$ edges that link the new vertex to $m$ different vertices already present in the network. To exhibit preferential attachment, the probability $\prod$ with which a new vertex will be connected to a vertex $i$ depends on the connectivity $k_i$ of that vertex, such that $\prod(k_i) = k_i / \sum_j k_j$. After $t$ time steps the model leads to a random network with $t + m_0$ vertices and $mt$ edges. This network is found to exhibit a power-law with exponent $2.9 \pm 0.1$.

Due to preferential attachment, a vertex that acquired more connections than another one will increase its connectivity at a higher rate, thus an initial difference in the connectivity between two vertices will increase further as the network grows. The rate at which a vertex acquires edges is $k_i/t = k_i/2t$, which gives $k_i(t) = m(t/t_i)^{0.5}$, where $t_i$ is the time at which vertex $i$ was added to the system. Thus older (smaller $t_i$) vertices increase their connectivity at the expense of the younger (larger $t_i$) ones, leading with time to some vertices that are highly connected, thus exhibiting a "rich-get-richer" phenomenon.

It is commonly known that the power-law distributions arise from decision-making across a population in the presence of cascades.

We will create the following model concerning the presence of hyperlinks between websites, to illustrate this:

1. Sites are created in order, and named $1, 2, 3, \ldots, N$.
2. When site $j$ is created, it produces a link to an earlier website according to the following probabilistic rule (probability $0 \leq p \leq 1$).
    a. With probability $p$, site $j$ chooses a site $i$ uniformly at random among all earlier sites, and creates a link to this site $i$.
    b. With probability $1 - p$, site $j$ instead chooses a site $i$ uniformly at random from among all earlier sites, and creates a link to the site that $i$ points to.
3. This describes the creation of a single link from site $j$. One can repeat this process to create multiple, independently generated links from site $j$.

Step 2(b) is the key because site $j$ is imitating the decision of site $i$. The main result about this model is that if we run it for many sites, the fraction of sites with $k$ in-links will be distributed approximately according to a power law $1/k^c$, where the value of the exponent $c$ depends on the choice of $p$. This dependence goes in an intuitive direction: as $p$ gets smaller, so that copying becomes more frequent, the exponent $c$ gets smaller as well, making one more likely to see extremely popular pages.

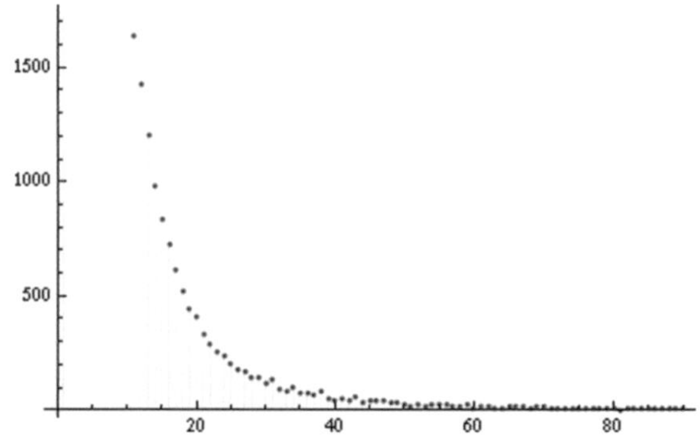


**Fig. 11.2** Distribution with a long tail

The process described in line 2(b) is an implementation of the *rich-get-richer* or *preferential attachment* phenomenon. It is called the rich-get-richer process because when $j$ copies the decision of $i$, the probability of linking to some site $l$ is directly proportional to the total number of sites that currently link to $l$. So, the probability that site $l$ experiences an increase in popularity is directly proportional to $l$'s current popularity. The term preferential attachment is given because the links are formed preferentially to pages that already have high popularity. Intuitively, this makes sense because the more well-known some website is, the more likely that name comes up in other websites, and hence it is more likely that websites will have a link to this well-known website.

This rich-get-richer phenomenon is not confined to settings governed by human-decision making. Instead the population of cities, the intensities of earthquakes, the sizes of power outages, and the number of copies of a gene in a genome are some instances of natural occurrences of this process.

Popularity distribution is found to have a *long tail* as shown in Fig. 11.2. This shows some nodes which have very high popularity when compared to the other nodes. This popularity however drops of to give a long set of nodes who have more or less the same popularity. It is this latter set of a long list of nodes which contribute to the long tail.

## 11.4 Analysis of Rich-Get-Richer Phenomenon

In this section, we will look at a heuristic argument that analyses the behaviour of the model concerning the presence of hyperlinks between websites presented in the previous section, to indicate why power law arises. This will also show us how power law exponent $c$ is related to more basic features of the model.

Let the number of in-links to node $j$ at time step $t \in j$ be a random variable $X_j(t)$. The following two conditions exist for $X_j(t)$:

1. *Initial condition*: Since node $j$ has no links when first created at time $j$, $X_j(j) = 0$.

2. *Expected change to* $X_j$ *over time*: At time step $t+1$, node $j$ gains an in-link if and only if a link from this new created node $t+1$ points to it. From step (2a) of the model, node $t+1$ links to $j$ with probability $1/t$. From step (2b) of the model, node $t+1$ links to $j$ with probability $X_j(t)/t$ since at the moment node $t+1$ was created, the total number of links in the network was $t$ and of these $X_j(t)$ point to $j$. Therefore, the overall probability that node $t+1$ links to node $j$ is as given in Eq. 11.4.

$$\frac{p}{t} + \frac{(1-p)X_j(t)}{t} \tag{11.4}$$

However, this deals with the probabilistic case. For the deterministic case, we define the time as continuously running from 0 to $N$ instead of the probabilistic case considered in the model. The function of time $X_j(t)$ in the discrete case is approximated in the continuous case as $x_j(t)$. The two properties of $x_j(t)$ are:

1. *Initial condition*: Since we had $X_j(j) = 0$ in the probabilistic case, the deterministic case gets $x_j(j) = 0$.
2. *Growth equation*: In the probabilistic case, when node $t+1$ arrives, the number of in-links to $j$ increases with probability given by Eq. 11.4. In the deterministic approximation provided by $x_j$, the rate of growth is modeled by the differential equation given in Eq. 11.5.

$$\frac{dx_j}{dt} = \frac{p}{t} + \frac{(1-p)x_j}{t} \tag{11.5}$$

Let $q = (1-p)$ in Eq. 11.5, then

$$\frac{dx_j}{dt} = \frac{p + qx_j}{t}$$

Dividing both sides by $p + qx_j$, we get

$$\frac{1}{p + qx_j}\frac{dx_j}{dt} = \frac{1}{t}$$

Integrating both sides

$$\int \frac{1}{p + qx_j}\frac{dx_j}{dt}dt = \int \frac{1}{t}dt$$

we get

$$ln(p + qx_j) = q\ ln\ t + c$$

for some constant $c$. Taking $A = e^c$, we get

$$p + qx_j = At^q$$

and hence

$$x_j(t) = \frac{1}{q}\left(At^q - p\right) \tag{11.6}$$

Using the initial condition, $x_j(j) = 0$ in Eq. 11.6, we get

$$0 = x_j(j) = \frac{1}{q}\left(Aj^q - p\right)$$

and hence $A = p/j^q$. Substituting this value for $A$ in Eq. 11.6, we get

$$x_j(t) = \frac{1}{q}\left(\frac{p}{j^q}t^q - p\right) = \frac{p}{q}\left[\left(\frac{t}{j}\right)^q - 1\right] \tag{11.7}$$

Now we ask the following question: For a given value of $k$, and time $t$, what fraction of all nodes have atleast $k$ in-links at time $t$? This can alternately be formulated as: For a given value of $k$, and time $t$, what fraction of all functions $x_j$ satisfy $x_j(t) \geq k$?

Equation 11.7 corresponds to the inequality

$$x_j(t) = \frac{1}{q}\left[\left(\frac{t}{j}\right)^q - 1\right] \geq k$$

This can be re-written as

$$j \leq \frac{1}{t}\left[\frac{q}{p}\cdot k + 1\right]^{-\frac{1}{q}}$$

we get

$$\frac{1}{t}\cdot t\left[\frac{q}{p}\cdot k + 1\right]^{-\frac{1}{q}} = \left[\frac{q}{p}\cdot k + 1\right]^{-\frac{1}{q}} \tag{11.8}$$

Since $p$ and $q$ are constants, the expression inside brackets is proportional to $k$ and so the fraction of $x_j$ that are atleast $k$ is proportional to $k^{-1/q}$.

Differentiating Eq. 11.8, we get

$$\frac{1}{q}\frac{q}{p}\left[\frac{q}{p}\cdot k + 1\right]^{-1-1/q}$$

From this, we can infer that the deterministic model predicts that the fraction of nodes with $k$ in-links is proportional to $k^{-(1+1/q)}$ with exponent

$$1 + \frac{1}{q} = 1 + \frac{1}{p}$$

With high probability over the random formation of links, fraction of nodes with $k$ in-links is proportional to $k^{(-1+1/(1-p))}$. When $p$ is close to 1, the link formation is mainly based on uniform random choices, and so the rich-get-richer dynamics is muted. On the other hand, when $p$ is close to 0, the growth of the network is strongly governed by rich-get-richer behaviour, and the power-law exponent decreases towards 2, allowing for many nodes with a very large number of in-links. The fact that 2 is a natural limit for the exponent as rich-get-richer dynamics become stronger also provides a nice way to think about the fact that many power-law exponents in real networks tend to be slightly above 2.

## 11.5 Modelling Burst of Activity

Reference [10] developed a formal approach for modelling "bursts of activity", the phenomenon where the appearance of a topic in a document stream grows in intensity for a period of time and then fades away. These bursts show certain features rising sharply in frequency as the topic emerges. Here, an organizational framework for robustly and efficiently identifying and analysing the content is developed. The approach is based on modelling the stream using an infinite-state automaton, in which bursts appear naturally as state transitions.

Suppose we are given a document stream, how do we identify the bursts of activity in the stream? On first thought, it would occur that bursts correspond to points at which the intensity of activity increases sharply. However, this intensity does not rise smoothly to a crescendo and then fall away, but rather exhibits frequent alternations of rapid flurries and longer pauses when examined closely. Thus, methods that analyse gaps between consecutive message arrivals in too simplistic a way can easily be pulled into identifying large numbers of short spurious bursts, as well as fragmenting long bursts into many smaller ones. It is worth noting that the intent is to extract global structure from a robust kind of data reduction, i.e, identifying bursts only when they have sufficient intensity, and in a way that allows a burst to persist smoothly across a fairly non-uniform pattern of message arrivals.

This paper models the generation of bursts by an automaton that is in one of two states, "low" and "high". The time gaps between consecutive events are distributed according to an exponential distribution whose parameter depend on the current state of the automaton. Thus, the high state is hypothesized as generating bursts of events. There is a cost associated with any state transition to discourage short bursts. Given a document stream, the goal is to find a low cost sequence that is likely to generate that stream. Finding an optimal solution to this problem is accomplished by dynamic programming.

In the case where each event in a stream is either *relevant* or *irrelevant*, this two-state model can be extended to generate events with a particular mix of these relevant and irrelevant events according to a binomial distribution. A sequence of events is considered bursty if the fraction of relevant events alternates between periods in which it is large and long periods in which it is small. Associating a weight with each burst, solves the problem of enumerating all the bursts by order of weight.

Reference [11] identify bursts in the Blogspace and propose techniques to generate bursty intra-community links.

It was found that within a community of interacting bloggers, a given topic may become the subject of intense debate for a period of time, then fade away. Simply identifying the bloggers contributing to this burst is not enough, the corresponding time interval of activity is also a requirement.

The paper uses a graph object called the *time graph*. A time graph $G = (V, E)$ consists of

1. A set $V$ of vertices where each vertex $v \in V$ has an associated interval $D(v)$ on the time axis called the duration of $v$.
2. A set $E$ of edges where each edge $e \in E$ is a triplet $(u, v, t)$ where $u$ and $v$ are vertices in $V$ and $t$ is a point in time in the interval $D(u) \cap D(v)$.

A vertex $v$ is said to be *alive* at time $t$ if $t \in D(v)$. This means that each edge is created at a point in time at which its two endpoints are alive.

Thus, tracking bursty communities on the Blogspace involves the following two steps:

1. Identify dense subgraphs in the time graph of the Blogspace which will correspond to all potential communities. However, this will result in finding all the clusters regardless of whether or not they are bursty.
2. Apply the work of [10] to perform burst analysis of each subgraph obtained in the previous step.

The time graph was generated for blogs from seven blog sites. The resulting graph consisted of 22299 vertices, 70472 unique edges and 777653 edges counting multiplicity. Applying the steps to this graph, the burstiness of the graph is as shown in Fig. 11.3.

## 11.6 Densification Power Laws and Shrinking Diameters

Reference [13] studied temporal graphs and found that most of these graphs densify over time with the number of edges growing superlinearly in the number of nodes. Also, the average distance between nodes is found to shrink over time.

It was observed that as graphs evolve over time,

$$|E|(t) \propto |V|(t)^a \tag{11.9}$$

where $|E|(t)$ and $|V|(t)$ denote the number of vertices and edges at time step $t$ and $a$ is an exponent that generally lies between 1 and 2. This relation is referred to as the *Densification power-law* or *growth power-law*.

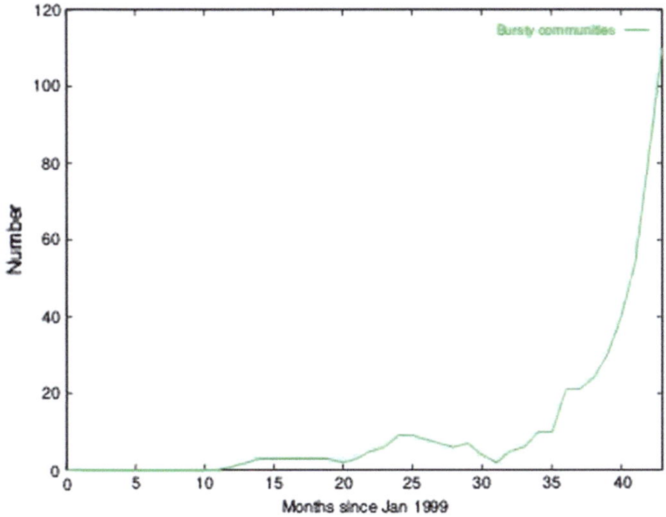


**Fig. 11.3** Burstiness of communities in the time graph of the Blogspace

Twelve different datasets from seven different sources were considered for the study. These included HEP-PH and HEP-TH arXiv citation graphs, a citation graph for U.S. utility patents, a graph of routers comprising the Internet, five bipartite affiliation graphs of authors with papers they authored for ASTRO-PH, HEP-TH, HEP-PH, COND-MAT and GR-QC, a bipartite graph of actors-to-movies corresponding to IMDB, a person to person recommendation graph, and an email communication network from an European research institution.

Figure 11.4 depicts the plot of average out-degree over time. We observe an increase indicating that graphs become dense. Figure 11.5 illustrates the log-log plot of the number of edges as a function of the number of vertices. They all obey the densification power law. This could mean that densification of graphs is an intrinsic phenomenon.

In this paper, for every $d \in \mathbb{N}$, $g(d)$ denotes the fraction of connected node pairs whose shortest connecting path has length atmost $d$. The *effective diameter* of the network is defined as the value of $d$ at which this function $g(d)$ achieves the value 0.9. So, if $D$ is a value where $g(D) = 0.9$, then the graph has effective diameter $D$. Figure 11.6 shows the effective diameter over time. A decrease in diameter can be observed from the plots. Since all of these plots exhibited a decrease in the diameter, it could be that the shrinkage was an inherent property of networks.

To verify that the shrinkage of diameters was not intrinsic to the datasets, experiments were performed to account for:

1. *Possible sampling problems*: Since computing shortest paths among all node pairs is computationally prohibitive for these graphs, several different approximate methods were applied, obtaining almost identical results from all of them.

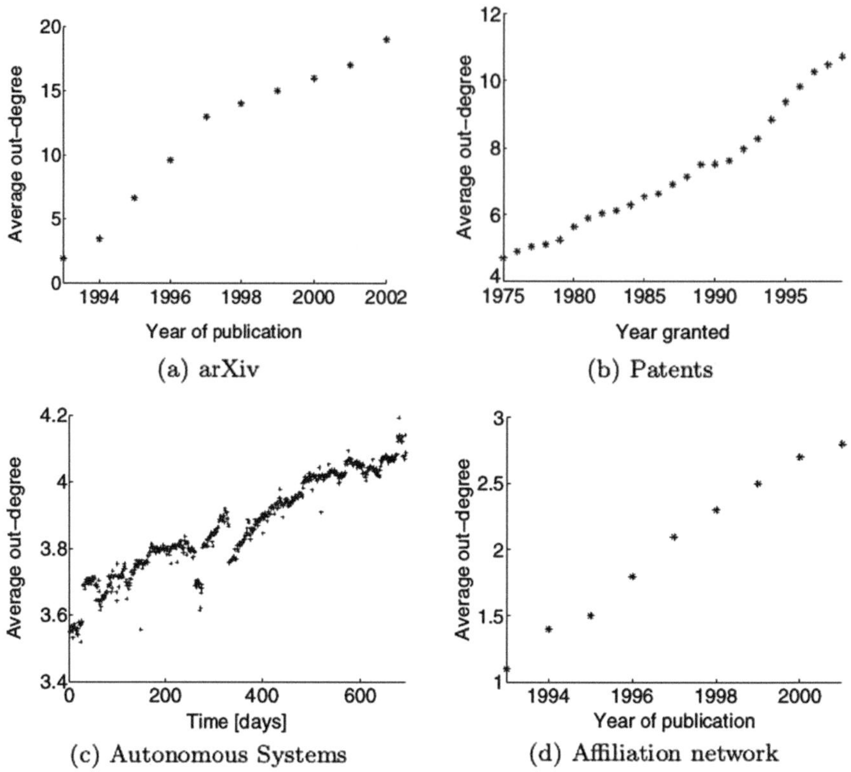


**Fig. 11.4** Average out-degree over time. Increasing trend signifies that the graph are densifying

2. *Effect of disconnected components*: These large graphs have a single giant component. To see if the disconnected components had a bearing on the diameter, the effective diameter for the entire graph and just the giant component were computed. The values were found to be the same.
3. *Effects of missing past*: With almost any dataset, one does not have data reaching all the way back to the network's birth. This is referred to as the problem of *missing past*. This means that there will be edges pointing to nodes prior to the beginning of the observation period. Such nodes and edges are referred to as *phantom nodes* and *phantom edges* respectively.
   To understand how the diameters of our networks are affected by this unavoidable problem, we perform the following test. We pick some positive time $t_0 > 0$ and determine what the diameter would look like as a function of time if this were the beginning of our data. We then put back in the nodes and the edges from before time $t_0$ and study how much the diameters change. If this change is small, then it provides evidence that the missing past is not influencing the overall result.
   $t_0$ were suitably set for the datasets and the results of three measurements were compared:

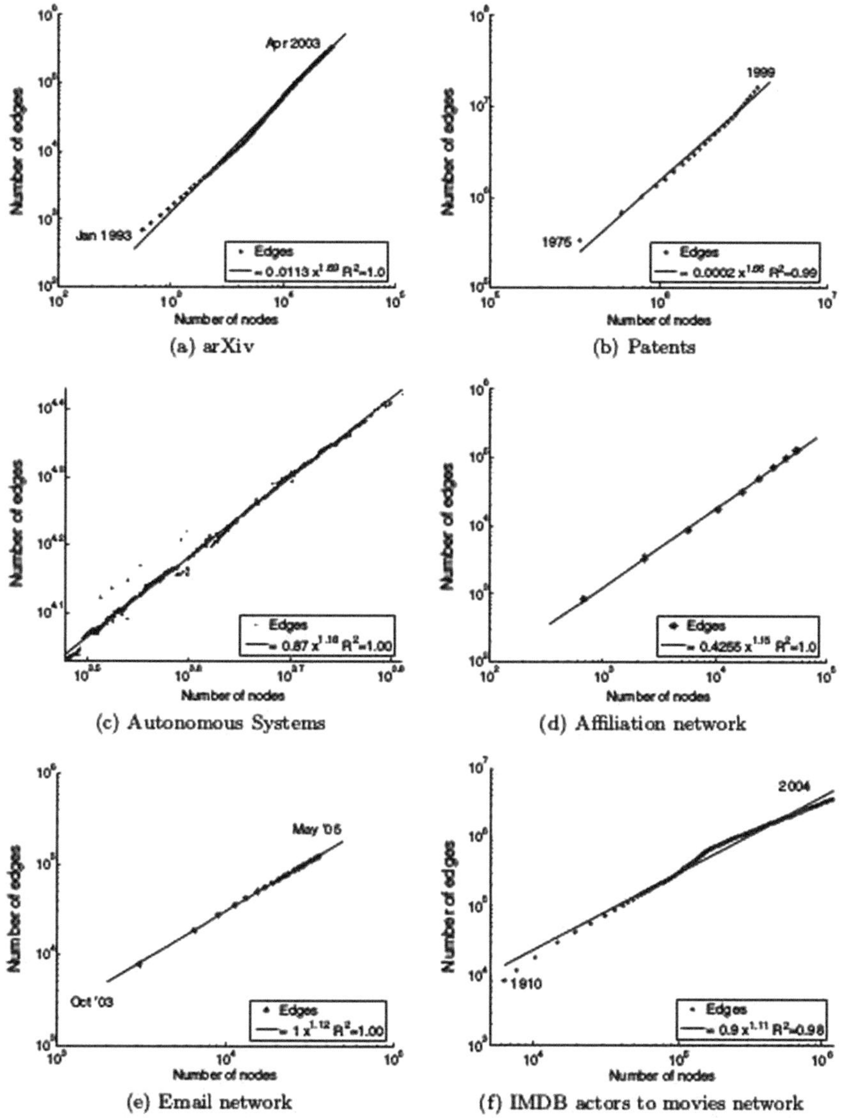


**Fig. 11.5** Number of edges as a function of the number of nodes in log-log scale. They obey the densification power law

a. *Diameter of full graph*: For each time $t$, the effective diameter of the graph's giant component was computed.
b. *Post-$t_0$ subgraph*: The effective diameter of the post-$t_0$ subgraph using all nodes and edges were computed. For each time $t (t > t_0)$, a graph using all nodes dated before $t$ was created. The effective diameter of the subgraph of

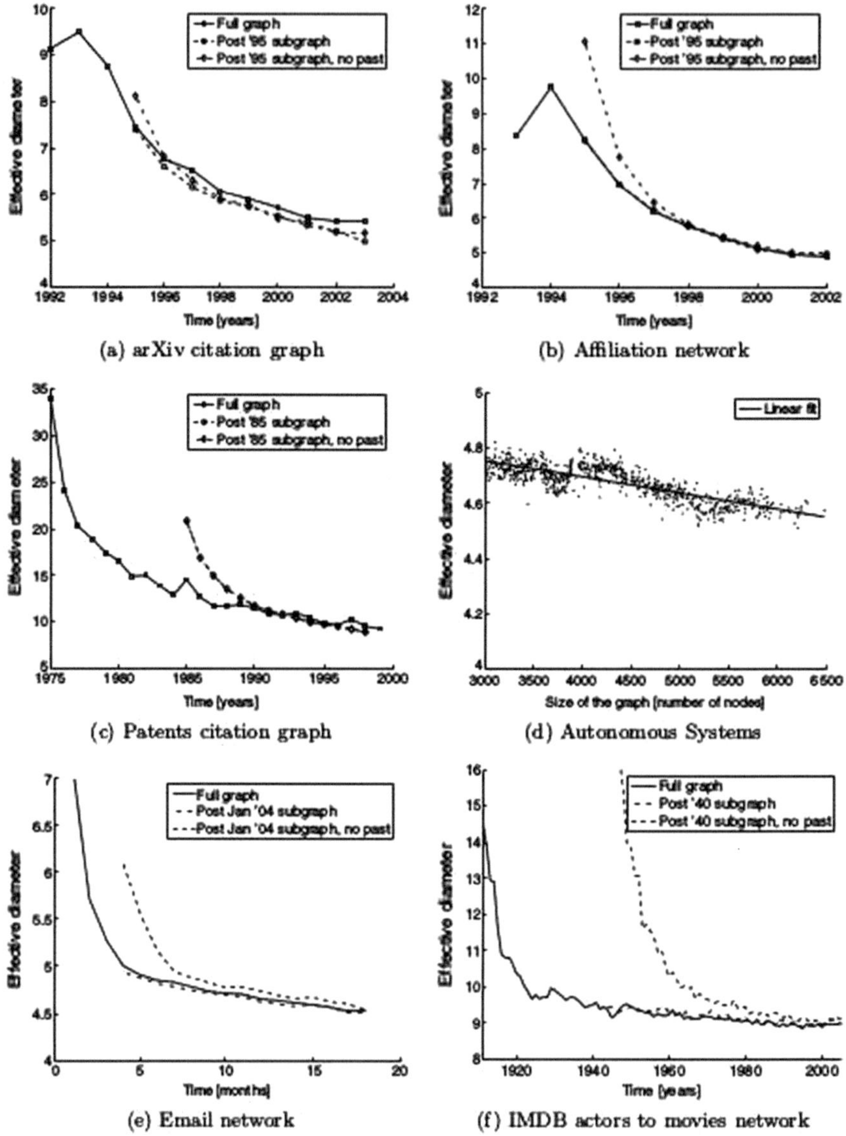


**Fig. 11.6** Effective diameter over time for 6 different datasets. There is a consistent decrease of the diameter over time

the nodes dated between $t_0$ and $t$ was computed. To compute the effective diameter, we can use all edges and nodes (including those dated before $t_0$). This means that we are measuring distances only among nodes dated between $t_0$ and $t$ while also using nodes and edges before $t_0$ as shortcuts or bypasses. The experiment measures the diameter of the graph if we knew the full

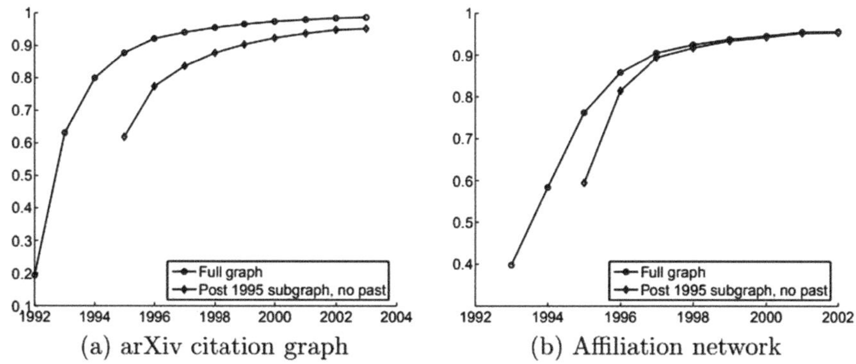


**Fig. 11.7** The fraction of nodes that are part of the giant connected component over time. Observe that after 4 years, 90% of all nodes in the graph belong to the giant component

(pre-$t_0$) past, the citations of the papers which we have intentionally excluded for this test.

c. *Post-$t_0$ subgraph, no past.* We set $t_0$ the same way as in the previous experiment, but then, for all nodes dated before $t_0$, we delete all their outlinks. This creates the graph we would have gotten if we had started collecting data only at time $t_0$.

In Fig. 11.6, we superimpose the effective diameters using the three different techniques. If the missing past does not play a large role in the diameter, then all three curves should lie close to one another. We observe this is the case for the arXiv citation graphs. For the arXiv paper-author affiliation graph and for the patent citation graph, the curves are quite different right at the cut-off time $t_0$, but they quickly align with one another. As a result, it seems clear that the continued decreasing trend in the effective diameter as time runs to the present is not the result of these boundary effects.

4. *Emergence of the giant component*: We have learnt in Chap. 3 that in the Erdös-Rényi random graph model, the diameter of the giant component is quite large when it first appears, and then it shrinks as edges continue to be added. Therefore, are shrinking diameters a symptom of the emergence of giant component?
Figure 11.7 shows us that this is not the case. In the plot of the size of the GCC for the full graph and for a graph where we had no past, i.e, where we delete all outlinks of the nodes dated before the cut-off time $t_0$. Because we delete the outlinks of the pre-$t_0$ nodes, the size of the GCC is smaller, but, as the graph grows, the effect of these deleted links becomes negligible.
Within a few years, the giant component accounts for almost all the nodes in the graph. The effective diameter, however, continues to steadily decrease beyond this point. This indicates that the decrease is happening in a mature graph and not because many small disconnected components are being rapidly glued together.

The models studied so far do not exhibit this densification and diameter shrinkage. The paper proposes the following models which can achieve these properties. The first model is the *Community Guided Attachment* where the idea is that if the nodes of a graph belong to communities-within-communities [6], and if the cost for cross-community edges is scale-free, then the densification power-law follows naturally. Also, this model exhibits a heavy-tailed degree distribution. However, this model cannot capture the shrinking effective diameters. To capture all of these, the *Forest Fire* model was proposed. In this model, nodes arrive in over time. Each node has a center-of-gravity in some part of the network and its probability of linking to other nodes decreases rapidly with their distance from this center-of-gravity. However, occasionally a new node will produce a very large number of outlinks. Such nodes will help cause a more skewed out-degree distribution. These nodes will serve as bridges that connect formerly disparate parts of the network, bringing the diameter down.

Formally, the forest fire model has two parameters, a *forward burning probability* $p$, and a *backward burning probability* $r$. Consider a node $v$ joining the network at time $t > 1$, and let $G_t$ be the graph constructed thus far. Node $v$ forms outlinks to nodes in $G_t$ according to the following process:

1. $v$ first chooses an ambassador node $w$ uniformly at random and forms a link to $w$.
2. Two random numbers, $x$ and $y$ are generated, that are geometrically distributed with means $p/(1-p)$ and $rp/(1-rp)$, respectively. Node $v$ selects $x$ out-links and $y$ in-links of $w$ incident to nodes that were not yet visited. Let $w_1$, $w_2$, ..., $w_{x+y}$ denotes the other ends of these selected links. If not enough in- or out-links are available, $v$ selects as many as it can.
3. $v$ forms out-links to $w_1$, $w_2$, ..., $w_{x+y}$, and then applies the previous step recursively to each of $w_1$, $w_2$, ..., $w_{x+y}$. As the process continues, nodes cannot be visited a second time, preventing the construction from cycling.

Thus, the burning of links in the Forest Fire model begins at $w$, spreads to $w_1$, ..., $w_{x+y}$, and proceeds recursively until it dies out. The model can be extended to account for isolated vertices and vertices with large degree by having newcomers choose no ambassadors in the former case (called *orphans*) and multiple ambassadors in the latter case (simply called *multiple ambassadors*). Orphans and multiple ambassadors help further separate the diameter decrease/increase boundary from the densification transition and so widen the region of parameter space for which the model produces reasonably sparse graphs with decreasing effective diameters.

Reference [12] proposed an *affiliation network* framework to generate models that exhibit these phenomena. Their intuition is that individuals are part of a certain society, therefore leading to a bipartite graph. By folding this bipartite graph $B$, the resultant folded graph $G$ is found to exhibit the following properties:

- $B$ has power-law distribution, and $G$ has a heavy-tailed distribution.
- $G$ has super-linear number of edges.
- The effective diameter of $G$ stabilizes to a constant.

## 11.7 Microscopic Evolution of Networks

Reference [14] proposed the use of model likelihood of individual edges as a way to evaluate and compare various network evolution models.

The following datasets were considered: (i) *FLICKR* (a photo- sharing website), (ii) *DELICIOUS* (a collaborative bookmark tagging website), (iii) *YAHOO! ANSWERS* (a knowledge sharing website), and (iv) *LINKEDIN* (a professional contacts website). Here, nodes represent people and edges represent social relationships. These datasets were considered particularly because they have the exact temporal information about individual arrival of nodes and edges. Thereby, we are able to consider edge-by-edge evolution of networks, and hence efficiently compute the likelihood that a particular model would have produced a particular edge, given the current state of the network.

There are three core processes to the models: (i) *Node arrival process*: This governs the arrival of new nodes into the network, (ii) *Edge initiation process*: Determines for each node when it will initiate a new edge, and (iii) *Edge destination selection process*: Determines the destination of a newly initiated edge.

Let $G_t$ denote a network composed from the earliest $t$ edges, $e_1, \ldots, e_t$ for $t \in \{1, \ldots, |E|\}$. Let $t_e$ be the time when edge $e$ is created, let $t(u)$ be the time when the node $u$ joined the network, and let $t_k(u)$ be the time when the $k^{th}$ edge of the node $u$ is created. Then $a_t(u) = t - t(u)$ denotes the age of the node $u$ at time $t$. Let $d_t(u)$ denote the degree of the node $u$ at time $t$ and $d(u) = d_T(u)$. $[\cdot]$ denotes a predicate (takes value of 1 if expression is true, else 0).

The maximum likelihood estimation (MLE) was applied to pick the best model in the following manner: the network is evolved in an edge by edge manner, and for every edge that arrives into this network, the likelihood that the particular edge endpoints would be chosen under some model is measured. The product of these likelihoods over all edges will give the likelihood of the model. A higher likelihood means a better model in the sense that it offers a more likely explanation of the observed data.

### 11.7.1 Edge Destination Selection Process

By the preferential attachment (PA) model, the probability $p_e(d)$ that a new edge chooses a destination node of degree $d$, normalized by the number of nodes of degree $d$ that exist just before this step is computed as

$$p_e(d) = \frac{\sum_t [e_t = (u, v) \wedge d_{t-1}(v) = d]}{\sum_t |\{u : d_{t-1}(u) = d\}|} \tag{11.10}$$

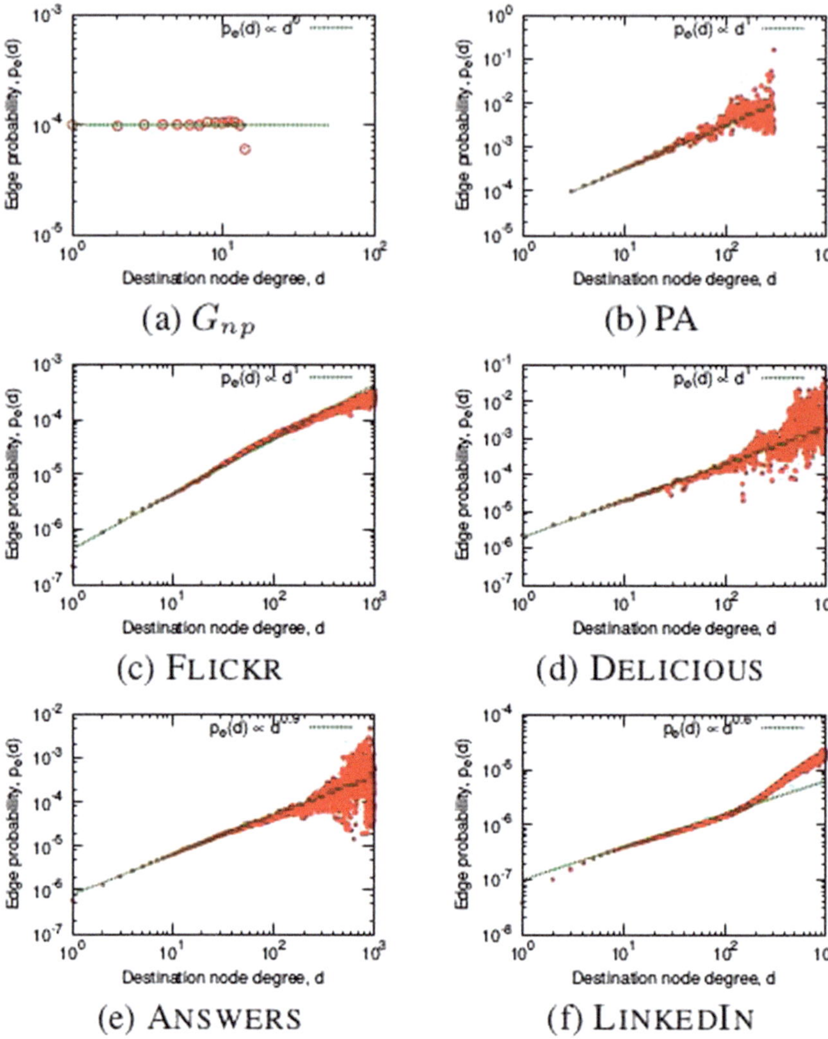


**Fig. 11.8** Probability $p_e(d)$ of a new edge $e$ choosing a destination at a node of degree $d$

Figure 11.8 shows the plot of $p_e(d)$ as a function of the node degree $d$. Figure 11.8a, b are for an Erdös-Rényi random graph and a preferential attachment model respectively. Figure 11.8c–f are for the datasets. Observe that they all follow $p_e(d) \propto d^{\tau}$ where the exponent $\tau \approx 1$ for all plots except the first.

The average number of edges, $e(a)$, created by nodes of age $a$, is the number of edges created by nodes of age $a$ normalized by the number of nodes that achieved age $a$ given in Eq. 11.11

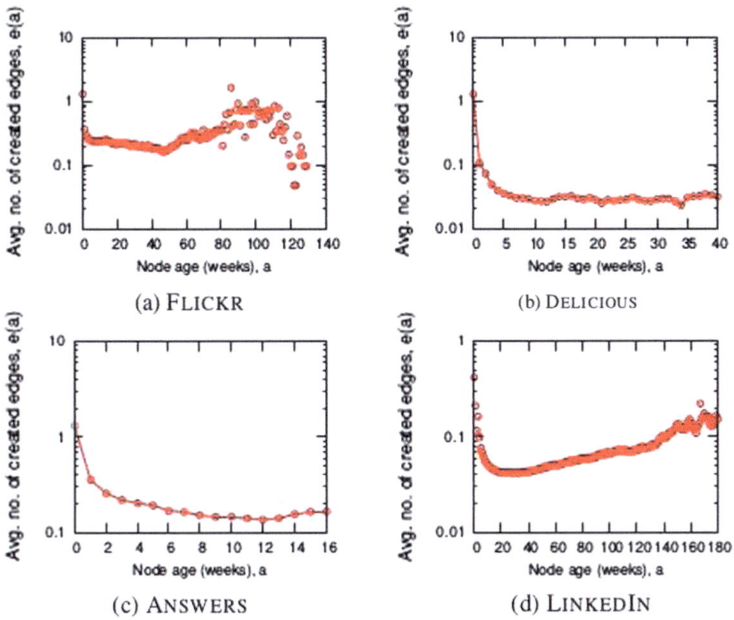


(a) Flickr (b) Delicious (c) Answers (d) LinkedIn

**Fig. 11.9** Average number of edges created by a node of age $a$

$$e(a) = \frac{|\{e = (u, v) : t(e) - t(u) = a\}|}{|\{t(u) : t_l - t(u) \geq a\}|} \tag{11.11}$$

where $t_l$ is the time when the last node in the network joined.

Figure 11.9 plots the fraction of edges initiated by nodes of a certain age. The spike at nodes of age 0 correspond to the people who receive an invite to join the network, create a first edge, and then never come back.

Using the MLE principle, the combined effect of node age and degree was studied by considering the following four parameterised models for choosing the edge endpoints at time $t$.

- $D$: The probability of selecting a node $v$ is proportional to its current degree raised to power $\tau : d_t(v)^{\tau}$.
- $DR$: With probability $\tau$, the node $v$ is selected preferentially (proportionally to its degree), and with probability $(1 - \tau)$, uniformly at random: $\tau \cdot d_t(v) + (1 - \tau) \cdot 1/N(t)$.
- $A$: The probability of selecting a node is proportional to its age raised to power $\tau : a_t(v)^{\tau}$.
- $DA$: The probability of selecting a node $v$ is proportional the product of its current degree and its age raised to the power $\tau : d_t(v) \cdot a_t(v)^{\tau}$.

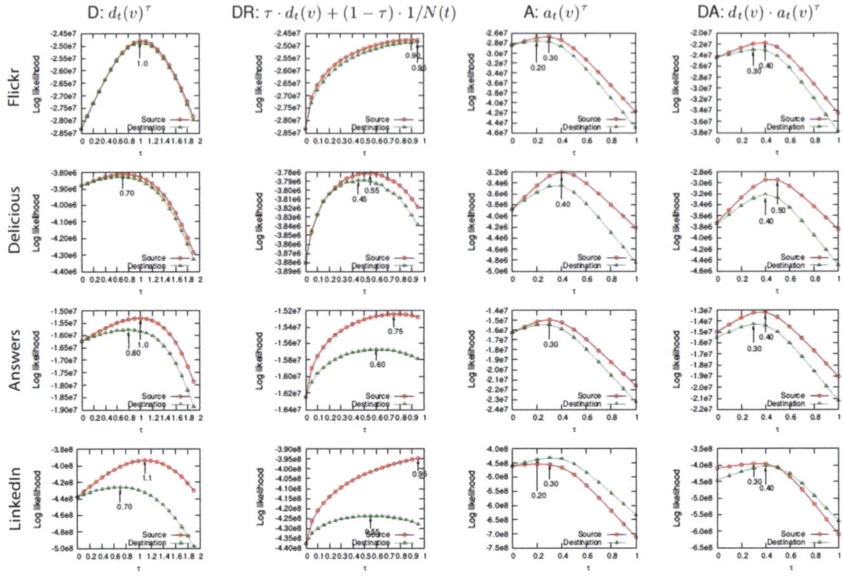


**Fig. 11.10** Log-likelihood of an edge selecting its source and destination node. Arrows denote $\tau$ at highest likelihood

Figure 11.10 plots the log-likelihood under the different models as a function of $\tau$. The red curve plots the log-likelihood of selecting a source node and the green curve for selecting the destination node of an edge.

In *FLICKR* the selection of destination is purely preferential: model *D* achieves the maximum likelihood at $\tau = 1$, and model $DA$ is very biased to model *D*, i.e, $\tau \approx 1$. Model *A* has worse likelihood but model $DA$ improves the overall log-likelihood by around 10%. Edge attachment in *DELICIOUS* seems to be the most "random": model *D* has worse likelihood than model $DR$. Moreover the likelihood of model $DR$ achieves maximum at $\tau = 0.5$ suggesting that about 50% of the *DELICIOUS* edges attach randomly. Model *A* has better likelihood than the degree-based models, showing edges are highly biased towards young nodes. For *YAHOO! ANSWERS*, models *D*, *A*, and $DR$ have roughly equal likelihoods (at the optimal choice of $\tau$), while model $DA$ further improves the log-likelihood by 20%, showing some age bias. In *LINKEDIN*, age-biased models are worse than degree-biased models. A strong degree preferential bias of the edges was also noted. As in *FLICKR*, model $DA$ improves the log-likelihood by 10%.

Selecting an edge's destination node is harder than selecting its source (the green curve is usually below the red). Also, selecting a destination appears more random than selecting a source, the maximum likelihood $\tau$ of the destination node (green curve) for models *D* and $DR$ is shifted to the left when compared to the source node (red), which means the degree bias is weaker. Similarly, there is a stronger bias towards young nodes in selecting an edge's source than in selecting its destination.

Based on the observations, model $D$ performs reasonably well compared to more sophisticated variants based on degree and age.

Even though the analysis suggests that model $D$ is a reasonable model for edge destination selection, it is inherently "non-local" in that edges are no more likely to form between nodes which already have friends in common. A detailed study of the locality properties of edge destination selection is required.

Consider the following notion of edge locality: for each new edge $(u, w)$, the number of hops it spans are measured, i.e., the length of the shortest path between nodes $u$ and $w$ immediately before the edge was created. Figure 11.11 shows the distribution of these shortest path values induced by each new edge for $G_{np}$ (with $p = 12/n$), $PA$, and the four social networks. (The isolated dot on the left counts the number of edges that connected previously disconnected components of the network). For $G_{np}$ most new edges span nodes that were originally six hops away, and then the number decays polynomially in the hops. In the PA model, we see a lot of long-range edges; most of them span four hops but none spans more than seven. The hop distributions corresponding to the four real-world networks look similar to one another, and strikingly different from both $G_{np}$ and $PA$. The number of edges decays exponentially with the hop distance between the nodes, meaning that most edges are created locally between nodes that are close. The exponential decay suggests that the creation of a large fraction of edges can be attributed to locality in the network structure, namely most of the times people who are close in the network (e.g., have a common friend) become friends themselves. These results involve counting the number of edges that link nodes certain distance away. In a sense, this over counts edges $(u, w)$ for which $u$ and $w$ are far away, as there are many more distant candidates to choose from, it appears that the number of long-range edges decays exponentially while the number of long-range candidates grows exponentially. To explore this phenomenon, the number of hops each new edge spans are counted but then normalized by the total number of nodes at $h$ hops, i.e, we compute

$$p_e(h) = \frac{\sum_t [e_t \; connects \; nodes \; at \; distance \; h \; in \; G_{t-1}]}{\sum_t (\# \; nodes \; at \; distance \; h \; from \; the \; source \; node \; of \; e_t)} \tag{11.12}$$

First, Fig. 11.12a, b show the results for $G_{np}$ and $PA$ models. (Again, the isolated dot at $h = 0$ plots the probability of a new edge connecting disconnected components.) In $G_{np}$, edges are created uniformly at random, and so the probability of linking is independent of the number of hops between the nodes. In $PA$, due to degree correlations short (local) edges prevail. However, a non-trivial amount of probability goes to edges that span more than two hops. Figure 11.12c–f show the plots for the four networks. Notice the probability of linking to a node $h$ hops away decays double-exponentially, i.e., $p_e(h) \propto exp(exp(-h))$, since the number of edges at $h$ hops increases exponentially with $h$. This behaviour is drastically different from both the $PA$ and $G_{np}$ models. Also note that almost all of the probability mass is

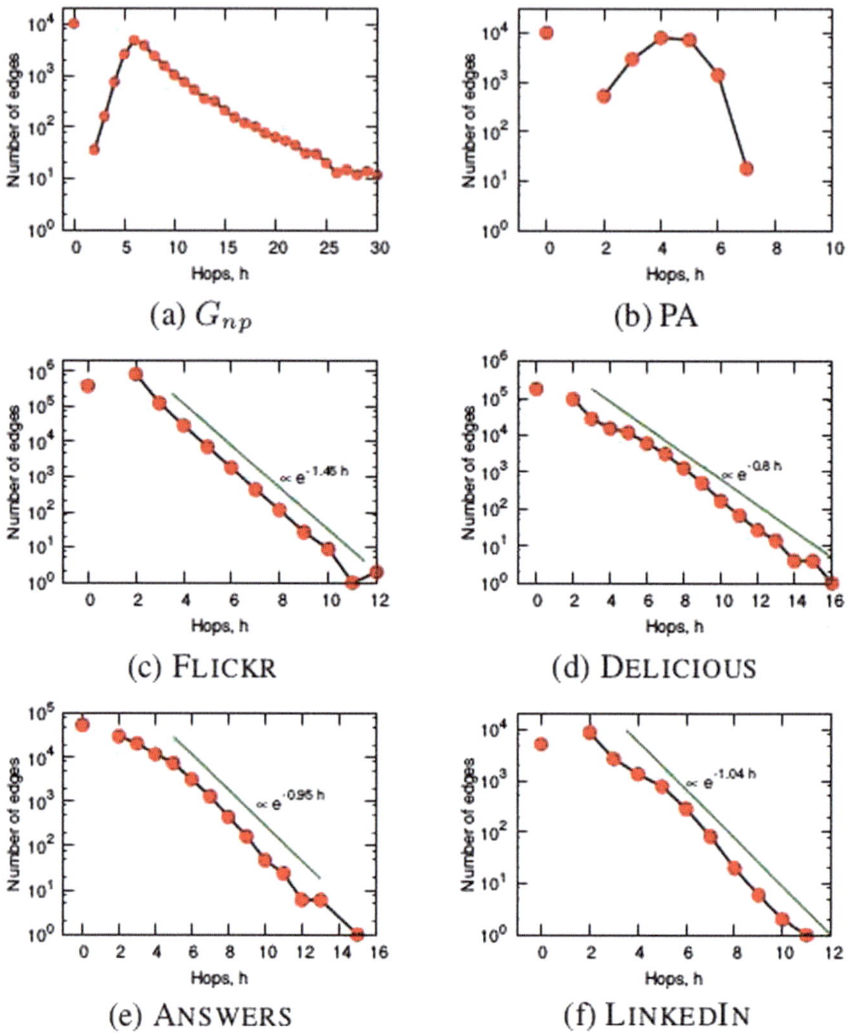


**Fig. 11.11** Number of edges $E_h$ created to nodes $h$ hops away. $h = 0$ counts the number of edges that connected previously disconnected components

on edges that close length-two paths. This means that edges are most likely to close triangles, i.e, connect people with common friends.

### *11.7.2 Edge Initiation Process*

Here, we assume that the sequence and timing of node arrivals is given, and we model the process by which nodes initiate edges. We begin by studying how long a node

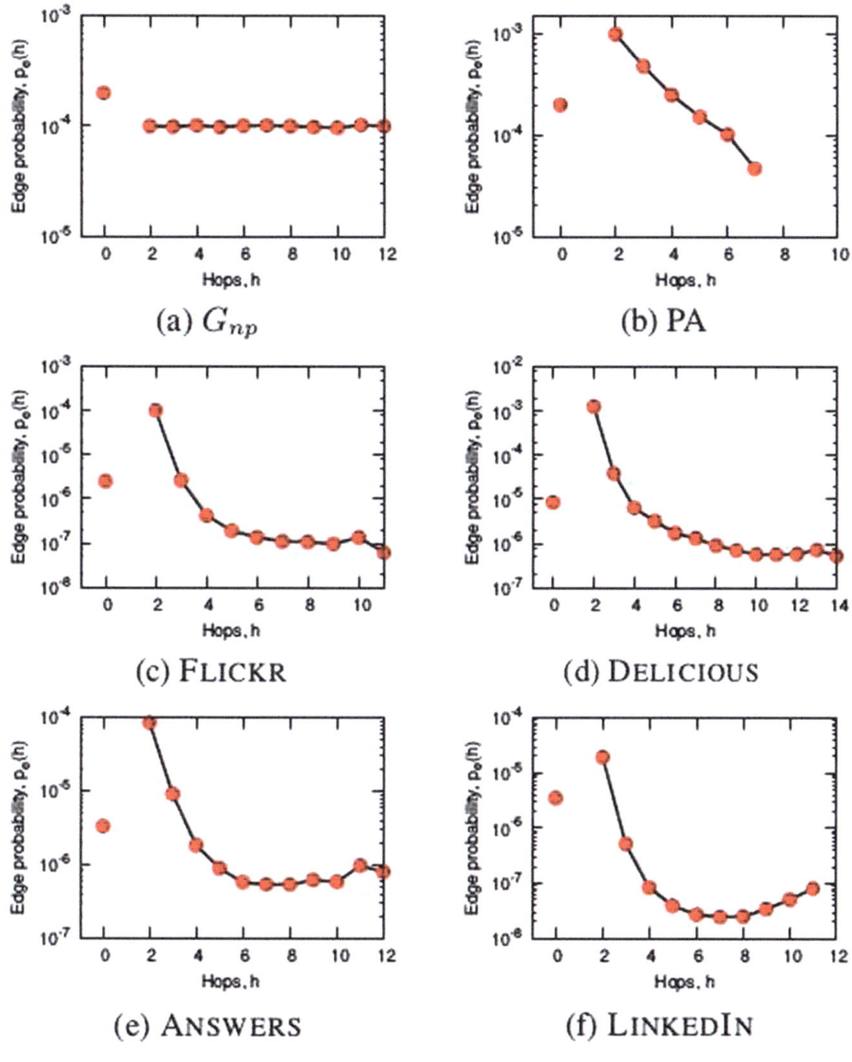


**Fig. 11.12** Probability of linking to a random node at $h$ hops from source node. Value at $h = 0$ hops is for edges that connect previously disconnected components

remains active in the social network, and then during this active lifetime, we study the specific times at which the node initiates new edges.

To avoid truncation effects, we only consider those nodes whose last-created edge is in the first half of all edges in the data. Recall that the lifetime of a node $u$ is $a(u) = t_{d(u)}(u) - t_1(u)$. We evaluate the likelihood of various distributions and observe that node lifetimes are best modeled by an exponential distribution, $p_l(a) = \lambda exp(-\lambda a)$. Figure 11.13 gives the plot of the data and the exponential fits, where time is measured

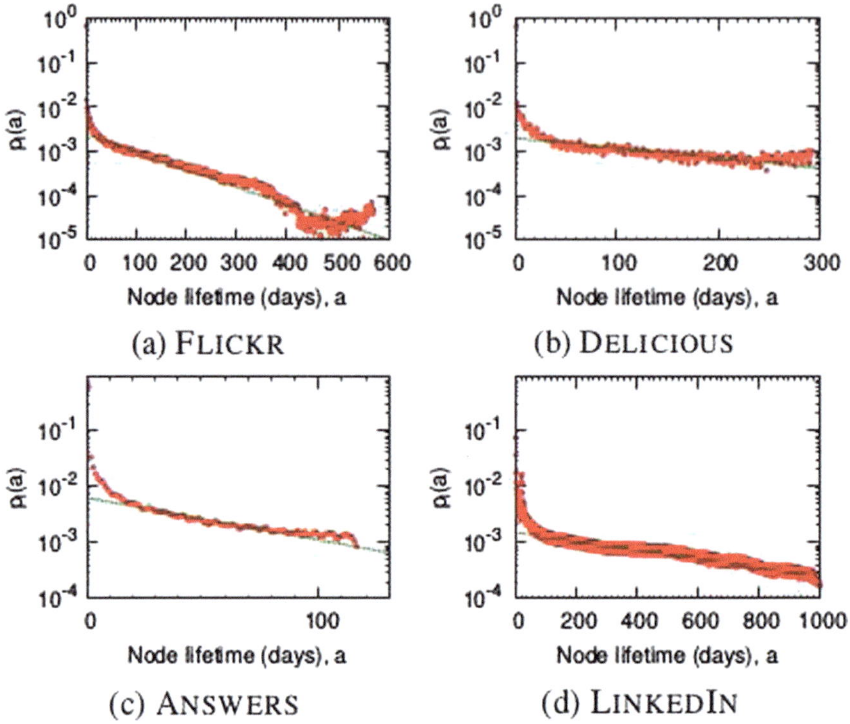


**Fig. 11.13** Exponentially distributed node lifetimes

in days. We find that the exponential distribution does not fit well the nodes with very short lifetimes, i.e, nodes that are invited into the network, create an edge and never return. But the distribution provides a very clean fit for nodes whose lifetime is more than a week.

Now that we have a model for the lifetime of a node $u$, we must model that amount of elapsed time between edge initiations from $u$. Let $\delta_u(d) = t_{d+1}(u) - t_d(u)$ be the time it takes for the node $u$ with current degree $d$ to create its $(d+1)$-st out-edge; we call $\delta_u(d)$ the edge gap. Again, we examine several candidate distributions to model edge gaps. The best likelihood is provided by a power law with exponential cut-off: $p_g(\delta(d); \alpha, \beta) \propto \delta(d)^{-\alpha} exp(-\beta\delta(d))$, where $d$ is the current degree of the node. These results are confirmed in Fig. 11.14, in which we plot the MLE estimates to gap distribution $\delta(1)$, i.e., distribution of times that it took a node of degree 1 to add the second edge. We find that all gaps distributions $\delta(d)$ are best modelled by a power law with exponential cut-off. For each $\delta(d)$ we fit a separate distribution and Fig. 11.15 shows the evolution of the parameters $\alpha$ and $\beta$ of the gap distribution, as a function of the degree $d$ of the node. Interestingly, the power law exponent $\alpha(d)$ remains constant as a function of $d$, at almost the same value for all four networks. On the other hand, the exponential cutoff parameter $\beta(d)$ increases linearly with $d$,

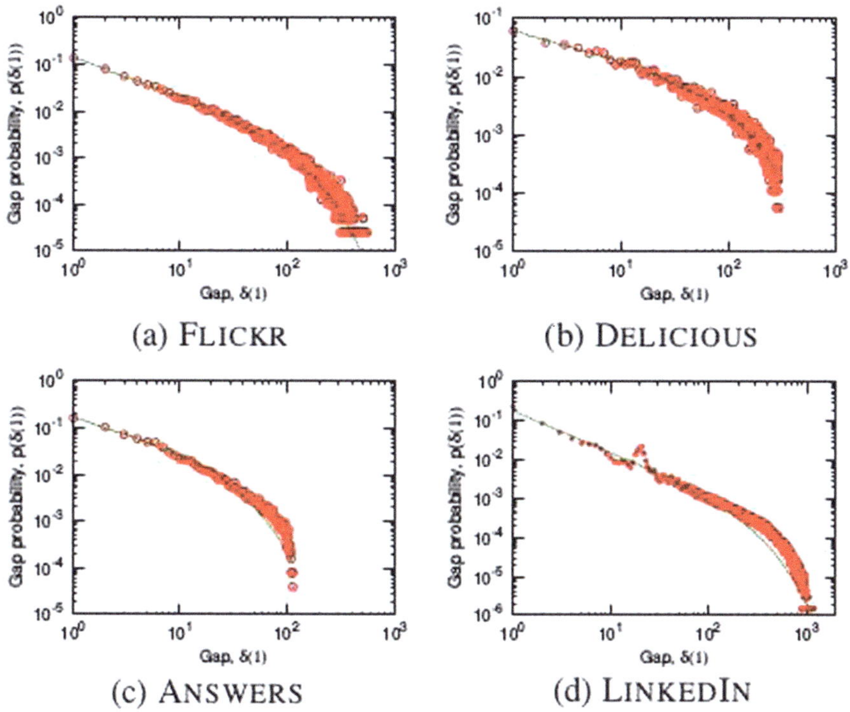


**Fig. 11.14** Edge gap distribution for a node to obtain the second edge, $\delta(1)$, and MLE power law with exponential cutoff fits

and varies by an order of magnitude across networks; this variation models the extent to which the "rich get richer" phenomenon manifests in each network. This means that the slope $\alpha$ of power-law part remains constant, only the exponential cutoff part (parameter $\beta$) starts to kick in sooner and sooner. So, nodes add their $(d + 1)$-st edge faster than their $d$th edge, i.e, nodes start to create more and more edges (sleeping times get shorter) as they get older (and have higher degree). So, based on Fig. 11.15, the overall gap distribution can be modelled by $p_g(\delta|d; \alpha, \beta) \propto \delta^{-\alpha} exp(-\beta d \delta)$.

### *11.7.3 Node Arrival Process*

Figure 11.16 shows the number of users in each of our networks over time. *FLICKR* grows exponentially over much of our network, while the growth of other networks is much slower. *DELICIOUS* grows slightly super-linearly, *LINKEDIN* quadratically, and *YAHOO! ANSWERS* sub-linearly. Given these wild variations we conclude the node arrival process needs to be specified in advance as it varies greatly across networks due to external factors.

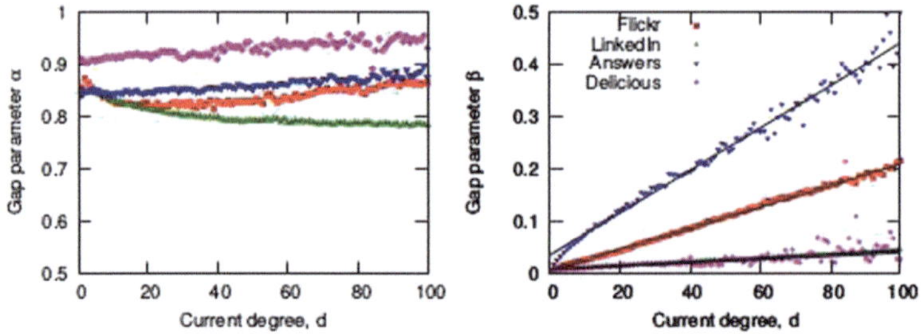


**Fig. 11.15** Evolution of the $\alpha$ and $\beta$ parameters with the current node degree $d$. $\alpha$ remains constant, and $\beta$ linearly increases

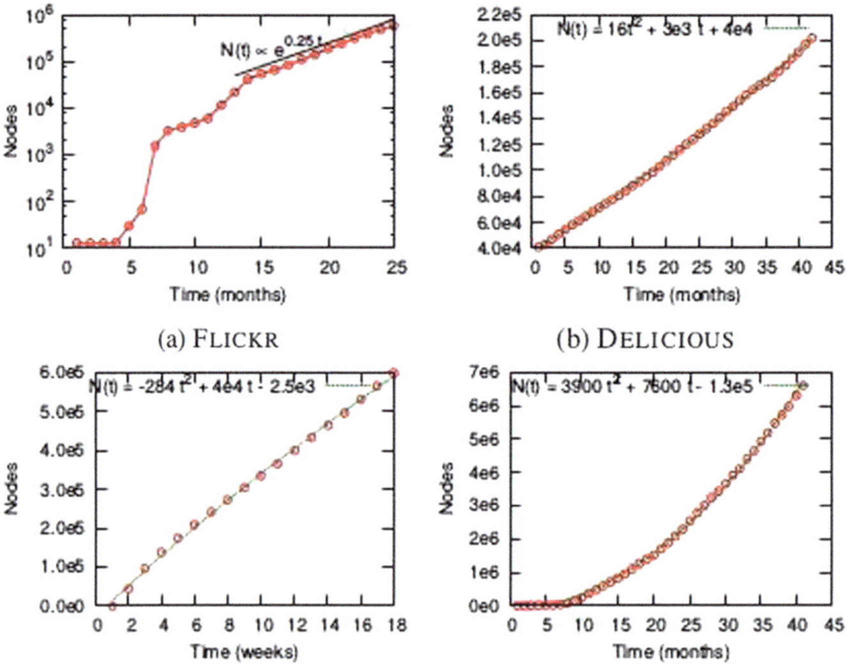


(a) FLICKR (b) DELICIOUS (c) ANSWERS (d) LINKEDIN

**Fig. 11.16** Number of nodes over time

## *11.7.4 Network Evolution Model*

From the observations so far, we now present a complete network evolution model. The model is parametrized by $N(\cdot)$, $\lambda$, $\alpha$, $\beta$, and operates as follows:

1. Nodes arrive using the node arrival function $N(\cdot)$.

2. Node $u$ arrives and samples its lifetime $a$ from the exponential distribution $p_l(a) = \lambda exp(-\lambda a)$.
3. Node $u$ adds the first edge to node $v$ with probability proportional to its degree.
4. A node $u$ with degree $d$ samples a time gap $\delta$ from the distribution $p_g(\delta|d; \alpha, \beta) = (1/Z)\delta^{-\alpha} exp(-\beta d\delta)$ and goes to sleep for $\delta$ time steps.
5. When a node wakes up, if its lifetime has not expired yet, it creates a two-hop edge using the random-random triangle-closing model.
6. If a node's lifetime has expired, then it stops adding edges; otherwise it repeats from step 4.

## Problems

Given that the probability density function (PDF) of a power-law distribution is given by Eq. 11.13.

$$P(X = x) = \frac{\alpha - 1}{x_{min}} \left(\frac{x}{x_{min}}\right)^{-\alpha} \tag{11.13}$$

where $x_{min}$ is the minimum value that $X$ can take.

**60** Derive an expression of $P(X \geq x)$, the Complementary Cumulative Distribution Function (CCDF), in terms of $\alpha$.

**61** Show how to generate a random sample from the power-law distribution using the CCDF derived and a uniform random sample $u \sim U(0, 1)$.

**62** Using this sampling technique, create a dataset of 10000 samples following the power-law distribution with exponent $\alpha = 2$ and $x_{min} = 1$. Plot the empirical distribution on a log-log scale by first rounding each sample to the nearest integer and then plotting the empirical PDF over these rounded values. Also plot the true probability density function for the power law (this will help verify that the data was generated correctly).

## References


1. Aiello, William, Fan Chung, and Linyuan Lu. 2002. Random evolution in massive graphs. In *Handbook of massive data sets*, 97–122. Berlin: Springer.
2. Barabási, Albert-László, and Réka Albert. 1999. Emergence of scaling in random networks. *Science* 286 (5439): 509–512.
3. Bollobás, Béla, Christian Borgs, Jennifer Chayes, and Oliver Riordan. 2003. Directed scale-free graphs. In *Proceedings of the fourteenth annual ACM-SIAM symposium on discrete algorithms*, 132–139. Society for Industrial and Applied Mathematics.
4. Brookes, Bertram C. 1969. Bradford's law and the bibliography of science. *Nature* 224 (5223): 953.

5. Clauset, Aaron, Cosma Rohilla Shalizi, and Mark E.J. Newman. 2009. Power-law distributions in empirical data. *SIAM Review* 51 (4): 661–703.
6. Fractals, Chaos. 1991. Power laws: Minutes from an infinite paradise.
7. Goel, Sharad, Andrei Broder, Evgeniy Gabrilovich, and Bo Pang. 2010. Anatomy of the long tail: Ordinary people with extraordinary tastes. In *Proceedings of the third ACM international conference on Web search and data mining*, 201–210. ACM.
8. Grünwald, Peter D. 2007. *The minimum description length principle*. Cambridge: MIT press.
9. Kass, Robert E., and Adrian E. Raftery. 1995. Bayes factors. *Journal of the American Statistical Association* 90 (430): 773–795.
10. Kleinberg, Jon. 2003. Bursty and hierarchical structure in streams. *Data Mining and Knowledge Discovery* 7 (4): 373–397.
11. Kumar, Ravi, Jasmine Novak, Prabhakar Raghavan, and Andrew Tomkins. 2005. On the bursty evolution of blogspace. *World Wide Web* 8 (2): 159–178.
12. Lattanzi, Silvio, and D. Sivakumar. 2009. Affiliation networks. In *Proceedings of the forty-first annual ACM symposium on Theory of computing*, 427–434. ACM.
13. Leskovec, Jure, Jon Kleinberg, and Christos Faloutsos. 2007. Graph evolution: Densification and shrinking diameters. *ACM Transactions on Knowledge Discovery from Data (TKDD)* 1 (1): 2.
14. Leskovec, Jure, Lars Backstrom, Ravi Kumar, and Andrew Tomkins. 2008. Microscopic evolution of social networks. In *Proceedings of the 14th ACM SIGKDD international conference on Knowledge discovery and data mining*, 462–470. ACM.
15. Lotka, Alfred J. 1926. The frequency distribution of scientific productivity. *Journal of the Washington Academy of Sciences* 16 (12): 317–323.
16. Mandelbrot, Benoit. 1960. The pareto-levy law and the distribution of income. *International Economic Review* 1 (2): 79–106.
17. Stone, Mervyn. 1977. An asymptotic equivalence of choice of model by cross-validation and Akaike's criterion. *Journal of the Royal Statistical Society. Series B (Methodological)* 39: 44–47.

# Chapter 12
# Kronecker Graphs

The graph models that we have learnt heretofore cater to specific network properties. We need a graph generator that can produce the long list of properties. These generated graphs can be used for simulations, scenarios and extrapolation, and the graphs draw a boundary over what properties to realistically focus on. Reference [4] proposed that such a realistic graph is the *Kronecker graph* which is generated using the Kronecker product.

The idea behind these Kronecker graphs is to create self-similar graphs recursively. Beginning with an initiator graph $G_1$, with $|V|_1$ vertices and $|E|_1$ edges, produce successively larger graphs $G_2, \ldots, G_n$ such that the $k$th graph $G_k$ is on $|V|_k = |V|_1^k$ vertices. To exhibit the densification power-law, $G_k$ should have $|E|_k = |E|_1^k$ edges. The Kronecker product of two matrices generates this recursive self-similar graphs.

Given two matrices $A = [a_{i,j}]$ and $B$ of sizes $n \times m$ and $n' \times m'$ respectively, the Kronecker product matrix $C$ of size $(n * n') \times (m * m')$ is given by Eq. 12.1.

$$C = A \otimes B = \begin{pmatrix} a_{1,1}B & a_{1,2}B & \ldots & a_{1,m}B \\ a_{2,1}B & a_{2,2}B & \ldots & a_{2,m}B \\ \vdots & \vdots & \ddots & \vdots \\ a_{n,1}B & a_{n,2}B & \ldots & a_{n,m}B \end{pmatrix} \tag{12.1}$$

So, the Kronecker product of two graphs is the Kronecker product of their adjacency matrices.

In a Kronecker graph, $Edge(X_{ij}, X_{kl}) \in G \otimes H$ iff $(X_i, X_k) \in G$ and $(X_j, X_l) \in H$ where $X_{ij}$ and $X_{kl}$ are vertices in $G \otimes H$, and $X_i, X_j, X_k$ and $X_l$ are the corresponding vertices in $G$ and $H$.

Figure 12.1 shows the recursive construction of $G \otimes H$, when $G = H$ is a 3-node path.

The $k$th power of $G_1$ is defined as the matrix $G_1^{[k]}$ (abbreviated to $G_k$), such that:

$$G_1^{[k]} = G_k = \underbrace{G_1 \otimes G_1 \otimes \ldots G_1}_{k\ times} = G_{k-1} \otimes G_1 \tag{12.2}$$



K. Raj P. M. et al., *Practical Social Network Analysis with Python*, Computer Communications and Networks,
https://doi.org/10.1007/978-3-319-96746-2_12

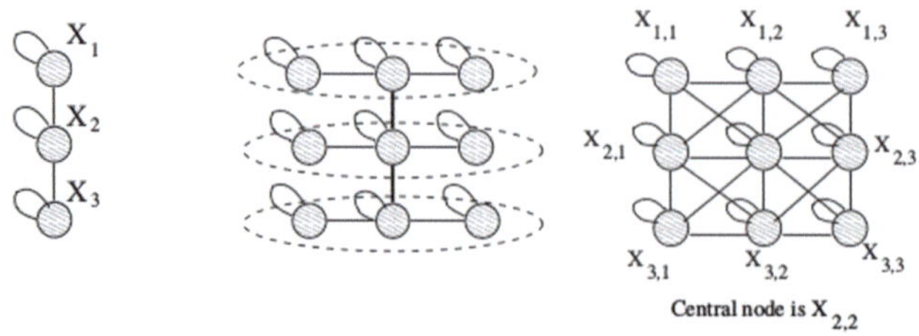


(a) Graph $G_1$ (b) Intermediate stage (c) Graph $G_2 = G_1 \otimes G_1$

| | | |
|---|---|---|
| 1 | 1 | 0 |
| 1 | 1 | 1 |
| 0 | 1 | 1 |

(d) Adjacency matrix of $G_1$

| | | |
|---|---|---|
| $G_1$ | $G_1$ | 0 |
| $G_1$ | $G_1$ | $G_1$ |
| 0 | $G_1$ | $G_1$ |

(e) Adjacency matrix of $G_2 = G_1 \otimes G_1$

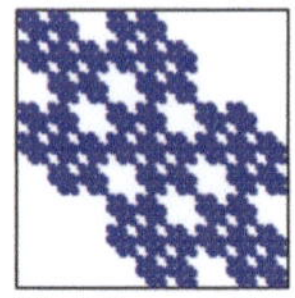

(f) Plot of $G_4$

**Fig. 12.1** Top: a "3-chain" and its Kronecker product with itself; each of the $X_i$ nodes gets expanded into 3 nodes, which are then linked. Bottom: the corresponding adjacency matrices, along with the matrix for the fourth Kronecker power $G_4$

The self-similar nature of the Kronecker graph product is clear: To produce $G_k$ from $G_{k-1}$, we "expand" (replace) each node of $G_{k-1}$ by converting it into a copy of $G$, and we join these copies together according to the adjacencies in $G_{k-1}$ (see Fig. 12.1). This process is intuitive: one can imagine it as positing that communities with the graph grow recursively, with nodes in the community recursively getting expanded into miniature copies of the community. Nodes in the subcommunity then link among themselves and also to nodes from different communities.

Kronecker graphs satisfy the following properties. The proofs for these theorems can be found in [4] or [5].

- **Theorem 20** *Kronecker graphs have multinomial degree distributions, for both in- and out-degrees.*
- **Theorem 21** *Kronecker graphs have a multinomial distribution for its eigenvalues.*
- **Theorem 22** *The components of each eigenvector of the Kronecker graph $G_k$ follow a multinomial distribution.*
- **Theorem 23** *If atleast one of $G$ and $H$ is a disconnected graph, then $G \otimes H$ is also disconnected.*
- **Theorem 24** *If both $G$ and $H$ are connected but bipartite, then $G \otimes H$ is disconnected, and each of the two connected components is again bipartite.*
- **Theorem 25** *Kronecker graphs follow the Densification Power Law (DPL) with densification exponent $a = log(E_1)/log(N_1)$.*
- **Theorem 26** *If $G$ and $H$ each have diameter at most $d$, and each has a self-loop on every node, then the Kronecker product $G \otimes H$ also has diameter at most $d$.*

*Therefore, if $G_1$ has diameter d and a self-loop on every node, then for every k, the graph $G_k$ also has diameter d.*
- **Theorem 27** *If $G_1$ has diameter d and a self-loop on every node, then for every q, the q-effective diameter of $G_k$ converges to d (from below) as k increases.*

## 12.1 Stochastic Kronecker Graph (SKG) Model

While the Kronecker power construction discussed thus far yields graphs with a range of desired properties, its discrete nature produces "staircase effects" in the degrees and spectral quantities, simply because individual values have large multiplicities. A stochastic version of Kronecker graphs that eliminates this effect is proposed.

We start with an $N_1 \times N_1$ probability matrix $\mathcal{P}_1$: the value $p_{ij}$ denotes the probability that edge $(i, j)$ is present. We compute its $k$th Kronecker power $\mathcal{P}_1^{[k]} = \mathcal{P}_k$; and then for each entry $p_{uv}$ of $P_k$, we include an edge between nodes $u$ and $v$ with probability $p_{u,v}$. The resulting binary random matrix $R = R(\mathcal{P}_k)$ will be called the *instance matrix* (or *realization matrix*).

In principle one could try choosing each of the $N_1^2$ parameters for the matrix $\mathcal{P}_1$ separately. However, we reduce the number of parameters to just two: $\alpha$ and $\beta$. Let $G_1$ be the initiator matrix (binary, deterministic); we create the corresponding probability matrix $\mathcal{P}_1$ by replacing each "1" and "0" of $G_1$ with $\alpha$ and $\beta$ respectively ($\beta \leq \alpha$). The resulting probability matrices maintain, with some random noise, the self-similar structure of the Kronecker graphs described earlier (called Deterministic Kronecker graphs for clarity).

The random graphs produced by this model continue to exhibit the desired properties of real datasets, and without the staircase effect of the deterministic version.

Formally, a SKG is defined by an integer $k$ and a symmetric $2 \times 2$ initiator matrix $\theta$: $\theta[1, 1] = \alpha, \theta[1, 0] = \theta[0, 1] = \beta, \theta[0, 0] = \gamma$, where $0 \leq \gamma \leq \beta \leq \alpha \leq 1$. The graph has $n = 2^k$ vertices, each vertex labelled by a unique bit vector of length $k$; given two vertices $u$ with label $u_1 u_2 \ldots u_k$ and $v$ with label $v_1 v_2 \ldots v_k$, the probability of edge $(u, v)$ existing, denoted by $P[u, v]$, is $\prod_i \theta[u_i, v_i]$, independent on the presence of other edges.

The SKG model is a generalization of the R-MAT model proposed by [2].

Reference [6] prove the following theorems for SKGs

- **Theorem 28** *The expected degree of a vertex u with weight l is $(\alpha+\beta)^l(\beta+\gamma)^{k-l}$.*
- **Theorem 29** *The necessary and sufficient condition for Kronecker graphs to be connected with high probability (for large k) is $\beta + \gamma > 1$ or $\alpha = \beta = 1, \gamma = 0$.*
- **Theorem 30** *The necessary and sufficient condition for Kronecker graphs to have a giant component of size $\Theta(n)$ with high probability is $(\alpha + \beta)(\beta + \gamma) > 1$, or $(\alpha + \beta)(\beta + \gamma) = 1$ and $\alpha + \beta > \beta + \gamma$.*
- **Theorem 31** *If $\beta + \gamma > 1$, the diameters of Kronecker graphs are constant with high probability.*
- **Theorem 32** *Kronecker graphs are not $n^{(1-\alpha)\log e}$-searchable.*

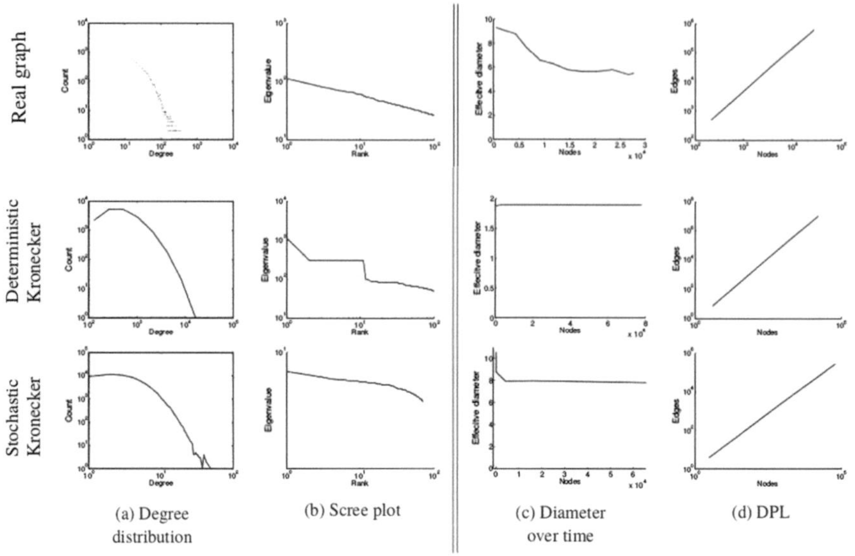

Fig. 12.2 CIT-HEP-TH: Patterns from the real graph (top row), the deterministic Kronecker graph with $K_1$ being a star graph on 4 nodes (center + 3 satellites) (middle row), and the Stochastic Kronecker graph ($\alpha = 0.41$, $\beta = 0.11$ - bottom row). Static patterns: **a** is the PDF of degrees in the graph (log-log scale), and **b** the distribution of eigenvalues (log-log scale). Temporal patterns: **c** gives the effective diameter over time (linear-linear scale), and **d** is the number of edges versus number of nodes over time (log-log scale)

- **Theorem 33** *If* $\beta + max(\alpha, \gamma) > 1$, *then Kronecker graphs are connected with high probability.*

Reference [4] show the results of deterministic and stochastic Kronecker graphs juxtaposed with real-world networks for the following datasets:

- *CIT-HEP-TH*: A citation graph for High-Energy Physics Theory research papers from pre-print archive ArXiv, with a total of $29,555$ papers and $352,807$ citations. One data-point for every month from January 1993 to April 2003 is present.
- *AS-ROUTEVIEWS*: A static data set consisting of a single snapshot of connectivity among Internet Autonomous Systems from January 2000 with $6,474$ nodes and $26,467$ edges.

Figure 12.2 shows the plots for the network properties of CIT-HEP-TH with that of the deterministic and the stochastic Kronecker graphs. Figure 12.3 depict the plots of network properties of AS-ROUTEVIEWS with that of stochastic Kronecker graphs. For reasons of brevity, the plots of the deterministic Kronecker graphs have been omitted. In both of these cases, the stochastic Kronecker graphs matches well the properties the real graphs.

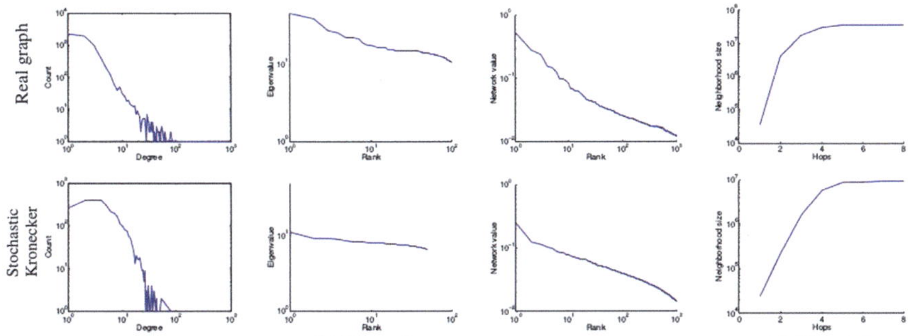


(a) Degree distribution (b) Scree plot (c) "Network value" distribution (d) "Hop-plot"

**Fig. 12.3** AS-ROUTEVIEWS: Real (top) versus Kronecker (bottom). Columns **a** and **b** show the degree distribution and the scree plot. Columns **c** shows the distribution of network values (principal eigenvector components, sorted, versus rank) and **d** shows the hop-plot (the number of reachable pairs $g(h)$ within $h$ hops or less, as a function of the number of hops $h$

### 12.1.1 *Fast Generation of SKGs*

Generating a SKG on $|V|$ vertices naively takes $O(|V|^2)$ time. Reference [5] presents a fast heuristic procedure that takes linear time in the number of edges to generate a graph. To arrive to a particular edge $(v_i, v_j)$ of $\mathcal{P}_k$ one has to make a sequence of $k$ decisions among the entries of $\mathcal{P}_1$, multiply the chosen entries of $\mathcal{P}_1$, and then placing the edge $(v_i, v_j)$ with the obtained probability.

Thus, instead of flipping $O(N^2) = O(N_1^{2k})$ biased coins to determine the edges in a graph, we place $E$ edges by directly simulating the recursion of the Kronecker product. Basically, we recursively choose sub-regions of matrix $K$ with probability proportional to $\theta_{ij}$, $\theta_{ij} \in \mathcal{P}_1$ until in $k$ steps we descend to a single cell of the big adjacency matrix $K$ and place an edge.

More generally, the probability of each individual edge of $\mathcal{P}_k$ follows a Bernoulli distribution, as the edge occurrences are independent. By the Central Limit Theorem the number of edges in $\mathcal{P}_k$ tends to a normal distribution with mean $(\sum_{i,j=1}^{N_1} \theta_{ij})^k = E_1^k$, where $\theta_{ij} \in \mathcal{P}_1$. So, given a stochastic initiator matrix $P_1$ we first sample the expected number of edges $E$ in $\mathcal{P}_k$. Then we place $E$ edges in a graph $K$, by applying the recursive descent for $k$ steps where at each step we choose entry $(i, j)$ with probability $\theta_{ij}/E_1$ where $E_1 = \sum_{ij} \theta_{ij}$. Since we add $E = E_1^k$ edges, the probability that edge $(v_i, v_j)$ appears in $K$ is exactly $\mathcal{P}_k[v_i, v_j]$. However, in practice it can happen that more than one edge lands in the same $(v_i, v_j)$ entry of big adjacency matrix $K$. If an edge lands in a already occupied cell we simply insert it again. Even though values of $\mathcal{P}_1$ are usually skewed, adjacency matrices of real networks are so sparse that collisions are not really a problem in practice as only around 1% of edges collide. It is due to these edge collisions the above procedure does not obtain exact samples from the graph distribution defined by the parameter matrix $P$. However, in practice graphs

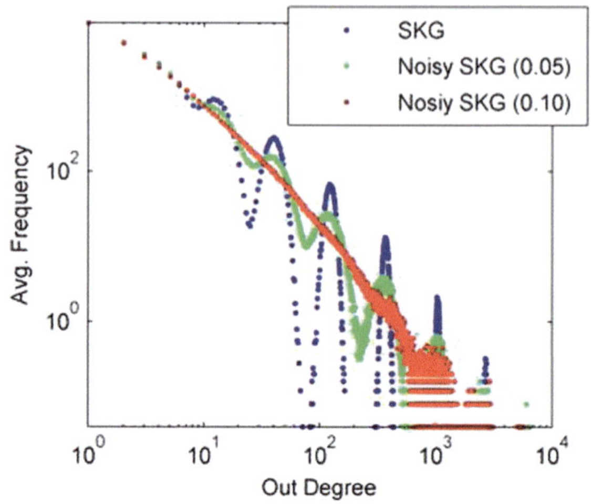


**Fig. 12.4** Comparison of degree distributions for SKG and two noisy variations

generated by this fast linear time ($O(E)$) procedure are basically indistinguishable from graphs generated with the exact exponential time ($O(N^2)$) procedure.

## 12.1.2 *Noisy Stochastic Kronecker Graph (NSKG) Model*

Reference [8] proved that the SKG model cannot generate a power-law distribution or even a lognormal distribution. However, by using random noise for smoothing, they proposed an enhanced model, Noisy SKG (NSKG), that is capable of exhibiting a lognormal distribution.

They found that the degree distributions of the SKG model oscillate between a lognormal and an exponential tail which is a disappointing feature. Real degree distributions do not have these large oscillations or the exponential tail behaviour. By adding small amount of noise, NSKG straightens out the degree distribution to be lognormal. Figure 12.4 shows the SKG and NSKG degree distributions.

If we consider the SKG model as having to generate a graph $G = (V, E)$ with an arbitrary square generator matrix with $|V|$ as a power of its size, the $2 \times 2$ generating matrix is defined as in Eq. 12.3.

$$T = \begin{bmatrix} t_1 & t_2 \\ t_3 & t_4 \end{bmatrix} \; with \; t_1 + t_2 + t_3 + t_4 = 1. \tag{12.3}$$

The NSKG model adds some noise to this matrix given as follows. Let $b$ be noise parameter $b \leq min((t_1 + t_4)/2, t_2)$. For each level $i \leq l$, define a new matrix $T_i$ in such a way that the expectation of $T_i$ is just $T$, i.e, for level $i$, choose $\mu_i$ to be a uniform random number in the range $[-b, +b]$. Set $T_i$ to be

$$T = \begin{bmatrix} t_1 - \frac{2\mu_i t_1}{t_1+t_4} & t_2 + \mu_i \\ t_3 + \mu_i & t_4 - \frac{2\mu_i t_4}{t_1+t_4} \end{bmatrix} \tag{12.4}$$

$T_i$ is symmetric with all its entries positive and summing to 1.

## 12.2 Distance-Dependent Kronecker Graph

Theorem 32 shows that Kronecker graphs are not searchable by a distributed greedy algorithm. Reference [1] propose an extension to the SKGs that is capable of generating searchable networks. By using a new "Kronecker-like" operation and a family of generator matrices, $\mathcal{H}$, both dependent upon the distance between two nodes, this generation method yields networks that have both a local (lattice-based) and global (distance-dependent) structure. This dual structure allows a greedy algorithm to search the network using only local information.

Kronecker graphs are generated by iteratively Kronecker-multiplying one initiator matrix with itself to produce a new adjacency or probability matrix. Here, a distance-dependent Kronecker operator is defined. Depending on the distance between two nodes $u$ and $v$, $d(u,v) \in \mathbb{Z}$, a different matrix from a defined family will be selected to be multiplied by that entry.

$$C = A \otimes_d \mathcal{H} = \begin{pmatrix} a_{11}H_{d(1,1)} & a_{12}H_{d(1,2)} & \dots & a_{1n}H_{d(1,n)} \\ a_{21}H_{d(2,1)} & a_{22}H_{d(2,2)} & \dots & a_{2n}H_{d(2,n)} \\ \dots & \dots & \ddots & \dots \\ a_{n1}H_{d(n,1)} & a_{n2}H_{d(n,2)} & \dots & a_{nn}H_{d(n,n)} \end{pmatrix} \quad where\ \mathcal{H} = \{H_i\}_{i \in \mathbb{Z}} \tag{12.5}$$

This makes the $k$th Kronecker power as in Eq. 12.6

$$G_k = \underbrace{G_1 \otimes_d \mathcal{H} \cdots \otimes_d \mathcal{H}}_{k\ times} \tag{12.6}$$

In this Kronecker-like multiplication, the choice of $H_i$ from the family $\mathcal{H}$, multiplying entry $(u, v)$, is dependent upon the distance $d(u, v)$. $d(u, v) = -d(v, u)$ and $H_{d(u,v)} = H'_{d(v,u)}$. This change to the Kronecker operation makes the model more complicated at the cost of some of the beneficial properties of Kronecker multiplication. Instead, we gain generality and the ability to create many different lattices and probability of long-range contacts.

Reference [1] explains how the conventional Kronecker graphs can be generated from these distance-dependent ones. Additionally, it is also mathematically proved that the Watts-Strogatz model cannot be generated from the original Kronecker graphs.

## 12.3 KRONFIT

Reference [5] presented KRONFIT, a fast and scalable algorithm for fitting Kronecker graphs by using the maximum likelihood principle. A Metropolis sampling algorithm was developed for sampling node correspondences, and approximating the likelihood of obtaining a linear time algorithm for Kronecker graph model parameter estimation that scales to large networks with millions of nodes and edges.

## 12.4 KRONEM

Reference [3] addressed the network completion problem by using the observed part of the network to fit a model of network structure, and then estimating the missing part of the network using the model, re-estimating the parameters and so on. This is combined with the Kronecker graphs model to design a scalable Metropolized Gibbs sampling approach that allows for the estimation of the model parameters as well as the inference about missing nodes and edges of the network.

The problem of network completion is cast into the *Expectation Maximisation* (EM) framework and the KRONEM algorithm is developed that alternates between the following two stages. First, the observed part of the network is used to estimate the parameters of the network model. This estimated model then gives us a way to infer the missing part of the network. Now, we act as if the complete network is visible and we re-estimate the model. This in turn gives us a better way to infer

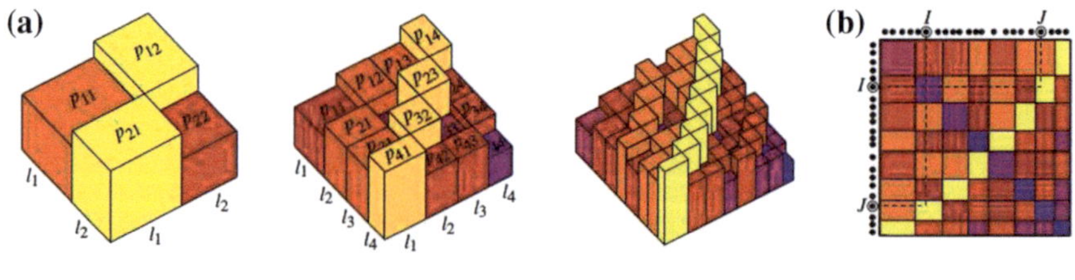


**Fig. 12.5** Schematic illustration of the multifractal graph generator. **a** The construction of the link probability measure. Start from a symmetric generating measure on the unit square defined by a set of probabilities $p_{ij} = p_{ji}$ associated to $m \times m$ rectangles (shown on the left). Here $m = 2$, the length of the intervals defining the rectangles is given by $l_1$ and $l_2$ respectively, and the magnitude of the probabilities is indicated by both the height and the colour of the corresponding boxes. The generating measure is iterated by recursively multiplying each box with the generating measure itself as shown in the middle and on the right, yielding $m^k \times m^k$ boxes at iteration $k$. The variance of the height of the boxes (corresponding to the probabilities associated to the rectangles) becomes larger at each step, producing a surface which is getting rougher and rougher, meanwhile the symmetry and the self similar nature of the multifractal is preserved. **b** Drawing linking probabilities from the obtained measure. Assign random coordinates in the unit interval to the nodes in the graph, and link each node pair $I$, $J$ with a probability given by the probability measure at the corresponding coordinates

(a) (b)

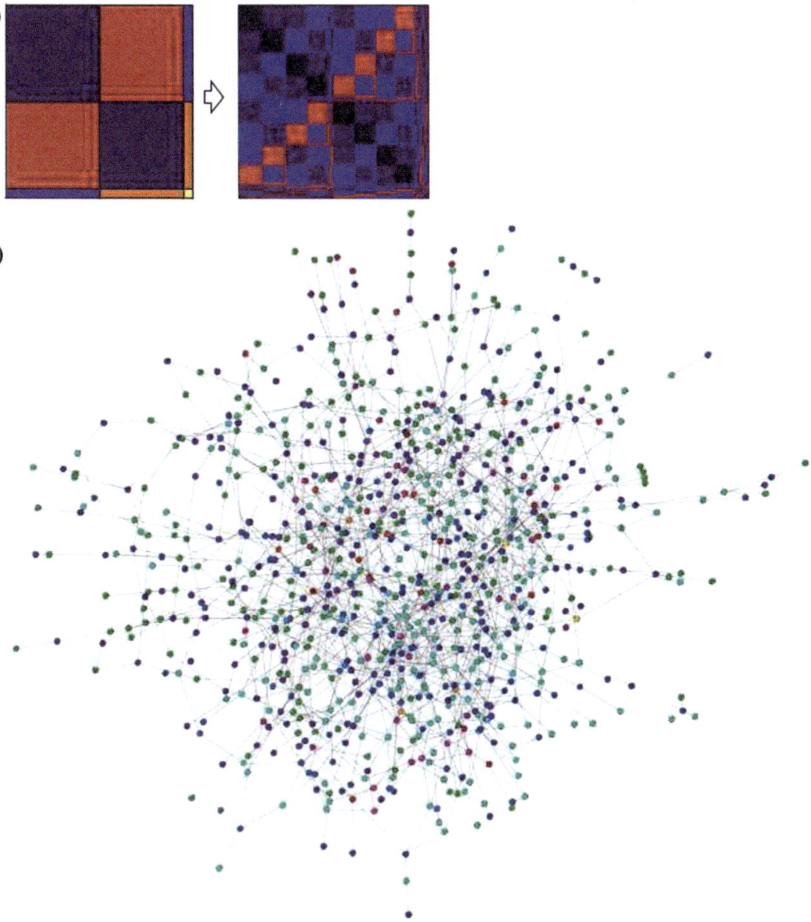

**Fig. 12.6** A small network generated with the multifractal network generator. **a** The generating measure (on the left) and the link probability measure (on the right). The generating measure consists of $3 \times 3$ rectangles for which the magnitude of the associated probabilities is indicated by the colour. The number of iterations, $k$, is set to $k = 3$, thus the final link probability measure consists of $27 \times 27$ boxes, as shown in the right panel. **b** A network with 500 nodes generated from the link probability measure. The colours of the nodes were chosen as follows. Each row in the final linking probability measure was assigned a different colour, and the nodes were coloured according to their position in the link probability measure. (Thus, nodes falling into the same row have the same colour)

the missing part of the network. We iterate between the model estimation step (the M-step) and the inference of the hidden part of the network (the E-step) until the model parameters converge.

The advantages of KronEM are the following: It requires a small number of parameters and thus does not overfit the network. It infers not only the model parameters but also the mapping between the nodes of the true and the estimated networks.

The approach can be directly applied to cases when collected network data is incomplete. It provides an accurate probabilistic prior over the missing network structure and easily scales to large networks.

## 12.5 Multifractal Network Generator

Reference [7] proposed the following network generator. This generator has three stages: First, a generating measure is defined on the unit square. Next, the generating measure is transformed into a link probability measure through a couple of iterations. Finally, links are drawn between the vertices using the link probability measure.

The generating measure is defined as follows: Both the $x$ and $y$ axis of the unit square are identically divided into $m$ (not necessarily equal) intervals, splitting it into $m^2$ rectangles. Each rectangle is assigned a probability $p_{ij}$. These probabilities must be normalized, $\sum p_{ij} = 1$ and symmetric $p_{ij} = p_{ji}$.

The link probability measure is obtained by recursively multiplying each rectangle with the generating measure $k$ times. This results in $m^{2k}$ rectangles, each associated with a linking probability $p_{ij}(k)$ equivalent to product of $k$ factors from the original generating $p_{ij}$.

$N$ points are distributed independently, uniformly at random on the [0, 1] interval, and each pair is linked with probability $p_{ij}(k)$ at the given coordinates.

Figure 12.5 illustrates the working of a multifactor generator. Figure 12.6 depicts the generation of a network using this generator.

## References

1. Bodine-Baron, Elizabeth, Babak Hassibi, and Adam Wierman. 2010. Distance-dependent kronecker graphs for modeling social networks. *IEEE Journal of Selected Topics in Signal Processing* 4 (4): 718–731.
2. Chakrabarti, Deepayan, Yiping Zhan, and Christos Faloutsos. 2004. R-mat: A recursive model for graph mining. In *Proceedings of the 2004 SIAM international conference on data mining*, 442–446. SIAM.
3. Kim, Myunghwan, and Jure Leskovec. 2011. The network completion problem: Inferring missing nodes and edges in networks. In *Proceedings of the 2011 SIAM International Conference on Data Mining*, 47–58. SIAM.
4. Leskovec, Jurij, Deepayan Chakrabarti, Jon Kleinberg, and Christos Faloutsos. 2005. Realistic, mathematically tractable graph generation and evolution, using Kronecker multiplication. In *European conference on principles of data mining and knowledge discovery*, 133–145. Berlin: Springer.
5. Leskovec, Jure, Deepayan Chakrabarti, Jon Kleinberg, Christos Faloutsos, and Zoubin Ghahramani. 2010. Kronecker graphs: An approach to modeling networks. *Journal of Machine Learning Research* 11 (Feb): 985–1042.
6. Mahdian Mohammad, and Ying Xu. 2007. Stochastic Kronecker graphs. In *International workshop on algorithms and models for the web-graph*, 179–186. Berlin: Springer.

7. Palla, Gergely, László Lovász, and Tamás Vicsek. 2010. Multifractal network generator. *Proceedings of the National Academy of Sciences* 107 (17): 7640–7645.
8. Seshadhri, Comandur, Ali Pinar, and Tamara G. Kolda. 2013. An in-depth analysis of stochastic Kronecker graphs. *Journal of the ACM (JACM)* 60 (2): 13.

# Chapter 13
# Link Analysis

## 13.1 Search Engine

A search engine is an application which takes as input a search query and returns a list of relevant Webpages. Reference [3] explains in detail the general architecture of a typical search engine as shown in Fig. 13.1.

Every engine requires a *crawler* module. A crawler is a small program that browses the Web by following links. The crawlers are given a starting set of pages. They then retrieve the URLs appearing in these pages and give it to the *crawl control* module. The crawl control module determines what links to visit next, and feeds the links to visit back to the crawler. The crawler also stores the retrieved pages in the *page repository*.

The *indexer* module extracts all the words from each page, and records the URL where each word occurred. The result is a very large "lookup table" that has URLs mapped to the pages where a given word occurs. This index is the *text index*. The indexer module could also generate a *structure index*, which reflects the links between pages. The *collection analysis module* is responsible for creating other kinds of indexes, such as the *utility index*. Utility indexes may provide access to pages of a given length, pages of a certain "importance", or pages with some number of images in them. The text and structure indexes may be used when creating utility indexes. The crawl controller can change the crawling operation based on these indexes.

The *query engine* module receives and files search requests from users. For the queries received by the query engine, the results may be too large to be directly displayed to the user. The *ranking* module is therefore tasked with the responsibility to sort the results.



K. Raj P. M. et al., *Practical Social Network Analysis with Python*,
Computer Communications and Networks,
https://doi.org/10.1007/978-3-319-96746-2_13

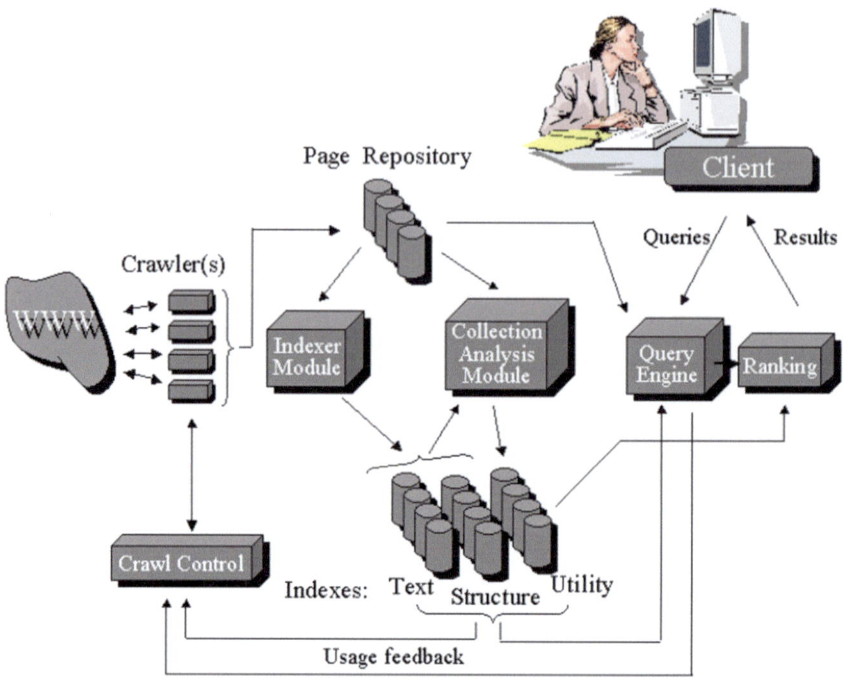


**Fig. 13.1** Typical search engine architecture

### 13.1.1 Crawling

The crawler module starts with an initial set of URLs $S_0$ which are initially kept in a priority queue. From the queue, the crawler gets a URL, downloads the page, extracts any URLs in the downloaded page, and puts the new URLs in the queue. This process repeats until the *crawl control* module asks the crawler to stop.

#### 13.1.1.1 Page Selection

Due to the sheer quantity of pages in the Web and limit in the available resources, the crawl control program has to decide which pages to crawl, and which not to. The "importance" of a page can be defined in one of the following ways:

1. *Interest Driven*: The important pages can be defined as those of "interest to" the users. This could be defined in the following manner: given a query $Q$, the importance of the page $P$ is defined as the textual similarity between $P$ and $Q$ [1]. This metric is referred to as $IS(\cdot)$.
2. *Popularity Driven*: Page importance depends on how "popular" a page is. Popularity can be defined in terms of a page's in-degree. However, a page's popularity

is the in-degree with respect to the entire Web. This can be denoted as $IB(\cdot)$. The crawler may have to instead provide an estimate $IB'(\cdot)$ with the in-degree from the pages seen so far.

3. *Location Driven*: This importance measure is computed as a function of a page's location instead of its contents. Denoted as $IL(\cdot)$, if URL $u$ leads to a page $P$, then $IL(P)$ is a function of $u$.

Therefore, the importance of a page $P$ can be defined as $IC(P) = k_1 IS(P) + k_2 IB(P) + k_3 IL(P)$, for constants $k_1$, $k_2$, $k_3$ and query $Q$.

Next, we will look at the performance of a crawler. The following ways may be used to compute the performance:

1. *Crawl and stop*: Under this method, a crawler $C$ starts at a page $P_0$ and stops after visiting $K$ pages. Here, $K$ denotes the number of pages that the crawler can download in one crawl. At this point a perfect crawler would have visited $R_1, \ldots, R_K$, where $R_1$ is the page with the highest importance value, $R_2$ is the next highest, and so on. These pages $R_1$ through $R_K$ are called the *hot pages*. The $K$ pages visited by our real crawler will contain only $M (\leq K)$ pages with rank higher than or equal to that of $R_K$. We need to know the exact rank of all pages in order to obtain the value $M$. The performance of the crawler $C$ is computed as $P_{CS}(C) = (M \cdot 100)/K$. Although the performance of the perfect crawler is 100%, a crawler that manages to visit pages at random would have a performance of $(K \cdot 100)/T$, where $T$ is the total number of pages in the Web.
2. *Crawl and stop with threshold*: Assume that a crawler visits $K$ pages. If we are given an importance target $G$, then any page with importance target greater than $G$ is considered hot. If we take the total number of hot pages to be $H$, then the performance of the crawler, $P_{ST}(C)$, is the percentage of the $H$ hot pages that have been visited when the crawler stops. If $K < H$, then an ideal crawler will have performance $(K \cdot 100)/H$. If $K \geq H$, then the ideal crawler has 100% performance. A purely random crawler that revisits pages is expected to visit $(H/T)K$ hot pages when it stops. Thus, its performance is $(k \cdot 100)/T$. Only if the random crawler visits all $T$ pages, is its performance expected to be 100%.

#### 13.1.1.2 Page Refresh

Once the crawler has downloaded the "important" pages, these pages must be periodically refreshed to remain up-to-date. The following strategies can be used to refresh the pages:

1. *Uniform refresh policy*: All pages are revisited at the same frequency $f$, regardless of how often they change.
2. *Proportional refresh policy*: The crawler visits a page proportional to its change. If $\lambda_i$ is the change frequency of a page $e_i$, and $f_i$ is the crawler's revisit frequency for $e_i$, then the frequency ratio $\lambda_i/f_i$ is the same for any $i$. Keep in mind that the crawler needs to estimate $\lambda_i$'s for each page, in order to implement this policy.

This estimation can be based on the change history of a page that the crawler can collect [9].

Reference [3] defines the "freshness" and "age" of a Webpage as follows:

1. *Freshness*: Let $S = \{e_1, \ldots, e_N\}$ be the collection of $N$ pages. The *freshness* of a local page $e_i$ at time $t$ is as given in Eq. 13.1

$$F(e_i; t) = \begin{cases} 1 \; if \; e_i \; is \; up - to - date \; at \; time \; t \\ 0 \; otherwise \end{cases} \tag{13.1}$$

Then the *freshness* of the local collection $S$ at time $t$ is as given in Eq. 13.2.

$$F(S; t) = \frac{1}{N} \sum_{i=1}^{N} F(e_i; t) \tag{13.2}$$

Since the pages get refreshed over time, the time average of the freshness of page $e_i$, $\overline{F}(e_i)$, and the time average of the freshness of collection $S$, $\overline{F}(S)$, are defined as in Eqs. 13.3 and 13.4.

$$\overline{F}(e_i) = \lim_{t \to \infty} \frac{1}{t} \int_0^t F(e_i; t) dt \tag{13.3}$$

$$\overline{F}(S) = \lim_{t \to \infty} \frac{1}{t} \int_0^t F(S; t) dt \tag{13.4}$$

2. *Age*: The *age* of the local page $e_i$ at time $t$ is as given in Eq. 13.5.

$$A(e_i; t) = \begin{cases} 0 \; if \; e_i \; is \; up - to - date \; at \; time \; t \\ t - modification \; time \; of \; e_i \; otherwise \end{cases} \tag{13.5}$$

Then the *age* of the local collection $S$ at time $t$ is as given in Eq. 13.6.

$$A(S; t) = \frac{1}{N} \sum_{i=1}^{N} A(e_i; t) \tag{13.6}$$

### 13.1.2 Storage

The storage repository of a search engine must perform two basic functions. First, it must provide an interface for the crawler to store pages. Second, it must provide an efficient access API that the indexer module and the collection analysis module can use to retrieve pages.

The issues a repository must deal with are as follows: First, it must be *scalable*, i.e, it must be capable of being distributed across a cluster of systems. Second, it must be capable of supporting both *random access* and *streaming access* equally efficiently. Random access for quickly retrieving a specific Webpage, given the page's unique identifier to serve out cached copies to the end-user. Streaming access to receive the entire collection as a stream of pages to provide pages in bulk for the indexer and analysis module to process and analyse. Third, since the Web changes rapidly, the repository needs to handle a high rate of modifications since pages have to be refreshed periodically. Lastly, the repository must have a mechanism of detecting and removing obsolete pages that have been removed from the Web.

A distributed Web repository that is designed to function over a cluster of interconnected *storage nodes* must deal with the following issues that affect the characteristics and performance of the repository. A detailed explanation of these issues are found in [15].

#### 13.1.2.1 Page Distribution Policies

Pages can be assigned to nodes using a number of different policies. In a *uniform distribution policy*, all nodes are treated identically, and a page can be assigned to any of these nodes, independent of its identifier. Thus each node will store portions of the collection proportionate to its storage capacity. On the other hand, a *hash distribution policy* allocates pages to nodes depending on the page identifiers. A page identifier would be hashed to yield a node identifier and the page would be allocated to the corresponding node.

#### 13.1.2.2 Physical Page Organization Methods

In essence, physical page organization at each node determines how well each node supports *page addition/insertion*, *high-speed streaming* and *random page access*.

A hash-based organization treats a disk as a set of hash-buckets, each of which is small enough to fit in memory. Pages are assigned to hash buckets depending on their page identifier. For page additions, a log-structured organization may be used in which the entire disk is treated as a large contiguous log to which incoming pages are appended. Random access is supported using a separate B-tree index that maps page identifiers to physical locations on disk. One can also devise a hybrid hashed-log organization, where storage is divided into large sequential "extents", as opposed to buckets that fit in memory. Pages are hashed into extents, and each extent is organized like a log-structured file.

#### 13.1.2.3 Update Strategies

The updates of the crawler can be structured in two ways:

1. *Batch-mode or steady crawler*: A batch-mode crawler is periodically executed and allowed to crawl for a certain amount of time or until a targeted set of pages have been crawled, and then stopped. In contrast, a steady crawler runs continuously, without pause, supplying updates and new pages to the repository.
2. *Partial or complete crawls*: A partial crawl recrawls only a specific set of pages, while a complete crawl performs a total crawl of all the pages. This makes sense only for a batch- mode crawler while a steady crawler cannot make such a distinction.
3. *In-place update or shadowing*: With in-place updates, pages received from the crawl are directly integrated into the repository's existing collection, probably replacing the older version. With shadowing, pages from a crawl are stored separate from the existing collection and updates are applied in a separate step.

   The advantage of shadowing is that the reading and updating tasks can be delegated to two separate nodes thereby ensuring that a node does not have to concurrently handle both page addition and retrieval. However, this is a two-edged sword. While avoiding conflict by simplifying implementation and improving performance, there is a delay between the time a page is retrieved by the crawler and the time it is available for access.

### *13.1.3 Indexing*

The indexer and the collection analysis modules are responsible for generating the text, structure and the utility indexes. Here, we describe the indexes.

#### 13.1.3.1 Structure Index

To build this index, the crawled content is modelled as a graph with nodes and edges. This index helps search algorithms by providing *neighbourhood information*: For a page $P$, retrieve the set of pages pointed to by $P$ or the set of pages pointing to $P$, and *sibling pages*: Pages related to a given page $P$.

An *inverted index* over a collection of Webpages consists of a set of *inverted lists*, one for each word. The inverted list for a term is a sorted collection of locations (page identifier and the position of the term in the page) where the term appears in the collection.

To make the inverted index scalable, there are two basic strategies for partitioning the inverted index across a collection of nodes.

In the *local inverted file* ($IF_L$) organization [21], each node is responsible for a disjoint subset of pages in the collection. A search query would be broadcast to all nodes, each of which would return disjoint lists of page identifiers containing the search terms.

*Global inverted file* ($IF_G$) organization [21] partitions on index terms so that each query server stores inverted lists only for a subset of the terms in the collection.

Reference [19] describes important characteristics of the $IF_L$ strategy that make this organization ideal for the Web search environment. Performance studies in [22] indicate that $IF_L$ organization uses system resources effectively and provides good query throughput in most cases.

#### 13.1.3.2 Text Index

Traditional information retrieval methods using suffix arrays, inverted indices and signature files, can be be used to generate these text index.

#### 13.1.3.3 Utility Index

The number and type of utility indexes built by the collection analysis module depends on the features of the query engine and the type of information used by the ranking module.

### *13.1.4 Ranking*

The query engine collects search terms from the user and retrieves pages that are likely to be relevant. These pages cannot be returned to the user in this format and must be ranked.

However, the problem of ranking is faced with the following issues. First, before the task of ranking pages, one must first retrieve the pages that are relevant to a search. This information retrieval suffers from problems of *synonymy* (multiple terms that more or less mean the same thing) and *polysemy* (multiple meanings of the same term, so by the term "jaguar", do you mean the animal, the automobile company, the American football team, or the operating system).

Second, the time of retrieval plays a pivotal role. For instance, in the case of an event such as a calamity, government and news sites will update their pages as and when they receive information. The search engine not only has to retrieve the pages repeatedly, but will have to re-rank the pages depending on which page currently has the latest report.

Third, with every one capable of writing a Web page, the Web has an abundance of information for any topic. For example, the term "social network analysis" returns a search of around 56 million results. Now, the task is to rank these results in a manner such that the most important ones appear first.

#### 13.1.4.1 HITS Algorithm

When you search for the term "msrit", what makes www.msrit.edu a good answer? The idea is that the page www.msrit.edu is not going to use the term "msrit" more frequently or prominently than other pages. Therefore, there is nothing in the page that makes it stand out in particular. Rather, it stands out because of features on other Web pages: when a page is relevant to "msrit", very often www.msrit.edu is among the pages it links to.

One approach is to first retrieve a large collection of Web pages that are relevant to the query "msrit" using traditional information retrieval. Then, these pages are voted based on which page on the Web receives the greatest number of in-links from pages that are relevant to msrit. In this manner, there will ultimately be a page that will be ranked first.

Consider the search for the term "newspapers". Unlike the case of "msrit", the position for a good answer for the term "newspapers" is not necessarily a single answer. If we try the traditional information retrieval approach, then we will get a set of pages variably pointing to several of the news sites.

Now we attempt to tackle the problem from another direction. Since finding the best answer for a query is incumbent upon the retrieved pages, finding good retrieved pages will automatically result in finding good answers. Figure 13.2 shows a set of retrieved pages pointing to newspapers.

We observe from Fig. 13.2 that among the sites casting votes, a few of them voted for many of the pages that received a lot of votes. Therefore, we could say that these pages have a sense where the good answers are, and to score them highly as lists. Thus, a page's value as a list is equal to the sum of the votes received by all pages that it voted for. Figure 13.3 depicts the result of applying this rule to the pages casting votes.

If pages scoring well as lists are believed to actually have a better sense for where the good results are, then we should weigh their votes more heavily. So, in particular, we could tabulate the votes again, but this time giving each page's vote a weight equal to its value as a list. Figure 13.4 illustrates what happens when weights are accounted for in the newspaper case.

This re-weighting can be done repeatedly.

The "good" answers that we were originally seeking for a query are called the *authorities* for the query and the high-value lists are called the *hubs* for the query. The goal here is to estimate a page $p$'s value as a potential authority and as a potential hub. Therefore, each page $p$ is assigned two numerical scores: $auth(p)$ and $hub(p)$. Each of these initially starts out at 1.

Now, $auth(p)$ and $hub(p)$ are updated according to the *Authority Update rule* and *Hub Update rule* respectively. The authority update rule states that for each page $p, auth(p)$ is computed as the sum of the hub scores of all pages that point to it. The hub update rule says that for each page $p$, $hub(p)$ is the sum of the authority scores of all pages that it points to.

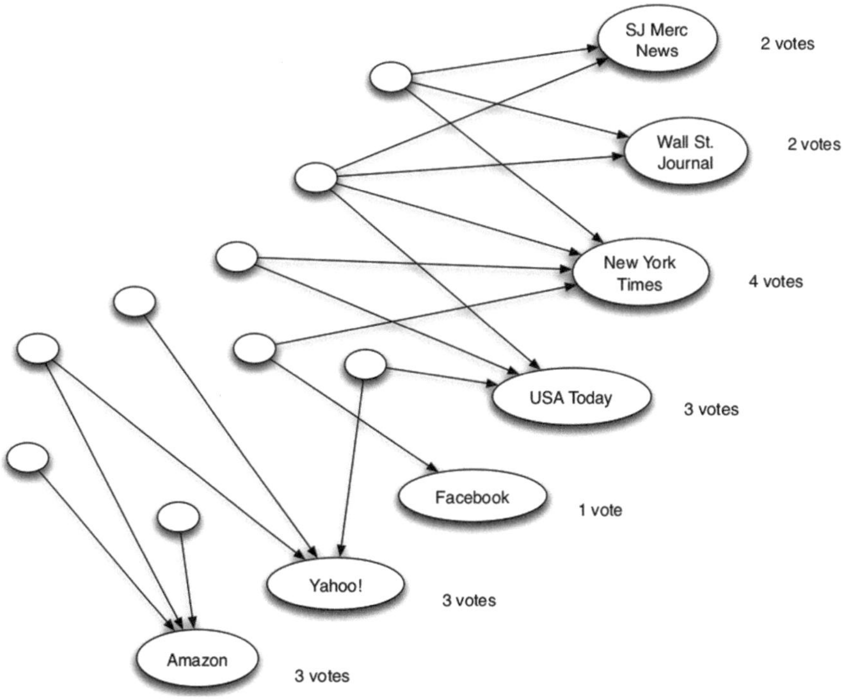


**Fig. 13.2** Counting in-links to pages for the query "newspapers"

By the principle of repeated improvement, we do the following:

1. Start with all hub and authority scores equal to 1.
2. Choose a number of steps $k$.
3. Perform a sequence of $k$ hub-authority updates. Each update works as follows:
   - Apply the Authority Update rule to the current set of scores.
   - Apply the Hub Update rule to the resulting set of scores.
4. The resultant hub and authority scores may involve numbers that are very large (as can be seen in Fig. 13.4). But we are concerned only with their relative size and therefore they can be normalized: we divide down each authority score by the sum of all authority scores, and divide down each hub score by the sum of all hub scores. Figure 13.5 shows the normalized scores of Fig. 13.4.

This algorithm is commonly known as the HITS algorithm [16].

However, as $k$ goes to infinity, the normalized values converge to a limit. Figure 13.6 depicts the limiting values for the "newspaper" query.

These limiting values correspond to a state of equilibrium where a page $p$'s authority score is proportional to the hub scores of the pages that point to $p$, and $p$'s hub score is proportional to the authority scores of the pages $p$ points to.

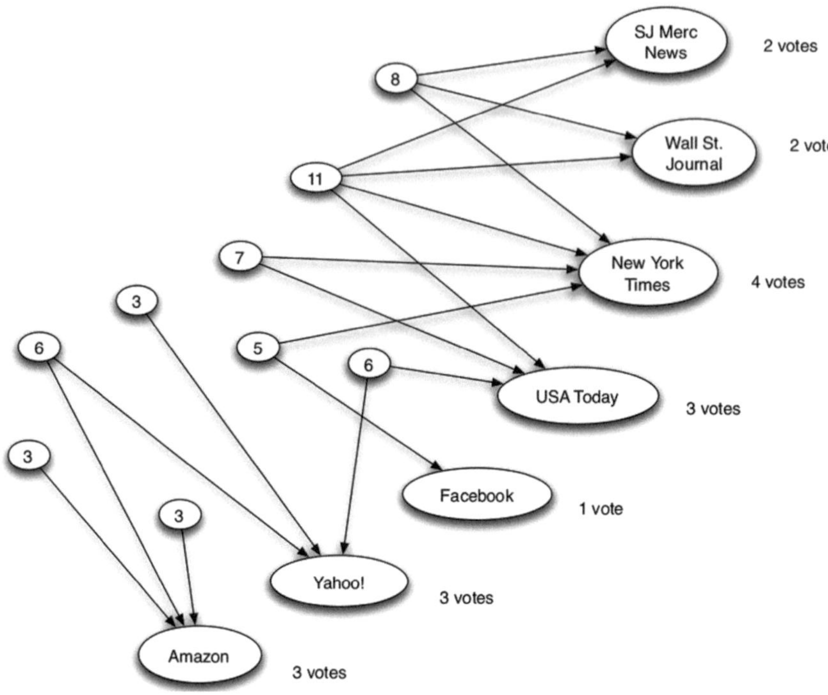


**Fig. 13.3** Finding good lists for the query "newspapers": each page's value as a list is written as a number inside it

When we intend to perform the spectral analysis of HITS algorithm, we will first represent the network of $n$ nodes as an adjacency matrix $M$. Although, it is not a very efficient way to represent a large network (as studied in Chap. 1), it is conceptually useful for analysis.

The hub and authority scores are represented as vectors in $n$ dimensions. The vector of hub scores is denoted as $h$ where the $i$th element represents the hub score of node $i$. On similar lines, we denote the vector of authority scores as $a$. Thus, the Hub Update rule can be represented by Eq. 13.7 and therefore the Authority Update rule can be represented by Eq. 13.8.

$$h \leftarrow M \cdot a \tag{13.7}$$

$$a \leftarrow M^T \cdot h \tag{13.8}$$

The $k$-step hub-authority computations for large values of $k$ is be described below: The initial authority and hub vectors are denoted as $a^{[0]}$ and $h^{[0]}$ each of which are equal to unit vectors. Let $a^{[k]}$ and $h^{[k]}$ represent the vectors of authority and hub

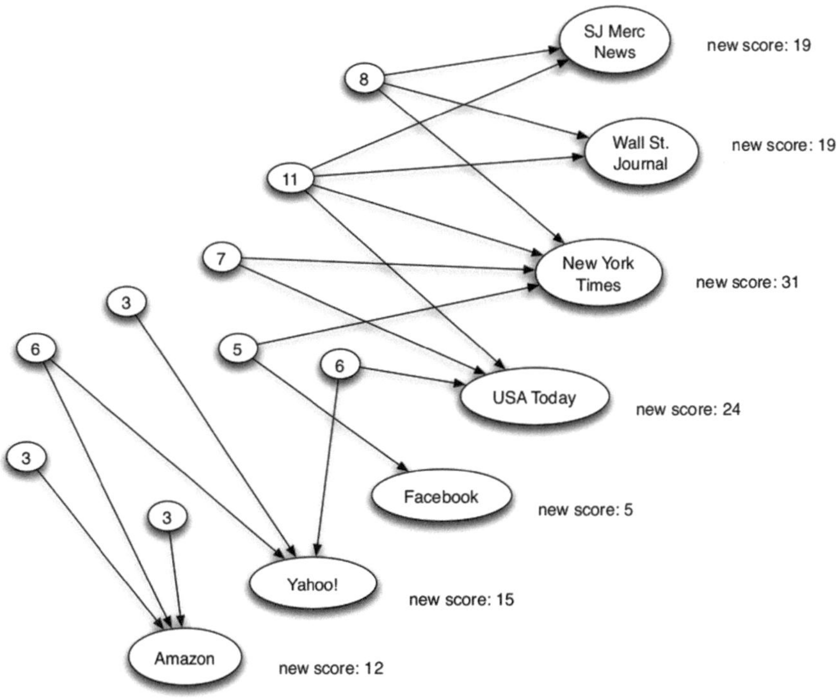


**Fig. 13.4** Re-weighting votes for the query "newspapers": each of the labelled page's new score is equal to the sum of the values of all lists that point to it

scores after $k$ applications of the Authority and Hub Update Rules in order. This gives us Eqs. 13.9 and 13.10.

$$a^{[1]} = M^T h^{[0]} \tag{13.9}$$

and

$$h^{[1]} = Ma^{[1]} = MM^T h^{[0]} \tag{13.10}$$

In the next step, we get

$$a^{[2]} = M^T h^{[1]} = M^T MM^T h^{[0]} \tag{13.11}$$

and

$$h^{[2]} = Ma^{[2]} = MM^T MM^T h^{[0]} = (MM^T)^2 h^{[0]} \tag{13.12}$$

For larger values of $k$, we have

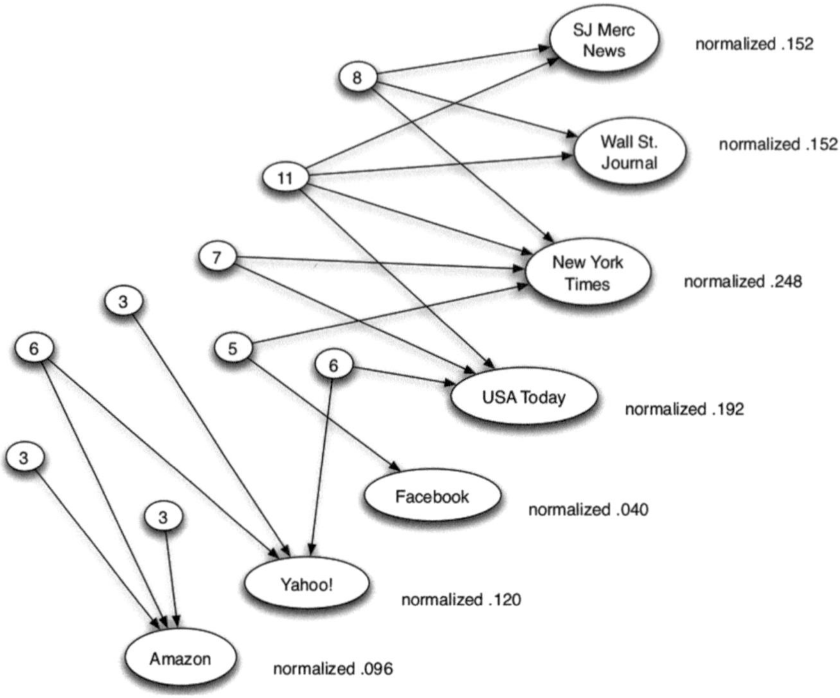


**Fig. 13.5** Re-weighting votes after normalizing for the query "newspapers"

$$a^{[k]} = (M^T M)^{k-1} M^T h^{[0]} \tag{13.13}$$

and

$$h^{[k]} = (M M^T)^k h^{[0]} \tag{13.14}$$

Now we will look at the convergence of this process.

Consider the constants $c$ and $d$. If

$$\frac{h^{[k]}}{c^k} = \frac{(M M^T)^k h^{[0]}}{c^k} \tag{13.15}$$

is going to converge to a limit $h^{[*]}$, we expect that at the limit, the direction of $h^{[*]}$ shouldn't change when it is multiplied by $(M M^T)$, although its length might grow by a factor of $c$, i.e, we expect that $h^*$ will satisfy the equation

$$(M M^T) h^{[*]} = c h^{[*]} \tag{13.16}$$

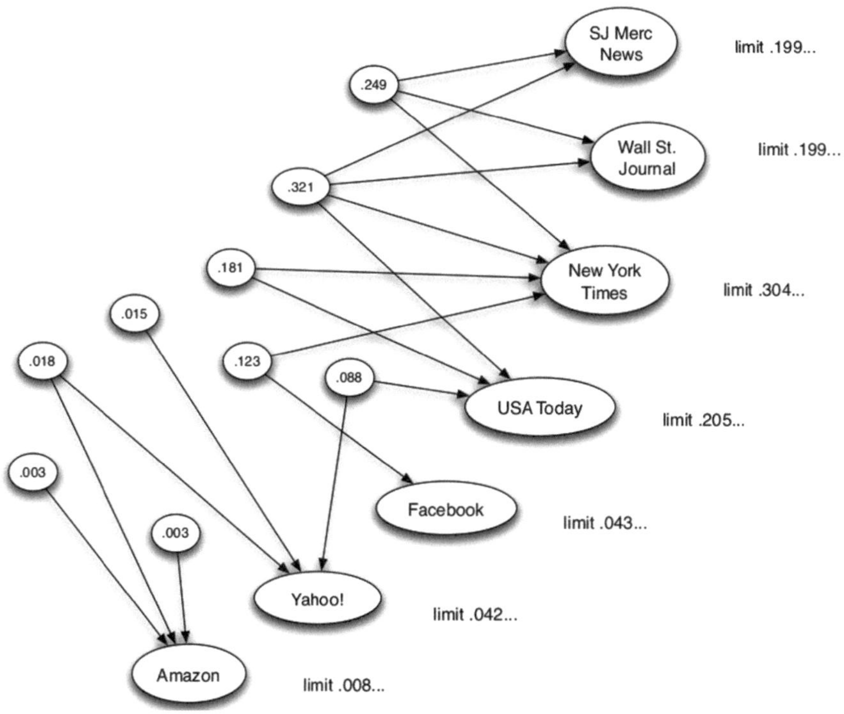


**Fig. 13.6** Limiting hub and authority values for the query "newspapers"

This means that $h^{[*]}$ is the eigenvector of the matrix $MM^T$, with $c$ a corresponding eigenvalue.

Any symmetric matrix with $n$ rows and $n$ columns has a set of $n$ eigenvectors that are all unit vectors and all mutually orthogonal, i.e, they form a basis for the space $\mathbb{R}^n$.

Since $MM^T$ is symmetric, we get the $n$ mutually orthogonal eigenvectors as $z_1, \ldots, z_n$, with corresponding eigenvalues $c_1, \ldots, c_n$. Let $|c_1| \geq |c_2| \geq \cdots \geq |c_n|$. Suppose that $|c_1| > |c_2|$, if we have to compute the matrix-vector product $(MM^T)x$ for any vector $x$, we could first write $x$ as a linear combination of the vectors $z_1, \ldots, z_n$, i.e, $x = p_1 z_1 + p_2 z_2 + \cdots + p_n z_n$ for coefficients $p_1, \ldots, p_n$. Thus

$$\begin{aligned} (MM^T)x &= (MM^T)(p_1 z_1 + p_2 z_2 + \cdots + p_n z_n) \\ &= p_1 MM^T z_1 + p_2 MM^T z_2 + \cdots + p_n MM^T z_n \\ &= p_1 c_1 z_1 + p_2 c_2 z_2 + \cdots + p_n c_n z_n \end{aligned} \tag{13.17}$$

$k$ multiplications of $MM^T$ of the matrix-vector product will therefore give us

$$(MM^T)^k x = c_1^k p_1 z_1 + c_2^k p_2 z_2 + \cdots + c_n^k p_n z_n \tag{13.18}$$

Applying Eq. 13.18 to the vector of hub scores, we get $h^{[k]} = (MM^T)h^{[0]}$. Since $h^{[0]}$ is just a starting unit vector, it can be represented in terms of the basis vectors $z_1, \ldots, z_n$ as some linear combination $h^{[0]} = q_1 z_1 + q_2 z_2 + \cdots + q_n z_n$. So,

$$h^{[k]} = (MM^T)^k h^{[0]} = c_1^k q_1 z_1 + c_2^k q_2 z_2 + \cdots + c_n^k q_n z_n \tag{13.19}$$

Dividing both sides by $c_1^k$, we get

$$\frac{h^{[k]}}{c_1^k} = q_1 z_1 + \left(\frac{c_2}{c_1}\right)^k q_2 z_2 + \cdots + \left(\frac{c_n}{c_1}\right)^k q_n z_n \tag{13.20}$$

Since $|c_1| > |c_2|$, as $k$ goes to infinity, every term on the right-hand side except the first is going to 0. This means that the sequence of vectors $\frac{h^{[k]}}{c_1^k}$ converges to the limit $q_1 z_1$ as $k$ goes to infinity.

What would happen if we began the computation from some starting vector $x$, instead of the unit vector $h^{[0]}$? If $x$ is a positive vector expressed as $x = p_1 z_1 + \cdots + p_n z_n$ for some coefficients $p_1, \ldots, p_n$, and so $(MM^T)^k x = c_1^k p_1 z_1 + \cdots + c_n^k p_n z_n$. Then, $\frac{h^{[k]}}{c_1^k}$ converges to $p_1 z_1$. Thus, we converge to a vector in the direction of $z_1$ even with this new starting vector.

Now we consider the case when the assumption $|c_1| > |c_2|$ is relaxed. Let's say that there are $l > 1$ eigenvalues that are tied for the largest absolute value, i.e, $|c_1| = \cdots = |c_l|$, and then $c_{l+1}, \ldots, c_n$, are all smaller in absolute value. With all the eigenvalues in $MM^T$ being non-negative, we have $c_1 = \cdots = c_l > c_{l+1} \geq \cdots \geq c_n \geq 0$. This gives us

$$\frac{h^{[k]}}{c_1^k} = \frac{c_1^k q_1 z_1 + \cdots + c_n^k q_n z_n}{c_1^k} = q_1 z_1 + \cdots + q_l z_l + \left(\frac{c_{l+1}}{c_l}\right)^k q_{l+1} z_{l+1} + \cdots + \left(\frac{c_n}{c_1}\right)^k q_n z_n \tag{13.21}$$

Terms $l + 1$ through $n$ of this sum go to zero, and so the sequence converges to $q_1 z_1 + \cdots + q_l z_l$. Thus, when $c_1 = c_2$, we still have convergence, but the limit to which the sequence converges might now depend on the choice of the initial vector $h^{[0]}$ (and particularly its inner product with each of $z_1, \ldots, z_l$). In practice, with real and sufficiently large hyperlink structures, one essentially always gets a matrix $M$ with the property that $MM^T$ has $|c_1| > |c_2|$.

This can be adapted directly to analyse the sequence of authority vectors. For the authority vectors, we are looking at powers of $(M^T M)$, and so the basic result is that the vector of authority scores will converge to an eigenvector of the matrix $M^T M$ associated with its largest eigenvalue.

**Table 13.1** PageRank values of Fig. 13.7

| Step | *A* | *B* | *C* | *D* | *E* | *F* | *G* | *H* |
|---|---|---|---|---|---|---|---|---|
| 1 | 1/2 | 1/16 | 1/16 | 1/16 | 1/16 | 1/16 | 1/16 | 1/8 |
| 2 | 3/16 | 1/4 | 1/4 | 1/32 | 1/32 | 1/32 | 1/32 | 1/16 |

#### 13.1.4.2 PageRank

PageRank [7] also works on the same principle as HITS algorithm. It starts with simple voting based on in-links, and refines it using the Principle of Repeated Improvement.

PageRank can be thought of as a "fluid" that circulates through the network, passing from node to node across edges, and pooling at the nodes that are most important. It is computed as follows:

1. In a network with $n$ nodes, all nodes are assigned the same initial PageRank, set to be $1/n$.
2. Choose a number of steps $k$.
3. Perform a sequence of $k$ updates to the PageRank values, using the following *Basic PageRank Update rule* for each update: Each page divides its current PageRank equally across its out-going links, and passes these equal shares to the pages it points to. If a page has no out-going links, it passes all its current PageRank to itself. Each page updates its new PageRank to be the sum of the shares it receives.

This algorithm requires no normalization because the PageRank values are just moved around with no chance of increase.

Figure 13.7 is an instance of a network with eight Webpages. All of these pages start out with a PageRank of $1/8$. Their PageRanks after the first two updates are as tabulated in Table 13.1.

Similar to the HITS algorithm, the PageRank values converge to a limit as $k$ goes to infinity. Figure 13.8 depicts the equilibrium PageRank values.

There is a problem with the PageRank rule in this form. Consider the network in Fig. 13.9, which is the same network as in Fig. 13.7 but with $F$ and $G$ pointing to one another rather than pointing to $A$. This causes the PageRanks to converge to $1/2$ for $F$ and $G$ with 0 for all other nodes.

This means that any network containing reciprocating links will have this clogging of PageRanks at such nodes. To prevent such a situation, the PageRank rule is updated by introducing a scaling factor $s$ that should be strictly between 0 and 1. This gives us the following *Scaled PageRank Update rule*. According to this rule, first apply the Basic PageRank Update rule. Then scale down all PageRank values by a factor of $s$, thereby shrinking the total PageRank from 1 to $s$. The residual $1 - s$ units of PageRank are divided equally over all the nodes, giving $(1 - s)/n$ to each.

This scaling factor makes the PageRank measure less sensitive to the addition or deletion of small number of nodes or edges.

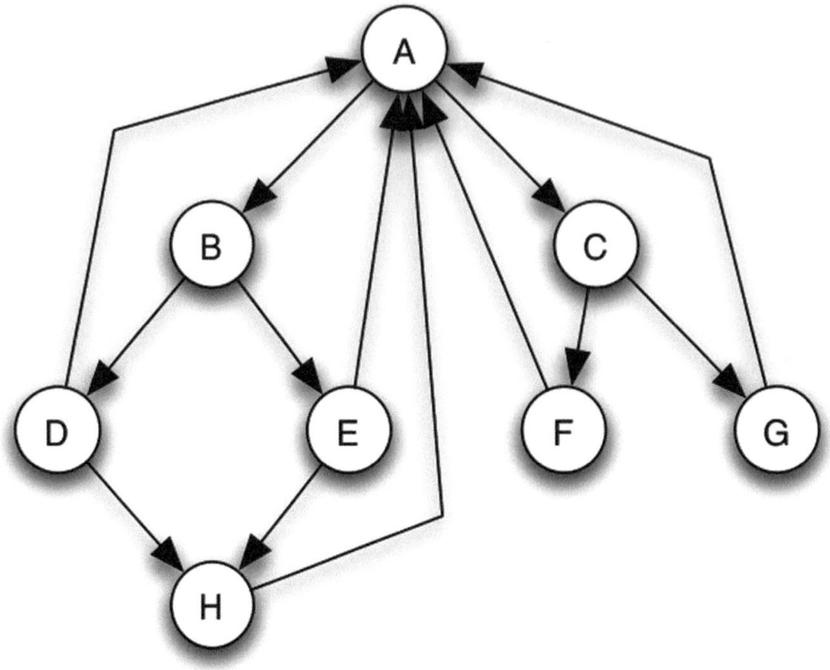


**Fig. 13.7** A collection of eight web pages

A survey of the PageRank algorithm and its developments can be found in [4].

We will first analyse the Basic PageRank Update rule and then move on to the scaled version. Under the basic rule, each node takes its current PageRank and divides it equally over all the nodes it points to. This suggests that the "flow" of PageRank specified by the update rule can be naturally represented using a matrix $N$. Let $N_{ij}$ be the share of $i$'s PageRank that $j$ should get in one update step. $N_{ij} = 0$ if $i$ doesn't link to $j$, and when $i$ links to $j$, then $N_{ij} = 1/l_i$, where $l_i$ is the number of links out of $i$. (If $i$ has no outgoing links, then we define $N_{ii} = 1$, in keeping with the rule that a node with no outgoing links passes all its PageRank to itself.)

If we represent the PageRank of all the nodes using a vector $r$, where $r_i$ is the PageRank of node $i$. In this manner, the Basic PageRank Update rule is

$$r \leftarrow N^T \cdot r \tag{13.22}$$

We can similarly represent the Scaled PageRank Update rule using the matrix $\hat{N}$ to denote the different flow of PageRank. To account for the scaling, we define $\hat{N_{ij}}$ to be $sN_{ij} + (1 - s)/n$, this gives the scaled update rule as

$$r \leftarrow \hat{N^T} \cdot r \tag{13.23}$$

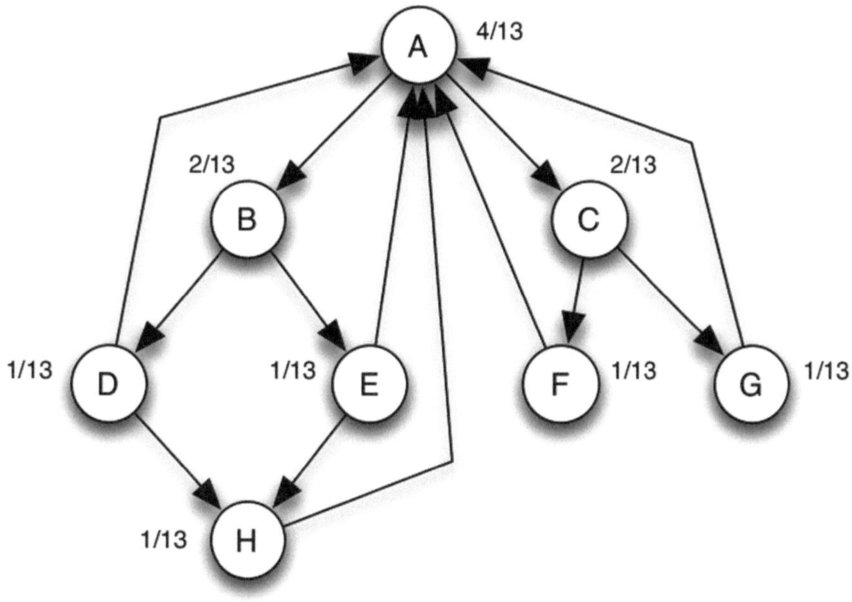


**Fig. 13.8** Equilibrium PageRank values for the network in Fig. 13.7

Starting from an initial PageRank vector $r^{[0]}$, a sequence of vectors $r^{[1]}, r^{[2]}, \ldots$ are obtained from repeated improvement by multiplying the previous vector by $\hat{N^T}$. This gives us

$$r^{[k]} = (\hat{N^T})^k r^{[0]} \tag{13.24}$$

This means that if the Scaled PageRank Update rule converges to a limiting vector $r^{[*]}$, this limit would satisfy $\hat{N^T} r^{[*]} = r^{[*]}$. This is proved using *Perron's Theorem* [18].

Reference [2] describes axioms that are satisfied by the PageRank algorithm, and that any page ranking algorithm that satisfies these must coincide with the PageRank algorithm.

#### 13.1.4.3 Random Walk

Consider the situation where one randomly starts browsing a network of Webpages. They start at a random page and pick each successive page with equal probability. The links are followed for a sequence of $k$ steps: in each step, a random out-going link from the current page is picked. (If the current page has no out-going links, they just stay where they are.)

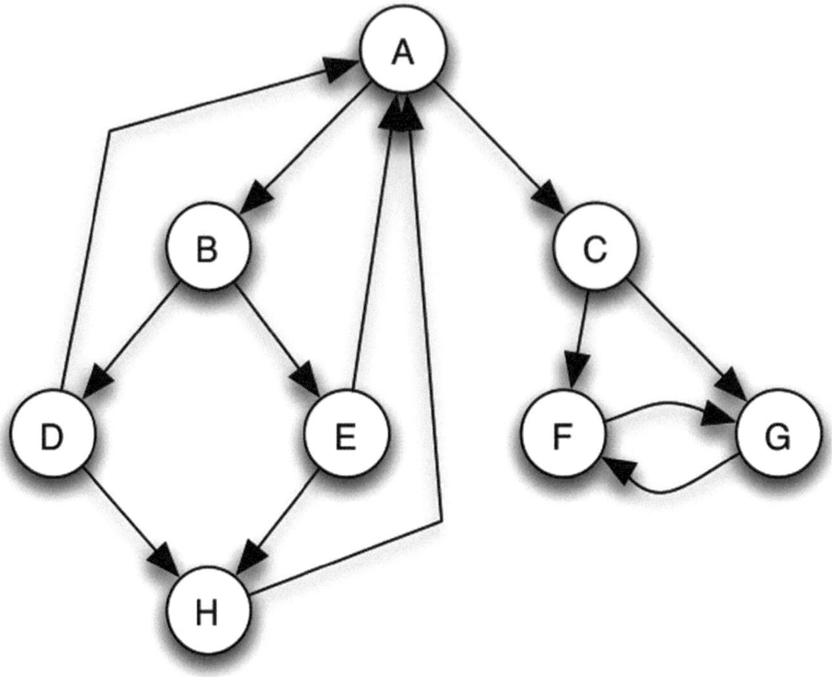


**Fig. 13.9** The same collection of eight pages, but $F$ and $G$ have changed their links to point to each other instead of to $A$. Without a smoothing effect, all the PageRank would go to $F$ and $G$

*Remark 1* Taking a random walk in this situation, the probability of being at a page $X$ after $k$ steps of this random walk is precisely the PageRank of $X$ after $k$ applications of the Basic PageRank Update rule.

*Proof* If $b_1, b_2, \ldots, b_n$ denote the probabilities of the walk being at nodes $1, 2, \ldots, n$ respectively in a given step, then the probability it will be at node $i$ in the next step is computed as follows:

1. For each node $j$ that links to $i$, if we are given that the walk is currently at node $j$, then there is a $1/l_j$ chance that it moves from $j$ to $i$ in the next step, where $l_j$ is the number of links out of $j$.
2. The walk has to actually be at node $j$ for this to happen, so node $j$ contributes $b_j(1/l_j) = b_j/l_j$ to the probability of being at $i$ in the next step.
3. Therefore, summing $b_j/l_j$ over all nodes $j$ that link to $i$ gives the probability the walk is at $b_i$ in the next step.

So the overall probability that the walk is at $i$ in the next step is the sum of $b_j/l_j$ over all nodes that link to $i$.

If we represent the probabilities of being at different nodes using a vector $b$, where the coordinate $b_i$ is the probability of being at node $i$, then this update rule can be written using matrix-vector multiplication as

$$b \leftarrow N^T \cdot b \tag{13.25}$$

This is exactly the same as Eq. 13.22. Since both PageRank values and random-walk probabilities start out the same (they are initially $1/n$ for all nodes), and they then evolve according to exactly the same rule, so they remain same forever. This justifies the claim.

*Remark 2* The probability of being at a page $X$ after $k$ steps of the scaled random walk is precisely the PageRank of $X$ after $k$ applications of the Scaled PageRank Update Rule.

*Proof* We go by the same lines as the proof of Remark 1. If $b_1, b_2, \ldots, b_n$ denote the probabilities of the walk being at nodes $1, 2, \ldots, n$ respectively in a given step, then the probability it will be at node $i$ in the next step, is the sum of $sb_j/l_j$, over all nodes $j$ that link to $i$, plus $(1-s)/n$. If we use the matrix $\hat{N}$, then we can write the probability update as

$$b \leftarrow \hat{N}^T b \tag{13.26}$$

This is the same as the update rule from Eq. 13.23 for the scaled PageRank values. The random-walk probabilities and the scaled PageRank values start at the same initial values, and then evolve according to the same update, so they remain the same forever. This justifies the argument.

A problem with both PageRank and HITS is *topic drift*. Because they give the same weights to all edges, the pages with the most in-links in the network being considered tend to dominate, whether or not they are most relevant to the query. References [8] and [5] propose heuristic methods for differently weighting links. Reference [20] biased PageRank towards pages containing a specific word, and [14] proposed applying an optimized version of PageRank to the subset of pages containing the query terms.

#### 13.1.4.4 SALSA Algorithm

Reference [17] proposed the SALSA algorithm which starts with a "Root Set" short list of Webpages relevant to the given query retrieved from a text-based search engine. This root set is augmented by pages which link to pages in the Root Set, and also pages which are linked to pages in the Root Set, to obtain a larger "Base Set" of Webpages. Perform a random walk on this base set by alternately (a) going uniformly to one of the pages which links to the current page, and (b) going uniformly to one of the pages linked to by the current page. The authority weights are defined to be the stationary distribution of the two-step chain first doing (a) and then (b), while the hub weights are defined to be the stationary distribution of the two-step chain first doing (b) and then (a).

Formally, let $B(i) = \{k : k \rightarrow i\}$ denote the set of all nodes that point to $i$, i.e, the nodes we can reach from $i$ by following a link backwards, and let $F(i) = \{k : i \rightarrow k\}$ denote the set of all nodes that we can reach from $i$ by following a forward link. The Markov Chain for the authorities has transition probabilities

$$P_a(i, j) = \sum_{k:k \in B(i) \cap B(j)} \frac{1}{|B(i)|} \frac{1}{|F(k)|} \tag{13.27}$$

If the Markov chain is irreducible, then the stationary distribution $a = (a_1, a_2, \ldots, a_N)$ of the Markov chain satisfies $a_i = |B(i)|/|B|$, where $B = \bigcup_i B(i)$ is the set of all backward links.

Similarly, the Markov chain for the hubs has transition probabilities

$$P_h(i, j) = \sum_{k:k \in F(i) \cap F(j)} \frac{1}{|F(i)|} \frac{1}{|B(k)|} \tag{13.28}$$

and the stationary distribution $h = (h_1, h_2, \ldots, h_N)$ of the Markov chain satisfies $h_i = |F(i)|/|F|$, where $F = \bigcup_i F(i)$ is the set of all forward links.

In the special case of a single component, SALSA can be viewed as a one-step truncated version of HITS algorithm, i.e, in the first iteration of HITS algorithm, if we perform the Authority Update rule first, the authority weights are set to $a = A^T u$, where $u$ is the vector of all ones. If we normalize in the $L_1$ norm, then $a_i = |B(i)|/|B|$, which is the stationary distribution of the SALSA algorithm. A similar observation can be made for the hub weights.

If the underlying graph of the Base Set consists of more than one component, then the SALSA algorithm selects a starting point uniformly at random, and performs a random walk within the connected component that contains that node. Formally, let $j$ be a component that contains node $i$, let $N_j$ denote the number of nodes in the component, and $B_j$ the set of (backward) links in component $j$. Then, the authority weight of node $i$ is

$$a_i = \frac{N_j}{N} \frac{|B(i)|}{|B_j|} \tag{13.29}$$

A simplified version of the SALSA algorithm where the authority weight of a node is the ratio $|B(i)|/|B|$, corresponds to the case that the starting point for the random walk is chosen with probability proportional to its in-degree. This variation of the SALSA algorithm is commonly referred to as pSALSA.

#### 13.1.4.5 PHITS Algorithm

Reference [10] proposed a statistical hubs and authorities algorithm called PHITS algorithm. A probabilistic model was proposed in which a citation $c$ of a document $d$ is caused by a latent "factor" or "topic", $z$. It is postulated that there are conditional distributions $P(c|z)$ of a citation $c$ given a factor $z$, and also conditional distributions $P(z|d)$ of a factor $z$ given a document $d$. In terms of these conditional distributions, they produce a likelihood function.

The EM Algorithm of [11] to assign the unknown conditional probabilities so as to maximize this likelihood function L, best explained the proposed data. Their algorithm requires specifying in advance the number of factors $z$ to be considered. Furthermore, it is possible that the EM algorithm could get stuck in a local maximum, without converging to the true global maximum.

#### 13.1.4.6 Breadth First Algorithm: A Normalized $n$-step Variant

Reference [6] proposed a BFS algorithm, as a generalization of the pSALSA algorithm, and a restriction of the HITS algorithm. The BFS algorithm extends the idea of in-degree that appears in pSALSA from a one link neighbourhood to a $n$-link neighbourhood. Here, we introduce the following notations. If we follow a link backwards, then we call this a $B$ path, and if we follow a link forwards, we call it a $F$ path. So, a $BF$ path is a path that first follows a link backwards, and then a link forward. $(BF)^n(i, j)$ denotes the set of $(BF)^n$ paths that go from $i$ to $j$, $(BF)^n(i)$ the set of $(BF)^n$ paths that leave node $i$, and $(BF)^n$ the set of all possible $(BF)^n$ paths. Similar sets can be defined for the $(FB)^n$ paths.

In this algorithm, instead of considering the number of $(BF)^n$ paths that leave $i$, it considers the number of $(BF)^n$ neighbours of node $i$. The contribution of node $j$ to the weight of node $i$ depends on the distance of the node $j$ from $i$. By adopting an exponentially decreasing weighting scheme, the weight of node $i$ is determined as:

$$a_i = 2^{n-1}|B(i)| + 2^{n-2}|BF(i)| + 2^{n-3}|BFB(i)| + \cdots + |(BF)^n(i)| \tag{13.30}$$

The algorithm starts from node $i$, and visits its neighbours in BFS order. At each iteration it takes a Backward or a Forward step (depending on whether it is an odd, or an even iteration), and it includes the new nodes it encounters. The weight factors are updated accordingly. Note that each node is considered only once, when it is first encountered by the algorithm.

#### 13.1.4.7 Bayesian Algorithm

Reference [6] also proposed a fully Bayesian statistical approach to authorities and hubs. If there are $M$ hubs and $N$ authorities, we suppose that each hub $i$ has a real parameter $e_i$, corresponding to its tendency to have hypertext links, and also a non-negative parameter $h_i$, corresponding to its tendency to have intelligent hypertext links to authoritative sites. Each authority $j$ has a non-negative parameter $a_j$, corresponding to its level of authority.

The statistical model is as follows. The a priori probability of a link from hub $i$ to authority $j$ is given by

$$P(i \rightarrow j) = \frac{exp(a_j h_i + e_i)}{1 + exp(a_j h_i + e_i)} \tag{13.31}$$

with the probability of no link from $i$ to $j$ given by

$$P(i \not\rightarrow j) = \frac{1}{1 + exp(a_j h_i + e_i)} \tag{13.32}$$

This states that a link is more likely if $e_i$ is large (in which case hub $i$ has large tendency to link to any site), or if both $h_i$ and $a_j$ are large (in which case $i$ is an intelligent hub, and $j$ is a high-quality authority).

We must now assign prior distributions to the $2M + N$ unknown parameters $e_i$, $h_i$, and $a_j$. To do this, we let $\mu = -5.0$ and $\sigma = 0.1$ be fixed parameters, and let each $e_i$ have prior distribution $N(\mu, \sigma^2)$, a normal distribution with mean $\mu$ and variance $\sigma^2$. We further let each $h_i$ and $a_j$ have prior distribution $exp(1)$, meaning that for $x \geq 0$, $P(h_i \geq x) = P(a_j \geq x) = exp(-x)$. The Bayesian inference method then proceeds from this fully-specified statistical model, by conditioning on the observed data, which in this case is the matrix $A$ of actual observed hypertext links in the Base Set. Specifically, when we condition on the data $A$ we obtain a posterior density $\prod : R^{2M+N} \rightarrow [0, \infty)$ for the parameters $(e_1, \ldots, e_M, h_1, \ldots, h_M, a_1, \ldots, a_N)$. This density is defined so that

$$\begin{aligned} &P((e_1, \ldots, e_M, h_1, \ldots, h_M, a_1, \ldots, a_N) \in S | \{A_{ij}\}) \\ &= \int_S \pi(e_1, \ldots, e_M, h_1, \ldots, h_M, a_1, \ldots, a_N) \\ &\qquad de_1 \ldots de_M dh_1 \ldots dh_M da_1 \ldots da_N \end{aligned} \tag{13.33}$$

for any measurable subset $S \subseteq R^{2M+N}$, and also

$$\begin{aligned} &E(g(e_1, \ldots, e_M, h_1, \ldots, h_M, a_1, \ldots, a_N) | \{A_{ij}\}) \\ &= \int_{R^{2M+N}} g(e_1, \ldots, e_M, h_1, \ldots, h_M, a_1, \ldots, a_N) \\ &\qquad \pi(e_1, \ldots, e_M, h_1, \ldots, h_M, a_1, \ldots, a_N) \\ &\qquad de_1 \ldots de_M dh_1 \ldots dh_M da_1 \ldots da_N \end{aligned} \tag{13.34}$$

for any measurable function $g : R^{2M+N} \rightarrow R$.

The posterior density for the model is given up to a multiplicative constant, by

$$\pi(e_1, \ldots, e_M, h_1, \ldots, h_M, a_1, \ldots, a_N) \propto \prod_{i=0}^{M-1} exp(-h_i)exp[-(e_i - \mu)^2/(2\sigma^2)]$$
$$\times \prod_{j=0}^{N-1} exp(-a_j) \times \prod_{(i,j):A_{ij}=1} exp(a_j h_i + e_i) / \prod_{all\ i,j} (1 + exp(a_j h_i + e_i)) \tag{13.35}$$

The Bayesian algorithm then reports the conditional means of the $2M + N$ parameters, according to the posterior density $\pi$, i.e, it reports final values $\hat{a_j}$, $\hat{h_i}$, and $\hat{e_i}$, where, for example

$$\hat{a_j} = \int_{R^{2M+N}} a_j \pi(e_1, \ldots, e_M, h_1, \ldots, h_M, a_1, \ldots, a_N)$$
$$de_1 \ldots de_M dh_1 \ldots dh_M da_1 \ldots da_N \tag{13.36}$$

A Metropolis algorithm is used to compute these conditional means.

This algorithm can be further simplified by replacing Eq. 13.31 with $P(i \rightarrow j) = (a_j h_i)/(1 + a_j h_i)$ and replacing Eq. 13.32 with $P(i \not\rightarrow j) = 1/(1 + a_j h_i)$. This eliminates the parameters $e_i$ entirely, so that prior values $\mu$ and $\sigma$ are no longer needed. This leads to the posterior density $\pi(\cdot)$, now given by $\pi : R^{M+N} \rightarrow R^{\geq 0}$ where

$$\pi(h_1, \ldots, h_M, a_1, \ldots, a_N) \propto \prod_{i=0}^{M-1} exp(-h_i) \times \prod_{j=0}^{N-1} exp(-a_j) \times \prod_{(i,j):A_{ij}=1} a_j h_i$$
$$/ \prod_{all\ i,j} (1 + a_j h_i) \tag{13.37}$$

Comparison of these algorithms can be found in [6].

## 13.2 Google

Reference [7] describes *Google*, a prototype of a large-scale search engine which makes use of the structure present in hypertext. This prototype forms the base of the Google search engine we know today.

Figure 13.10 illustrates a high level view of how the whole system works. The paper states that most of Google was implemented in C or C++ for efficiency and was available to be run on either Solaris or Linux.

The *URL Server* plays the role of the crawl control module here by sending the list of URLs to be fetched by the crawlers. The *Store Server* receives the fetched pages and compresses them before storing it in the repository. Every Webpage has an associated ID number called a docID which is assigned whenever a new URL is parsed out of a Webpage. The *Indexer* module reads the repository, uncompresses the

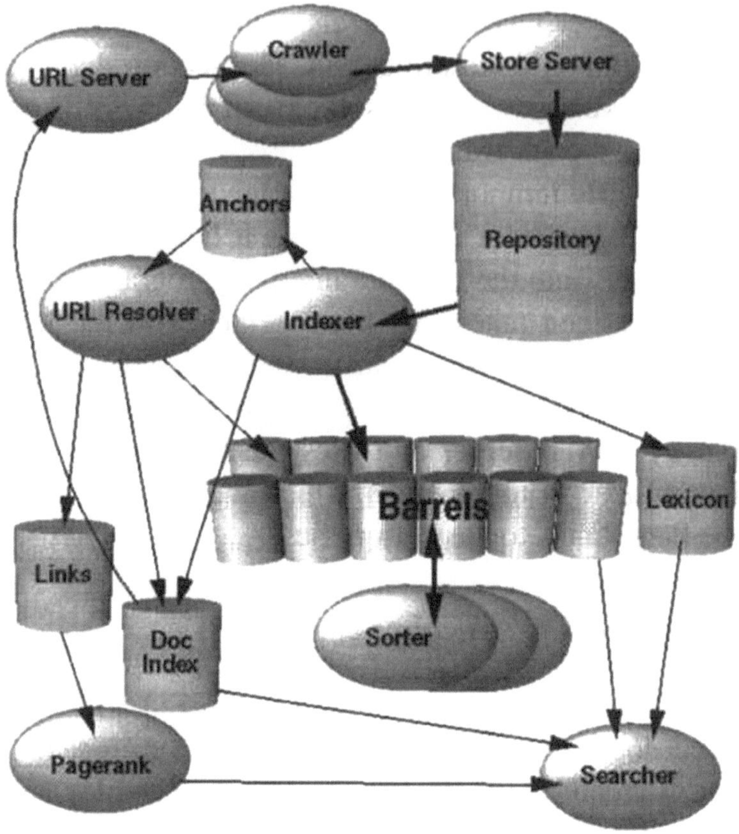


**Fig. 13.10** High level Google architecture

documents and parses them. Each of these documents is converted to a set of word occurrences called hits. The hit record the word, position in document, approximation of the font size and capitalization. These hits are then distributed into a set of *Barrels*, creating a partially sorted forward index. The indexer also parses out all the links in every Webpage and stores important information about them in anchor files placed in *Anchors*. These anchor files contain enough information to determine where each link points from and to, and the text of the link.

The *URL Resolver* reads these anchor files and converts relative URLs into absolute URLs and in turn into docIDs. These anchor texts are put into the forward index, associated with the docID that the anchor points to. It also generates a database of links which are pairs of docIDs. The *Links* database is used to compute PageRanks for all the documents. The *Sorter* takes the barrels, which are sorted by docID, and resorts them by wordID to generate the inverted index. The sorter also produces a list of wordIDs and offsets into the inverted index. A program called *DumpLexicon* takes this list together with the lexicon produced by the indexer and generates a new lexicon to be used by the searcher. The *Searcher* is run by a Web server and uses the lexicon built by DumpLexicon together with the inverted index and the *PageRanks* to answer queries.

### *13.2.1 Data Structures*

Almost all of the data is stored in BigFiles which are virtual files that can span multiple file systems and support compression. The raw HTML repository uses roughly half of the necessary storage. It consists of concatenation of the compressed HTML of every page, preceded by a small header. The *DocIndex* keeps information about each document. The DocIndex is a fixed width Index Sequential Access Mode (ISAM) index, ordered by docID. The information stored in each entry includes the current document status, a pointer into the repository, a document checksum, and various statistics. Variable width information such as URL and title is kept in a separate file. There is also an auxiliary index to convert URLs into docIDs. The lexicon has several different forms for different operations. They all are memory-based hash tables with varying values attached to each word.

Hit lists account for most of the space used in both the forward and the inverted indices. Because of this, it is important to represent them as efficiently as possible. Therefore, a hand optimized compact encoding is used which uses two bytes for every hit. To save space, the length of the hit list is stored before the hits and is combined with the wordID in the forward index and the docID in the inverted index.

The forward index is actually already partially sorted. It is stored in a number of barrels. Each barrel holds a range of wordIDs. If a document contains words that fall into a particular barrel, the docID is recorded into the barrel, followed by a list of wordIDs with hitlists which correspond to those words. This scheme requires slightly more storage because of duplicated docIDs but the difference is very small for a reasonable number of buckets and saves considerable time and coding complexity in the final indexing phase done by the sorter. The inverted index consists of the same barrels as the forward index. Except that they have been processed by the sorter. For every valid wordID, the lexicon contains a pointer into the barrel that wordID falls into. It points to a list of docIDs together with their corresponding hit lists. This list is called a doclist and represents all the occurrences of that word in all documents.

An important issue is in what order the docIDs should appear in the doclist. One simple solution is to store them sorted by docID. This allows for quick merging of different doclists for multiple word queries. Another option is to store them sorted by a ranking of the occurrence of the word in each document. This makes answering one word queries trivial and makes it likely that the answers to multiple word queries are near the start. However, merging is much more difficult. Also, this makes development much more difficult in that a change to the ranking function requires a rebuild of the index. A compromise between these options was chosen, keeping two sets of inverted barrels - one set for hit lists which include title or anchor hits and another set for all hit lists. This way, we check the first set of barrels first and if there are not enough matches within those barrels we check the larger ones.

### *13.2.2 Crawling*

Crawling is the most fragile application since it involves interacting with hundreds of thousands of Web servers and various name servers which are all beyond the control of the system. In order to scale to hundreds of millions of Webpages, Google has a fast distributed crawling system. A single URLserver serves lists of URLs to a number of crawlers. Both the URLserver and the crawlers were implemented in Python. Each crawler keeps roughly 300 connections open at once. This is necessary to retrieve Web pages at a fast enough pace. At peak speeds, the system can crawl over 100 Web pages per second using four crawlers. A major performance stress is DNS lookup so each crawler maintains a DNS cache. Each of the hundreds of connections can be in a number of different states: looking up DNS, connecting to host, sending request. and receiving response. These factors make the crawler a complex component of the system. It uses asynchronous IO to manage events, and a number of queues to move page fetches from state to state.

### *13.2.3 Searching*

Every hitlist includes position, font, and capitalization information. Additionally, hits from anchor text and the PageRank of the document are factored in. Combining all of this information into a rank is difficult. The ranking function so that no one factor can have too much influence. For every matching document we compute counts of hits of different types at different proximity levels. These counts are then run through a series of lookup tables and eventually are transformed into a rank. This process involves many tunable parameters.

## 13.3 Web Spam Pages

Web spam pages are notorious for using techniques to achieve higher-than-deserved rankings in a search engine's results. Reference [12] proposed a technique to semi-automatically separate reputable pages from spam. First, a small set of seed pages are evaluated to be good by a human expert. Once these reputable seed pages have been identified, the link structure of the Web is used to discover other pages that are likely to be good.

Humans can easily identify spam pages and a number of search engine companies have been known to recruit people who have expertise in identifying spam, and regularly scan the Web looking for such pages. However, this is an expensive and time-consuming process but nevertheless has to be done in order to ensure the quality of the search engine's result.

The algorithm first selects a small seed set of pages whose spam status needs to be determined by a human. Using this, the algorithm identifies other pages that are likely to be good based on their connectivity with the good seed pages.

The human checking of a page for spam is formalized as a *oracle function* $O$ over all pages $p \in V$

$$O(p) = \begin{cases} 0 \; if \; p \; is \; bad \\ 1 \; if \; p \; is \; good \end{cases} \tag{13.38}$$

Since oracle evaluations over all pages is an expensive ordeal, this is avoided by asking the human to assign oracle values for just a few of the pages.

To evaluate pages without relying on $O$, the likelihood that a given page $p$ is good is estimated using a *trust function* $T$ which yields the probability that a page is good, i.e, $T(p) = P[O(p) = 1]$.

Although it would be difficult to come up with a function $T$, such a function would be useful in ordering results. These functions could be defined in terms of the following properties. We first look at the *ordered trust property*

$$\begin{aligned} T(p) < T(q) &\Leftrightarrow P[O(p) = 1] < P[O(q) = 1] \\ T(p) = T(q) &\Leftrightarrow P[O(p) = 1] = P[O(q) = 1] \end{aligned} \tag{13.39}$$

By introducing a threshold value $\delta$, we define the *threshold trust property* as

$$T(p) > \delta \Leftrightarrow O(p) = 1 \tag{13.40}$$

A binary function $I(T, O, p, q)$ to signal if the ordered trust property has been violated.

$$I(T, O, p, q) = \begin{cases} 1 \; if \; T(p) \geq T(q) \; and \; O(p) < O(q) \\ 1 \; if \; T(p) \leq T(q) \; and \; O(p) > O(q) \\ 0 \; otherwise \end{cases} \tag{13.41}$$

We now define a set of $\mathcal{P}$ of ordered pairs of pages $(p, q)$, $p \neq q$, and come up with the *pairwise orderedness* function that computes the fraction of pairs for which $T$ did not make a mistake

$$pairord(T, O, \mathcal{P}) = \frac{|\mathcal{P}| - \sum_{(p,q) \in \mathcal{P}} I(T, O, p, q)}{|\mathcal{P}|} \tag{13.42}$$

If $pairord$ equals 1, there are no cases when misrated a pair. In contrast, if $pairord$ equals 0, then $T$ misrated all the pairs.

We now proceed to define the trust functions. Given a budget $L$ of $O$-invocations, we select at random a seed set $\mathcal{S}$ of $L$ pages and call the oracle on its elements. The subset of good and bad seed pages are denoted as $\mathcal{S}^+$ and $\mathcal{S}^-$, respectively. Since the remaining pages are not checked by human expert, these are assigned a trust score of $1/2$ to signal our lack of information. Therefore, this scheme is called the *ignorant trust function* $T_0$ defined for any $p \in V$ as

$$T_0(p) = \begin{cases} O(p)\, if\ p \in \mathcal{S} \\ 1/2\ otherwise \end{cases} \tag{13.43}$$

Now we attempt to compute the trust scores, by taking advantage of the approximate isolation of good pages. We will select at random the set $\mathcal{S}$ of $L$ pages that we invoke the oracle on. Then, expecting that good pages point to other good pages only, we assign a score of 1 to all pages that are reachable from a page in $\mathcal{S}^+$ in $M$ or fewer steps. The *M-step trust function* is defined as

$$T_M(p) = \begin{cases} O(p)\, if\ p \in \mathcal{S} \\ 1\ if\ p \notin \mathcal{S}\ and\ \exists q \in \mathcal{S}^+ : q \rightsquigarrow_M p \\ 1/2\ otherwise \end{cases} \tag{13.44}$$

where $q \rightsquigarrow_M p$ denotes the existence of a path of maximum length of $M$ from page $q$ to page $p$. However, such a path must not include bad seeds.

To reduce trust as we move further away from the good seed pages, there are two possible schemes. The first is called the *trust dampening*. If a page is one link away from a good seed page, it is assigned a dampened trust score of $\beta$. A page that can reach another page with score $\beta$, gets a dampened score of $\beta \cdot \beta$.

The second technique is called *trust splitting*. Here, the trust gets split if it propagates to other pages. If a page $p$ has a trust score of $T(p)$ and it points to $\omega(p)$ pages, each of the $\omega(p)$ pages will receive a score fraction $T(p)/\omega(p)$ from $p$. In this case, the actual score of a page will be the sum of the score fractions received through its in-links.

The next task is to identify pages that are desirable for the seed set. By desirable, we mean pages that will be the most useful in identifying additional good pages. However, we must ensure that the size of the seed set is reasonably small to limit the number of oracle invocations. There are two strategies for accomplishing this task.

The first technique is based on the idea that since trust flows out of the good seed pages, we give preference to pages from which we can reach many other pages. Building on this, we see that seed set can be built from those pages that point to many pages that in turn point to many pages and so on. This approach is the inverse of the PageRank algorithm because the PageRank ranks pages based on its in-degree while here it is based in the out-degree. This gives the technique the name *inverted PageRank*. However, this method is a double-edged sword. While it does not guarantee maximum coverage, its execution time is polynomial in the number of pages.

The other technique is to take pages with high PageRank as the seed set, since high-PageRank pages are likely to point to other high- PageRank pages.

Piecing all of these elements together gives us the *TrustRank* algorithm. The algorithm takes as input the graph. At the first step, it identifies the seed set. The pages in the set are re-ordered in decreasing order of their desirability score. Then, the oracle function is invoked on the $L$ most desirable seed pages. The entries of the static score distribution vector $d$ that correspond to good seed pages are set to 1. After normalizing the vector $d$ so that its entries sum to 1, the TrustRank scores are evaluated using a biased PageRank computation with $d$ replacing the uniform distribution.

Reference [13] complements [12] by proposing a novel method for identifying the largest *spam farms*. A spam farm is a group of interconnected nodes involved in link spamming. It has a single *target node*, whose ranking the spammer intends to boost by creating the whole structure. A farm also contains *boosting nodes*, controlled by the spammer and connected so that they would influence the PageRank of the target. Boosting nodes are owned either by the author of the target, or by some other spammer. Commonly, boosting nodes have little value by themselves; they only exist to improve the ranking of the target. Their PageRank tends to be small, so serious spammers employ a large number of boosting nodes (thousands of them) to trigger high target ranking.

In addition to the links within the farm, spammers may gather some external links from reputable nodes. While the author of a reputable node $y$ is not voluntarily involved in spamming, "stray" links may exist for a number of reasons. A spammer may manage to post a comment that includes a spam link in a reputable blog. Or a *honey pot* may be created, a spam page that offers valuable information, but behind the scenes is still part of the farm. Unassuming users might then point to the honey pot, without realizing that their link is harvested for spamming purposes. The spammer may purchase domain names that recently expired but had previously been reputable and popular. This way he/she can profit of the old links that are still out there.

A term called *spam mass* is introduced which is a measure of how much PageRank a page accumulates through being linked to by spam pages. The idea is that the target pages of spam farms, whose PageRank is boosted by many spam pages, are expected to have a large spam mass. At the same time, popular reputable pages, which have high PageRank because other reputable pages point to them, have a small spam mass.

In order to compute this spam mass, we partition the Web into a set of reputable node $V^+$ and a set of spam nodes $V^-$, with $V^+ \cup V^- = V$ and $V^+ \cap V^- = \phi$. Given this partitioning, the goal is to detect web nodes $x$ that gain most of their PageRank through spam nodes in $V^-$ that link to them. Such nodes $x$ are called spam farm target nodes.

A simple approach would be that, given a node $x$, we look only at its immediate in-neighbours. If we are provided information about whether or not these in-neighbours are reputable or spam, we could infer whether or not $x$ is good or spam.

In a first approach, if majority of $x$'s links comes from spam nodes, $x$ is labelled a spam target node, otherwise it is labelled good. This scheme could easily mislabel spam. An alternative is to look not only at the number of links, but also at what amount of PageRank each link contributes. The contribution of a link amounts to the change in PageRank induced by the removal of the link. However, this scheme does not look beyond the immediate in-neighbours of $x$ and therefore could succumb to mislabelling. This paves a way for a third scheme where a node $x$ is labelled considering all the PageRank contributions of other nodes that are directly or indirectly connected to $x$.

The *PageRank contribution* of $x$ to $y$ over the *walk* $W$ is defined as

$$q_y^W = s^k \pi(W)(1-s)v_x \tag{13.45}$$

where $v_x$ is the probability of a random jump to $x$, and $\pi(W)$ is the weight of the walk.

$$\pi(W) = \prod_{i=0}^{k-1} \frac{1}{out(x_i)} \tag{13.46}$$

This weight can be interpreted as the probability that a Markov chain of length $k$ starting in $x$ reaches $y$ through the sequence of nodes $x_1, \ldots, x_{k-1}$.

This gives the total PageRank contribution of $x$ to $y$, $x \neq y$, over all walks from $x$ to $y$ as

$$q_y^x = \sum_{W \in W_{xy}} q_y^W \tag{13.47}$$

For a node's contribution to itself, a virtual cycle $Z_x$ that has length zero and weight 1 is considered such that

$$\begin{aligned} q_x^x = \sum_{W \in W_{xx}} q_x^W &= q_x^{Z_x} + \sum_{V \in W_{xx}, |V| \geq 1} q_x^V \\ &= (1-s)v_x + \sum_{V \in W_{xx}, |V| \geq 1} q_x^V \end{aligned} \tag{13.48}$$

If a node $x$ does not participate in cycles, $x$'s contribution to itself is $q_x^x = (1-s)v_x$, which corresponds to the random jump component. If these is no walk from node $x$ to $y$ then the PageRank contribution $q_y^x$ is zero.

This gives us that the PageRank *score* of a node $y$ is the sum of the contributions of all other nodes to $y$

$$p_y = \sum_{x \in V} q_y^x \tag{13.49}$$

Under a given random jump distribution $v$, the vector $q^x$ of contributions of a node $x$ to all nodes is the solution of the linear PageRank system for the core-based random jump vector $v^x$

$$v_y^x = \begin{cases} v_x \ if \ x = y \\ 0 \ otherwise \end{cases} \implies q^x = PR(v^x) \tag{13.50}$$

From this, we can compute the PageRank contribution $q^U$ of any subset of nodes $U \subseteq V$ by computing the PageRank using the random jump vector $v^U$ defined as

$$v_y^U = \begin{cases} v_y \ if \ y \in U \\ 0 \ otherwise \end{cases} \tag{13.51}$$

We will now use this to compute the spam mass of a page. For a given partitioning $\{V^+, V^-\}$ of $V$ and for any node $x$, $p_x = q_x^{V^+} + q_x^{V^-}$, i.e, $x$'s PageRank is the sum of the contributions of good and that of spam nodes. The *absolute spam mass* of a node $x$, denoted by $M_x$, is the PageRank contribution that $x$ receives from spam nodes, i.e, $M_x = q_x^{V^-}$. Therefore, the spam mass is a measure of how much direct or indirect in-neighbour spam nodes increase the PageRank of a node. The *relative spam mass* of node $x$, denoted by $m_x$, is the fraction of $x$'s PageRank due to contributing spam nodes, i.e, $m_x = q_x^{V^-}/p_x$.

If we assume that only a subset of the good nodes $\tilde{V^+}$ is given, we can compute two sets of PageRanks scores. $p = PR(v)$ is the PageRank of nodes based on the uniform random jump distribution $v = (1/n)^n$, and $p' = PR(v^{\tilde{V^+}})$ is a core-based PageRank with a random jump distribution $v^{\tilde{V^+}}$

$$v_x^{\tilde{V^+}} = \begin{cases} 1/n \ if \ x \in \tilde{V^+} \\ 0 \ otherwise \end{cases} \tag{13.52}$$

Given the PageRank scores $p_x$ and $p'_x$, the estimated absolute spam mass of node $x$ is

$$\tilde{M_x} = p_x - p'_x \tag{13.53}$$

and the estimated spam mass of $x$ is

$$\tilde{m_x} = (p_x - p'_x)/p_x = 1 - p'_x/p_x \tag{13.54}$$

Instead, if $\tilde{V^-}$ is provided, the absolute spam mass can be estimated by $\hat{M} = PR(v^{\tilde{V^-}})$. When both $V^-$ and $V^+$ are known, the spam mass estimates could be derived by simply computing the average $(\tilde{M} + \hat{M})/2$.

Now, we consider the situation where the core $\tilde{V^+}$ is significantly smaller than the actual set of good nodes $V^+$, i.e, $|\tilde{V^+}| << |V^+|$ and thus $||v^{\tilde{V^+}}|| << ||v||$. Since $p = PR(v)$, $||p|| \leq ||v||$ and similarly $||p'|| \leq ||v^{\tilde{V^+}}||$. This means that $||p'|| << ||p||$, i.e, the total estimated good contribution is much smaller than the total PageRank of nodes. Therefore, we will have $||p - p'|| \approx ||p||$ with only a few nodes that have absolute mass estimates differing from their PageRank scores.

To counter this problem, we construct a uniform random sample of nodes and manually label each sample node as spam or good. This way it is possible to roughly approximate the prevalence of spam nodes on the Web. We introduce $\gamma$ to denote the fraction of nodes that we estimate that are good, so $\gamma n \approx |V^+|$. Then, we scale the core-based random jump vector $v^{\tilde{V^+}}$ to $w$, where

$$w_x = \begin{cases} \gamma/|\tilde{V^+}| \; if \; x \in \tilde{V^+} \\ 0 \; otherwise \end{cases} \tag{13.55}$$

Note that $||w|| = \gamma \approx ||v^{V^+}||$, so the two random jump vectors are of the same order of magnitude. Then, we can compute $p'$ based on $w$ and expect that $||p'|| \approx ||p^{V^+}||$, so we get a reasonable estimate of the total good contribution.

Using $w$ in computing the core-based PageRank leads to the following: as $\tilde{V^+}$ is small, the good nodes in it will receive an unusually high random jump ($\gamma/|\tilde{V^+}|$ as opposed to $1/n$). Therefore, the good PageRank contribution of these known reputable nodes will be overestimated, to the extent that occasionally for some node $y$, $p'_y$ will be larger than $p_y$. Hence, when computing $\tilde{M}$, there will be nodes with *negative spam mass*. In general, a negative mass indicates that a node is known to be good in advance (is a member of $\tilde{V^+}$) or its PageRank is heavily influenced by the contribution of nodes in the good core.

Now we can discuss the mass-based spam detection algorithm. It takes as input a good core $\tilde{V^+}$, a threshold $\tau$ to which the relative mass estimates are compared, and a PageRank threshold $\rho$. If the estimated relative mass of a node is equal to or above this $\tau$ then the node is labelled as a spam candidate. Only the relative mass estimates of nodes with PageRank scores larger than or equal to $\rho$ are verified. Nodes with PageRank less than $\rho$ are never labelled as spam candidates.

## Problems

Download the Wikipedia hyperlinks network available at
https://snap.stanford.edu/data/wiki-topcats.txt.gz.

**63** Generate the graph of the network in this dataset.

**64** Compute the PageRank, hub score and authority score for each of the nodes in the graph.

**65** Report the nodes that have the top 3 PageRank, hub and authority scores respectively.

# References


1. Agirre, Eneko, Mona Diab, Daniel Cer, and Aitor Gonzalez-Agirre. 2012. Semeval-2012 task 6: a pilot on semantic textual similarity. In *Proceedings of the first joint conference on lexical and computational semantics-volume 1: Proceedings of the main conference and the shared task, and Volume 2: Proceedings of the sixth international workshop on semantic evaluation*, 385–393. Association for Computational Linguistics.
2. Altman, Alon, and Moshe Tennenholtz. 2005. Ranking systems: the pagerank axioms. In *Proceedings of the 6th ACM conference on electronic commerce*, 1–8. ACM.
3. Arasu, Arvind, Junghoo Cho, Hector Garcia-Molina, Andreas Paepcke, and Sriram Raghavan. 2001. Searching the web. *ACM Transactions on Internet Technology (TOIT)* 1 (1): 2–43.
4. Berkhin, Pavel. 2005. A survey on pagerank computing. *Internet Mathematics* 2 (1): 73–120.
5. Bharat, Krishna, and Monika R. Henzinger. 1998. Improved algorithms for topic distillation in a hyperlinked environment. In *Proceedings of the 21st annual international ACM SIGIR conference on research and development in information retrieval*, 104–111. ACM.
6. Borodin, Allan, Gareth O. Roberts, Jeffrey S. Rosenthal, and Panayiotis Tsaparas. 2001. Finding authorities and hubs from link structures on the world wide web. In *Proceedings of the 10th international conference on World Wide Web*, 415–429. ACM.
7. Brin, Sergey, and Lawrence Page. 1998. The anatomy of a large-scale hypertextual web search engine. *Computer networks and ISDN systems* 30 (1–7): 107–117.
8. Chakrabarti, Soumen, Byron Dom, Prabhakar Raghavan, Sridhar Rajagopalan, David Gibson, and Jon Kleinberg. 1998. Automatic resource compilation by analyzing hyperlink structure and associated text. *Computer Networks and ISDN Systems* 30 (1–7): 65–74.
9. Cho, Junghoo, and Hector Garcia-Molina. 2003. Estimating frequency of change. *ACM Transactions on Internet Technology (TOIT)* 3 (3): 256–290.
10. Cohn, David, and Huan Chang. 2000. Learning to probabilistically identify authoritative documents. In *ICML*, 167–174. Citeseer.
11. Dempster, Arthur P., Nan M. Laird, and Donald B. Rubin. 1977. Maximum likelihood from incomplete data via the em algorithm. *Journal of the Royal Statistical Society. Series B (methodological)* 1–38.
12. Gyöngyi, Zoltán, Hector Garcia-Molina, and Jan Pedersen. 2004. Combating web spam with trustrank. In *Proceedings of the thirtieth international conference on very large data bases-volume 30*, 576–587. VLDB Endowment.
13. Gyongyi, Zoltan, Pavel Berkhin, Hector Garcia-Molina, and Jan Pedersen. 2006. Link spam detection based on mass estimation. In *Proceedings of the 32nd international conference on very large data bases*, 439–450. VLDB Endowment.
14. Haveliwala, Taher H. 2002. Topic-sensitive pagerank. In *Proceedings of the 11th international conference on World Wide Web*, 517–526. ACM.
15. Hirai, Jun, Sriram Raghavan, Hector Garcia-Molina, and Andreas Paepcke. 2000. Webbase: a repository of web pages. *Computer Networks* 33 (1–6): 277–293.
16. Kleinberg, Jon M. 1998. Authoritative sources in a hyperlinked environment. In *In Proceedings of the ACM-SIAM symposium on discrete algorithms*, Citeseer.
17. Lempel, Ronny, and Shlomo Moran. 2000. The stochastic approach for link-structure analysis (salsa) and the tkc effect1. *Computer Networks* 33 (1–6): 387–401.
18. MacCluer, Charles R. 2000. The many proofs and applications of perron's theorem. *Siam Review* 42 (3): 487–498.
19. Melink, Sergey, Sriram Raghavan, Beverly Yang, and Hector Garcia-Molina. 2001. Building a distributed full-text index for the web. *ACM Transactions on Information Systems (TOIS)* 19 (3): 217–241.
20. Rafiei, Davood, and Alberto O. Mendelzon. 2000. What is this page known for? computing web page reputations. *Computer Networks* 33 (1–6): 823–835.

21. Ribeiro-Neto, Berthier A., and Ramurti A. Barbosa. 1998. Query performance for tightly coupled distributed digital libraries. In *Proceedings of the third ACM conference on digital libraries*, 182–190. ACM.
22. Tomasic, Anthony, and Hector Garcia-Molina. 1993. Performance of inverted indices in shared-nothing distributed text document information retrieval systems. In *Proceedings of the second international conference on parallel and distributed information systems*, 8–17. IEEE.

# Chapter 14
# Community Detection

## 14.1 Strength of Weak Ties

As part of his Ph.D. thesis research in the late 1960s, Mark Granovetter interviewed people who had recently changed employers to learn how they discovered their new jobs [4]. He learnt that many of them learnt about the jobs through personal contacts. These personal contacts were more often than not an acquaintance rather than a close friend. Granovetter found this rather surprising because one would suppose that close friends are the most motivated in helping a person find a job, so why is it that acquaintances are actually the ones who help land the job?

The answer that Granovetter proposed links two different perspectives on acquaintanceship. One is structural, focusing on the way the connections span different portions of the full network; and the other is interpersonal, which is concerned with the local consequences that follow from the friendship. Before dwelling any further on this question, we will go over an important concept.

### *14.1.1 Triadic Closure*

The triadic closure property states that if two individuals in a social network have a mutual friend, then there is an increased likelihood that they will become friends themselves. Figure 14.1 shows a graph with vertices $A$, $B$, $C$ and $D$ with edges between $A$ and $B$, $B$ and $C$, $C$ and $D$, and $A$ and $D$. By triadic closure property, edges $A$ and $C$ will be formed because of the presence of mutual friends $B$ and $D$. Similarly, due to $A$ and $C$, an edge will exist between $B$ and $D$. These edges are depicted in Fig. 14.2.

Granovetter postulated that triadic closure was one of the most crucial reason why acquaintances are the ones to thank for a person's new job. Consider the graph in Fig. 14.3, $B$ has edges to the tightly-knit group containing $A$, $D$ and $C$, and also has



K. Raj P. M. et al., *Practical Social Network Analysis with Python*,
Computer Communications and Networks,
https://doi.org/10.1007/978-3-319-96746-2_14

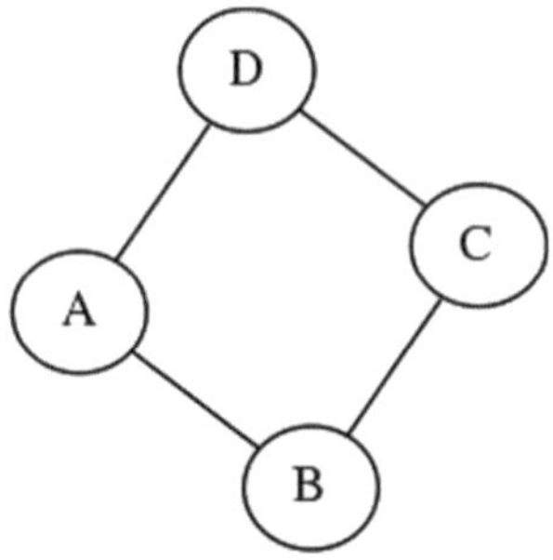


**Fig. 14.1** Undirected graph with four vertices and four edges. Vertices *A* and *C* have a mutual contacts *B* and *D*, while *B* and *D* have mutual friend *A* and *C*

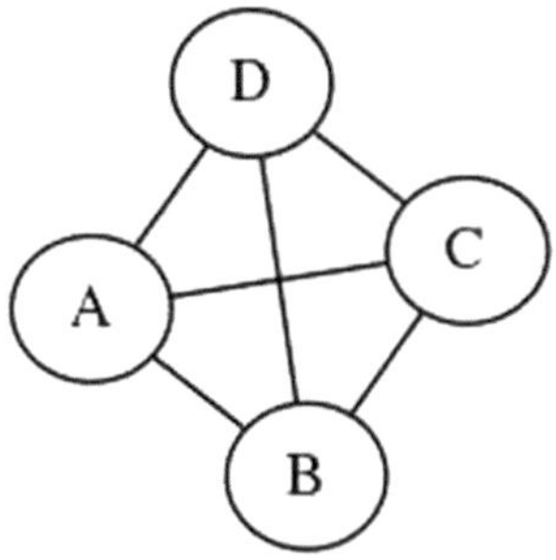


**Fig. 14.2** Figure 14.1 with an edge between *A* and *C*, and *B* and *D* due to triadic closure property

an edge to $E$. The connection of $B$ to $E$ is qualitatively different from the links to the tightly-knit group, because the opinions and information that $B$ and the group have access to are similar. The information that $E$ will provide to $B$ will be things that $B$ will not necessarily have access to.

We define an edge to be a *local bridge* is the end vertices of the edge do not have mutual friends. By this definition, the edge between $B$ and $E$ is a local bridge. Observe that local bridge and triadic closure are conceptually opposite term. While triadic closure implies an edge between vertices having mutual friends, local bridge does not form an edge between such vertices. So, Granovetter's observation was that acquaintances connected to an individual by local bridges can provide information such as job openings which the individual might otherwise not have access to because the tightly-knit group, although with greater motivation to find their buddy a job, will know roughly the same things that the individual is exposed to.

When going about edges in formal terms, acquaintanceships are considered as *weak ties* while friendships in closely-knit groups are called *strong ties*. Let us assume that we are given the strength of each tie in Fig. 14.3 (shown in Fig. 14.4). So, if a vertex $A$ has edges to both $B$ and $C$, then the $B$-$C$ edge is likely to form if $A$'s edges to $B$ and $C$ are both strong ties. This could be considered a similarity to the theory of structural balance studied in Chap. 7, where the affinity was to keep triads balanced by promoting positive edges between each pair of vertices in the triangle.

This gives us the following statement: If a node $A$ in a network satisfies the Strong Triadic Closure property and is involved in at least two strong ties, then any local bridge it is involved in must be a weak tie.

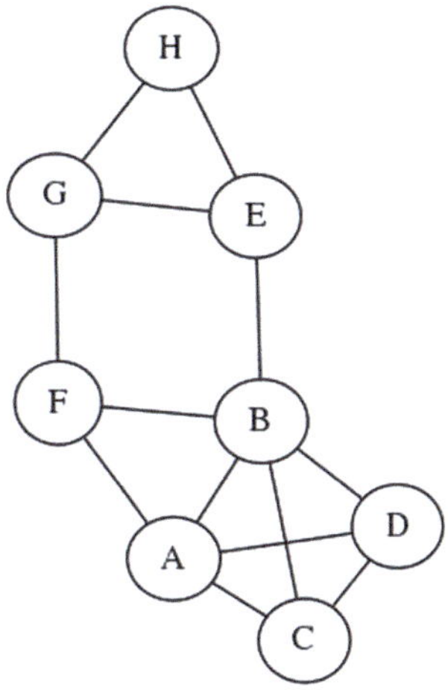


**Fig. 14.3** Graph with a local bridge between $B$ and $E$

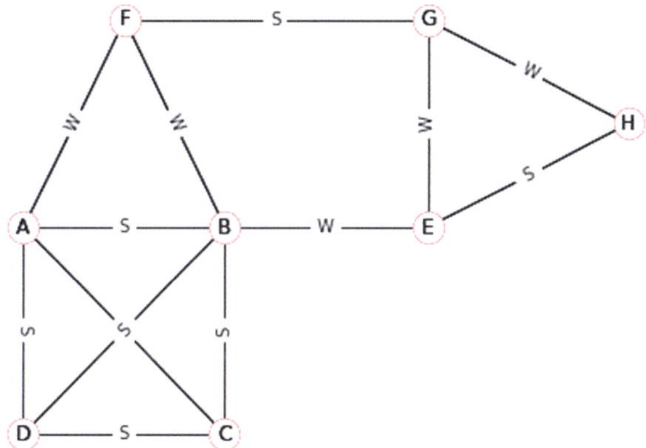


**Fig. 14.4** Each edge of the graph in Fig 14.3 is labelled either as a strong tie(S) or a weak tie(W). The labelling in the figure satisfies the Strong Triadic Closure property

Putting all of this together, we get that an edge is either a strong tie or a weak tie, and it is either a local bridge or it isn't.

The *neighbourhood overlap* of an edge connecting two nodes $A$ and $B$ is defined to be the ratio

$$\frac{number\ of\ vertices\ who\ are\ neighbours\ of\ both\ A\ and\ B}{number\ of\ vertices\ who\ are\ neighbours\ of\ at\ least\ one\ of\ A\ or\ B} \tag{14.1}$$

Consider the edge $(B, F)$ in Fig. 14.3. The denominator of the neighbourhood overlap is determined by the vertices $A$, $C$, $D$, $E$ and $G$, since they are the neighbours of either $B$ or $F$. Of these only $A$ is a neighbour of both $B$ and $F$. Therefore, the neighbourhood overlap of $(B, F)$ is $1/5$.

Similarly, the neighbourhood overlap of $(B, E)$ is zero. This is because these vertices have no neighbour in common. Therefore, we can conclude that a local bridge has zero neighbourhood overlap.

The neighbourhood overlap can be used as a quantitative way of determining the strength of an edge in the network.

## 14.2 Detecting Communities in a Network

To identify groups in a network we will first have to formulate an approach to partition the graph.

One class of methods to partition graphs is to identify and remove the "spanning" links between densely-connected regions. Once these links are removed, the graph breaks into disparate pieces. This process can be done recursively. These methods are referred to as *divisive* methods of graph partitioning.

An alternate class of methods aims at identifying nodes that are likely to belong to the same region and merge them together. This results in a large number of chunks, each of which are then merged in a bottom-up approach. Such methods are called *agglomerative* methods of graph partitioning.

One traditional method of agglomerative clustering is *hierarchical clustering*. In this technique, we first calculate the weight $W_{ij}$ for each pair $i,j$ of vertices in the network, which gives a sense of how similar these two vertices are when compared to other vertices. Then, we take the $n$ vertices in the network, with no edge between them, and add edges between pairs one after another in order of their weights, starting with the pair with the strongest weight and progressing to the weakest. As edges are added, the resulting graph shows a nested set of increasingly large components, which are taken to be the communities. Since the components are properly nested, they can all be represented using a tree called "dendrograms", in which the lowest level at which two vertices are connected represents the strength of the edge which resulted in their first becoming members of the same community. A "slice" through this tree at any level gives the communities which existed just before an edge of the corresponding weight was added.

Several different weights have been proposed for the hierarchical clustering algorithm. One possible definition of the weight is the *number of node-independent paths* between vertices. Two paths which connect the same pair of vertices are said to be node-independent if they share none of the same vertices other than their initial and final vertices. The number of node-independent paths between vertices $i$ and $j$ in a graph is equal to the minimum number of vertices that need be removed from the graph in order to disconnect $i$ and $j$ from one another. Thus this number is in a sense a measure of the robustness of the network to deletion of nodes.

Another possible way to define weights between vertices is to count the total number of paths that run between them. However, since the number of paths between any two vertices is infinite (unless it is zero), we typically weigh paths of length $l$

by a factor $\alpha^l$ with $\alpha$ small, so that the weighted count of the number of paths converges. Thus long paths contribute exponentially less weight than short ones. If $A$ is the adjacency matrix of the network, such that $A_{ij}$ is 1 if there is an edge between vertices $i$ and $j$ and 0 otherwise, then the weights in this definition are given by the elements of the matrix

$$W = \sum_{l=0}^{\infty}(\alpha A)^l = [I - \alpha A]^{-1} \tag{14.2}$$

In order for the sum to converge, we must choose $\alpha$ smaller than the reciprocal of the largest eigenvalue of $A$.

However, these definitions of weights are less successful in certain situations. For instance, if a vertex is connected to the rest of a network by only a single edge then, to the extent that it belongs to any community, it should clearly be considered to belong to the community at the other end of that edge. Unfortunately, both the numbers of node-independent paths and the weighted path counts for such vertices are small and hence single nodes often remain isolated from the network when the communities are formed.

### *14.2.1 Girvan-Newman Algorithm*

Reference [2] proposed the following method for detecting communities. The *betweenness* value of an edge is defined as the number of shortest paths between pairs of vertices that pass through it. If there is more than one shortest path between a pair of vertices, each of these paths is given equal weight such that the total weight of all the paths is unity. The intuition is that if a network contains communities or groups that are only loosely connected by a few inter-group edges, then all shortest paths between different communities must go along one of these few edges. Thus, the edges connecting communities will have high edge betweenness. By removing these edges, the groups are separated from one another and so the underlying community structure of the graph is revealed.

The algorithm for identifying communities using the edge betweenness values is called the *Girvan-Newman* algorithm and is stated as follows:

1. Calculate the betweenness values for all the edges in the network.
2. Remove the edge with the highest betweenness value.
3. Recalculate the betweenness for all edges affected by the removal.
4. Repeat from step 2 until no edges remain.

The algorithm in [5] can calculate the betweenness for all the $|E|$ edges in a graph of $|V|$ vertices in time $O(|V||E|)$. Since the calculation has to be repeated once for the removal of each edge, the entire algorithm runs in worst-case time $O(|E|^2|V|)$.

However, Girvan-Newman algorithm runs in $O(|V|^3)$ time on sparse graphs, which makes it impractical for very large graphs.

### 14.2.2 Modularity

Reference [2] proposed a measure called "modularity" and suggested that the optimization of this quality function over the possible divisions of the network is an efficient way to detect communities in a network. The modularity is, up to a multiplicative constant, the number of edges falling within groups minus the expected number in an equivalent network with edges placed at random. The modularity can be either positive or negative, with positive values indicating the possible presence of community structure. Thus, we can search for community structure precisely by looking for the divisions of a network that have positive, and preferably large, values of the modularity.

Let us suppose that all the vertices in our graph belongs to one of two groups, i.e, $s_i = 1$ if vertex $i$ belongs to group 1 and $s_i = -1$ if it belongs to group 2. Let the number of vertices between vertices $i$ and $j$ be $A_{ij}$, which will normally be 0 or 1, although larger values are possible for graphs with multiple edges. The expected number of edges between vertices $i$ and $j$ if edges are placed at random is $k_i k_j/2|E|$ where $k_i$ and $k_j$ are the degrees of vertices $i$ and $j$ respectively, and $E = \sum_i k_i/2$. The modularity $Q$ is given by the sum of $A_{ij} - k_i k_j/2|E|$ over all pairs of vertices $i$ and $j$ that fall in the same group.

Observing that the quantity $\frac{1}{2}(s_i s_j + 1)$ is 1 if $i$ and $j$ are in the same group and 0 otherwise, the modularity is formally expressed as

$$Q = \frac{1}{4|E|}\sum_{ij}\left(A_{ij} - \frac{k_i k_j}{2|E|}\right)(s_i s_j + 1) = \frac{1}{4|E|}\sum_{ij}\left(A_{ij} - \frac{k_i k_j}{2|E|}\right) s_i s_j \quad (14.3)$$

where the second equality follows from the observation that $2|E| = \sum_i k_i = \sum_{ij} A_{ij}$.

Equation 14.3 can be written in matrix form as

$$Q = \frac{1}{4|E|} s^T B s \quad (14.4)$$

where $s$ is the column vector whose elements are $s_i$ and have defined a real symmetric matrix $B$ with elements

$$B_{ij} = A_{ij} - \frac{k_i k_j}{2|E|} \quad (14.5)$$

which is called the *modularity matrix*. The elements of each of its rows and columns sum to zero, so that it always has an eigenvector $(1, 1, 1, \ldots)$ with eigenvalue zero.

Given Eq. 14.4, $s$ can be written as a linear combination of the normalized eigenvectors $u_i$ of $B$ so that $s = \sum_{i=1}^{|V|} a_i u_i$ with $a_i = u_i^T \cdot s$, we get

$$Q = \frac{1}{4|E|} \sum_i a_i u_i^T B \sum_j a_j u_j = \frac{1}{4|E|} \sum_{i=1}^{|V|} (u_i^T \cdot s)^2 \beta_i \qquad (14.6)$$

where $\beta_i$ is the eigenvalue of $B$ corresponding to eigenvector $u_i$.

Assume that the eigenvalues are labelled in decreasing order, $\beta_1 \geq \beta_2 \geq \cdots \geq \beta_{|V|}$. To maximize the modularity, we have to choose the value of $s$ that concentrates as much weight as possible in terms of the sum in Eq. 14.6 involving the largest eigenvalues. If there were no other constraints on the choice of $s$, this would be an easy task: we would simply chose $s$ proportional to the eigenvector $u_1$. This places all of the weight in the term involving the largest eigenvalue $\beta_1$, the other terms being automatically zero, because the eigenvectors are orthogonal.

There is another constraint on the problem imposed by the restriction of the elements of $s$ to the values $\pm 1$, which means $s$ cannot normally be chosen parallel to $u_1$ . To make it as close to parallel as possible, we have to maximize the dot product $u_1^T \cdot s$. It is straightforward to see that the maximum is achieved by setting $s_i = +1$ if the corresponding element of $u_1$ is positive and $s_i = -1$ otherwise. In other words, all vertices whose corresponding elements are positive go in one group and all of the rest in the other. This gives us the algorithm for dividing the network: we compute the leading eigenvector of the modularity matrix and divide the vertices into two groups according to the signs of the elements in this vector.

There are some satisfying features of this method. First, it works even though the sizes of the communities are not specified. Unlike conventional partitioning methods that minimize the number of between-group edges, there is no need to constrain the group sizes or artificially forbid the trivial solution with all vertices in a single group. There is an eigenvector $(1, 1, 1, \ldots)$ corresponding to such a trivial solution, but its eigenvalue is zero. All other eigenvectors are orthogonal to this one and hence must possess both positive and negative elements. Thus, as long as there is any positive eigenvalue this method will not put all vertices in the same group.

It is, however, possible for there to be no positive eigenvalues of the modularity matrix. In this case the leading eigenvector is the vector $(1, 1, 1, \ldots)$ corresponding to all vertices in a single group together. But this is precisely the correct result: the algorithm is in this case telling us that there is no division of the network that results in positive modularity, as can immediately be seen from Eq. 14.6, because all terms in the sum will be zero or negative. The modularity of the undivided network is zero, which is the best that can be achieved. This is an important feature of the algorithm. The algorithm has the ability not only to divide networks effectively, but also to refuse to divide them when no good division exists. The networks in this latter case will be called *indivisible*, i.e, a network is indivisible if the modularity matrix has no positive eigenvalues. This idea will play a crucial role in later developments.

The algorithm as described makes use only of the signs of the elements of the leading eigenvector, but the magnitudes convey information, too. Vertices corresponding to elements of large magnitude make large contributions to the modularity, Eq. 14.6, and conversely for small ones. Alternatively, if we take the optimal division of a network into two groups and move a vertex from one group to the other, the vector element for that vertex gives an indication of how much the modularity will decrease: vertices corresponding to elements of large magnitude cannot be moved without incurring a large modularity penalty, whereas those corresponding to smaller elements can be moved at relatively little cost. Thus, the elements of the leading eigenvector measure how firmly each vertex belongs to its assigned community, those with large vector elements being strong central members of their communities, whereas those with smaller elements are more ambivalent.

When dealing with networks that can be divided into more than two communities, we use the algorithm of the previous section first to divide the network into two parts, then divide those parts, and so forth. However, after first dividing a network in two, it is not correct to simply delete the edges falling between the two parts and then apply the algorithm again to each subgraph. This is because the degrees appearing in the definition, Eq. 14.3, of the modularity will change if edges are deleted, and any subsequent maximization of modularity would thus maximize the wrong quantity. Instead, the correct approach is to write the additional contribution $\Delta Q$ to the modularity upon further dividing a group $g$ of size $|V|_g$ in two as

$$\begin{aligned}
\Delta Q &= \frac{1}{2|E|}\left[\frac{1}{2}\sum_{i,j\in g} B_{ij}(s_i s_j + 1) - \sum_{i,j\in g} B_{ij}\right] \\
&= \frac{1}{4|E|}\left[\sum_{i,j\in g} B_{ij} s_i s_j - \sum_{i,j\in g} B_{ij}\right] \\
&= \frac{1}{4|E|}\sum_{i,j\in g}\left[B_{ij} - \delta_{ij}\sum_{k\in g} B_{ik}\right] s_i s_j \\
&= \frac{1}{4|E|} s^T B^{(g)} s
\end{aligned} \tag{14.7}$$

where $\delta_{ij}$ is the Kronecker $\delta$-symbol, $B^{(g)}$ is the $n_g \times n_g$ matrix with elements indexed by the labels $i, j$ of vertices within group $g$ and having values

$$B_{ij}^{(g)} = B_{ij} - \delta_{ij}\sum_{k\in g} B_{ik} \tag{14.8}$$

Since Eq. 14.7 has the same form as Eq. 14.4, we can now apply the spectral approach to this generalized modularity matrix, just as before, to maximize $\Delta Q$. Note that the rows and columns of $B^{(g)}$ still sum to zero and that $\Delta Q$ is correctly zero if group $g$ is undivided. Note also that for a complete network Eq. 14.8 reduces to the previous definition of the modularity matrix, Eq. 14.5, because $\sum_k B_{ik}$ is zero in that case.

In repeatedly subdividing the network, an important question we need to address is at what point to halt the subdivision process. A nice feature of this method is that it provides a clear answer to this question: if there exists no division of a subgraph that will increase the modularity of the network, or equivalently that gives a positive value for $\Delta Q$, then there is nothing to be gained by dividing the subgraph and it should be left alone; it is indivisible in the sense of the previous section. This happens when there are no positive eigenvalues to the matrix $B^{(g)}$, and thus the leading eigenvalue provides a simple check for the termination of the subdivision process: if the leading eigenvalue is zero, which is the smallest value it can take, then the subgraph is indivisible.

Note, however, that although the absence of positive eigenvalues is a sufficient condition for indivisibility, it is not a necessary one. In particular, if there are only small positive eigenvalues and large negative ones, the terms in Eq. 14.6 for negative $\beta_i$ may outweigh those for positive. It is straightforward to guard against this possibility, however; we simply calculate the modularity contribution $\Delta Q$ for each proposed split directly and confirm that it is greater than zero.

Thus the algorithm is as follows. We construct the modularity matrix, Eq. 14.5, for the network and find its leading (most positive) eigenvalue and the corresponding eigenvector. We divide the network into two parts according to the signs of the elements of this vector, and then repeat the process for each of the parts, using the generalized modularity matrix, Eq. 14.8. If at any stage we find that a proposed split makes a zero or negative contribution to the total modularity, we leave the corresponding subgraph undivided. When the entire network has been decomposed into indivisible subgraphs in this way, the algorithm ends.

An alternate method for community detection is a technique that bears a striking resemblance to the *Kernighan-Lin* algorithm. Suppose we are given some initial division of our vertices into two groups. We then find among the vertices the one that, when moved to the other group, will give the biggest increase in the modularity of the complete network, or the smallest decrease if no increase is possible. We make such moves repeatedly, with the constraint that each vertex is moved only once. When all the vertices have been moved, we search the set of intermediate states occupied by the network during the operation of the algorithm to find the state that has the greatest modularity. Starting again from this state, we repeat the entire process iteratively until no further improvement in the modularity results.

Although this method by itself only gives reasonable modularity values, the method really comes into its own when it is used in combination with the spectral method introduced earlier. The spectral approach based on the leading eigenvector of the modularity matrix gives an excellent guide to the general form that the communities should take and this general form can then be fine-tuned by the vertex moving method to reach the best possible modularity value. The whole procedure is repeated to subdivide the network until every remaining subgraph is indivisible, and no further improvement in the modularity is possible.

The most time-consuming part of the algorithm is the evaluation of the leading eigenvector of the modularity matrix. The fastest method for finding this eigenvector is the simple power method, the repeated multiplication of the matrix into a trial vector. Although it appears at first glance that matrix multiplications will be slow, taking $O(n^2)$ operations each because the modularity matrix is dense, we can in fact perform them much faster by exploiting the particular structure of the matrix. Writing $B = A - kk^T/2|E|$, where $A$ is the adjacency matrix and $k$ is the vector whose elements are the degrees of the vertices, the product of $B$ and an arbitrary vector $x$ can be written

$$Bx = Ax - \frac{k(k^T \cdot x)}{2|E|} \tag{14.9}$$

The first term is a standard sparse matrix multiplication taking time $O(|V| + |E|)$. The inner product $k^T \cdot x$ takes time $O(|V|)$ to evaluate and hence the second term can be evaluated in total time $O(|V|)$ also. Thus the complete multiplication can be performed in $O(|V| + |E|)$ time. Typically $O(|V|)$ such multiplications are needed to converge to the leading eigenvector, for a running time of $O[(|V| + |E|)|V|]$ overall. Often we are concerned with sparse graphs with $|E| \propto |V|$, in which case the running time becomes $O(|V|^2)$. It is a simple matter to extend this procedure to find the leading eigenvector of the generalized modularity matrix, Eq. 14.8, also.

Although we will not go through the details here, it is straight-forward to show that the fine-tuning stage of the algorithm can also be completed in $O[(|V| + |E|)|V|]$ time, so that the combined running time for a single split of a graph or subgraph scales as $O[(|V| + |E|)|V|]$, or $O(|V|^2)$ on a sparse graph.

We then repeat the division into two parts until the network is reduced to its component indivisible subgraphs. The running time of the entire process depends on the depth of the tree or "dendrogram" formed by these repeated divisions. In the worst case the dendrogram has depth linear in $|V|$, but only a small fraction of possible dendrograms realize this worst case. A more realistic figure for running time is given by the average depth of the dendrogram, which goes as $\log |V|$, giving an average running time for the whole algorithm of $O(|V|^2 \log |V|)$ in the sparse case. This is considerably better than the $O(|V|^3)$ running time of the betweenness algorithm, and slightly better than the $O(|V|^2 \log 2|V|)$ of the extremal optimization algorithm.

### *14.2.3 Minimum Cut Trees*

Reference [1] introduces a simple graph clustering method based on minimum cuts within the graph.

The idea behind the minimum cut clustering techniques is to create clusters that have small inter-cluster cuts and relatively large intra-cluster cuts. The clustering algorithm used in this paper is based on inserting an artificial sink into a graph that gets connected to all nodes in the network.

For a weighted graph $G(V, E)$, we define a *cut* in this graph as $(A, B)$ where $A$ and $B$ are two subsets of $V$, such that $A \cup B = V$ and $A \cap B = \phi$. The sum of the weights of the edges crossing the cut defines its value. A real function $c$ is used to represent the value of a cut, i.e, cut$(A, B)$ has value $c(A, B)$. $c$ can also be applied when $A$ and $B$ don't cover $V$, but $A \cup B \subset V$.

For this graph $G$, there exists a weighted graph $T_G$, which is called the *minimum cut tree* of $G$. This minimum cut tree has the property that the minimum cut between two vertices $s$ and $t$ in $G$ can be found by inspecting the path that connects $s$ and $t$ in $T_G$. The edge of minimum capacity on that path corresponds to the minimum cut. The capacity of the edge is equal to the minimum cut value, and its removal yields two sets of nodes in $T_G$, and also in $G$ corresponding to the two sides of the cut. Reference [3] provides algorithms for computing minimum cut trees.

Let $(S, \overline{S})$ be a cut in $G$. The *expansion* of the cut is defined as

$$\psi(S) = \frac{\sum\limits_{u \in S, v \in \overline{S}} w(u, v)}{min\{|S|, |\overline{S}|\}} \tag{14.10}$$

where $w(u, v)$ is the weight of the edge $(u, v)$. The expansion of a (sub)graph is the minimum expansion over all the cuts of the (sub)graph. The expansion of a clustering of $G$ is the minimum expansion over all its clusters. The larger the expansion of the clustering, the higher its quality.

The *conductance* for the cut $(S, \overline{S})$ is defined as

$$\phi(S) = \frac{\sum\limits_{u \in S, v \in \overline{S}} w(u, v)}{min\{c(S), c(\overline{S})\}} \tag{14.11}$$

where $c(S) = c(S, V) = \sum\limits_{u \in S} \sum\limits_{v \in V} w(u, v)$. The conductance of a graph is the minimum conductance over all the cuts of the graph. For a clustering of $G$, let $C \subseteq V$ be a cluster and $(S, C - S)$ a cluster within $C$, where $S \subseteq C$. The conductance of $S$ in $C$ is

$$\phi(S, C) = \frac{\sum\limits_{u \in S, v \in C - S} w(u, v)}{min\{c(S), c(C - S)\}} \tag{14.12}$$

The conductance of a cluster $\phi(C)$ is the smallest conductance of a cut within the cluster; for a clustering, the conductance is the minimum conductance of its clusters.

The main difference between expansion and conductance is that expansion treats all nodes as equally important while the conductance gives greater importance to nodes with higher degree and adjacent edge weight.

However, both expansion and conductance are insufficient by themselves as clustering criteria because neither enforces qualities pertaining to inter-cluster weight, nor the relative size of clusters. Moreover, these are both NP-hard and require approximations.

The paper present a *cut clustering algorithm*. Let $G(V, E)$ be a graph and let $s, t \in V$ be two nodes of $G$. Let $(S, T)$ be the minimum cut between $s$ and $t$, where $s \in S$ and $t \in T$. $S$ is defined to be the *community* of $s$ in $G$ w.r.t $t$. If the minimum cut between $s$ and $t$ is not unique, we choose the minimum cut that maximises the size of $S$.

The paper provides proofs for the following theorems.

Here, a community $S$ is defined as a collection of nodes that has the property that all nodes of the community predominantly links to other community nodes.

- **Theorem 34** *For an undirected graph $G(V, E)$, let $S$ be a community of $s$ w.r.t $t$. Then*
$$\sum_{v \in S} w(u, v) > \sum_{v \in \overline{S}} w(u, v), \forall u \in S - \{s\} \tag{14.13}$$

- **Theorem 35** *Let $G(V, E)$ be a graph and $k > 1$ an integer. The problem of partitioning $G$ into $k$ communities is NP-complete.*

When no $t$ is given, an artificial node $t$ called the *artificial sink* is introduced. The artificial sink is connected to all nodes of $G$ via an undirected edge of capacity $\alpha$.

- **Theorem 36** *Let $G(V, E)$ be an undirected graph, $s \in V$ a source, and connect an artificial sink $t$ with edges of capacity $\alpha$ to all nodes. Let $S$ be the community of $s$ w.r.t $t$. For any non-empty $P$ and $Q$, such that $P \cup Q = S$ and $P \cap Q = \phi$, the following bounds always hold:*
$$\frac{c(S, V - S)}{|V - S|} \leq \alpha \leq \frac{c(P, Q)}{min(|P|, |Q|)} \tag{14.14}$$

- **Theorem 37** *Let $s, t \in V$ be two nodes of $G$ and let $S$ be the community of $s$ w.r.t $t$. Then, there exists a minimum cut tree $T_G$ of $G$, and an edge $(a, b) \in T_G$, such that the removal of $(a, b)$ yields $S$ and $V - S$.*
- **Theorem 38** *Let $T_G$ be a minimum cut tree of a graph $G(V, E)$, and let $(u, w)$ be an edge of $T_G$. Edge $(u, w)$ yields the cut $(U, W)$ in $G$, with $u \in U$, $w \in W$. Now, take any cut $(U_1, U_2)$ of $U$, so that $U_1$ and $U_2$ are non-empty, $u \in U_1$, $U_1 \cup U_2 = U$, and $U_1 \cap U_2 = \phi$. Then,*
$$c(W, U_2) \leq c(U_1, U_2) \tag{14.15}$$

- **Theorem 39** *Let $G_\alpha$ be the expanded graph of $G$, and let $S$ be the community of $s$ w.r.t the artificial sink $t$. For any non-empty $P$ and $Q$, such that $P \cup Q = S$ and $P \cap Q = \phi$, the following bound always holds:*
$$\alpha \leq \frac{c(P, Q)}{min(|P|, |Q|)} \tag{14.16}$$

- **Theorem 40** *Let $G_\alpha$ be the expanded graph of $G(V, E)$ and let $S$ be the community of $s$ w.r.t the artificial sink $t$. Then, the following bound always holds:*

$$\frac{c(S, V - S)}{|V - S|} \leq \alpha \tag{14.17}$$

The cut clustering algorithm is as given in Algorithm 8

**Algorithm 8** Cut clustering algorithm

```
procedure CUTCLUSTERINGALGORITHM(G(V, E), α)
    Let V' = V ∪ t
    for all nodes v ∈ V do
        Connect t to v with edge of weight α
    end for
    Let G'(V', E') be the expanded graph after connecting t to V
    Calculate the minimum-cut tree T' of G'
    Remove t from T'
    Return all connected components as the clusters of G
end procedure
```

- **Theorem 41** *For a source $s$ in $G_{\alpha_i}$, where $\alpha_i \in \{\alpha_1, \ldots, \alpha_{max}\}$, such that $\alpha_1 < \alpha_2 < \cdots < \alpha_{max}$, the communities $S_1, \ldots, S_{max}$ are such that $S_1 \subseteq S_2 \subseteq \cdots \subseteq S_{max}$, where $S_i$ is the community of $s$ w.r.t $t$ in $G_{\alpha_i}$.*
- **Theorem 42** *Let $v_1, v_2 \in V$ and $S_1, S_2$ be their communities w.r.t $t$ in $G_\alpha$. Then either $S_1$ and $S_2$ are disjoint or the one is a subset of the other.*
- **Theorem 43** *Let $\alpha_1 > \alpha_2 > \cdots > \alpha_{max}$ be a sequence of parameter values that connect $t$ to $V$ in $G_{\alpha_i}$. Let $\alpha_{max+1} \leq \alpha_{max}$ be small enough to yield a single cluster in $G$ and $\alpha_0 \geq \alpha_1$ be large enough to yield all singletons. Then all $\alpha_{i+1}$ values, for $0 \leq i \leq max$, yield clusters in $G$ which are supersets of the clusters produced by each $\alpha_i$, and all clusterings together form a hierarchical tree over the clusterings of $G$.*

## 14.3 Tie Strengths in Mobile Communication Network

Reference [6] examined the communication patterns of millions of mobile phone users and found that social networks are robust to the removal of the strong ties but fall apart after a phase transition if the weak ties are removed.

A significant portion of a country's communication network was reconstructed from 18 weeks of all mobile phone call records among ≈20% of the country's entire population, 90% of whose inhabitants had a mobile phone subscription. To translate this phone log data into a network representation that captures the characteristics of the underlying communication network, the two users were connected with an undirected link if there had been at least one reciprocated pair of phone calls between them and the *strength*, $w_{AB} = w_{BA}$, of a tie is defined as the aggregated duration of calls between users $A$ and $B$. The resulting *mobile call graph* (MCG) contains 4.6 million nodes and 7 million links, 84.1% of which belonged to a giant component.

Figure 14.5a shows that the MCG has a skewed degree distribution with a long tail, indicating that although most users communicate with only a few individuals, a small minority talks with dozens. If the tail is approximated by a power law, which appears to fit the data better than an exponential distribution, the obtained exponent $\gamma_k = 8.4$. Figure 14.5b indicates that the tie strength distribution is broad but decaying with exponent $\gamma_w = 1.9$, so that although the majority of ties correspond to a few minutes of airtime, a small fraction of users spend hours chatting with each other. Figure 14.5c measures the relative topological overlap of the neighbourhood of two users $v_i$ and $v_j$, representing the proportion of their common friends $O_{ij} = n_{ij}/((k_i - 1) + (k_j - 1) - n_{ij})$, where $n_{ij}$ is the number of common neighbours of $v_i$ and $v_j$, and $k_i(k_j)$ denotes the degree of node $v_i(v_j)$. If $v_i$ and $v_j$ have no common acquaintances, then we have $O_{ij} = 0$, the link between $i$ and $j$ representing potential bridges between two different communities. If $i$ and $j$ are part of the same circle of friends, then $O_{ij} = 1$. Figure 14.5d shows that permuting randomly the tie strengths between links results in $O_{ij}$ that is independent of $w_{ij}$.

Figure 14.6a depicts the network in the vicinity of a randomly selected individual, where the link colour corresponds to the strength of each tie. We observe from the figure that the network consists of clusters, typically grouped around a high degree individual. The majority of strong ties are found within the clusters, indicating that users spend most of their on-air time talking to members of their immediate circle of friends. On the contrary, most links connecting different communities are visibly weaker than the links within communities. Figure 14.6b shows that when the link strengths among the connected user pairs are randomly permuted, more weak ties are found to connect vertices within communities and more strong ties connect distant communities. Figure 14.6c shows what it would look like if, inter-community ties were strong and intra-community ties were weak.

Figures 14.5 and 14.6 suggest that instead of tie strength being determined by the characteristics of the individuals it connects or by the network topology, it is determined solely by the network structure in the tie's immediate vicinity.

To evaluate this suggestion, we explore the network's ability to withstand the removal of either strong or weak ties. For this, we measure the relative size of the giant component $R_{gc}(f)$, providing the fraction of nodes that can all reach each other through connected paths as a function of the fraction of removed links, $f$. Figure 14.7a, b shows that removing in rank order the weakest (or smallest overlap) to strongest (or greatest overlap) ties leads to the network's sudden disintegration at $f^w = 0.8(f^O = 0.6)$. However, removing first the strongest ties will shrink the network but will not rapidly break it apart. The precise point at which the network disintegrates can be determined by monitoring $\tilde{S} = \sum_{s<s_{max}} n_s s^2/N$, where $n_s$ is the number of clusters containing $s$ nodes. Figure 14.7c, d shows that $\tilde{S}$ develops a peak if we start with the weakest links. Finite size scaling, a well established technique

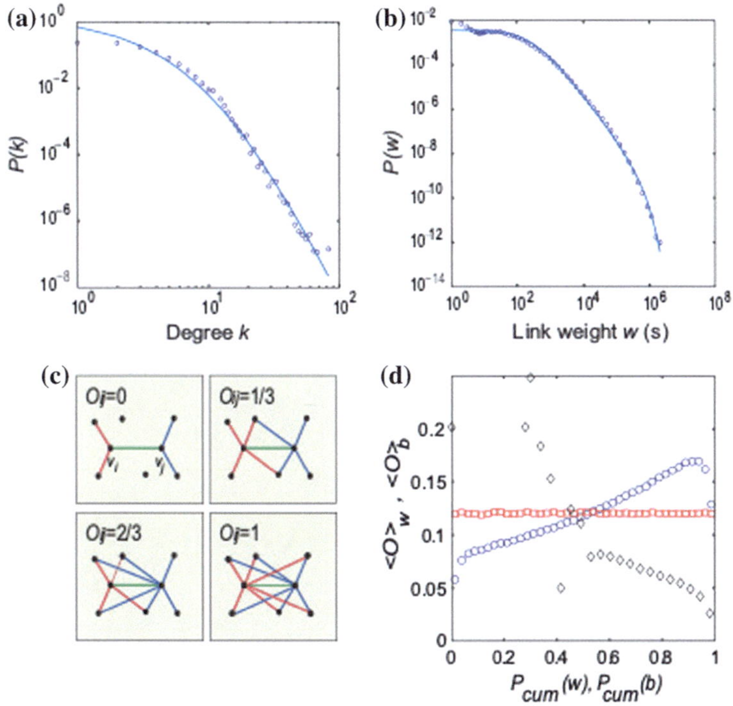


**Fig. 14.5** **a** Degree distribution. **b** Tie strength distribution. The blue line in **a** and **b** correspond to $P(x) = a(x + x_0)^{-x} exp(-x/x_c)$, where $x$ corresponds to either $k$ or $w$. The parameter values for the fits in (A) are $k_0 = 10.9$, $\gamma_k = 8.4$, $k_c = \infty$, and for the fits in (B) are $w_0 = 280$, $\gamma_w = 1.9$, $w_c = 3.45 \times 10.5$. **c** Illustration of the overlap between two nodes, $v_i$ and $v_j$, its value being shown for four local network configurations. **d** In the real network, the overlap $< O >_w$ (blue circles) increases as a function of cumulative tie strength $P_{cum}(w)$, representing the fraction of links with tie strength smaller than $w$. The dyadic hypothesis is tested by randomly permuting the weights, which removes the coupling between $< O >_w$ and $w$ (red squares). The overlap $< O >_b$ decreases as a function of cumulative link betweenness centrality $b$ (black diamonds)

for identifying the phase transition, indicates that the values of the critical points are $f_c^O(\infty) = 0.62 \pm 0.05$ and $f_c^w(\infty) = 0.80 \pm 0.04$ for the removal of the weak ties, but there is no phase transition when the strong ties are removed first.

This finding gives us the following conclusion: Given that the strong ties are predominantly within the communities, their removal will only locally disintegrate a community but not affect the network's overall integrity. In contrast, the removal of the weak links will delete the bridges that connect different communities, leading to a phase transition driven network collapse.

To see whether this observation affects global information diffusion, at time 0 a randomly selected individual is infected with some novel information. It is assumed that at each time step, each infected individual, $v_i$, can pass the information to his/her contact, $v_j$, with effective probability $P_{ij} = xw_{ij}$, where the parameter $x$ controls

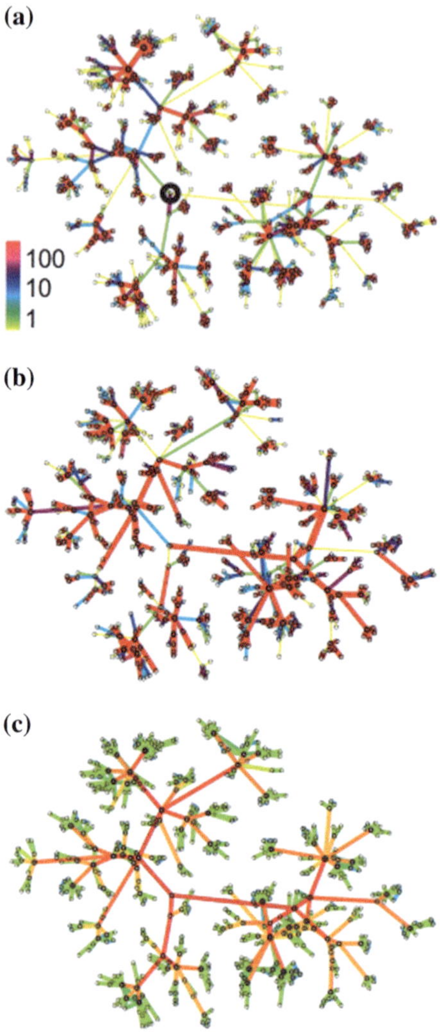


**Fig. 14.6** Each link represents mutual calls between the two users, and all nodes are shown that are at distance less than six from the selected user, marked by a circle in the center. **a** The real tie strengths, observed in the call logs, defined as the aggregate call duration in minutes. **b** The dyadic hypothesis suggests that the tie strength depends only on the relationship between the two individuals. To illustrate the tie strength distribution in this case, we randomly permuted tie strengths for the sample in **a**. **c** The weight of the links assigned on the basis of their betweenness centrality $b_{ij}$ values for the sample in $A$ as suggested by the global efficiency principle. In this case, the links connecting communities have high $b_{ij}$ values (red), whereas the links within the communities have low $b_{ij}$ values (green)

the overall spreading rate. Therefore, the more time two individuals spend on the phone, the higher the chance that they will pass on the monitored information. The spreading mechanism is similar to the susceptible-infected model of epidemiology in which recovery is not possible, i.e., an infected individual will continue transmitting information indefinitely. As a control, the authors considered spreading on the same network, but replaced all tie strengths with their average value, resulting in a constant transmission probability for all links.

Figure 14.8a shows the real diffusion simulation, where it was found that information transfer is significantly faster on the network for which all weights are equal, the difference being rooted in a dynamic trapping of information in communities. Such

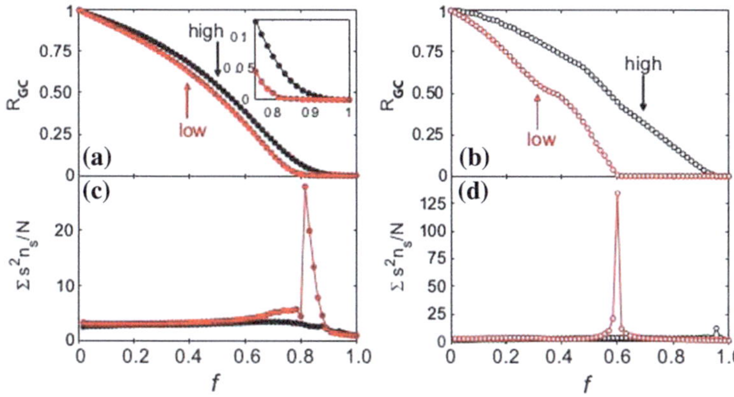


**Fig. 14.7** The control parameter $f$ denotes the fraction of removed links. **a** and **c** These graphs correspond to the case in which the links are removed on the basis of their strengths ($w_{ij}$ removal). **b** and **d** These graphs correspond to the case in which the links were removed on the basis of their overlap ($O_{ij}$ removal). The black curves correspond to removing first the high-strength (or high $O_{ij}$) links, moving toward the weaker ones, whereas the red curves represent the opposite, starting with the low-strength (or low $O_{ij}$) ties and moving toward the stronger ones. **a** and **b** The relative size of the largest component $R_{GC}(f) = N_{GC}(f)/N_{GC}(f = 0)$ indicates that the removal of the low $w_{ij}$ or $O_{ij}$ links leads to a breakdown of the network, whereas the removal of the high $w_{ij}$ or $O_{ij}$ links leads only to the network's gradual shrinkage. **a** Inset Shown is the blowup of the high $w_{ij}$ region, indicating that when the low $w_{ij}$ ties are removed first, the red curve goes to zero at a finite $f$ value. **c** and **d** According to percolation theory, $\tilde{S} = \sum_{s<s_{max}} n_s s^2/N$ diverges for $N \rightarrow \infty$ as we approach the critical threshold $f_c$, where the network falls apart. If we start link removal from links with low $w_{ij}$ (**c**) or $O_{ij}$ (**d**) values, we observe a clear signature of divergence. In contrast, if we start with high $w_{ij}$ (**c**) or $O_{ij}$ (**d**) links, there the divergence is absent

trapping is clearly visible if the number of infected individuals in the early stages of the diffusion process is monitored (as shown in Fig. 14.8b). Indeed, rapid diffusion within a single community was observed, corresponding to fast increases in the number of infected users, followed by plateaus, corresponding to time intervals during which no new nodes are infected before the news escapes the community. When all link weights are replaced with an average value $w$ (the control diffusion simulation) the bridges between communities are strengthened, and the spreading becomes a predominantly global process, rapidly reaching all nodes through a hierarchy of hubs.

The dramatic difference between the real and the control spreading process begs the following question: Where do individuals get their information? Figure 14.8c shows that the distribution of the tie strengths through which each individual was first infected has a prominent peak at $w \approx 10^2$ s, indicating that, in the vast majority of cases, an individual learns about the news through ties of intermediate strength. The distribution changes dramatically in the control case, however, when all tie strengths are taken to be equal during the spreading process. In this case, the majority of infections take place along the ties that are otherwise weak (as depicted in Fig. 14.8d). Therefore, both weak and strong ties have a relatively insignificant role as conduits for information, the former because the small amount of on-air time offers little chance of information transfer and the latter because they are mostly confined within communities, with little access to new information.

To illustrate the difference between the real and the control simulation, Fig. 14.8e, f show the spread of information in a small neighbourhood. First, the overall direction of information flow is systematically different in the two cases, as indicated by the large shaded arrows. In the control runs, the information mainly follows the shortest paths. When the weights are taken into account, however, information flows along a strong tie backbone, and large regions of the network, connected to the rest of the network by weak ties, are only rarely infected.

## Problems

The *betweenness centrality* of an edge $(u, v) \in E$ in $G(V, E)$ is given by Eq. 14.18.

$$B(u, v) = \sum_{(s,t)\in V^2} \frac{\sigma_{st}(u, v)}{\sigma_{st}} \tag{14.18}$$

where $\sigma_{st}$ is the number of shortest paths between $s$ and $t$, and $\sigma_{st}(u, v)$ is the number of shortest paths between $s$ and $t$ that contain the edge $(u, v)$. This is assuming that the graph $G$ is connected.

The betweenness centrality can be computed in the following manners.

## 14.4 Exact Betweenness Centrality

For each vertex $s \in V$, perform a BFS from $s$, which gives the BFS tree $T_s$. For each $v \in V$, let $v$'s *parent set* $P_s(v)$ be defined as the set of nodes $u \in V$ that immediately precede $v$ on some shortest path from $s$ to $v$ in $G$. During the BFS, compute, for every $v \in V$, the number $\sigma_{sv}$ of shortest paths between $s$ and $v$, according to recurrence

$$\sigma_{sv} = \begin{cases} 1 & \text{if } v = s \\ \sum\limits_{u\in P_s(v)} \sigma_{su} & \text{otherwise} \end{cases} \tag{14.19}$$

After the BFS is finished, compute the *dependency* of $s$ on each edge $(u, v) \in E$ using the recurrence

$$\delta_s(u, v) = \begin{cases} \frac{\sigma_{su}}{\sigma_{sv}} & \text{if } v \text{ is a leaf of } T_s \\ \frac{\sigma_{su}}{\sigma_{sv}}(1 + \sum\limits_{x:w\in P_s(x)} \delta_s(w, x)) & \text{otherwise} \end{cases} \tag{14.20}$$

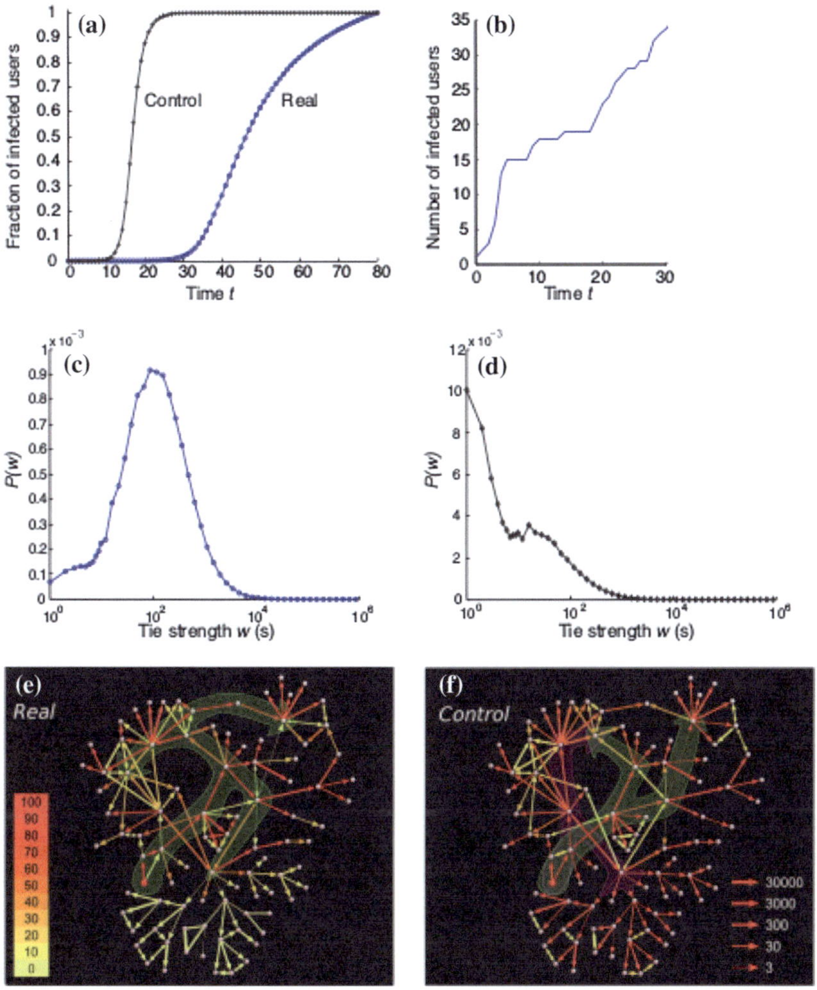


**Fig. 14.8** The dynamics of spreading on the weighted mobile call graph, assuming that the probability for a node $v_i$ to pass on the information to its neighbour $v_j$ in one time step is given by $P_{ij} = xw_{ij}$, with $x = 2.59 \times 10^{-4}$. **a** The fraction of infected nodes as a function of time $t$. The blue curve (circles) corresponds to spreading on the network with the real tie strengths, whereas the black curve (asterisks) represents the control simulation, in which all tie strengths are considered equal. **b** Number of infected nodes as a function of time for a single realization of the spreading process. Each steep part of the curve corresponds to invading a small community. The flatter part indicates that the spreading becomes trapped within the community. **c** and **d** Distribution of strengths of the links responsible for the first infection for a node in the real network (**c**) and control simulation (**d**). **e** and **f** Spreading in a small neighbourhood in the simulation using the real weights (E) or the control case, in which all weights are taken to be equal (**f**). The infection in all cases was released from the node marked in red, and the empirically observed tie strength is shown as the thickness of the arrows (right-hand scale). The simulation was repeated 1,000 times; the size of the arrowheads is proportional to the number of times that information was passed in the given direction, and the colour indicates the total number of transmissions on that link (the numbers in the colour scale refer to percentages of 1, 000). The contours are guides to the eye, illustrating the difference in the information direction flow in the two simulations

Since the $\delta$ values are only really defined for edges that connect two nodes, $u$ and $v$, where $u$ is further away from $s$ than $v$, assume that $\delta$ is 0 for cases that are undefined (i.e., where an edge connects two nodes that are equidistant from $s$).

Do not iterate over all edges when computing the dependency values. It makes more sense to just look at edges that are in some BFS tree starting from $s$, since other edges will have zero dependency values (they are not on any shortest paths). (Though iterating over all edges is not technically wrong if you just set the dependency values to 0 when the nodes are equidistant from $s$.)

The betweenness centrality of $(u, v)$ or $B(u, v)$ is

$$B(u, v) = \sum_{s \in V} \delta_s(u, v) \tag{14.21}$$

This algorithm has a time complexity of $O(|V||E|)$. However, the algorithm requires the computation of the betweenness centrality of all edges even if only the values in some edges are to required to be computed.

## 14.5 Approximate Betweenness Centrality

This is an approximation of the previous algorithm with the difference that it does not start a BFS from every node but rather samples starting nodes randomly with replacement. Also, it can approximate betweenness for any edge $e \in E$ without necessarily having to compute the centrality of all other edges as well.

Repeatedly sample a vertex $v_i \in V$ and perform a BFS from $v_i$ and maintain a running sum $\Delta_e$ of the dependency scores $\delta_{v_i}(e)$ (one $\Delta_e$ for each edge $e$ of interest). Sample until $\Delta_e$ is greater than $cn$ for some constant $c \geq 2$. Let the total number of samples be $k$. The estimated betweenness centrality score of $e$ is given by $\frac{n}{k}\Delta_e$.

In this exercise, do the following:

**66** Generate a preferential attachment model on 1000 nodes and degree of 4.

**67** Implement the exact betweenness centrality algorithm and compute the values for all edges $e \in E$.

**68** Implement the approximate betweenness centrality algorithm and compute the values for all edges $e \in E$. Use $c = 5$ and sample at most $\frac{|V|}{10}$ random starting nodes $v_i$.

**69** Each algorithm induces an ordering over edges with respect to betweenness centrality. Plot one curve for the exact betweenness centrality algorithm and one for the approximate betweenness centrality algorithm, overlaid in the same plot. If the edge with the $x$th largest betweenness centrality (according to the respective algorithm) has betweenness centrality $y$, draw a dot with co-ordinates $(x, y)$. Use a logarithmic $y$-axis.

## References

1. Flake, Gary William, Robert E. Tarjan, and Kostas Tsioutsiouliklis. 2002. Clustering methods based on minimum-cut trees. Technical report, technical report 2002–06, NEC, Princeton, NJ.
2. Girvan, Michelle, and Mark E.J. Newman. 2002. Community structure in social and biological networks. *Proceedings of the National Academy of Sciences* 99 (12): 7821–7826.
3. Gomory, Ralph E., and Tien Chung Hu. 1961. Multi-terminal network flows. *Journal of the Society for Industrial and Applied Mathematics* 9 (4): 551–570.
4. Granovetter, Mark S. 1977. The strength of weak ties. In *Social networks*, 347–367. Elsevier.
5. Newman, Mark E.J. 2011. Scientific collaboration networks. II. Shortest paths, weighted networks, and centrality. *Physical Review E* 64 (1): 016132.
6. Onnela, J.-P., Jari Saramäki, Jorkki Hyvönen, György Szabó, David Lazer, Kimmo Kaski, János Kertész, and A.-L. Barabási. 2007. Structure and tie strengths in mobile communication networks. *Proceedings of the National Academy of Sciences* 104 (18): 7332–7336.

# Chapter 15
# Representation Learning on Graphs

Machine learning on social network applications is now ubiquitous with tasks ranging from recommendation networks to spam detection. These applications have traditionally relied on hand-engineered heuristics to extract features from the graph to exploit machine learning models. However, recent developments in the field of deep learning have led to advancements in representation learning which automatically encode the graph structure into low-dimensional embeddings.

Reference [15] provides a brief review of the representation learning techniques that can embed individual nodes as well as subgraphs.

The major problem of applying traditional machine learning techniques to graphs is finding a way to incorporate the information about the structure of the graph into the machine learning model. For instance, in the case of link prediction in a social network, one has to first encode the pairwise properties between nodes such as the strength of relationships or number of common friends. However, there is no straightforward approach to encode this information into a feature vector. This means that to extract these vectors, the vectors depend on hand-engineered features which are inflexible because they cannot adapt during the learning process, and can be time-consuming and expensive to design.

This is where representation learning approaches are an advantage. They seek to learn representations that encode structural information about the graph by learning a mapping that embeds nodes, or entire subgraphs, as points in a low-dimensional vector space, $\mathbb{R}^d$. The goal is to optimize this mapping so that geometric relationships in this learned space reflect the structure of the original graph. After optimizing the embedding space, the learned embeddings can be used as feature inputs for machine learning tasks. The key distinction between these representation learning approaches and hand-engineering tasks is how they deal with the problem of capturing structural information about the graph. Hand-engineering techniques deal with this problem as a pre-processing step, while representation learning approaches treat it as a machine learning task in itself, using a data-driven approach to learn embeddings that encode graph structure.



K. Raj P. M. et al., *Practical Social Network Analysis with Python*,
Computer Communications and Networks,
https://doi.org/10.1007/978-3-319-96746-2_15

We assume that the representation learning algorithm takes as input an undirected graph $G = (V, E)$, its corresponding binary adjacency matrix $A$ and a real-valued matrix of node attributes $X \in \mathbb{R}^{m \times |V|}$. The goal is to use this information contained in $A$ and $X$ to map each node, or subgraph, to a vector $z \in \mathbb{R}^d$, where $d << |V|$.

There are two perspectives to consider before deciding how to optimize this mapping. First is the purview of *unsupervised learning* where only the information in $A$ and $X$ are considered without accounting for the downstream machine learning task. Second is the arena of *supervised learning* where the embeddings are considered as regression and classification tasks.

## 15.1 Node Embedding

In node embedding, the goal is to encode nodes as low-dimensional vectors that summarize their graph position and the structure of their local graph neighbourhood. These low-dimensional embeddings can be viewed as encoding, or projections of nodes into a latent space, where geometric relations in this latent space correspond to connections in the original graph.

First, we will look at the *encoder-decoder* framework which consists of two main mapping functions: an *encoder*, which maps each node to a low-dimensional vector or embedding, and a *decoder*, which decodes structural information about the graph from these learned embeddings. The idea behind this framework is that if we can learn to decode high-dimensional graph information from the encoded low-dimensional embeddings, then these embeddings should be sufficient for the downstream machine learning tasks.

Formally, the encoder is a function

$$ENC : V \rightarrow \mathbb{R}^d \tag{15.1}$$

that maps nodes to vector embeddings, $z_i \in \mathbb{R}^d$ (where $z_i$ corresponds to the embedding vector for the node $v_i \in V$).

A decoder must accept a set of node embeddings as input and decode user-specified graph statistics from these embeddings. Although there are several ways to accomplish this task, one of the most commonly used is a basic *pairwise decoder*

$$DEC : \mathbb{R}^d \times \mathbb{R}^d \rightarrow \mathbb{R}^+ \tag{15.2}$$

that maps pairs of node embeddings to a real-valued graph proximity measure, which quantifies the proximity of the two nodes in the original graph.

When we apply the pairwise decoder to a pair of embeddings $(z_i, z_j)$ we get a reconstruction of the proximity between $v_i$ and $v_j$ in the original graph, and the goal is to optimize the encoder and decoder mappings to minimize the error, or loss, in this reconstruction so that:

$$DEC(ENC(v_i), ENC(v_j)) = DEC(z_i, z_j) \approx s_G(v_i, v_j) \tag{15.3}$$

where $s_G$ is a user-defined, graph-based proximity measure between nodes, defined over $G$.

Most approaches realize the reconstruction objective (Eq. 15.3) by minimizing an empirical loss, $\mathcal{L}$, over a set of training node pairs, $\mathcal{D}$

$$\mathcal{L} = \sum_{(v_i, v_j) \in \mathcal{D}} l(DEC(z_i, z_j), s_G(v_i, v_j)). \tag{15.4}$$

where $l : \mathbb{R} \times \mathbb{R} \to \mathbb{R}$ is a user-specified loss function, which measures the discrepancy between the decoded proximity values, $DEC(z_i, z_j)$, and the true values, $s_G(v_i, v_j)$.

Once the encoder-decoder system has been optimised, we can use the trained encoder to generate embeddings for nodes, which can then be used as a feature inputs for downstream machine learning tasks.

### 15.1.1 Direct Encoding

In this direct encoding approach, the encoder function is simply an embedding lookup:

$$ENC(v_i) = Zv_i \tag{15.5}$$

where $Z \in \mathbb{R}^{d \times |V|}$ is a matrix containing the embedding vectors for all nodes and $v_i \in \mathbb{I}_V$ is a one-hot indicator vector indicating the column of $Z$ corresponding to node $v_i$. The set of trainable parameters for direct encoding methods is simply $\Theta_{ENC} = \{Z\}$, i.e. the embedding matrix $Z$ is optimized directly.

### 15.1.2 Factorization-Based Approaches

Early methods for learning representations for nodes largely focused on matrix-factorization approaches, which are directly inspired by classic techniques for dimensionality reduction.

#### 15.1.2.1 Laplacian Eigenmaps

This technique can be viewed as a direct encoding approach in which the decoder is defined as

$$DEC(z_i, z_j) = ||z_i - z_j||_2^2 \tag{15.6}$$

and the loss function weights pairs of nodes according to their proximity in the graph

$$\mathcal{L} = \sum_{(v_i, v_j) \in \mathcal{D}} DEC(z_i, z_j) \cdot s_G(v_i, v_j) \tag{15.7}$$

#### 15.1.2.2 Inner-Product Methods

There are a large number of embedding methodologies based on a pairwise, inner-product decoder

$$DEC(z_i, z_j) = z_i^T z_j \tag{15.8}$$

where the strength of the relationship between two nodes is proportional to the dot product of their embeddings. This decoder is commonly paired with the mean-squared-error (MSE) loss

$$\mathcal{L} = \sum_{(v_i, v_j) \in \mathcal{D}} ||DEC(z_i, z_j) - s_G(v_i, v_j)||_2^2 \tag{15.9}$$

Graph Factorization (GF) algorithm [1], GraRep [4], and HOPE [22] fall under this category. These algorithms share the same decoder function as well as the loss function, but differ in the proximity measure. The GF algorithm defines proximity measure directly based on the adjacency matrix, i.e, $s_G(v_i, v_j) \triangleq A_{i,j}$. GraRep uses higher-order adjacency matrix as a definition of the proximity measure, (e.g., $s_G(v_i, v_j) \triangleq A^2_{i,j}$. The HOPE algorithm supports general proximity measures.

These methods are generally referred to as matrix-factorization approaches because, averaging across all nodes, they optimize loss function of the form:

$$\mathcal{L} = ||Z^T Z - S||_2^2 \tag{15.10}$$

where $S$ is a matrix containing pairwise proximity measures (i.e., $S_{i,j} \triangleq s_G(v_i, v_j)$) and $Z$ is the matrix of node embeddings. Intuitively, the goal of these methods is simply to learn embeddings for each node such that the inner product between the learned embedding vectors approximates some deterministic measure of graph proximity.

### *15.1.3 Random Walk Approaches*

In this method, the node embeddings are learnt from random walks statistics. The idea is to optimize the node embeddings so that nodes have similar embeddings if they tend to co-occur on short random walks over the graph. Thus, instead of using a deterministic measure of graph proximity, these random walk methods employ a flexible, stochastic measure of graph proximity.

#### 15.1.3.1 DeepWalk and node2vec

DeepWalk [23] and node2vec [13] rely on direct encoding and use a decoder based on the inner product. However, instead of trying to decode a fixed deterministic distance measure, these approaches optimize embeddings to encode the statistics of random walks. The idea behind these approaches is to learn embeddings so that:

$$DEC(z_i, z_j) \triangleq \frac{e^{z_i^T z_j}}{\sum\limits_{v_k \in V} e^{z_i^T z_k}} \approx p_{G,T}(v_j|v_i) \tag{15.11}$$

where $p_{G,T}(v_j|v_i)$ is the probability of visiting $v_j$ on a length-$T$ random walk starting at $v_i$, with $T$ usually defined to be in the range $T \in \{2, \ldots, 10\}$. $p_{G,T}(v_j|v_i)$ is both stochastic and symmetric.

More formally, these approaches attempt to minimize the following cross-entropy loss:

$$\mathcal{L} = \sum_{(v_i,v_j)\in\mathcal{D}} -log(DEC(z_i, z_j)) \tag{15.12}$$

where in this case the training set, $\mathcal{D}$, is generated by sampling random walks starting from each node (i.e., where $N$ pairs for each node, $v_i$, are sampled from the distribution $(v_i, v_j) \sim p_{G,T}(v_j|v_j)$). However, naively evaluating this loss is of order $O(|D||V|)$ since evaluating the denominator of Eq. 15.11 has time complexity $O(|V|)$. Thus, DeepWalk and node2vec use different optimizations and approximations to compute the loss in Eq. 15.12. DeepWalk employs a "hierarchical softmax" technique to compute the normalizing factor, using a binary-tree structure to accelerate the computation. In contrast, node2vec approximates Eq. 15.12 using "negative sampling": instead of normalizing over the full vertex set, node2vec approximates the normalizing factor using a set of random "negative samples".

The key distinction between node2vec and DeepWalk is that node2vec allows for a flexible definition of random walks, whereas DeepWalk uses simple unbiased random walks over the graph. In particular, node2vec introduces two random walk hyper-parameters, $p$ and $q$, that bias the random walk. The hyper-parameter $p$ controls the likelihood of the walk immediately revisiting a node, while $q$ controls the likelihood of the walk revisiting a node's one-hop neighbourhood. By introducing these hyper-parameters, node2vec is able to smoothly interpolate between walks that

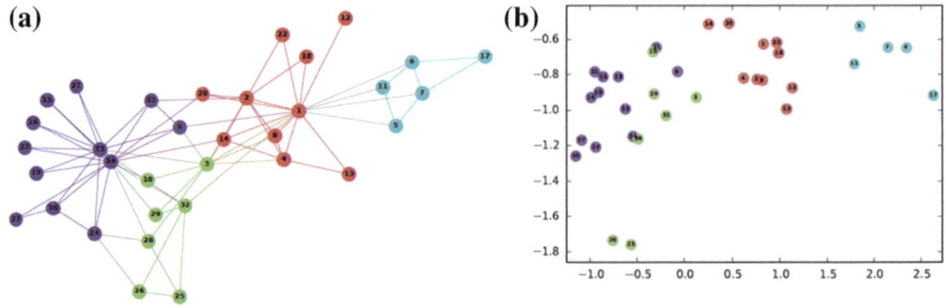


**Fig. 15.1** **a** Graph of the Zachary Karate Club network where nodes represent members and edges indicate friendship between members. **b** Two-dimensional visualization of node embeddings generated from this graph using the DeepWalk method. The distances between nodes in the embedding space reflect proximity in the original graph, and the node embeddings are spatially clustered according to the different colour-coded communities

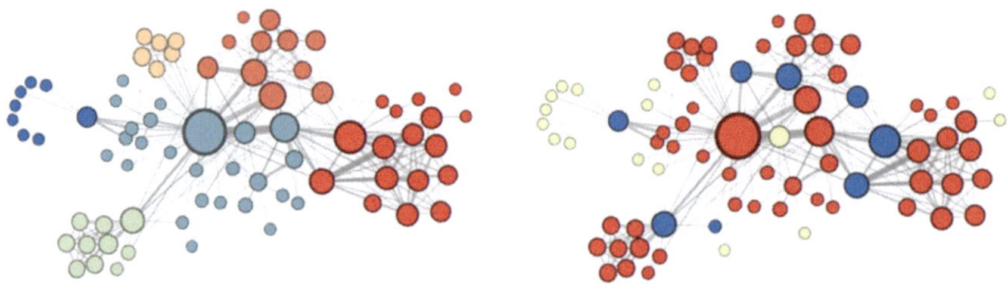

**Fig. 15.2** Graph of the Les Misérables novel where nodes represent characters and edges indicate interaction at some point in the novel between corresponding characters. (Left) Global positioning of the nodes. Same colour indicates that the nodes belong to the same community. (Right) Colour denotes structural equivalence between nodes, i.e, they play the same roles in their local neighbourhoods. Blue nodes are the articulation points. This equivalence where generated using the node2vec algorithm

are more akin to breadth-first or depth-first search. Reference [13] found that tuning these parameters allowed the model to trade-off between learning embeddings that emphasize community structures or embeddings that emphasize local structural roles.

Figure 15.1 depicts the DeepWalk algorithm applied to the Zachary Karate Club network to generate its two-dimensional embedding. The distance between nodes in this embedding space reflects proximity in the original graph.

Figure 15.2 illustrates the node2vec algorithm applied to the graph of the characters of the Les Misérables novel where colour depict the nodes which have structural equivalence.

#### 15.1.3.2 Large-Scale Information Network Embeddings (LINE)

Another highly successful direct encoding approach, which is not based on random walks but is often compared with DeepWalk and node2vec, is the LINE method [28]. LINE combines two encoder-decoder objectives that optimize "first-order" and "second-order" graph proximity, respectively. The first-order objective uses a decoder based on the sigmoid function,

$$DEC(z_i, z_j) = \frac{1}{1 + e^{-z_i^T z_j}} \tag{15.13}$$

and an adjacency-based proximity measure. The second-order encoder-decoder objective is similar but considers two-hop adjacency neighbourhoods and uses an encoder identical to Eq. 15.11. Both the first-order and second-order objectives are optimized using loss functions derived from the KL-divergence metric [28]. Thus, LINE is conceptually related to node2vec and DeepWalk in that it uses a probabilistic decoder and loss, but it explicitly factorizes first- and second-order proximities, instead of combining them in fixed-length random walks.

#### 15.1.3.3 Hierarchical Representation Learning for Networks (HARP)

Reference [7] introduced a "meta-strategy", called HARP, for improving various random-walk approaches via a graph pre-processing step. In this approach, a graph coarsening procedure is used to collapse related nodes in $G$ together into "supernodes", and then DeepWalk, node2vec, or LINE is run on this coarsened graph. After embedding the coarsened version of $G$, the learned embedding of each supernode is used as an initial value for the random walk embeddings of the supernode's constituent nodes (in another round of non-convex optimization on a "finer-grained" version of the graph). This general process can be repeated in a hierarchical manner at varying levels of coarseness, and has been shown to consistently improve performance of DeepWalk, node2vec, and LINE.

These direct encoding approaches that we have discussed so far train unique embedding vectors for each node independently and hence have the following drawbacks:

1. No parameters are shared between nodes in the encoder. This can be statistically inefficient, since parameter sharing can act as a powerful form of regularization, and it is also computationally inefficient, since it means that the number of parameters in direct encoding methods necessarily grows as $O(|V|)$.
2. Direct encoding also fails to leverage node attributes during encoding. In many large graphs, nodes have attribute information (e.g., user profiles) that is often highly informative with respect to the node's position and role in the graph.
3. Direct encoding methods can only generate embeddings for nodes that were present during the training phase, and they cannot generate embeddings for pre-

viously unseen nodes unless additional rounds of optimization are performed to optimize the embeddings for these nodes. This is highly problematic for evolving graphs, massive graphs that cannot be fully stored in memory, or domains that require generalizing to new graphs after training.

A number of approaches have been proposed for dealing with the aforementioned drawbacks.

## 15.2 Neighbourhood Autoencoder Methods

Deep Neural Graph Representations (DNGR) [5] and Structural Deep Network Embeddings (SDNE) [30] address the first problem. Unlike the direct encoding methods, they directly incorporate graph structure into the encoder algorithm. These approaches use autoencoders [16] to compress information about a node's local neighbourhood. Additionally, the approaches use a unary decoder instead of a pairwise one.

In these approaches, each node, $v_i$, is associated with a neighbourhood vector, $s_i \in \mathbb{R}^{|V|}$, which corresponds to $v_i$'s row in the matrix $S$. The $s_i$ vector contains $v_i$'s pairwise graph proximity with all other nodes and functions as a high-dimensional vector representation of $v_i$'s neighbourhood. The autoencoder objective for DNGR and SDNE is to embed nodes using the $s_i$ vectors such that the $s_i$ vectors can then be reconstructed from these embeddings:

$$DEC(ENC(s_i)) = DEC(z_i) \approx s_i \tag{15.14}$$

The loss for these methods takes the following form:

$$\mathcal{L} = \sum_{v_i \in V} ||DEC(z_i) - s_i||_2^2 \tag{15.15}$$

As with the pairwise decoder, we have that the dimension of the $z_i$ embeddings is much smaller than $|V|$, so the goal is to compress the node's neighbourhood information into a low-dimensional vector. For both SDNE and DNGR, the encoder and decoder functions consist of multiple stacked neural network layers: each layer of the encoder reduces the dimensionality of its input, and each layer of the decoder increases the dimensionality of its input.

SDNE and DNGR differ in the similarity functions they use to construct the neighborhood vectors $s_i$ and also how the autoencoder is optimized. DNGR defines $s_i$ according to the pointwise mutual information of two nodes co-occurring on random walks, similar to DeepWalk and node2vec. SDNE sets $s_i \triangleq A_i$ and combines the autoencoder objective with the Laplacian eigenmaps objective.

However, the autoencoder objective depends on the input $s_i$ vector, which contains information about $v_i$'s local graph neighbourhood. This dependency allows SDNE

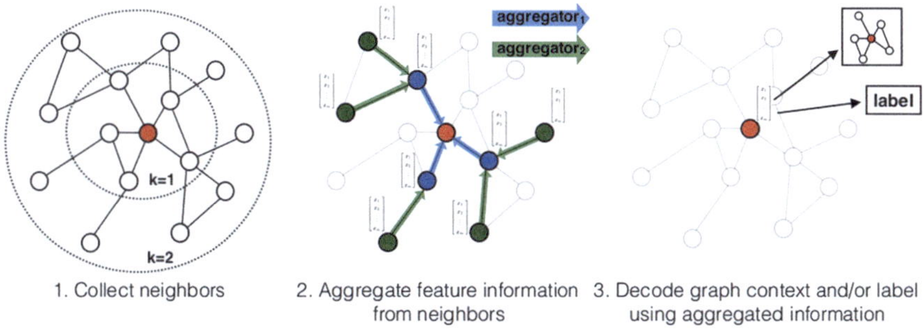


**Fig. 15.3** Illustration of the neighbourhood aggregation methods. To generate the embedding for a node, these methods first collect the node's k-hop neighbourhood. In the next step, these methods aggregate the attributes of node's neighbours, using neural network aggregators. This aggregated neighbourhood information is used to generate an embedding, which is then fed to the decoder

and DNGR to incorporate structural information about a node's local neighbourhood directly into the encoder as a form of regularization, which is not possible for the direct encoding approaches. However, despite this improvement, the autoencoder approaches still suffer from some serious limitations. Most prominently, the input dimension to the autoencoder is fixed at $|V|$, which can be extremely costly and even intractable for very large graphs. In addition, the structure and size of the autoencoder is fixed, so SDNE and DNGR cannot cope with evolving graphs, nor can they generalize across graphs.

## 15.3 Neighbourhood Aggregation and Convolutional Encoders

Another way to deal with the limitations of direct encoding is by designing encoders that rely on a node's local neighbourhood instead of the entire graph. These approaches attempt to generate embeddings by aggregating information from a node's local neighbourhood (as shown in Fig. 15.3).

These *neighbourhood aggregation* algorithms rely on node features or attributes (denoted $x_i \in \mathbb{R}^m$) to generate embeddings. The neighbourhood aggregation methods leverage this attribute information to inform their embeddings. In cases where attribute data is not given, these methods can use simple graph statistics as attributes or assign each node a one-hot indicator vector as an attribute. These methods are often called *convolutional* because they represent a node as a function of its surrounding neighbourhood, in a manner similar to the receptive field of a center-surround convolutional kernel in computer vision [18].

In the encoding phase, the neighbourhood aggregation methods build up the representation for a node in an iterative, or recursive fashion. First, the node embeddings are initialized to be equal to the input node attributes. Then at each iteration of the encoder algorithm, nodes aggregate the embeddings of their neighbours, using an aggregation function that operates over sets of vectors. After this aggregation, every node is assigned a new embedding, equal to its aggregated neighbourhood vector combined with its previous embedding from the last iteration. Finally, this combined embedding is fed through a dense neural network layer and the process repeats. As the process iterates, the node embeddings contain information aggregated from further and further reaches of the graph. However, the dimensionality of the embeddings remains constrained as the process iterates, so the encoder is forced to compress all the neighbourhood information into a low dimensional vector. After $K$ iterations the process terminates and the final embedding vectors are output as the node representations.

Graph convolutional networks (GCN) [18, 19, 27, 29], column networks [24], and the GraphSAGE algorithm [14] are some of the algorithms that follow this approach. A set of aggregation functions and a set of weight matrices $\{W^k, \forall k \in [1, K]\}$ specify how to aggregate information from a node's local neighbourhood and, unlike the direct encoding approaches, these parameters are shared across nodes. The same aggregation function and weight matrices are used to generate embeddings for all nodes, and only the input node attributes and neighbourhood structure change depending on which node is being embedded. This parameter sharing increases efficiency, provides regularization, and allows this approach to be used to generate embeddings for nodes that were not observed during training.

GraphSAGE, column networks, and the various GCN approaches all follow this algorithm but differ primarily in how the aggregation and vector combination are performed. GraphSAGE uses concatenation and permits general aggregation functions; the authors experiment with using the element-wise mean, a max-pooling neural network and LSTMs [17] as aggregators, and they found the the more complex aggregators, especially the max-pooling neural network, gave significant gains. GCNs and column networks use a weighted sum and a (weighted) element-wise mean.

Column networks also add an additional "interpolation" term, setting

$$h_v^{k'} = \alpha h_v^k + (1 - \alpha) h_v^{k-1} \tag{15.16}$$

where $\alpha$ is an interpolation weight computed as a non-linear function of $h_v^{k-1}$ and $h_{\mathcal{N}(v)}^{k-1}$. This interpolation term allows the model to retain local information as the process iterates.

In principle, the GraphSAGE, column network, and GCN encoders can be combined with any of the previously discussed decoders and loss functions, and the entire system can be optimized using Stochastic Gradient Descent.

At a high level, these approaches solve the four main limitations of direct encoding: they incorporate graph structure into the encoder; they leverage node attributes; their parameter dimension can be made sub-linear in $|V|$; and they can generate embeddings for nodes that were not present during training.

## 15.4 Binary Classification

In cases where nodes have an associated binary classification label, the following approach can be used. It should be noted that this approach can be easily extended to more complex classification settings.

Assume that we have a binary classification label, $y_i \in \mathbb{Z}$, associated with each node. To learn to map nodes to their labels, we can feed our embedding vectors, $z_i$, through a logistic, or sigmoid, function $\hat{y}_i = \sigma(z_i^T \theta)$, where $\theta$ is a trainable parameter vector. We can then compute the cross-entropy loss between these predicted class probabilities and the true labels:

$$\mathcal{L} = \sum_{v_i \in V} y_i log(\sigma(ENC(v_i)^T \theta)) + (1 - y_i) log(1 - \sigma(ENC(v_i)^T \theta)) \tag{15.17}$$

The gradient computed according to Eq. 15.17 can then be backpropagated through the encoder to optimize its parameters. This task-specific supervision can completely replace the reconstruction loss computed using the decoder, or it can be included along with the decoder loss.

## 15.5 Multi-modal Graphs

The previous sections have all focused on simple, undirected graphs. However many real-world graphs have complex multi-modal, or multi-layer, structures (e.g., heterogeneous node and edge types). In this section we will look at strategies that cope with this heterogeneity.

### *15.5.1 Different Node and Edge Types*

When dealing with graphs that contain different types of nodes and edges, a general strategy is to (i) use different encoders for nodes of different types [6], and (ii) extend pairwise decoders with type-specific parameters [21, 27]. The standard inner product edge decoder can be replaced with a bilinear form:

$$DEC_{\tau}(z_i, z_j) = z^T A_{\tau} z \tag{15.18}$$

where $\tau$ indexes a particular edge type and $A_{\tau}$ is a learned parameter specific to edges of type $\tau$. The matrix, $A_{\tau}$, in Eq. 15.18 can be regularized in various ways, which can be especially useful when there are a large number of edge types, as in the case for embedding knowledge graphs. Indeed, the literature on knowledge-graph completion, where the goal is predict missing relations in knowledge graphs, contains many related techniques for decoding a large number of edge types.

Recently, [10] also proposed a strategy for sampling random walks from heterogeneous graphs, where the random walks are restricted to only transition between particular types of nodes. This approach allows many of the methods in Sect. 15.1.3 to be applied on heterogeneous graphs and is complementary to the idea of including type-specific encoders and decoders.

### *15.5.2 Node Embeddings Across Layers*

When graphs have multiple "layers" that contain copies of the same nodes, such as in protein-protein interaction networks derived from different tissues (e.g., brain or liver tissue), some proteins occur across multiple tissues. In these cases it can be beneficial to share information across layers, so that a node's embedding in one layer can be informed by its embedding in other layers. Reference [31] offer one solution to this problem, called OhmNet, that combines node2vec with a regularization penalty that ties the embeddings across layers. Assuming that we have a node $v_i$, which belongs to two distinct layers $G_1$ and $G_2$, the standard embedding loss on this node can be augmented as follows:

$$\mathcal{L}(v_i)' = \mathcal{L}(v_i) + \lambda||z_i^{G_1} - z_i^{G_2}|| \tag{15.19}$$

where $\mathcal{L}$ denotes the usual embedding loss for that node, $\lambda$ denotes the regularization strength, and $z_i^{G_1}$ and $z_i^{G_2}$ denote $v_i$'s embeddings in the two different layers, respectively.

Reference [31] further extend this idea by exploiting hierarchies between graph layers. For example, in protein-protein interaction graphs derived from various tissues, some layers correspond to interactions throughout large regions (e.g., interactions that occur in any brain tissue) while other interaction graphs are more fine-grained (e.g., only interactions that occur in the frontal lobe). To exploit this structure, embeddings can be learned at the various levels of the hierarchy, and the regularization in Eq. 15.19 can recursively be applied between layers that have a parent-child relationship in the hierarchy.

## 15.6 Embedding Structural Roles

In many tasks it is necessary to learn representations that correspond to the structural roles of the nodes, independent of their global graph positions. The node2vec approach offers one solution to this problem. It was found that biasing the random walks allows the model to better capture structural roles. However, [11, 25] have developed node embedding approaches that are specifically designed to capture structural roles.

Reference [25] propose struc2vec, which involves generating a a series of weighted auxiliary graphs $G'_k$, $k = \{1, 2, \dots\}$ from the original graph $G$, where the auxiliary graph $G'_k$ captures structural similarities between nodes' $k$-hop neighbourhoods. In particular, letting $R_k(v_i)$ denote the ordered sequence of degrees of the nodes that are exactly $k$-hops away from $v_i$, the edge-weights, $w_k(v_i, v_j)$, in auxiliary graph $G'_k$ are recursively defined as

$$w_k(v_i, v_j) = w_{k-1}(v_i, v_j) + d(R_k(v_i), R_k(v_j)) \tag{15.20}$$

where $w_0(v_i, v_j) = 0$ and $d(R_k(v_i), R_k(v_j))$ measures the distance between the ordered degree sequences $R_k(v_i)$ and $R_k(v_j)$. After computing these weighted auxiliary graphs, struc2vec runs biased random walks over them and uses these walks as input to the node2vec optimization algorithm.

Reference [11] takes an approach called GraphWave to capture structural roles. It relies on spectral graph wavelets and heat kernels. Let $L$ denote the graph Laplacian, i.e, $L = D - A$ where $D$ contains node degrees on the diagonal and $A$ is the adjacency matrix. Also, let $U$ and $\lambda_i$, $i = 1 \dots |V|$ denote the eigenvector matrix and eigenvalues of $L$, respectively. Finally, we define a heat kernel, $g(\lambda) = e^{-s\lambda}$, with pre-defined scale $s$. Using $U$ and $g(\lambda)$, GraphWave computes a vector, $\psi_{v_i}$, corresponding to the structural role of node, $v_i \in V$, as

$$\psi_{v_i} = UGU^T v_i \tag{15.21}$$

where $G = diag([g(\lambda_1), \dots, g(\lambda_{|V|})])$ and $v_i$ is a one-hot indicator vector corresponding to $v_i$'s row/column in the Laplacian. The paper shows that these $\psi_{v_i}$ vectors implicitly relate to topological quantities, such as $v_i$'s degree and the number of $k$-cycles $v_i$ is involved in. With a proper choice of scale, $s$, the WaveGraph is able to effectively capture structural information about a node's role in a graph.

Node embeddings find applications in visualization, clustering, node classification, link prediction and pattern discovery.

## 15.7 Embedding Subgraphs

Now that we have looked at ways of embedding nodes, we will now turn to the task of embedding subgraphs. Here, the goal is to learn a continuous vector representation, $z_S \in \mathbb{R}^d$, of an induced subgraph $G[S]$ of the graph $G$, where $S \subseteq V$. This embedding, $z_S$, can then be used to make predictions about the entire subgraph.

Most of the methods discussed in node embeddings can be extended to subgraphs. The node embeddings and convolutional approaches discussed earlier is used to generate embeddings for nodes and then additional modules are applied to aggregate sets of node embeddings corresponding to subgraphs. The primary distinction between the different approaches is how they aggregate the set of node embeddings corresponding to a subgraph.

### 15.7.1 Sum-Based Approaches

Reference [12] introduced "convolutional molecular fingerprinting" to represent subgraphs in molecular graph representations by summing all the individual node embeddings in the subgraph

$$z_S = \sum_{v_i \in S} z_i \tag{15.22}$$

Reference [8] constructive intermediate embeddings, $\eta_{i,j}$, corresponding to edges, $(i, j) \in \mathcal{E}$

$$\eta_{i,j}^k = \sigma(W_{\mathcal{E}}^k \cdot COMBINE(x_i, AGGREGATE(\{\eta_{l,i}^{k-1}, \forall v_l \in \mathcal{N}(v_i) \setminus v_j\}))) \tag{15.23}$$

These edge embeddings are then aggregated to form the node embeddings:

$$z^i = \sigma(W_V^k \cdot COMBINE(x_i, AGGREGATE(\{\eta_{i,l}^K, \forall v_l \in \mathcal{N}(v_i)\}))) \tag{15.24}$$

Once these embeddings are computed, a simple element-wise sum to combine the node embeddings for a subgraph.

### 15.7.2 Graph-Coarsening Approaches

References [3, 9] also employ convolutional approaches, but instead of summing the node embeddings for the whole graph, they stack convolutional and graph coarsening layers. In the graph coarsening layers, the nodes are clustered together, and the clustered node embeddings are combined using element-wise max-pooling. After clustering, the new coarser graph is again fed through a convolutional encoder and the process repeats.

Unlike the previous discussed convolutional approaches, there is considerable emphasis placed on designing convolutional encoders based upon the graph Fourier transform. However, because the graph Fourier transform requires identifying and manipulating the eigenvectors of the graph Laplacian, naive versions of these approaches are necessarily $O(|V|^3)$. State-of-the-art approximations to these spectral approaches are discussed in [2].

## 15.8 Graph Neural Networks

Reference [26] discuss the graph neural network (GNN) where instead of aggregating information from neighbours, the idea is that subgraphs can be viewed as specifying a compute graph, i.e, a recipe for accumulating and passing information between nodes.

Every node, $v_i$, is initialized with a random embedding, $h_i^0$, and at each iteration of the GNN algorithm, nodes accumulate inputs from their neighbours using simple neural network layers

$$h_i^k = \sum_{v_j \in \mathcal{N}(v_i)} \sigma(W h_j^{k-1} + b) \tag{15.25}$$

where $W \in \mathbb{R}^{d \times d}$ and $b \in \mathbb{R}^d$ are trainable parameters and $\sigma$ is a non-linearity. Equation 15.25 is repeatedly applied in a recursive fashion until the embeddings converge, and special care must be taken during initialization to ensure convergence. Once the embeddings have converged, they are aggregated for the entire (sub)graph and this aggregated embedding is used for subgraph classification. The paper suggests that the aggregation can be done by introducing a "dummy" super-node that is connected to all nodes in the target subgraph.

Reference [20] extend and modify the GNN framework to use Gated Recurrent Units and back propagation through time, which removes the need to run the recursion in Eq. 15.25 to convergence. Adapting the GNN framework to use modern recurrent units also allows the leverage of node attributes and to use the output of intermediate embeddings of subgraphs.

The GNN framework is highly expressive, but it is also computationally intensive compared to the convolutional approaches, due to the complexities of ensuring convergence or running back propagation through time. Thus, unlike the convolutional approaches, which are most commonly used to classify molecular graphs in large datasets, the GNN approach has been used for more complex, but smaller scale, tasks, e.g., for approximate formal verification using graph-based representations of programs.

## References

1. Ahmed, Amr, Nino Shervashidze, Shravan Narayanamurthy, Vanja Josifovski, and Alexander J. Smola. Distributed large-scale natural graph factorization. In *Proceedings of the 22nd international conference on World Wide Web*, 37–48. ACM, 2013.
2. Bronstein, Michael, M., Joan Bruna, Yann LeCun, Arthur Szlam, and Pierre Vandergheynst. 2017. Geometric deep learning: Going beyond Euclidean data. *IEEE Signal Processing Magazine* 34 (4): 18–42.
3. Bruna, Joan, Wojciech Zaremba, Arthur Szlam, and Yann LeCun. 2013. Spectral networks and locally connected networks on graphs. arXiv:1312.6203.

4. Cao, Shaosheng, Wei Lu, and Qiongkai Xu. 2015. Grarep: Learning graph representations with global structural information. In *Proceedings of the 24th ACM international on conference on information and knowledge management*, 891–900. ACM.
5. Cao, Shaosheng, Wei Lu, and Qiongkai Xu. 2016. Deep neural networks for learning graph representations. In *AAAI*, 1145–1152.
6. Chang, Shiyu, Wei Han, Jiliang Tang, Guo-Jun Qi, Charu C. Aggarwal, and Thomas S. Huang. 2015. Heterogeneous network embedding via deep architectures. In *Proceedings of the 21st ACM SIGKDD international conference on knowledge discovery and data mining*, 119–128. ACM.
7. Chen, Haochen, Bryan Perozzi, Yifan Hu, and Steven Skiena. 2017. Harp: Hierarchical representation learning for networks. arXiv:1706.07845.
8. Dai, Hanjun, Bo Dai, and Le Song. 2016. Discriminative embeddings of latent variable models for structured data. In *International conference on machine learning*, 2702–2711.
9. Defferrard, Michaël, Xavier Bresson, and Pierre Vandergheynst. 2016. Convolutional neural networks on graphs with fast localized spectral filtering. In *Advances in neural information processing systems*, 3844–3852.
10. Dong, Yuxiao, Nitesh V. Chawla, and Ananthram Swami. 2017. metapath2vec: Scalable representation learning for heterogeneous networks. In *Proceedings of the 23rd ACM SIGKDD international conference on knowledge discovery and data mining*, 135–144. ACM.
11. Donnat, Claire, Marinka Zitnik, David Hallac, and Jure Leskovec. 2017. Spectral graph wavelets for structural role similarity in networks. arXiv:1710.10321.
12. Duvenaud, David K., Dougal Maclaurin, Jorge Iparraguirre, Rafael Bombarell, Timothy Hirzel, Alán Aspuru-Guzik, and Ryan P. Adams. 2015. Convolutional networks on graphs for learning molecular fingerprints. In *Advances in neural information processing systems*, 2224–2232.
13. Grover, Aditya, and Jure Leskovec. 2016. node2vec: Scalable feature learning for networks. In *Proceedings of the 22nd ACM SIGKDD international conference on knowledge discovery and data mining*, 855–864. ACM.
14. Hamilton, Will, Zhitao Ying, and Jure Leskovec. 2017. Inductive representation learning on large graphs. In *Advances in neural information processing systems*, 1025–1035.
15. Hamilton, William L., Rex Ying, and Jure Leskovec. 2017. Representation learning on graphs: Methods and applications. arXiv:1709.05584.
16. Hinton, Geoffrey E., and Ruslan R Salakhutdinov. 2006. Reducing the dimensionality of data with neural networks. *Science* 313 (5786): 504–507.
17. Hochreiter, Sepp, and Jürgen Schmidhuber. 1997. Long short-term memory. *Neural Computation* 9 (8): 1735–1780.
18. Kipf, Thomas N., and Max Welling. 2016. Semi-supervised classification with graph convolutional networks. arXiv:1609.02907.
19. Kipf, Thomas N., and Max Welling. 2016. Variational graph auto-encoders. arXiv:1611.07308.
20. Li, Yujia, Daniel Tarlow, Marc Brockschmidt, and Richard Zemel. 2015. Gated graph sequence neural networks. arXiv:1511.05493.
21. Nickel, Maximilian, Kevin Murphy, Volker Tresp, and Evgeniy Gabrilovich. 2016. A review of relational machine learning for knowledge graphs. *Proceedings of the IEEE* 104 (1): 11–33.
22. Ou, Mingdong, Peng Cui, Jian Pei, Ziwei Zhang, and Wenwu Zhu. 2016. Asymmetric transitivity preserving graph embedding. In *Proceedings of the 22nd ACM SIGKDD international conference on knowledge discovery and data mining*, 1105–1114. ACM.
23. Perozzi, Bryan, Rami Al-Rfou, and Steven Skiena. 2014. Deepwalk: Online learning of social representations. In *Proceedings of the 20th ACM SIGKDD international conference on knowledge discovery and data mining*, 701–710. ACM.
24. Pham, Trang, Truyen Tran, Dinh Q. Phung, and Svetha Venkatesh. 2017. Column networks for collective classification. In *AAAI*, 2485–2491.
25. Ribeiro, Leonardo FR., Pedro HP. Saverese, and Daniel R. Figueiredo. 2017. struc2vec: Learning node representations from structural identity. In *Proceedings of the 23rd ACM SIGKDD international conference on knowledge discovery and data mining*, 385–394. ACM.

26. Scarselli, Franco, Marco Gori, Ah Chung Tsoi, Markus Hagenbuchner, and Gabriele Monfardini. 2009. The graph neural network model. *IEEE Transactions on Neural Networks* 20 (1): 61–80.
27. Schlichtkrull, Michael, Thomas N. Kipf, Peter Bloem, Rianne van den Berg, Ivan Titov, and Max Welling. 2017. Modeling relational data with graph convolutional networks. arXiv:1703.06103.
28. Tang, Jian, Meng Qu, Mingzhe Wang, Ming Zhang, Jun Yan, and Qiaozhu Mei. 2015. Line: Large-scale information network embedding. In *Proceedings of the 24th international conference on World Wide Web*, 1067–1077. (International World Wide Web Conferences Steering Committee).
29. van den Berg, Rianne, Thomas N. Kipf, and Max Welling. 2017. Graph convolutional matrix completion. *Statistics* 1050: 7.
30. Wang, Daixin, Peng Cui, and Wenwu Zhu. 2016. Structural deep network embedding. In *Proceedings of the 22nd ACM SIGKDD international conference on knowledge discovery and data mining*, 1225–1234. ACM.
31. Zitnik, Marinka, and Jure Leskovec. 2017. Predicting multicellular function through multi-layer tissue networks. *Bioinformatics* 33 (14): i190–i198.

# Index





K. Raj P. M. et al., *Practical Social Network Analysis with Python*,
Computer Communications and Networks,
https://doi.org/10.1007/978-3-319-96746-2

**Q**



**R**

MIX
Papier aus verantwortungsvollen Quellen
Paper from responsible sources
FSC® C105338

If you have any concerns about our products,
you can contact us on
**ProductSafety@springernature.com**

In case Publisher is established outside the EU,
the EU authorized representative is:
**Springer Nature Customer Service Center GmbH**
**Europaplatz 3, 69115 Heidelberg, Germany**

Printed by Libri Plureos GmbH
in Hamburg, Germany